The Free Mind

Essays and Poems in Honour of Barry Spurr

Barry Spurr delivering the Occasional Address at the English Honours graduation in the Great Hall, University of Sydney, soon after his appointment as Australia's first Professor of Poetry and Poetics (May, 2011)

The Free Mind

Essays and Poems in Honour of Barry Spurr

Edited by
Catherine A. Runcie

www.edwinhlowepublishing.com

Copyright © in this collection Catherine A. Runcie 2016.

Copyright © in the individual chapters remains with the individual authors.

All rights reserved. This book is copyright. Apart from any fair dealing for the purpose of private study, research, criticism or review, as permitted under the Copyright Act 1968, no part may be reproduced or stored by any process without prior written permission of the publisher.

Grateful acknowledgement is made to copyright holders of materials reproduced in this book. The publisher would be grateful to be informed of any inadvertent errors or omissions in the use of copyright material and would be pleased to correct them in any forthcoming editions

National Library of Australia Cataloguing-in-Publication entry
The free mind. : essays and poems in honour of Barry Spurr / edited by Catherine A. Runcie.

9780994168214 (paperback)
Spurr, Barry.
Higher education--Australia.
English essays.
Australian poetry--20th century.
Runcie, Catherine, editor.
378.10094

Edwin H. Lowe Publishing, Sydney.
www.edwinlowepublishing.com
contact@edwinlowepublishing.com
Edwin H. Lowe Publishing is the trading name of Edwin Hulme Lowe. ABN 60 901 995 995

ISBN-13: 978-0-9941682-1-4
ISBN-10: 0-9941682-1-7

Cover Image: Radcliffe Camera, Bodleian Library, the University of Oxford.
© Jo Hocking 2011.

Available from edwinhlowepublishing.com, Amazon.com and other book stores.
Printed by Createspace.

Acknowledgements

This book would not have been possible without the assistance of many people, including the patient advice of Dr Beverley Sherry on early modern English literature, and the dedicated assistance of Annette Krausmann. I wish to thank my loving family for their patience too – my husband Neil, computer trouble-shooters Michael and Emma, and my grandchildren. Granddaughter Ava's curiosity about Shakespeare always acted as an inspiring reminder of how long the western tradition is, and how alive it is still to lively young minds.

In particular I wish also to thank the following for their generous assistance in the use of copyright material: Professor Mark Eaton, *Christianity & Literature*, and Sage Publications Ltd; Professor Carole Cusack, *Literature & Aesthetics* and the Sydney Society of Literature and Aesthetics; Dr Jane Potter, the Wilfred Owen Association and the Wilfred Owen Royalties Trust.

The free mind has access to all the knowledge and speculation of its age, and nothing cramps it like a taboo.

Joint letter of E.M. Forster and Virginia Woolf to *Nation and Athenaeum* 43 (September, 1928)

A true university serves neither political purposes nor social programmes, necessarily partisan and transitory. Above all, it rebukes censorship and correctness of any kind.... And it should honour anarchic provocation.

George Steiner, 'Universitas' Lecture, Part III

Contents

Foreword — 1
Catherine A. Runcie

The Strategy of Shakespeare's *Sonnets* — 3
G.A. Wilkes

**Shakespeare's Moral Wisdom and Political Insight:
Dual Power in *Coriolanus*** — 30
David Brooks

Milton's *Samson Agonistes*: A Political Reading — 59
Michael Wilding

Reading Aloud — 76
Bruce Dawe

The Legacy of T. S. Eliot to Milton Studies — 78
Beverley Sherry

Why Study the Humanities? — 92
Stephen Prickett

On Professing Poetry in Australia in the 21st Century — 100
Simon Haines

**'Pour forth thy fervours for a healthful mind':
Pagan and Christian Views of Courage** — 113
David Daintree

State of the Arts — 121
Jonathan Mills

Four Sonnets	132
Stephen McInerney	
Eliot's Rose-Garden: Some Phenomenology and Theology in "Burnt Norton"	136
Kevin Hart	
The Call of Canterbury: The Festival Plays of T.S. Eliot and Charles Williams (1935-1936)	159
Bradley M. Wells	
The Sea-Wall	174
Robert Gray	
Knowing Oneself and the Aesthetic Shaping of Character: German Romantic Anthropology	177
Stephen Gaukroger	
Do Not Forget: Memory and Moral Obligation in *Little Dorrit*	187
Jennifer Gribble	
A Reading of Wilfred Owen's 'Dulce et Decorum Est'	199
Lyn Ashcroft	
The Lizard	211
Christine Townend	
Liturgy and Language	212
David Jasper	
Calumniation and Payback Theory: Wars of Words in the Breakdown of the Warrior Ethos	221
Garry W. Trompf	
Two Poems	236
Ivan Head	

An Introduction to St Philip Neri Ivan Francis Head	237
The Pen of a Ready Writer: The Psalms of Myles Coverdale John Bunyan	241
Spurred On John Bunyan	252
The Cultic Milieu in Australia: Deviant Religiosity in the Novels of Carmel Bird Carole M. Cusack	253
Small Child and Art Installation Geoffrey Lehmann	269
The Future of the Humanities Michael Warren Davis	271
The Supervisor – Student Relationship Henry Cooper	278
O Where Are the Sounds? Inviting Poetry Back into the Lives of Learners Karina Hepner	283
Imagery for the End of the Day Devika Brendon	292
Occasional Address Barry Spurr	295
List of Publications of Barry Spurr	298
List of Contributors	315
Photographs	294

Foreword

Professor Barry Spurr retired from the University of Sydney in July 2015, after 40 years on the academic staff of the Department of English. He began as a Teaching Fellow in 1974, and on returning from postgraduate study at Oxford in 1976, he took up a lectureship in English, being promoted to Senior Lecturer in 1984 and Associate Professor in 2007. In 2011, he was appointed to a Personal Chair as Australia's first Professor of Poetry and Poetics. Concurrent with his university post, Professor Spurr was also (from 1978 to 1987) Senior Tutor and Tutor in English at St Paul's College within the University. And for a year in 1992, he was the Inaugural University of Sydney Fellow in English at Sydney Grammar. In 2007, Professor Spurr was elected a Fellow of the Australian College of Educators for 'outstanding contributions to education'.

Barry Spurr's appointment to a Personal Chair recognized his distinguished record in published scholarship, his reputation as an exceptionally gifted lecturer and his conspicuous service to the University and to the wider community as a public intellectual. In his research (see 'List of Publications' at the end of this book), Professor Spurr's contribution to scholarship in English literature covers a wide historical range and variety of authors from the early modern period to contemporary Australian poetry. His particular interest in Renaissance religious poetry (such as John Donne's) and his principal study, over many years, of the life and work of the leading Modernist poet, T.S. Eliot, have secured his international reputation as a leading scholar of poetry and poetics. His book, *Anglo-Catholic in Religion: T. S. Eliot and Christianity* (2010), described by the *Times Literary Supplement* as a 'wonderful journey' into its subject, is the authoritative study of Eliot's religious faith and its influence in his poetry. An earlier book, *See the Virgin Blest* (2007) is similarly ground-breaking in describing representations of the Virgin Mary in English poetry, from the mediaeval period to today, while the textbook, *Studying Poetry* (2006), is now in its second edition. But Professor Spurr's research and scholarship are by no means confined to poetry. Another book is a study of Lytton Strachey's prose style, and yet another, *The Word in the Desert* (1995), is an account of liturgical language.

This collection, *The Free Mind. Essays and Poems in Honour of Barry Spurr*, is very privileged by the breadth and depth of the range of contributions. Emeritus Professor G.A. Wilkes's essay on Shakespeare begins the collection fittingly, as Professor Wilkes, Australia's first Professor of Australian Literature and then Challis Professor of English at the University of Sydney, was the principal mentor of Barry Spurr, initially as an undergraduate, then as a junior member of the academic staff.

Many other essays and poems follow from scholars and poets who share Barry Spurr's interests. There are essays on literary criticism, ranging from the works of Shakespeare to John Milton, Charles Dickens, Wilfred Owen and T.S. Eliot. Other essays explore how the power of words connects with ideas in politics and in religion. Yet others explore the role of the humanities and the arts in the ever shifting contemporary world and the contemporary university.

Among these essays is one from Michael Wilding, a scholar who has been awarded the Prime Minister's Literary Award (2015) for non-fiction, and a poem from Geoffrey Lehmann, awarded the Prime Minister's Literary Award (2015) for poetry. From international professors to high school teachers, from Barry's teachers to Barry's students, the contributions are a bounty of work of the finest, coinciding with Barry's unfaltering belief in the role of the university in engendering and safeguarding disinterested learning, free debate, leading to genuine knowledge that stands the test of time.

As editor may I allow myself the privilege of praising the 'Festschrifters', their affectionate loyalty, their perspicacity and far sightedness, their deep scholarship and their poetic talents; they gave of their best to celebrate Barry Spurr, beloved teacher, mentor, colleague, scholar and friend, who never faltered in the pursuit of the intellectual ideals incumbent upon a university.

Catherine A. Runcie
Sydney 2016

The Strategy of Shakespeare's *Sonnets*

G.A. Wilkes

Anyone who has "taught" Shakespeare's sonnets (always a privilege) over a period of time will have encountered various approaches to the topic. To apply the term "strategy" may seem presumptuous. But it reflects my basic conviction, that when Shakespeare set out on this venture, it was to produce a sequence that would be true to the genre, but unlike anything that had gone before. The intent was exploratory, and interrogative. This I shall try to demonstrate, but as the term "strategy" did not come into the English language until after Shakespeare's death, I take as a starting-point two of the earliest references to Shakespeare as a literary figure in his lifetime, to provide some perspective.

The first reference has an Australian connection which has gone almost unnoticed. In 1592 Robert Greene was one of a group of dramatists later dubbed the University Wits (Lyly and Nashe were included, sometimes Marlowe) who resented others who were not graduates of Oxford or Cambridge, who were competing successfully with them in the theatre. In his *Groats-worth of witte, bought with a million of Repentance* (1592), Greene attacked "those Puppets ... that spake from our mouths, those Anticks garnisht in our colours"...

> Yes trust them not for there is an upstart Crow, beautified with our feathers, that with his *Tygers hart wrapt in a Players hyde*, supposes he is as well able to bombast out a blanke verse as the best of you: and beeing an absolute *Johannes fac totum*, is in his owne conceit the onely Shake-scene in a countrey. (A3^v)

Greene's *Groats-worth of Witte* was entered in the Stationers Register in September 1592, and Greene died before it appeared, so that other hands may have been involved. Shakespeare is attacked as an actor (player) who bombasts out a blank verse as well as the best of you, and possibly as a plagiarist, if he appropriates York's denunciation of Queen Margaret as "a tiger's heart wrapped in a woman's hide" (3 *Henry VI*, I.iv.135).[1] The authorship of that play is now attributed to Shakespeare, which may deepen the offence.

---

[1] All references to Shakespeare's works other than the Sonnets are from William Shakespeare, *The Complete Works*, eds. Stanley Wells and Gary Taylor (Oxford: Oxford University Press, 1986).

Greene's main charge is that this nondescript, this factotum in the theatrical world, is "in his owne conceit the onely Shake-scene in a country". "Shake" at this time meant "steal". It faded from polite usage in England in that sense, but not before it had been exported to Australia with the convicts. Professor H. J. Oliver of the University of New South Wales contributed an article on this to *Notes & Queries* in 1979, but I have not found any awareness of it in the northern hemisphere.[2] The whole point of Greene's "Shake-scene" is that Shakespeare is a purloiner of scenes.

The second of these early references to Shakespeare as a literary figure is more genteel. It comes in 1598 in the *Palladis Tamia* of Francis Meres, where the pseudo-Latin title may suggest Pallas the goddess of wisdom, while the subtitle *Wits Treasury* aspires to the compendium or the cultural handbook. The entry on Shakespeare declares that "the sweete wittie soule of *Ouid* lives, in mellifluous hony-tongued *Shakespeare*, witnes his *Venus* and *Adonis*, his *Lucrece*; his sugred Sonnets among his priuate friends, &c".[3] This reference seems to assign Shakespeare to the leisured class of sonneteers, probably accomplished in dancing and swordplay, who saw writing of sonnets as a courtly pursuit. They would not be writing for publication, but could submit their efforts to their private friends. This would be in keeping for someone who had dedicated his *Venus and Adonis* and *Lucrece* to the Earl of Southampton, then in his twenties.

The only difficulty with Meres' reference to Shakespeare is that modern scholars never quote it in full. Meres continues:

> As *Plautus* and *Seneca* are accounted the best for Comedy and Tragedy among the Latines: so *Shakespeare* among the English is the most excellent in both kinds for the stage; for Comedy, witnes his *Gentlemen of Verona*, his *Errors*, his *Loue labors lost*, his *Loue labours wonne*, his *Midsummers night dreame*, & his *Merchant of Venice*: for Tragedy his *Richard the 2. Richard the 3. Henry the 4. King John, Titus Andronicus* and his *Romeo and Juliet*. (Oo2ʳ)

By 1598 Shakespeare, as a literary figure, had become rather more than a writer of sugared sonnets. His ventures into drama had also opened a playground there for the sonnet itself. In *Two Gentlemen of Verona*, Thurio is tutored at some length in the writing of "wailful sonnets" in his wooing of Silvia (III.ii.68-95); in *Love's Labour's Lost* there is much "sonneting" (IV.iii.156) by the courtiers who have denied themselves the company of women; in *Much*

---

[2] H.J. Oliver, "Shakespeare the Shake-scene", *Notes & Queries*, 26.2 (1979), 115. I have encountered fourteen instances of "shake" in the sense of "steal" in Australian writing from 1812 to 1998, including a character in Patrick White: "You don't think I'd shake anything off Ern? 'E's my mate!" *Four Plays* (London: Eyre & Spottiswoode, 1965), 105. The Second Edition of the OED (1989) has an entry for "Shakescene", with the citation from Greene, and the comment "Of uncertain or vague meaning".

[3] Francis Meres, *Palladis Tamia. Wits Treasury* (1598).

Ado About Nothing (which belongs to this time) when Beatrice and Benedick are finally reconciled, each is found to have privately been writing a sonnet to the other. In *Romeo and Juliet*, editors have observed that the fourteen or so lines the two exchange (I.v.92-105) are on the page in the shape of their meeting lips.

Meres and *Palladis Tamia* have one more contribution to make, which is the entry on *Epigrammatists*. The epigram was an important classical form, and Meres lists five English names, of which the fifth is "Davies". As we are concerned with the literary climate to which Shakespeare's sonnets belong, I move forward to June 1599, when the Archbishop of Canterbury and the Bishop of London ordered the burning of books of satires and epigrams, and decreed that no more be published. There were two proclamations, one on 1 June 1599, with a list including "Davyes *Epigrams* with Marlowes *Elegyes*", and a second list dated 1-4 June 1599, including "Davies *Epigrames*" (with the note that "Theis bookes presently thereuppon were burnte in the hall").[4] Davies was eventually to become Sir John Davies, but at this time he was a law student banished from the Middle Temple, and seeking to redeem himself as the author of *Nosce Teipsum* (entered in the Stationers Register on 14 April 1599), followed by *Hymnes of ASTRÆA in Acrosticke Verse* on 17 November.

Davies would have been most active as a writer of epigrams in 1594-1595. Copies surviving the fire and the proclamations are few and incomplete, but modern editors have recovered a series of 48 epigrams from printed texts, and extended it to 62 from manuscript sources.[5] Epigram 1 introduces "the gull", and the second epigram goes on to explain "this new terme" through examples, concluding:

> But to define a gull in termes precise
> A gull is he which semes, and is not wise.

Davies pursued a separate manuscript sequence titled *Gullinge Sonnets*, dedicated to Sir Anthony Cooke (who was not knighted until 1596), and sonnet 5 may provide an example:

> Mine Eye, myne eare, my will, my witt, my harte,
> Did see, did heare, did like, discerne, did love,
> Her face, her speche, her fashion, judgement, arte,
> Which did charme, please, delighte, confounde and move.
> Then fancie, humor, love, conceipte, and thought
> Did soe drawe, force, intyse, perswade, devise,
> That she was wonne, mov'd, caryed, compast, wrought,

---

[4] See Edward Arber, *Transcripts* of the Stationers Register, London, 1875-1894, iii.677-678.
[5] See Robert Krueger, ed., *The Poems of Sir John Davies* (Oxford: Oxford University Press, 1975).

> To thinck me kinde, true, comelie, valiant, wise,
> That heaven, earth, hell, my folly and her pride
> Did worke, contrive, labor, conspire and sweare
> To make me scorn'd, vile, cast off, bace, defied
> With her my love, my lighte, my life, my deare;
> So that my harte, my witt, will, eare, and eye
> Doth greive, lament, sorrowe, dispaire and dye.[6]

How might such an approach as this be applied to the *blazon* of a mistress's beauty?

I refer to the vogue of epigrams and satires at this time to indicate a particular context for the sonnets. In 1599 Shakespeare himself was an established member of the King's Men, the owner of property at Stratford, and considering his eligibility for a coat of arms. His exposure to the rough and tumble of the literary scene was however demonstrated in 1599 with the publication by William Jaggard of *The Passionate Pilgrime*, described as *"By W Shakespeare"*, who knew nothing about it. It contained two sonnets by Shakespeare, "When my love swears that she is made of truth" and "Two loves I have, of comfort and despair", later to appear as sonnets 138 and 144. "If love make me forsworn, how shall I swear to love" is from *Love's Labour's Lost* (IV.ii.106-119) without acknowledgement, and "Did not the heavenly rhetoric of thine eye" is Longueville's sonnet to Maria from the same source (IV.iii.57-70), with Dumaine's "sonnet" to follow ("On a day (alack the day)", (IV.iii.99-118). There are four sallies from the world of *Venus and Adonis*, designed to be titillating, but not by Shakespeare, and two poems by Richard Barnfield. This pirated text was evidently very successful, as it was reprinted almost immediately, and no complete copy of the first edition has survived.

It is time to move from 1599 to the quarto text of 1609. It has *Shakespeare's Sonnets* on the title page, and on the verso the dedication "To the onlie begetter of these insuing sonnets Mr. W. H." (not yet identified) by "The well-wishing adventurer in setting forth. T. T." (Thomas Thorpe, the printer). In this text certain groupings of poems have been claimed, such as "The Friend", "The Friend's Fault", "The Rival Poet" and "The Dark Lady". Significant changes of mood have been found in the sequence, and signs of improvisation also appear. I hope to deal with these features as we go along.

In any study of the strategy of the sonnets, it is imperative to understand the code in which the text is presented. The belief that the experiences recorded in the sequence were undergone by "Shakespeare" has faded. He is regarded as "the author", in the legal sense. The person engaged in composing the text may be referred to as "the poet". The task of conveying the text is given to "the speaker". This is an emancipation, because "the

---

[6] *Ibid.*, 165.

speaker" at times may seem to be adopting a standpoint of his own. If this becomes marked, the term "persona" may suggest itself, but that offer is best declined. I prefer the title "fictive speaker", as employed by Professor Helen Vendler.[7]

Professor Vendler made the most comprehensive attempt to codify these practices in *The Art of Shakespeare's Sonnets* (1997), a task on which she had been engaged for the previous nine years.[8] Her edition includes a commentary on all 154 sonnets along these lines, sometimes with diagrams to illustrate them, and concepts such as "Couplet Tie" and "Key Word" to analyse the inner structure of each poem.

It is possible for a system to become too intricate. I have adopted the simple tabulation already described, but I propose one addition to the code. This is the role of the "non-speaker". As a literary form, the sonnet has a confessional aspect. It seems designed for the expression of private thoughts, and may seem to invite a similar response. Do we sometimes assume an addressee? The influence of the non-speaker may be felt when the speaker seems to change tack in the course of an argument. The Petrarchan sonnet is hospitable to this effect through the *volta*, the "turn", when the case being argued in the octave is countered in the sestet, and possibly taken to a different conclusion. In Shakespeare the effect is not so restricted, and might well come as a comment at the end. Again I shall try to demonstrate this as we go on.

"Strategy" is a very inclusive term. When I suggested that Shakespeare's approach to the sonnet sequence was exploratory and interrogative, I might have added that he was also engaged in mocking its institutions. In 1609 a reader of *Shake-speare's Sonnets* "Never before Imprinted" would probably have expected to encounter a mistress. A tradition had been set by Petrarch and Laura, Sidney with *Astrophil and Stella*, Samuel Daniel's *Delia*, and possibly Fulke Greville's *Cælica* (encompassing *Myra* and *Cynthia*). The opening sonnets in Shakespeare's sequence are calculated with this expectation in mind. The first poem, "From fairest creatures we desire increase", with "beauty's rose" in the second line, could in some sense involve a mistress, though in the second sonnet the opening line "When forty winters shall besiege thy brow" would have been unexpected, until in the third poem, the invitation "Look in thy glass" yields to the question:

---

[7] I am not sure to whom I am indebted for the "fictive speaker". I had encountered "fictive" presences in Thomas P. Roche, *Petrarch and the English Sonnet Sequence* (New York: AMS Press, 1989) as though the term was then current (e.g. 390). I find that in 1986, in a paper on quite a different topic, I myself had used the concept of "the fictional self", though not in relation to Shakespeare. See G.A. Wilkes, "The Role of the Critic - and the Language of Criticism" in *Proceedings* (Canberra: Australian Academy of the Humanities, 1986), 75-85.

[8] Helen Vendler, *The Art of Shakespeare's Sonnets* (Cambridge MA: Harvard University Press, 1997).

> For where is she so faire whose uneared womb
> Disdains the tillage of thy husbandry?

The addressee is male, a young man being urged to marry so that his beauty may be perpetuated. Beauty is a paramount value, which in some form – "beauty's legacy", "beauty's treasure", "beauteous" – will be mentioned twenty times by sonnet 14.[9] Procreation is a constant theme. Questions are being put, as early as sonnet 4:

> Unthrifty loveliness, why dost thou spend
> Upon thyself thy beauty's legacy?

where "spend" may refer to masturbation ("having traffic with thyself alone" - 4.9). In sonnet 9 these urgings are turning towards reproof, the young man is accused of "beauty's waste", and visited with "murd'rous shame". In sonnet 10, admitting he is "beloved of many", he is so possessed with "murd'rous hate" that the speaker makes a pronouncement:

> For shame deny that thou bear'st love to any,
> Who for thyself art so unprovident;
> Grant, if thou wilt, thou art beloved of many,
> But that thou none lov'st is most evident:
> For thou art so possessed with murd'rous hate
> That 'gainst thyself thou stick'st not to conspire,
> Seeking that beauteous roof to ruinate
> Which to repair should be thy chief desire:
> O change thy thought, that I may change my mind;
> Shall hate be fairer lodged than gentle love?
> Be as thy presence is, gracious and kind;
> Or to thyself at least kind-hearted prove,
>   Make thee another self for love of me,
>   That beauty still may live in thine or thee.

"O change thy thought, that I may change my mind" is a personal intervention, the poet changing his role from advocate to lover. "Make thee another self for love of me" is the request, and by sonnet 13 the "fair youth" is being addressed as "love" in the first line, and as "dear my love" at the close. He vows to resist "Time's scythe" (12.13), and in that war "As he takes from you, I engraft you new" (15.14).

This is the first strategic move in the sequence, and it is to be completed in sonnet 18. So far as my enquiries have extended, most readers have

---

[9] All references to the Sonnets are from William Shakespeare, *Shakespeare's Sonnets* (Arden Shakespeare: Third Series), ed. Katherine Duncan-Jones (London: Thomson Learning, 2004)

encountered sonnet 18 for the first time in an anthology, and have assumed that it is addressed to a young woman. But it is addressed to a young man, and on a summer's day in England, at a time when, in the English calendar, summer extended into June, so that May was regarded as a summer month.

18

> Shall I compare thee to a summer's day?
> Thou art more lovely and more temperate:
> Rough winds do shake the darling buds of May,
> And summer's lease hath all too short a date:
> Sometime too hot the eye of heaven shines,
> And often is his gold complexion dimmed;
> And every fair from fair sometime declines,
> By chance, or nature's changing course, untrimmed:
> But thy eternal summer shall not fade,
> Nor lose possession of that fair thou ow'st,
> Nor shall death brag thou wander'st in his shade
> When in eternal lines to time thou grow'st:
> > So long as men can breathe or eyes can see,
> > So long lives this, and this gives life to thee.

That "Thou art more lovely" is the case to be made. "More temperate" depends on the weather conditions which may be encountered in summer. In May the "darling buds" may be exposed to rough winds, and the lease negotiated by summer with the other seasons falls short. On a given summer's day, the sun (the eye of heaven to the fair youth) may be "too hot", or too clouded ("his gold complexion dimmed"). The youth seems to have various exemptions and immunities, through no exertion of his own, just as he seems insulated from the rough winds that shake the darling buds of May – indeed they seem to be drawn into his ambience. In what dimension does the young man exist?

At this point the argument starts to move from these effortless effects to actual attainments:

> And every fair from fair sometime declines,
> By chance, or nature's changing course, untrimmed.

"Every fair" refers to everyone so regarded, for their beauty of person or character, who must "sometime" lapse from that standard. "By chance" needs no explanation, but by "nature's changing course, untrimmed" refers to the "trimming" of a boat, which may be upset by the distribution of the cargo or some failure in the steering. I resist the interpretation that by "nature's changing course, untrimmed" refers to the onset of menstruation (certainly the young man would be unscathed) because it can hardly be taken as an example of how "fair from fair" declines.

"But" then introduces the sestet, taking the argument to another level. It invokes the *monumentum aere perennius*, the monument more lasting than bronze (Horace, *Odes* 111.30). Through this sonnet the young man's "eternal summer" will grow into "eternal lines to time":

> So long as men can breathe or eyes can see,
> So long lives this, and this gives life to thee.

The poet is not of course at this moment presenting a monument more lasting than bronze; he is endorsing the principle, he is enlisting in that cause. In its sheer accomplishment, this sonnet is typical of the poems with which Shakespeare marks a stage in the sequence, and indicates the distance travelled.

The poem immediately following asserts that "My love shall in my verse ever live young", but already sonnet 20 is on the way.

20

> A woman's face with Nature's own hand painted
> Hast thou, the master mistress of my passion;
> A woman's gentle heart, but not acquainted
> With shifting change, as is false women's fashion;
> An eye more bright than theirs, less false in rolling,
> Gilding the object whereupon it gazeth;
> A man in hue, all hues in his controlling,
> Which steals men's eyes and women's souls amazeth;
> And for a woman wert thou first created,
> Till Nature as she wrought thee fell a-doting,
> And by addition me of thee defeated,
> By adding one thing to my purpose nothing:
> > But since she pricked thee out for women's pleasure,
> > Mine be thy love, and thy love's use their treasure.[10]

This sonnet is the pronouncement of one speaker, pursued through a single sentence. It is addressed to the young man – "thou, the master mistress of my passion" – and this focus does not change, however the argument proceeds. I take the local difficulties as they present themselves in the text, in an effort to maintain its coherence.

"with Nature's own hand painted". Everywhere else in the sonnets, "painted" is something derivative or second-hand. Here we are dealing with no copyist, but Nature herself.

"the master mistress of my passion": the "mistress" of this first sonnet sequence is a) a male, and b) a master in that role. "passion": a new element.

---

[10] I deviate from the 1609 text by spelling "Nature" with a capital letter.

"A woman's gentle heart": Nature's second gift (after a woman's face) is "gentle", but it still impugns its provenance. Any feminine characteristic which is so transferred exposes shortcomings in the stock from which it is taken. The young man's gentle heart is "not acquainted / With shifting change, as is false women's fashion". It is feasible here that "quaint" in "not acquainted" could refer to "cunt", but unlikely that "shifting change" could refer to menstruation, as has been suggested. "An eye more bright than theirs" will be "less false in rolling", and less apt to gild "the object whereupon it gazeth".

At this point the young man seems to be brought forward as an exhibit, the ideal to be aimed at:

A man in hue, all hues in his controlling

where "hue" would refer to his manly appearance and disposition, and "all hues in his controlling" to the command which that gives him over others. It is a style which both "steals men's eyes and women's souls amazeth".

The octave is completed, but the semi-colon holds it in suspension. The speaker then moves to his own defeat and the betrayal:

And for a woman wert thou first created,
Till Nature as she wrought thee fell a-doting,
And by addition me of thee defeated,
By adding one thing to my purpose nothing:

Here "nothing" must be allowed its first and simplest meaning. The "addition" would not rule out a homosexual relationship, but "to my purpose nothing" does. (I do not engage with the contrary body of opinion, but simply acknowledge it.) The defeat which the speaker suffers is that at the last moment a doting Nature reserved the young man for herself and her sex. The speaker's long pronouncement is still however incomplete. The sestet has its closing couplet, which I see as his rejoinder:

But since she pricked thee out for women's pleasure,
Mine be thy love, and thy love's use their treasure.

"Mine be thy love" takes it to a higher plane, beyond the physical. "Thy love's use" is at the lower physical level, and then, at a level lower still, suited to "women's pleasure", as defined.

After this abrasive episode, the series comes to focus more on the private world of the two lovers. An exchange of hearts has been effected in sonnet 22, and in sonnet 26 the young man is addressed as "Lord of my love", by the poet in a state of "vassalage". The concern with procreation seems to have abated. There are two reflective pieces, "When in disgrace with fortune and men's eyes" (29) and "When to the sessions of sweet silent thought" (30), which are eloquent with the consolations of love in adversity. So sonnet 30 concludes:

> But if the while I think on thee, dear friend,
> All losses are restored, and sorrows end.

This "dear friend" is on the brink of what has been termed "The Friend's Fault".

The designation "The Friend's Fault" is not from Shakespeare. Its intrusion here (or anywhere) can be misleading, because there is no telling which sonnets are involved and which are not, and no clear account of the offence itself. This event is approached and accomplished in two sonnets, 33 and 34, "Full many a glorious morning have I seen" and "Why didst thou promise such a beauteous day", with the elements of nature colluding. A disciple of E. R. Curtius might feel a *topos* coming on. The morning sun of sonnet 33 flatters the mountain tops, kisses the green meadows, and gilds pale streams with "heavenly alchemy". So it was "one early morn" in the poet's experience, when the sun shone with "all triumphant splendour on my brow" – but for one hour only, then being overtaken and obscured by cloud. So the inquiry is pursued into sonnet 34. The speaker is the injured party, the young man is the miscreant:

34

> Why didst thou promise such a beauteous day
> And make me travail forth without my cloak,
> To let base clouds o'ertake me, in my way,
> Hiding thy brav'ry in their rotten smoke?
> 'Tis not enough that through the cloud thou break,
> To dry the rain on my storm-beaten face,
> For no man well of such a salve can speak
> That heals the wound and cures not the disgrace;
> Nor can thy shame give physic to my grief;
> Though thou repent, yet I have still the loss;
> Th'offender's sorrow lends but weak relief
> To him that bears the strong offence's loss.
>   Ah, but those tears are pearl which thy love sheds,
>   And they are rich, and ransom all ill deeds.

It is not clear whether this account is literal or figurative. But it is presented as a betrayal. The "beauteous day" had become a promise, giving the incentive to go forth without a cloak, enhancing the delusive garden *topos*, and encouraging a "brav'ry" of attire. The discourse continues, in a manner that is more skilful and calculated. It is agreed that the sun breaking through on to a rain-beaten face is not a sufficient recompense, that any salve applied to a wound cannot cure the disgrace, that shame is no "physic" for grief, that "sorrow" cannot recoup such a loss. In each instance there is evidence of a practical effort to help, an admission of the disgrace, shame and sorrow incurred, and mention of repentance, pointing the way to forgiveness. The rebuke is taking a positive aspect, but the concluding couplet is more positive still. The young man's contrition will bring him (has already brought him?) to tears, and "those tears are pearl", and ransom all ill deeds. (References to scripture are on offer, but are better left reverently undisturbed – as again at 42.12.)

A basic problem is that we are not told what the young man's "fault" actually was. Are we to imagine him in dalliance in the shrubbery on this "beauteous day", surprised by a change in the weather, with recrimination and apologies to follow? Sonnet 34 has communicated the offence, and at the same time prescribed the remedy. Sonnet 35 takes the exculpation a stage further:

35

No more be grieved at that which thou hast done;
Roses have thorns, and silver fountains mud;
Clouds and eclipses stain both moon and sun,
And loathsome canker lives in sweetest bud.
All men make faults, and even I, in this,
Authorizing thy trespass with compare,
Myself corrupting, salving thy amiss,
Excusing these sins more than these sins are:
For to thy sensual fault I bring in sense;
Thy adverse party is thy advocate,
And 'gainst myself a lawful plea commence:
Such civil war is in my love and hate
    That I an accessory needs must be
    To that sweet thief which sourly robs from me.

The speaker is not only excusing the young man, but transferring the blame to himself: "Myself corrupting, salving thy amiss". Engaging with "thy sensual fault", he undertakes to act for both prosecution and defence, moving to end the "civil war" between "my love and hate".

Sonnet 36 reports on the success of the mission:

Let me confess that we two must be twain,
Although our undivided loves are one

without explaining how its terms are to be met. The impression is that the transaction is now complete and the future secure. This is confirmed rather cleverly in sonnet 37, by presenting the new order in retrospect, as seen by a "decrepit father" who has taken delight in having "my love engrafted to this store". These poems, as numbered, mark the end of "The Friend's Fault".

Sonnet 38 resumes with a sense of emancipation and resurgence. It is strange that this poem has received so little attention, given its relevance to the enterprise as a whole. The poet addresses the young man as though speaking from the bond which unites them. The key terms are the verb "invent" in the first line and the noun "invention" in line 8, "Invention" comes from the Latin *invenire*, "to come upon, discover, find out, devise, contrive" and for the Elizabethans it had the sense later to be conveyed by the Romantics in such terms as "originality" and "inspiration". So the poet counts himself as fortunate:

> 38
>
> How can my Muse want subject to invent
> While thou dost breathe, that pour'st into my verse
> Thine own sweet argument, too excellent
> For every vulgar paper to rehearse?
> O give thyself the thanks, if aught in me
> Worthy perusal stand against thy sight:
> For who's so dumb, that cannot write to thee,
> When thou thyself dost give invention light?
> Be thou the tenth Muse, ten times more in worth
> Than those old nine which rhymers invocate;
> And he that calls on thee, let him bring forth
> Eternal numbers to outlive long date.
>   If my slight Muse do please these curious days,
>   The pain be mine, but thine shall be the praise.

Here the poet and the young man seem to be renewing their relationship. The poet rejoices that his Muse will never "want subject to invent" so long as the young man can breathe, and pour into his verse "thine own sweet argument". The youth could become the tenth muse, superseding the old nine and relegating the "rhymers" who perpetuate them. This eloquence is checked in the concluding couplet, as though a non-speaker may be exerting a custodial influence. If the speaker's own "slight Muse" (as he puts it) should figure at all in the future envisaged, it would only be evidence of his own humble toil, while praise for achievement would belong to others.

If "invention" is the key term being demonstrated in this poem, the compelling phrase applied to the young man is "thine own sweet argument". At the outset he had been identified with "beauty", but "sweetness" was already being remarked in sonnet 4; with his "sweet semblance" in sonnet 13, his "sweet love remembered" in sonnet 29. What of "thine own sweet argument"? An "argument" can be a topic, a theme for discussion, or whatever, but here it seems like a complex of exceptional qualities, endearing personality traits, generosity of spirit and creative talent, an inspiration to poets, and all this expressed with "sweetness". For the poet, the appeal to the "sweet argument" will become talismanic. This spirit is retained in the following sonnet 39, but then comes the jolt of the second instalment of "The Friend's Fault".

The Friend has formed a liaison with the poet's mistress. The poet was not known to have a mistress, but he is the complainant:

40

Take all my loves, my love; yea, take them all;
What hast thou then more than thou hadst before?
No love, my love, that thou mayst true love call;
All mine was thine, before thou hadst this more:
Then if for my love thou my love receivest,
I cannot blame thee, for my love thou usest;
But yet be blamed, if thou thyself deceivest
By wilful taste of what thyself refusest.
I do forgive thy robb'ry, gentle thief,
Although thou steal thee all my poverty;
And yet love knows it is a greater grief
To bear love's wrong, than hate's known injury.
    Lascivious grace, in whom all ill well shows,
    Kill me with spites; yet we must not be foes.

The speaker is indignant and wounded, and yet already re-adjusting the relationships into a more acceptable pattern. His next argument concerns the vulnerability of young men who are "gentle" and "beauteous" in situations "when a woman woos" – "what woman's son / Will sourly leave her till he have prevailed?"

41

Those pretty wrongs that liberty commits
When I am sometime absent from thy heart,
Thy beauty and thy years full well befits;
For still temptation follows where thou art.
Gentle thou art, and therefore to be won;
Beauteous thou art, therefore to be assailed;
And when a woman woos, what woman's son
Will sourly leave her till he have prevailed?
Ay me, but yet thou mightst my seat forbear,
And chide thy beauty and thy straying youth
Who lead thee in their riot even there
Where thou art forced to break a twofold truth:
    Hers by thy beauty tempting her to thee,
    Thine by thy beauty being false to me.

In the third sonnet the speaker is reliving the pain which these defections have caused, but by line 5 he is recommending a better accounting system that can be applied.

42

That thou hast her it is not all my grief,
And yet it may be said I loved her dearly;
That she hath thee is of my wailing chief,
A loss in love that touches me more nearly.
Loving offenders, thus I will excuse ye:
Thou dost love her, because thou knowst I love her,
And for my sake even so doth she abuse me,
Suff'ring my friend for my sake to approve her;
If I lose thee, my loss is my love's gain,
And losing her, my friend hath found that loss;
Both find each other, and I lose both twain,
And both for my sake lay on me this cross:
    But here's the joy, my friend and I are one;
    Sweet flattery! Then she loves but me alone.

The "loving offenders" should appreciate this outcome (while admiring the dexterity).

What is the relevance of "The Friend's Fault" to the strategy of Shakespeare's sonnets? The answer is a simple one. We are never to know what the offence was. The events could be interpreted as one man's taking the blame for the actions of another, selflessly taking over the management of the crisis, and resolving it. The same process could be seen as an exercise in duplicity and connivance, relying on deceit at every stage. Readers may be drawn to make individual judgments, but we are never to know what the "fault" was. Some of the cleverest writing in the sonnets is devoted to ensuring this strategic outcome.

The "narrative" resumes at sonnet 43, with the poet and the fair youth taking up their fractured relationship. We may be reminded of sonnet 27, described by Professor Vendler in her *Commentary* at the time of its first appearance as "the first of the travel sonnets; the first instance of insomnia", and a study of "unrepose".[11] The insomnia now threatens in sonnet 43 and "Injurious distance" strikes at 44.2. Separation inflicts the pains of travel, extending particularly to the sufferings of the horse (50.9). As before, there are declarations from a state of "vassalage":

---

[11] Vendler, *op.cit*. 152.

> That god forbid, that made me first your slave,
> I should in thought control your times of pleasure (58.1-2)

though these are now more likely to conclude with some retaliatory comment.

In this pervading fretfulness, the mature reflections of "Like as the waves make for the pebbled shore" (60) stand out, reviving the spirit of

> Not marble, nor the gilded monuments
> Of princes, shall outlive this powerful rhyme (55.1-2).

It is therefore a little unnerving to encounter "Tired with all these for restful death I cry (66), "No longer mourn for me when I am dead" (71), and "After my death (dear love) forget me quite" (72.3).

Sonnet 76 is more spirited.

76

> Why is my verse so barren of new pride,
> So far from variation or quick change?
> Why with time do I not glance aside
> To new-found methods and to compounds strange?
> Why write I still all one, ever the same,
> And keep invention in a noted weed,
> That every word almost doth tell my name,
> Showing their birth, and where they did proceed?
> O know, sweet love, I always write of you,
> And you and love are still my argument:
> So all my best is dressing old words new,
> Spending again what is already spent:
> > For as the sun is daily new and old,
> > So is my love still telling what is told.

The key word is "invention" in line 6. This reaches back to sonnet 38, when in between the first and second instalments of The Friend's Fault, the poet insisted his "Muse" would "never" want subject to "invent" so long as the young man poured "into my verse" his own "sweet argument". Now he asks:

> Why write I still all one, ever the same,
> And keep invention in a noted weed,
> That every word almost doth tell my name?

Invention in "a noted weed" would be in a fabric of good quality, tailored in a distinctive style, and now identifying the wearer as out of date. The "sweet argument" is still invoked:

> O know, sweet love, I always write of you,
> And you and love are still my argument:

but its efficacy may now be coming into question.

The sagacity of sonnet 77 may have been intended to allay these concerns, but sonnet 78 is quite confronting. The poet is in a reproving mood.

> 78
>
> So oft have I invoked thee for my Muse,
> And found such fair assistance in my verse,
> As every alien pen hath got my use,
> And under thee their poesy disperse.
> Thine eyes, that taught the dumb on high to sing,
> And heavy ignorance aloft to fly,
> Have added feathers to the learned's wing,
> And given grace a double majesty.
> Yet be most proud of that which I compile,
> Whose influence is thine, and born of thee:
> In others' works thou dost but mend the style,
> And arts with thy sweet graces graced be;
>   But thou art all my art, and dost advance,
>   As high as learning, my rude ignorance.

Here the speaker, addressing the fair youth, remarks "so oft have I invoked thee for my Muse". His recital recalls events with which the young man is already familiar, and of which the Muse is already cognisant, but it is the young man whose role is consistently scrutinised, in the constant references to "thou", "thee", "thy" and "thine".

"So oft as I have invoked thee for my Muse" could be an expression of gratitude, as again for finding "such fair assistance for my verse". That "every alien pen hath got my use" is hardly a commendation. It implies that an alien culture is intruding on our own, and "hath got my use" reinforces this, with the "authentic" articles becoming very hard to distinguish. In the expression "hath got my use" there is a sense of the second rate, or the second hand, or something more distasteful, as at 20.14. "Disperse" implies "dispose of", appropriate for the marketing style "under thee".

There is an acrobatic leap in the second quatrain – into the past. With "Thine eyes", the speaker recalls for the young man a joint foray of theirs, in which the fair youth had excelled. There were four achievements, which seem to be encoded now in terms of overcoming limitations of any kind (some sort of "uplift" is being suggested). Thus the (dumb?) birds were taught to sing "on high", those held back by ignorance were raised to fly "aloft", the learned were taken up another grade (adding feathers to their wings), and those already "graced" were further enhanced in status. The tone of the recital is now more positive.

In another acrobatic leap, in the third quatrain, the speaker and the fair youth are brought back to the present. They find themselves to be on the same mission, (which seems to include the writing of this poem). The speaker looks back on the past record, and then addresses the fair youth again:

> Yet be most proud of that which I compile,
> Whose influence is thine, and born of thee:
> In others' works thou dost but mend the style,
> And arts with thy sweet graces graced be;
>> But thou are all my art, and dost advance
>> As high as learning, my rude ignorance.

The key term here is "influence". It is used in the sense of a heavenly body "flowing in" to another, or into an earthly one, pervading and transforming it. This influence is "thine", the poet affirms (to the young man): thou can "mend the style" of others' works, and enhance the art of others, but "thou art all my art", and this relationship eclipses any other.

In trying to provide an exegesis of sonnet 78, one may begin to wonder "How do I extricate myself from all this?" Or "Is this the end of poetry as we know it?" or "Do we now have to rely on astral influences?" It so happens that the next set of sonnets engages in different ways with the question of whether poetry is still possible.

Collisions will occur. Indeed it almost seems as though the strategy now is to devise a series of collisions, to propel the movement forward. Sonnet 79 goes back to the beginning of the relationship of the poet and the young man, which is now at a critical stage: "My sick Muse doth give another place".

79

> Whilst I alone did call upon thy aid
> My verse alone had all thy gentle grace;
> But now my gracious numbers are decayed,
> And my sick Muse doth give another place.
> I grant, sweet love, thy lovely argument
> Deserves the travail of a worthier pen;
> Yet what of thee thy poet doth invent
> He robs thee of, and pays it thee again;
> He lends thee virtue, and he stole that word
> From thy behaviour; beauty doth he give,
> And found it in thy cheek; he can afford
> No praise to thee, but what in thee doth live:
>> Then thank him not for that which he doth say,
>> Since what he owes thee, thou thyself dost pay.

The mode of address is significant:

> I grant, sweet love, thy lovely argument
> Deserves the travail of a worthier pen.

The "sweet love" and "thy lovely argument" go back to the indispensable pact of sonnet 38, with the talismanic "sweet argument". Given that the transition is assured, sonnet 79 assumes the authoritative tone of the non-speaker. Presumably any "worthier pen" will continue to take his inspiration from the young man, in realising the "lovely argument".

The arrival of the Rival Poet (a title not known in Shakespeare's vocabulary) is notified in sonnet 80. It is communicated to the young man by the (incumbent) Poet, who seems rather rattled.

80

> O how I faint when I of you do write,
> Knowing a better spirit doth use your name,
> And in the praise thereof spends all his might,
> To make me tongue-tied speaking of your fame.
> But since your worth, wide as the ocean is,
> The humble as the proudest sail doth bear,
> My saucy bark, inferior far to his,
> On your broad main doth wilfully appear.
> Your shallowest help will hold me up afloat,
> Whilst he upon your soundless deep doth ride;
> Or, being wracked, I am a worthless boat,
> He of tall building, and of goodly pride.
>   Then if he thrive, and I be cast away,
>   The worst was this: my love was my decay.

Here the poet is still the speaker, and his addressee is still the fair youth. The newcomer is "a better spirit" who so extols the young man that the speaker finds himself tongue-tied when he himself wishes to extol him. In line 5 the speaker reminds the young man that "your worth" is as wide as the ocean, which "the humble as the proudest sail doth bear". The speaker in his own "saucy bark" has "wilfully" ventured on to "your broad main", where "Your shallowest help will hold me up afloat". The Rival Poet is presumably the rival captain, "upon your soundless deep".

We seem to be in a hypothetical nautical contest, with The Rival Poet (the intrusive newcomer) on one side and the Poet and the young man on the other.

The Rival Poet will be referred to later, but the problems engaging the Poet himself are immediate, as he is addressing the young man.

82

> I grant thou wert not married to my Muse,
> And therefore mayst without attaint o'erlook
> The dedicated words which writers use
> Of their fair subject, blessing every book.
> Thou art as fair in knowledge as in hue,
> Finding thy worth a limit past my praise,
> And therefore art enforced to seek anew
> Some fresher stamp of the time-bettering days,
> And do so love; yet when they have devised
> What strained touches rhetoric can lend,
> Thou, truly fair, wert truly sympathized
> In true plain words, by thy true-telling friend;
> > And their gross painting might be better used
> > Where cheeks need blood; in thee it is abused.

This is a disagreement which is already at an advanced stage, and will be carried further in later sonnets. In his relationship with the young man, the poet has hitherto had the role of mentor. This is now under challenge. There are two key statements. The first is that the poet says that the youth's own work has reached "a limit past my praise". The youth therefore has felt "enforced" to seek "some fresher stamp" to carry him forward. The second key statement, from the mentor, is "And do so love". An advocate of "true plain words", he warns of the "strained touches" that rhetoric can lend, the "gross painting" that is indulged in (excoriated since 21.2), with the risks of the "modern quill".

It seems that the young man, for his part, makes "praise" a requirement. The poet apologizes for having "slept in your report" (83.5) – but goes on to say that, had he undertaken the review, it would have been adverse. He is more positive in sonnet 84, apparently referring to a more favourable notice,

> But he that writes of you, if he can tell
> That you are you, so dignifies his story.
> Let him but copy what in you is writ,
> Not making worse what nature made so clear.

but then spoils it by adding:

> You to your beauteous blessings add a curse,
> Being fond on praise, which makes your praises worse.

The poet eventually becomes embarrassed (sonnet 85) when he hears the young man praised, and if he joins in, feels like the "unlettered clerk" who in church cannot read the lesson, but joins in the stock responses, such as "Amen".

> Hearing you praised, I say, " 'Tis so, 'tis true",
> And to the most of praise add something more;
> But that is in my thought, whose love to you
> (Though words come hindmost) holds his rank before;
> The others for the breath of words respect,
> Me for my dumb thought, speaking in effect.

This goes on, with a genuine difference of opinion, exaggerated by obstinacy and resentment on both sides, until it has disastrous consequences.

The next intersection proves to be critical, because the speaker is the Poet, who seems to have set himself up as an interrogator, investigating the episode of the Rival Poet and the folklore associated with it. The sonnet takes the form of a series of questions.

86

> Was it the proud full sail of his great verse,
> Bound for the prize of all-too-precious you,
> That did my ripe thoughts in my brain in-hearse,
> Making their tomb the womb wherein they grew?
> Was it his spirit, by spirits taught to write
> Above a mortal pitch, that struck me dead?
> No, neither he, nor his compeers by night,
> Giving him aid, my verse astonished.
> He, nor that affable familiar ghost
> Which nightly gulls him with intelligence,
> As victors of my silence cannot boast;
> I was not sick of any fear from thence,
>   But when your countenance filled up his line,
>   Then lacked I matter, that enfeebled mine.

The proud full sail of his great verse recalls the nautical metaphor of sonnet 80, where the proud full sail belonged to the Rival Poet, and the fair youth was the "all-too-precious you". The nautical metaphor here is concerned with the proud full sail of his "great verse", which is hard to represent poetically. No-one has explained what verse this might be, but apparently the thought of it "in-hearsed" the "ripe thoughts" in the Poet's brain at the time.

> Was it his spirit, by spirits taught to write
> Above a mortal pitch, that struck me dead?

The "spirits" known to The Rival Poet were spirited individuals or individual spirits, nightly visitants, some able to write "above a mortal pitch". These seem to be strange acquaintances for a Rival Poet to have. He was not troubled by that "affable familiar ghost" which nightly gulled others with intelligence. None of these can boast to be "victors of my silence", the Poet insists:

> But when your countenance filled up his line,
> Then lacked I matter, that enfeebled mine.

"Countenance" can mean "give countenance to", or that the young man put forward his own work, which the Poet rejected.

This marks the disintegration of the relationship of the Poet and the Fair Youth. It is the demise of the sweet argument.

The sonnet sequence made provision for the farewell to love. Sidney had written "Leave me, O love which reachest but to dust". Samuel Daniel had renounced Delia, Drayton was to write

> Since there's no help, come let us kiss and part.
> Nay, I have done; you get no more of me.

So Shakespeare offered his tribute:

87

> Farewell, thou art too dear for my possessing,
> And like enough thou knowst thy estimate;
> The charter of thy worth give thee releasing;
> My bonds in thee are all determinate.
> For how do I hold thee but by thy granting,
> And for that riches where is my deserving?
> The cause of this fair gift in me is wanting,
> And so my patent back again is swerving.
> Thyself thou gav'st, thy own worth then not knowing,
> Or me, to whom thou gav'st it, else mistaking;
> So thy great gift upon misprision growing
> Comes home again, on better judgement making.
>   Thus have I had thee as a dream doth flatter,
>   In sleep a king, but waking no such matter.

This is couched in legal language, as though a contract had expired, and some details remain to be settled.

Shakespeare is being more venturesome. The aftermath takes on an identity of its own. The intent of the first half-dozen of the sonnets that follow is given in the conclusion of the first one:

> Such is my love, to thee I so belong,
> That for thy right myself will bear all wrong. (88.13-14)

This persists in "Thy love is better than high birth to me" (91.9), as in the exclamation "Happy to have thy love, happy to die!" (92.12). But in sonnet 93 the beloved is being compared to "Eve's apple":

93

So shall I live, supposing thou art true,
Like a deceived husband; so love's face
May still seem love to me, though altered new,
Thy looks with me, thy heart in other place;
For there can live no hatred in thine eye,
Therefore in that I cannot know thy change.
In many's looks, the false heart's history
Is writ in moods and frowns and wrinkles strange;
But heaven in thy creation did decree
That in thy face sweet love should ever dwell;
Whate'er thy thoughts or thy heart's workings be,
Thy looks should nothing thence but sweetness tell.
    How like Eve's apple doth thy beauty grow,
    If thy sweet virtue answer not thy show.

In Sonnet 94 we are told that "Lilies that fester smell far worse than weeds", then with a sigh (95.9–11):

O what a mansion have those vices got,
Which for their habitation chose out thee.

The occupation of writing poetry now seems to come under threat, and the "truant Muse" is summoned (101.1) and reproached "O blame me not if I no more can write!" (103.5), until a more limited power of "invention" is accepted (105.11).

A certain perspective is established in sonnet 104, with the relationship now three years old. The passage of time has been regularly measured in terms of the seasons, especially winter as a time of absence (97), and spring as a time of promise or renewal. These occasions stay in the memory:

          three winters cold
Have from the forests shook three summers' pride;
Three beauteous springs to yellow autumn turned
In process of the seasons I have seen
Three April perfumes in three hot Junes burned,
Since first I saw you fresh, which yet art green (104.3–8)

In sonnet 107 the speaker is defying death ("Since 'spite of him I'll live in this poor rhyme") (107.11) and in sonnet 121 resisting slander. This context may give a rather different effect to such a poem as "Let me not to the marriage of true minds / Admit impediments" (116), which might elsewhere seem one of the general reflective pieces.

There is a more personal note in the last sonnet in this series, addressed to "O thou my lovely Boy".[12]

126

O thou my lovely Boy, who in thy power
Dost hold Time's fickle glass, his sickle hour,
Who hast by waning grown, and therein show'st
Thy lover's withering, as thy sweet self grow'st;
If Nature, sovereign mistress over wrack,
As thou goest onwards still will pluck thee back,
She keeps thee to this purpose: that her skill
May Time disgrace, and wretched minutes kill.
Yet fear her, O thou minion of her pleasure:
She may detain, but not still keep, her treasure!
Her audit, though delayed, answered must be,
And her quietus is to render thee.
    (   )
    (   ) (126.10–12)

Nature, who was influential at the outset, is a "sovereign mistress" now, but she is subject to Time. Nature, "As thou goest onwards still will pluck thee back", the poet declares, but "She may detain, but still not keep, her treasure!" In now losing the "lovely Boy", the Poet may be allowed this small victory over Nature.

Sonnet 126, as printed, is two lines short, as indicated by the printer's marks at the end. The next sonnet is simply numbered 127.

The series following has taken its identity from the Dark Lady, once again a title not conferred by Shakespeare and not found in his vocabulary. For some time golden hair was considered to be beautiful, as a compliment to the Queen, who was a redhead. Lady Rich, Astrophil's Stella, had eyes that were gleaming black, and in *Love's Labours Lost* Biron had declared his love for "the heavenly Rosaline", one of the ladies attending the Princess of France, prompting the King to interject, "By heaven, thy love is black as ebony", and Biron to respond, "Is ebony like her? O word divine!", concluding "No face is fair that is not full so black" (IV.iii.219–51).

This courtly approach was available to Shakespeare, but he chose to introduce the series with a speaker who is disgruntled and inexpert.

---

[12] Capitals have been supplied for "Nature" and "Time".

127

In the old age black was not counted fair,
Or if it were, it bore not beauty's name;
But now is black beauty's successive heir,
And beauty slandered with a bastard shame:
For since each hand hath put on nature's power,
Fairing the foul with art's false borrowed face,
Sweet beauty hath no name, no holy bower,
But is profaned, if not lives in disgrace.
Therefore my mistress' eyes are raven black,
Her eyes so suited, and they mourners seem
At such who, not born fair, no beauty lack,
Sland'ring creation with a false esteem;
    Yet so they mourn, becoming of their woe,
    That every tongue says beauty should look so.

Sonnet 128 is unremarkable, but 129 is one of those "disquisitions" that Shakespeare makes from time to time, as though defining a theme.

129

Th'expense of spirit in a waste of shame
Is lust in action; and till action, lust
Is perjured, murd'rous, bloody, full of blame,
Savage, extreme, rude, cruel, not to trust;
Enjoyed no sooner but despised straight;
Past reason hunted, and no sooner had,
Past reason hated as a swallowed bait,
On purpose laid to make the taker mad;
Mad in pursuit, and in possession so,
Had, having, and in quest to have, extreme;
A bliss in proof, and proved, a very woe;
Before, a joy proposed; behind, a dream.
    All this world well knows, yet none knows well
    To shun the heaven that leads men to this hell.

Here "waste" is an alternative spelling of "waist", and a "waist of shame" identifies a prostitute. So lust is defined as sex with a prostitute, in a quite clinical analysis (though "hell" is a mark of disapproval).

A disquisition, certainly. But does sonnet 129 also signal a change of attitude, a change of strategy, at this point? The series takes on an unflinching quality, and the odd celebratory poem will be hard to find. Sonnet 130 may seem to be offering one.

130

My mistress' eyes are nothing like the sun;
Coral is far more red than her lips' red;
If snow be white, why then her breasts are dun;
If hairs be wires, black wires grow on her head;
I have seen roses damasked, red and white,
But no such roses see I in her cheeks;
And in some perfumes is there more delight
Than in the breath that from my mistress reeks.
I love to hear her speak, yet well I know
That music hath a far more pleasing sound;
I grant I never saw a goddess go;
My mistress when she walks treads on the ground.
    And yet, by heaven, I think my love as rare
    As any she belied by false compare.

In my earlier account of the literary climate of 1590–1610, I referred to the vogue of the gulling sonnet, and cited an example by John Davies. Another such sonnet attributed to him might be introduced now:

Faith (wench) I cannot court thy sprightly eyes,
With the base Viall placed betweene my Thighes;
I cannot lispe, nor to some Fiddle sing,
Nor run uppon a high strecht Minikin.
I cannot whine in puling Elegies,
Intombing Cupid with sad obsequies.
I am not fashioned for these amorous times,
To court thy beutie with lascivious rimes.
I cannot dally, caper, daunce and sing,
Oyling my saint with supple sonneting.
I cannot crosse my armes, or sigh ay me,
Ay me Forlorne: egregious Fopperie.
I cannot busse thy fist, play with thy hayre,
Swearing by Jove, Thou are most debonaire.
    Not I by Cock, but shall I tel thee roundly,
    Hark in thine eare, zounds I can ( ) thee soundly.[13]

I find it hard to believe that either of these poems refers to an actual woman. The one exhibited by Shakespeare is a playful aside, because his concern is with the "tyrannous" mistress of sonnet 131, where the speaker is the one introduced in 127, to be caught in successive encounters with the "black" of his mistress's reputation. In sonnets 133 and 134 she has recruited as lovers

---

[13] Krueger ed., *The Poems of Sir John Davies*, 180

both the Poet and the Friend from the main series, and the original suitor declares (sonnet 147):

> For I have sworn thee fair, and thought thee bright,
> Who art as black as hell, and dark as night.

There is an insistence in the strategy of these later poems that is felt even in the comic interlude which Shakespeare allowed himself on the cult of anonymity in the sonnets. There was a time when readers had to guess the identities of *Astrophil* and *Stella*, or who in real life was Samuel Daniel's *Delia*, and speculation continues on the *Caelica*, *Cynthia* and *Myra* of Fulke Greville's poems. The name Will may stand for William, or for the noun will as a legal document, or will as in willpower, or for the male member or the female genitalia. Or William Shakespeare. One example should suffice.

135

> Whoever hath her wish, thou hast thy Will,
> And Will to boot, and Will in overplus;
> More than enough am I, that vex thee still,
> To thy sweet will making addition thus.
> Wilt thou, whose will is large and spacious,
> Not once vouchsafe to hide my will in thine?
> Shall will in others seem right gracious,
> And in my will no fair acceptance shine?
> The sea, all water, yet receives rain still,
> And in abundance addeth to his store;
> So thou, being rich in Will, add to thy Will
> One will of mine, to make thy large Will more:
>   Let no unkind, no fair beseechers kill;
>   Think all but one, and me in that one Will.

The series resumes with 138 ("When my love swears that she is made of truth") and 144 ("Two loves I have, of comfort and despair") which had first been published in 1599. The speaker addresses his soul in sonnet 146, and in 147 declares "Past cure I am, now reason is past care", though going on in sonnet 149 to urge "But, love, hate on, for now I know thy mind". This is a descent into nullity.

The issue now is what is left of the relationship. In 151 the speaker declares that on his side it is a question of tumescence and detumescence.

>   flesh stays no further reason,
> But rising at thy name doth point out thee …
> He is contented thy poor drudge to be,
> To stand in thy affairs, fall by thy side. (151.8-12)

Sonnet 152 takes up the issue of who has broken more oaths in the relationship.

152

> In loving thee thou knowst I am forsworn;
> But thou art twice forsworn to me love swearing,
> In act thy bed-vow broke and new faith torn,
> In vowing new hate after new love bearing.
> But why of two oaths' breach do I accuse thee,
> When I break twenty? I am perjured most,
> For all my vows are oaths but to misuse thee,
> And all my honest faith in thee is lost:
> For I have sworn deep oaths of thy deep kindness,
> Oaths of thy love, thy truth, thy constancy,
> And to enlighten thee gave eyes to blindness,
> Or made them swear against the thing they see:
> > For I have sworn thee fair: more perjured eye,
> > To swear against the truth so foul a lie.

The speaker seems to blame himself.

> But why of two oaths' breach do I accuse thee,
> When I break twenty?

Twenty would seem enough, but the real guilt is that his oaths are guaranteeing "thy love, thy truth, thy constancy".

> For I have sworn thee fair: more perjured eye,
> To swear against the truth so foul a lie.

Shakespeare is making the point that human existence at this level is not worth continuing. This is a termination.

There are two sonnets appended, numbered 153 and 154, which provide a coda. They are based on a conceit from *The Greek Anthology* (among other sources). Three points are being made. The first is that love (in some form) will always be part of human experience. The second is that as Cupid is in charge, there will always be mishaps. The third point is rather conjectural, as it depends on the outcome of any positive action Cupid may now take. It may be helpful if there is a fountain or flowing river nearby. But the success rate is only fifty percent.

FINIS.

Shakespeare's Moral Wisdom and Political Insight: Dual Power in *Coriolanus*

David Brooks

I

In his essay "Reflections on Clarendon's *History of the Rebellion*" (1948) L. C. Knights draws a comparison between Clarendon and Trotsky as historians, much to Trotsky's disadvantage.[1]

Knights indeed recognises the deficiencies of Clarendon's *History* as offering an explanation for the English Civil War or "Great Rebellion". Clarendon ignores the profounder social forces that were reshaping English society, and that were bound to have repercussions in political life. As Knights writes:

> But we look in vain in the *History* for any recognition of the deeper motives that united large masses of men in fundamental opposition to king and bishop. He was completely unaware of the widespread shift in economic power that gave significance to the parliamentary slogan, 'Property and liberty'. He had no understanding of the sober strength of Puritanism: he saw only its fanatical and intolerant side.[2]

But, for Knights, these deficiencies count for little in comparison with Clarendon's positive qualities. Clarendon displays an interest in individual characters that is grounded in, and expresses a profound wisdom about human nature and society, a wisdom that is both moral and political.

> What interests Clarendon is the essential bent of a man's mind, the motives that, ingrained in character, issue in significant action. He does not simplify. He has a special relish in revealing inconsistencies and in reconciling them.

---

[1] L. C. Knights, *Further Explorations* (Stanford: Stanford University Press, 1965), 121-137.

[2] *Ibid.*, 121. Edward Hyde, first Earl of Clarendon (b. 1608), wrote his *History* partly between 1646 and 1648, and partly in exile between 1667 and his death in 1674. It was published posthumously in three volumes in 1702, 1703 and 1704 as *The True Historical Narrative of the Rebellion and the Civil Wars in England*. It is generally known as *The History of the Rebellion*. See Clarendon, *Selections from the History of the Rebellion and The Life by Himself*, ed. G. Huehns with a new introduction by Hugh Trevor-Roper (Oxford: Oxford University Press, 1978), [iv], vi-x.

Each of his characters is judged; there is an explicit or implicit moral evaluation. The judgment is not always, we may feel, a fair one; but it is always based on Clarendon's own sense of the person. It is not – or not as a rule – imposed; it issues from a cultivated awareness in which moral taste and psychological acumen are combined.[3]

After quoting Clarendon's remarks on the value of "public debates in Council", debates which allow for the maximum of wisdom to be expressed from a multiplicity of counsellors, Knights comments:

Here, we may say, is political wisdom springing from a lifetime of political experience. True; but my point is that it is more than *political* wisdom.[4]

Knights now quotes Clarendon on how a minister should respond to envy and detraction with patience, resignation and self-control rather than with anger and indignation, and comments:

This is moral wisdom; and it underlies – is one with – the political wisdom. It is this, I think, that constitutes Clarendon's greatness as an historian: that there is a constant reference beyond politics – beyond, that is, the conflict of forces – to the human ground.[5]

Thus, Clarendon represents for Knights an approach to society and history that focuses on individuals and the morality of their conduct, because only in individuals and their personal relations does the "concrete actuality" of human life exist. For Knights politics must be subordinated to ethics; and both must be grounded in a conception of human nature that recognises the moral and spiritual dimensions of life, and not just the struggle for power. Political wisdom is impossible without moral wisdom.

Inevitably, for Knights, Trotsky represents the very opposite of what Clarendon typifies, that is, the complete absence of moral wisdom, the immoral pursuit of power for its own sake, and the dissolution of the individual in the abstract and the general. Commenting on Trotsky's *History of the Russian Revolution*, Knights writes:

Trotsky, like Marx, from whom his historical method is derived, is clearly the product of an age dominated by the idea of scientific law. His vigorous intellect works in terms of masses and social forces, and the slightest fluctuation in the main course of events is caught and pinned into place as a logically necessary exception.

---

[3] Knights, *Further Explorations*, 123.
[4] *Ibid.*, 129. Italics in original.
[5] *Ibid.*, 130.

If we feel that Clarendon sometimes mistakenly attributes representative acts to purely personal motives, in reading Trotsky we are constantly aware of the absence of the personal – especially of the irrational, or non-rational – motives that certainly played a part in the actions he describes.

Nor is there a single person – not even Lenin – who appears in the book as anything more than a bloodless embodiment of political will or of some social category.

The result is that although the *History of the Russian Revolution* is packed with detail the total effect is of something abstract and schematized. One cannot resist the conclusion that the pattern, so vigorously asserted in its complex detail, is to a large extent imposed.[6]

Knight's condemnatory judgment is representative:

The blindness to everything in life but some schematized abstractions is the disease of a mind that thinks solely in terms of power and that therefore, of necessity, propagates the idea of power as the sole concern of political man. Trotsky is the embodiment of political will masquerading as destiny or impersonal law.[7]

Thus, Trotsky abandons traditional wisdom in the pursuit of science (and power), and fails to achieve even science.

II

In this essay I do not intend to criticise Knights or to defend Trotsky. I only wish to suggest that Knights's view of the humane approach to politics is partial and one-sided, and needs to be complemented by some such view as Trotsky's that recognises that social forces are objects in their own right, distinct from, although arising out of, and reacting upon the actions and interactions of individuals.

Knights's view may be described as primarily idealist, and only to a limited extent realist. It is idealist in that it judges the actions of individuals from the standpoint of an ideal moral order. Its realism is limited to the

---

[6] *Ibid.*, 133-134. Trotsky wrote *The History of the Russian Revolution* in 1930. See Victor Serge and Natalia Sedova Trotsky, *The Life and Death of Leon Trotsky*, tr. Arnold J. Pomerans (London: Wildwood House Ltd, 1975), 165. The English translation of Trotsky's *History* by Max Eastman was published by Victor Gollancz Ltd in three volumes, 1932-1933, and in one volume in 1934. This was the translation used by Knights. See Leon Trotsky, *The History of the Russian Revolution*, translated from the Russian by Max Eastman (London: Pluto Press Ltd, 1977), [4]. I have used this reissued edition, to which my references are made.
[7] Knights, *Further Explorations*, 135.

patterns of cause and effect in the actions and interactions of individuals, and does not extend to the causes and consequences of social forces, or of the creation, operation and dissolution of social institutions.

Trotsky's view, by contrast, is primarily realist in that he is overwhelmingly concerned with the patterns of cause and effect in the political sphere, both in relation to individuals, and in relation to social forces and social institutions. His view is only sporadically idealist when he judges individuals as to their political effectiveness or ineffectiveness. The ideal order to which he refers is certainly political, and not moral.

The point of these generalities is that Knights finds in Shakespeare's *Coriolanus* the same approach to politics that he attributes (persuasively) to Clarendon. He writes:

> In *Coriolanus* the main subject is the relation between a member of the ruling class, a Governor, and the political society to which he belongs; and the handling of it results in a breaking-down of any over-simple distinction we might be tempted to make between what is 'individual', on the one hand, and what is 'social' and 'political' on the other.[8]

But the merging of the categories of "individual" and "social/political" turns out to be a matter of seeing the social and political in terms of the individual. Thus:

> What the play emphasizes is the challenge of difference and diversity. There is no suggestion that the social distinctions between patricians and plebeians ought not to exist: it is suggested that the diversified social group, the body politic, is in danger of corruption to the extent that *what lies behind diversity* is lost sight of. 'What lies behind' is of course simple humanity. It is Coriolanus' defective humanity that makes him a defective governor.[9]

> The play is an experiment in *concrete* political thinking, and one of the things that it demonstrates so superbly is that disruption in the state – the body politic – is related to individual disharmony by something more palpable than an Elizabethan trick of metaphor, that the public crisis is rooted in the personal and habitual.[10]

For Knights, the actuality of political life is not the struggle for power, but the web of relationships amongst the individual political actors.

---

[8] *Ibid.*, 20 ("Shakespeare's Politics: with Some Reflections on the Nature of Tradition").
[9] *Ibid.*, 21 ("Shakespeare's Politics"). Italics in original.
[10] *Ibid.*, 62 ("Poetry, Politics and the English Tradition"). Italics in original.

> And it seems to me an indication of the humanizing value of literary studies that an attempt to understand, say, *Coriolanus*, should at least bring into view ways of thinking about politics and society that do not begin with questions of power, and forms of social life in which direct relationships are obviously more important than impersonal techniques.[11]

Moreover, to focus on individuals and their relationships is to negate any generalising approach to politics.

> The reason why Shakespeare's political plays can so refresh and invigorate our own thinking is that they embody not doctrines but specific insights: they are a perpetual warning against simplification and abstraction, a solvent of mechanical and rigid formulae.[12]

Shakespeare, thus, stands with Clarendon, in implicit opposition to Trotsky.

I do not wish to reverse this verdict, although I think it is itself a gross simplification. I only wish to suggest that Shakespeare and Trotsky have something in common, which Knights completely ignores. This something is crucial to an understanding of the depiction of political life in *Coriolanus*. It is, of course, an interest in social classes, in the ways in which social classes enter into conflict, in how their conflict produces a political crisis, and how that crisis is resolved in what is in fact a revolution.

Shakespeare's depiction of this crisis in the first three acts of the play is a realist study of the struggle for power. It is a struggle for power between classes, and not just individuals, however much the working out of the crisis is mediated by the actions and character of individuals, and however much the individuals are implicitly judged morally, as Knights correctly suggests.

Shakespeare could transcend and reconcile the oppositions that Knights finds between Clarendon and Trotsky, because in Shakespeare's time there had not yet occurred that tearing of the social fabric that was to place Clarendon on one side of the Civil War. Shakespeare could make use of the representations of class conflict in his sources, Livy and Plutarch, whereas Clarendon (who, presumably, was familiar with these and other ancient authors) would have recoiled from them. For Clarendon, the rebellion of the English people against their king was just monstrous, hardly capable of rational understanding.[13]

---

[11] *Ibid.*, 72 ("Poetry, Politics and the English Tradition").

[12] *Ibid.*, 62 ("Poetry, Politics and the English Tradition").

[13] Clarendon affirms "all this bulk of misery to have proceeded, and to have been brought upon us, from the same natural causes and means, which have usually attended kingdoms, swoln with long plenty, pride and excess, towards some signal mortifications, and castigation of Heaven". But his emphasis is on the irrational and the supernatural: "And then, though the hand and judgment of God will be very visible, in the infatuating a people (as ripe and prepared for destruction) into all the perverse actions of folly and madness...." See Clarendon, *Selections*, 1, 2.

There is further reason for considering the concept of a struggle for power in *Coriolanus*, because it helps us to understand even those parts of the play that focus on the moral conduct of individuals, and their relationships. Power is not something separate from either passion or virtue, but a characteristic or condition of them. The ideas that we bring from Trotsky to the study of the class conflict in *Coriolanus* will turn out to have some relevance to the study of the personal relations between the central characters.

But it is not just the general idea of class conflict that we must take from Trotsky. It is specifically the concept of the *dual power*.

III

Trotsky's concept of the *dual power* applies to the political relations between social classes during a period of revolution, and especially to the changes in power relations in the sphere of the state.[14] But it may be considered as a specification and development of the general dialectical concept of the unity of opposites. For the sake of clarifying the analogies between the political and the personal aspects of *Coriolanus* it may be useful to unfold the concept in its general, abstract form.

A unity of opposites will be a totality whose opposing sides will sometimes be in a state of harmony and co-operation, and sometimes in a state of antagonism, portending rupture. If rupture does not occur, the old form of the totality may be restored. If rupture does occur, the totality may be reconstituted in a new form, or dissolved altogether.

So much is commonplace. What Trotsky's innovation does implicitly is to expand the notion of antagonism and rupture by introducing the idea of single and dual power-centres.

In order to function harmoniously the totality will need a single centre of power, which will maintain relations of dominance and subordination between the two opposing sides. But under the impact of internal development, and perhaps external conditions, the two opposing sides of the totality may move from a harmonious relationship into a state of antagonism. At this point, the hitherto subordinate side may throw up a new centre of power of its own, so that the totality now has two centres of power, in uneasy relations with each other, rendering the totality unstable and prone to collapse. One of these centres of power must defeat the other, if the totality is to be restabilised, whether in the old form or, after rupture, in a new form.[15]

The application of all this to class relations and revolution will be obvious. According to Marxian theory, a society composed of ruling and ruled classes

---

[14] Trotsky expounds his theory of the dual power in chapter XI ("Dual Power") of his *History*, 223-232. But the whole book is devoted to applying the concept to the analysis of the course of events in 1917.
[15] Trotsky, *History*, 224-225.

may develop to the point where the ruling classes can no longer maintain their rule. The normal patterns of dominance and subordination lapse, as the society enters a period of revolutionary crisis. The old ruling classes are overthrown, and a new society is constituted with one of the former subordinate classes as the new ruling class.

Trotsky's innovation is to analyse the process of revolutionary crisis as involving a dual power regime, or a series of such regimes.[16] One of the subordinate classes creates a new centre of state power which co-exists for a time with the old centre of state power. The co-existence of two power-centres is necessarily unstable, and cannot last. It must be resolved by the defeat of one by the other.[17] If the social and material conditions exist for the old ruling class to re-establish its rule, then the revolution will be defeated, and the old order will be restored. If these social and material conditions no longer exist, then the old ruling class will be defeated, and a new order will be established, with a new ruling class.

In the case of the Russian Revolution of 1917, failure of the war-effort, and discontent in the Russian armed forces, combined with popular opposition in the streets, cause the old ruling classes to withdraw their support from the Czar, who abdicates, thus initiating the period of revolutionary crisis. Elements of the State Duma form a Provisional Government, which represents the interests of the owners of large-scale property, while workers and soldiers set up the Petrograd Soviet, and subsequently other soviets in Moscow, and throughout Russia. The demands of the workers and soldiers for "peace, land and bread" are incompatible with the Provisional Government's policy of continuing the war, and preserving property relations in land suitable to the interests of landlords. The Provisional Government thus becomes paralysed. Economic deterioration and the advance of the German army on Petrograd force the Provisional Government and the Soviet into violent conflict. In July 1917 the Soviet is temporarily defeated. But it re-groups, defeats an attempted coup from the Right by General Kornilov, and overthrows the Provisional Government in October. The dual power regime comes to an end with the establishment of a new Bolshevik government, elected by the Soviet, the Council of People's Commissars.[18]

---

[16] For example, Trotsky notes that in the case of the English Civil War there is first a dual power regime between the King and Parliament (supported by the City of London). But then, a second dual power regime emerges between the Parliament and the Army. A third dual power system between the leadership of the Army and its lower ranks fails to develop, as the Levellers, the leaders of the lower ranks, are crushed. Out of this process comes the dictatorship of Cromwell. See Trotsky, *History*, 225-226. Trotsky makes a similar analysis of the course of the French Revolution of 1789 (226-228).
[17] Trotsky, *History*, 224-225.
[18] After some preliminaries Trotsky's *History* moves from the February Revolution of 1917 to the October Revolution. For a convenient account of the year of revolution, see Sheila Fitzpatrick, *The*

As we shall see, the concept of the dual power is vividly illustrated in Shakespeare's depiction of the crisis between patricians and plebeians in the first three acts of *Coriolanus*. The concept is not only implicit in what happens, providing the pattern for the unfolding of events. It is actually articulated in the dialogue.

IV

Shakespeare's sources, Livy and Plutarch, both give a clear view of class conflict in Ancient Rome, and of the facts concerning the dual power regime between consuls and senate on one side, and tribunes on the other – even if neither author has a single term for the idea of dual power.[19]

Livy shows how the common people of Rome – peasants and artisans – are subjected to a dialectic of impoverishment: poverty leads to debt; an incapacity to repay debts leads to enslavement. Constant warfare with neighbouring cities exacerbates the situation by interrupting agriculture and commerce, plunging the people further into poverty and debt. The patrician class and the senate are limited in what they can do to provide debt relief because the creditors are to be found in their own ranks. Incompatible class interests produce endless crises and political struggles.[20]

Livy also shows the characteristic political strategies and tactics of each side. The people's habitual tactic is the strike, especially the refusal to enlist in the army, just at the time when Rome's enemies are launching an attack. The senate is routinely faced with a choice between taking a hardline against the people's demands, a policy of coercion, and making concessions, a policy of conciliation. In Livy's account, Martius is a spokesman for the hardliners.[21]

Russian Revolution, 1917-1932 (Oxford: Oxford University Press, 1982), ch. 2 (34-60) ("1917: The Revolutions of February and October").

[19] We know from verbal echoes that Shakespeare read the "fable of the belly" in Philemon Holland's translation of Livy: *The Roman Historie written by T. Livius of Padua* (1600). It is unlikely that Shakespeare would not have read the rest of the story of Martius. Sir Thomas North's Plutarch translation, *The Lives of the noble Grecians and Romans, compared together by that grave learned Philosopher and Historiographer, Plutarch of Chaeronea*, was first published in 1579. Second and third editions appeared in 1595 and 1603. It is uncertain which of these editions Shakespeare used.

[20] Livy, *The Early History of Rome, Books I-V of The History of Rome from its Foundation*, translated by Aubrey de Sélincourt with an Introduction by R. M. Ogilvie (Harmondsworth Middlesex: Penguin Books Ltd, 1971), 129-144. Livy depicts the "Struggle of the Orders" as between the patricians and the plebeians. The former were an aristocracy descended from the *patres*, the heads of families who originally formed the senate. Exactly who should be included in the category of the plebeians remains uncertain. See Livy, *Early History*, 26. See also the magisterial study by G. E. M. de Ste Croix, *The Class Struggle in the Ancient Greek World from the Archaic Age to the Arab Conquests* (London: Gerald Duckworth & Company Ltd, 1981), 332-337.

[21] Livy, *Early History*, 131-144. See also de Ste Croix, *Class Struggle*, 335.

Events unfold in this way: a crisis develops during the consulship of Appius Claudius, a hardliner. Claudius recognises that a situation of dual power has already arisen from the common people having been granted the right of appeal to their own assembly against the oppression of the consuls. A dictator is appointed who offers to introduce a measure of debt relief, but this is sabotaged by the senate. The plebeians respond by secession – they withdraw to the Sacred Mount. The conciliators in the senate send Menenius Agrippa to appease the secessionists. The bargain that ends the crisis includes the creation of the tribunate, a new magistracy whose function is to protect the people against the consuls. The dual power regime of Rome has taken a new and more dangerous form, with consuls and tribunes facing each other, with contradictory powers. This is the situation when Martius makes his intervention in the senate.[22]

Plutarch, as a biographer, is more interested in the life of his protagonist than in the political situation in Rome, but even Plutarch sets out clearly, if rather summarily, the general outlines of the class conflicts in the city, their basis in opposed interests, and the strategy and tactics of both sides.[23] As a biographer, concerned with characteristic mentalities, Plutarch has a distinctive contribution to make in his accounts of the class consciousness of the two classes: the abject passive-aggression of the plebeians, and the complacent pride of rank, and self-belief of the patricians.[24]

However, Plutarch articulates more clearly than Livy the fact of dual power, and the danger that it represents to the unity of Rome. This can be seen in the speech that Plutarch gives to Martius, when Martius is denouncing the people and the tribunes in the senate. Referring to the distribution of corn to relieve the poor, Martius rails:

> Therefore it were a great folly for us, methinks, to do it. Yea, shall I say more? We should, if we were wise, take from them their Tribuneship, which most manifestly is the embasing of the Consulship and the cause of the division of the city; the state whereof, as it standeth, is not now as it was wont to be; but becometh dismembered in two factions, which maintains always civil dissension and discord between us, and will never suffer us again to be united into one body.[25]

---

[22] Livy, *Early History*, 127-146. The story of Martius is probably legendary. See Livy, *Early History*, 13.
[23] T. J. B. Spencer ed., *Shakespeare's Plutarch: The Lives of Julius Caesar, Brutus, Marcus Antonius and Coriolanus in the translation of Sir Thomas North* (Harmondsworth, Middlesex: Penguin Books Ltd, 1964), 300-305, 314-317. Spencer's text is that of the 1595 edition of North/Plutarch. See also Plutarch, *The Lives of the Noble Grecians and Romans*, translated by John Dryden and revised by Arthur Hugh Clough (New York: Random House Inc., n.d.), 265-266, 270-271. This "Modern Library" edition is a reprint of Clough's, which was published in 1864.
[24] Spencer ed., *Shakespeare's Plutarch*, 302-305, 321; Plutarch, *Lives*, 265-266, 272.
[25] Spencer ed., *Shakespeare's Plutarch*, 323-324. See also Plutarch, *Lives*, 273.

Martius, thus, calls for the abolition of the tribunate, as incompatible with the established authority of the consuls. This is counter-revolutionary politics, and it leads to the coup of the tribunes and the people against him.

Shakespeare, then, can hardly have been unaware of the class nature of the political situation in Rome, or of the dual power regime that leads to the banishment and exile of Martius.

V

Shakespeare follows Livy and Plutarch in his depiction of the general situation of Rome, although he makes some changes of emphasis, presumably to render the political scene in Rome more familiar to his audience.[26]

Rome and its neighbours are in a situation of continual warfare. Rome, therefore, needs both a military elite, and a reliable army of common soldiers. But this division of Roman society itself leads to conflict, as the nobles look down on the people with contempt, while the people, when aroused, view the nobles with hatred. Both classes need to co-operate to ensure Rome's security, but that co-operation is continually under threat.

This class animosity is exacerbated by the difference of class interests. In this respect Shakespeare emphasises the shortage of food, although he does vaguely allude to the issues of debt and enslavement.[27]

In Shakespeare's depiction of the polity of Rome, the city seems to have become an elective monarchy, with only one consul.[28] The consul is chosen by the senate, but the consul-elect must be endorsed by the people. This situation already exhibits a degree of dual power, but the dual power regime undergoes a significant development with the creation of the tribunate.

In relation to the changes introduced into Roman political life by the institution of the tribunate, we can distinguish between the "old politics" and the "new politics". Before the tribunes are instituted, the senate must respond to any disaffection of the common people with either force or conciliation. This choice of possibilities is mirrored on the side of the plebeians, who also have their hardliners and their conciliators. In the first

---

[26] I have used the Arden edition of *Coriolanus*, edited by Philip Brockbank (London: Methuen & Co. Ltd, 1976). All references are to this edition.

[27] I. i. 78-85. Although Shakespeare's plebeians are urban artisans, he was probably partly moved to consider the story of Martius by the Midlands peasant insurrection of 1607. See E. C. Pettet, "*Coriolanus* and the Midlands Insurrection of 1607", *Shakespeare Survey* 3 (1950), 34-42.

[28] The evidence of the play is inconsistent. At II. ii. 1-2 First Officer asks, "How many stand for consulships?" And at III. i. 107 Martius exclaims, "It makes the consuls base...." But, in II. ii. a stage direction (probably Shakespeare's), between lines 36 and 37, refers to "Cominius the Consul", and later in the same scene at line 43 Menenius refers to "[t]he present consul". Shakespeare, presumably, did not care about this.

scene of the play all four alternatives are on display. First Citizen, who already wants to have Martius killed, represents the plebeian hardline, while Second Citizen, who demurs, is the conciliator. On the patrician side, Martius's desire to use his sword on the mob represents the use of force, while Menenius Agrippa's "fable of the belly" is an attempt at conciliation.

But this general situation is about to be superseded, because, offstage, the senate has made a revolutionary concession: five tribunes have been granted to the people, to defend the people's interests against the established social and political order. The "old politics" are about to be replaced by the new. This development, and the dangers of dual power to the unity of the state are immediately seen by Martius, who tells Menenius of

> ... a petition granted them, a strange one,
> To break the heart of generosity
> And make bold power look pale ...
>
> Five tribunes to defend their vulgar wisdoms,
> Of their own choice ...
>   ... it will in time
> Win upon power and throw forth greater themes
> For insurrection's arguing.
>   (I. i. 209-211, 214-215, 218-220)

The essence of a dual power regime is its instability. The two poles of power can co-exist for a time, but only uneasily. Because the two authorities are basically incompatible, there must always be the possibility of some event triggering a crisis. In this case, the event is Martius's "run" for the consulship.

It is not merely the personalities of Martius and of the tribunes, Brutus and Sicinius, that are in question. The clash of these personalities occurs within the context of the elite military ethos of the patricians. It is a contradiction in Rome's culture that extreme military prowess will both qualify such an individual as Martius for the highest office, the consulship, and tempt that individual into excessive pride and contempt, which will provoke the common people, and produce disaffection.

But, beside these subjective factors – individual and collective – there is the objective contradiction between the two authorities. Just as Martius sees the tribuneship as a threat to the authority of the senate and consuls, so Brutus and Sicinius see Martius, as consul, to be a threat to their authority as tribunes. When Sicinius predicts that Martius will promptly become consul, Brutus responds:

>   Then our office may,
> During his power, go sleep.
>   (II. i. 220-221)

Realising this, the tribunes begin their intrigue to prevent Martius from becoming consul. In their plans we can see the new style of plebeian politics which has been born with the dual power regime. It is a new style of crowd control, and a new style of managing meetings. In its deviousness, and its organisational power, it makes Menenius' traditional modes of flattery and deference seem amateurish. The tribunes will set Martius and their own plebeian supporters against each other. Martius will be provoked to insolence, and this will provoke the people to turn against him.[29] This is neither coercion nor conciliation. It is conspiracy and manipulation. But the aim of the manipulation is now only partly to defend the interests of the plebeians. It is primarily to solidify and defend the power of the tribunes. Rome has entered a more modern, less noble era. The nobility of patrician culture is about to be undermined by deliberate baseness. But the spontaneous power of the plebeians is also to be subordinated to the organisational power of the tribunes.

Martius receives the *agnomen* "Coriolanus" for his exploits during the battle for Corioli, in the war against the Volscians, and is urged by his mother and his fellow-patricians to stand for the consulship.[30] Martius reluctantly agrees, and is duly elected by the senate.[31] But he must also receive the endorsement of the people of Rome, and this involves the custom of the consul-elect showing his battle-wounds to the people, and entreating their approval. Loathing the people, Martius must shrink from fulfilling this custom.

When Menenius reminds Martius that he must speak to the people, Martius cannot resist revealing his desire that the custom should be abolished.

> It is a part
> That I shall blush in acting, and might well
> Be taken from the people.
> (II. ii. 144-146)

It should be noted that the tribunes have hardly begun to provoke Martius at this point. Moreover, the custom for the consul-elect to speak to the people, and show his wounds is not a recent innovation, like the tribuneship. It is an established custom. Martius's reaction is therefore extreme, and might be judged revolutionary. It must suggest to the tribunes that Martius does indeed desire to reduce the people's political rights. This desire on Martius's part may be said to represent the "new politics" on the side of the patricians.

---

[29] II. i. 203-268.
[30] I. ix. 57-65; II. i. 161-166, 196-200; II. ii. 132-133. Brockbank in his Arden edition at page 93, note 1 explains the system of names for Roman males: *praenomen*, *nomen*, *cognomen* and *agnomen*.
[31] II. ii. 132-144.

This new politics is, strictly speaking, reactionary, since it involves taking back from the people political concessions already made.

Martius allows himself to be persuaded to follow the custom, and, wearing the "gown of humility", he goes to the Forum. He ungraciously asks individual citizens for their support, but fails to show his wounds. Nonetheless, the people good-naturedly give him their endorsement.[32] All would now be well, were it not for the tribunes.

Brutus and Sicinius arouse the people's indignation against Martius by dwelling on the fact that Martius refused to show his wounds. The tribunes then criticize the people for not following the tribunes' instructions: the people failed to extract from Martius a promise of good will to the people. Such a promise would have tested Martius's disposition. If the promise were given, the people could in future demand that it be kept. If it were not given, then Martius's ill-will would be obvious, and the people might have refused their endorsement.[33]

Thus, the tribunes' first attempt at crowd control has failed, and the people cannot be considered reliable from the standpoint of their new leaders. But the tribunes can save the situation.

They now urge the people to take back their endorsement, as the official confirmation in the assembly has still to be given.[34] As the people storm off, Sicinius sums up the relation between the tribunes and their plebeian constituents. Referring to the coming "mutiny", Sicinius remarks:

> And this shall seem, as partly 'tis, their own,
> Which we have goaded onwards.
> (II. iii. 260-261)

This is the new plebeian politics of "managed spontaneity".

The climax of this whole dynamic comes in the first scene of Act III, in which the tribunes achieve the first stage of their coup against Martius. The plebeians angrily reject Martius as consul, and the tribunes bring against him the charge of treason. The coup would have ended here in Martius's death, were it not that the concourse of plebeians and patricians lapses into riots, in which the patricians succeed in temporarily overcoming the plebeians.

This scene both shows the contradictions of dual power in action, and gives clear articulation to the notion of dual power.

As Martius and the patricians are coming to the Forum, where Martius's election is to be officially confirmed, their way is barred by the tribunes, who

---

[32] II. iii. 41-147.
[33] II. iii. 153-197.
[34] II. iii. 197-253.

announce that Martius does not have the endorsement of the people.[35] This change of mind by the people infuriates Martius and the patricians, and the altercation that develops inevitably focuses on the issue of dual power.

Martius denounces the fickleness of the people, and their participation in the power of the state.

> For the mutable, rank-scented meinie, let them
> Regard me as I do not flatter, and
> Therein behold themselves. I say again,
> In soothing them, we nourish 'gainst our senate
> The cockle of rebellion, insolence, sedition,
> Which we ourselves have plough'd for, sow'd, and scatter'd,
> *By mingling them with us*, the honour'd number
> Who lack not virtue, no, nor *power, but that*
> *Which they have given to beggars.*
> (III. i. 65-73; italics added)

When Sicinius declares that the "poison" of Martius's mind shall do no further harm in Rome, but remain ineffective, Martius responds to the implied assumption that the tribunician power is absolute.

> Shall remain!
> Hear you this Triton of the minnows? Mark you
> His absolute 'shall'?
> (III. i. 87-89)

Martius now rushes on, indignant against what he perceives as the presumption of the tribunes, but also clearly expressing for his fellow-patricians both the fact of dual power, and the implications of that for the Roman state.

> O good but most unwise patricians: why,
> You grave but reckless senators, have you thus
> Given Hydra here to choose an officer,
> That with his peremptory 'shall', being but
> The horn and noise o'th'monster's, wants not spirit
> To say he'll turn your current in a ditch
> And make your channel his? If he have power,
> Then vail your ignorance; if none, awake
> Your dangerous lenity. If you are learn'd,
> Be not as common fools; if you are not,
> Let them have cushions by you. You are plebeians
> If they be senators; and they are no less

---

[35] III. i. 21-32.

> *When, both your voices blended, the great'st taste*
> *Most palates theirs.* They choose their magistrate,
> And such a one as he, who puts his 'shall',
> His popular 'shall', against a greater bench
> Than ever frown'd in Greece. By Jove himself,
> It makes the consuls base; and my soul aches
> To know, *when two authorities are up,*
> *Neither supreme, how soon confusion*
> *May enter 'twixt the gap of both and take*
> *The one by th'other.*
>
> (III. i. 90-111; italics added)

It is remarkable that in Rome it is only Martius and the tribunes who recognise that the political situation has radically changed. Neither the plebeians nor the patricians seem to have any awareness of this. But it is natural that Martius and the tribunes should have this awareness, since it is their authorities that are at stake.

Martius is now so enraged that he must express everything with which his heart is full. From denouncing the distribution of corn to the people, he returns to the issue of dual power, warns that the state is in peril, and at last calls for the abolition of the tribuneship.

> This *double worship,*
> Where one part does disdain with cause, the other
> Insult without all reason: *where gentry, title, wisdom,*
> *Cannot conclude but by the yea and no*
> *Of general ignorance,* it must omit
> Real necessities, and give way the while
> To unstable slightness. Purpose so barr'd, it follows
> Nothing is done to purpose. Therefore, beseech you –
> You that will be less fearful than discreet,
> That love the *fundamental part of state*
> More than you doubt the change on't; that prefer
> A noble life before a long, and wish
> To jump a body with a dangerous physic
> That's sure of death without it — *at once pluck out*
> *The multitudinous tongue*: let them not lick
> The sweet which is their poison. Your dishonour
> Mangles true judgment, and *bereaves the state*
> *Of that integrity which should become't;*
> *Not having the power to do the good it would,*
> *For th'ill which doth control't.*
>
> (III. i. 141-160; italics added)

Martius's call for the abolition of the tribuneship gives Sicinius the opportunity to denounce Martius as a traitor. But this only provokes Martius to make his call more clearly.

> In a rebellion,
> When what's not meet, but what must be, was law,
> Then were they chosen. In a better hour,
> Let what is meet be said it must be meet,
> *And throw their power i' th' dust.*
> (III. i. 165-169; italics added)

What follows is the working out of the dual power in action. The tribunes enact their authority by arresting Martius. The patricians resist the arrest, and there is a riot. The tribunes urge on the people, and warn that the people are about to lose their liberties. When some of the patricians plead that Sicinius's appeal to the people is the way to "unbuild the city, and to lay all flat" (III. i. 195), Sicinius responds with a cry that anticipates the revolutionary sentiment of 1789:

What is the city but the people?

All the plebeians join in the cry:

> True,
> The people are the city.
> (III. i. 196-198)

Rome's identity as a united society, and its polity have been put in question. Unity has given way to civil strife. The conflict must be resolved, which means that one side must defeat the other.[36]

Sicinius calls for the death penalty for Martius. Brutus, seeing that their authority is at stake, demands that it be carried out immediately, without trial.

> Or let us stand to our authority
> Or let us lose it: we do here pronounce,
> Upon the part o' th' people, in whose power
> We were elected theirs, Martius is worthy
> Of present death.
> (III. i. 206-210)

Sicinius orders Martius to be carried to execution.

---

[36] Cf. Trotsky, *History*, 224-225.

>   Therefore lay hold of him.
> Bear him to th' rock Tarpeian, and from thence
> Into destruction cast him.
>   (III. i. 210-212)

The tribunes are now offering to exercise supreme power in Rome, and against a consul-elect. As so often happens during a revolution, the power exercised is arbitrary. Legal process is ignored, and resort is made to pure force.

Force is now met with force. Martius draws his sword, and there is another riot. The patricians beat away the plebeians, but the plebeians return. At the tribunes' urging, the people once more refuse Martius the consulship.[37]

Menenius pleads for due process, and promises to bring Martius to the Forum for trial. The tribunes agree, perhaps owing to their failure to overcome the patricians in the riots.[38] Nonetheless, the tribunes have already succeeded in exerting their authority over that of the senate by having a consul-elect put on trial.

In this scene the crisis of the dual power regime has come to a head, the two authorities have come into conflict, and civil strife has erupted. But the conflict has not been resolved by force. It remains for the tribunes to secure victory by intrigue.

In the following scene (III. ii.) Martius is persuaded by his family and friends, although much against his will, to return to the Forum to stand trial. I shall consider the psychological dynamics of Martius's relation with his mother Volumnia below. Here I only wish to point out that, politically, the patricians in this scene are astonishingly naive. They believe that the "old politics" of conciliation will still work. Martius even promises his mother that he will "return consul".[39] The patricians walk into the tribunes' trap blindly.

The trial in the Forum (in III. iii) is to be a hearing in the assembly of the people. This means it is a public meeting that the tribunes can arrange to manage. Before the plebeians and patricians arrive, the tribunes discuss tactics. They rely on psychological manipulation of Martius, on number-crunching, on exploiting procedure, and on having plants in the assembly to make appropriate interjections.[40]

Martius is to be charged with affecting tyrannical power, with ill-will towards the people, and with failing to distribute war booty. The first and third of these charges are guaranteed to provoke Martius to arrogance and

---

[37] III. i. 221-278.
[38] III. i. 279-331.
[39] III. ii. 135.
[40] III. iii. 1-30.

insolence, so that he alienates his judges. But the verdict of the trial is not to be left to chance.

The tribunes have "done the numbers" already.

> Have you a catalogue
> Of all the voices that we have procur'd,
> Set down by th' poll?
> (III. iii. 8-10)

The tribunes have also determined that the assembly will meet as "tribes".

> Have you collected them by tribes?
> (III. iii. 11)

The significance of this, as Shakespeare would have learned from Plutarch, is that if the trial were to be held in an assembly based on "centuries" (*comitia centuriata*), the wealthier citizens composing the centuries would be more likely to favour Martius; whereas, if the assembly is based on tribes (*comitia curiata*), the assembly will include all the poor who loathe Martius. The former assembly might acquit Martius; the latter will certainly convict him.[41]

Finally, the tribunes order their aedile to pass on instructions to the people for them to follow the tribunes' lead.

> *Sic.* Assemble presently the people hither:
> And when they hear me say, 'It shall be so
> I'th'right and strength o'th'commons,' be it either
> For death, for fine, or banishment, then let them
> If I say fine, cry 'Fine', if death, cry 'Death',
> Insisting on the old prerogative
> And power i' th' truth o' th' cause …
>
> *Bru.* And when such time they have begun to cry,
> Let them not cease, but with a din confus'd
> Enforce the present execution
> Of what we chance to sentence.
> (III. iii. 12-18, 19-22)

The trial therefore is rigged, and the verdict a foregone conclusion.

When the patricians arrive in the Forum, Martius tries to be conciliatory, but the tribunes easily succeed in provoking him. With the insight of political manipulators, Sicinius makes the accusation guaranteed to enrage Martius.

---

[41] Spencer ed., *Shakespeare's Plutarch*, 331-332; Plutarch, *Lives*, 276.

Sicinius accuses Martius of being, not a traitor to Rome, but a "traitor to the people" (III. iii. 66). Martius explodes:

> The fires i' th' lowest hell fold in the people!
> Call me their traitor!
> (III. iii. 68-69)

The people cry for Martius to be taken to the Tarpeian Rock, and Sicinius prepares to pronounce sentence.

At this point the tribunes retreat somewhat, and sentence Martius to banishment rather than death. But they emphasise that they are acting on their authority, and in the name of the people. Their authority has triumphed over that of the senate. Martius is banished as a class enemy of the people.

> For that he has,
> As much as in him lies, from time to time
> Envied against the people, seeking means
> To pluck away their power, as now at last
> Given hostile strokes, and that not in the presence
> Of dreaded justice, but on the ministers
> That doth distribute it—in the name o' th' people,
> And in the power of us the tribunes, we,
> Ev'n from this instant, banish him our city,
> In peril of precipitation
> From off the rock Tarpeian, never more
> To enter our Rome gates. I' th' people's name,
> I say it shall be so.
> (III. iii. 93-105)

The plebeians endorse the sentence with acclamation. Martius leaves with his defiant, but childish "I banish you!" (III. iii. 123).

The scene ends with a mark of the tribunes' triumph, when Sicinius orders, "Let a guard / Attend us through the city." (III.iii. 140-141).

The crisis of the dual power regime has ended with a victory of the plebeians, although the real power now obviously lies with the tribunes. However, the hegemony of the tribunes does not last long. The force of Rome's external relations of continual war reasserts itself, as Martius defects to the Volscians, and leads a Volscian army to besiege Rome. In Shakespeare's version of the story the plebeians turn against the tribunes, beat up Brutus, and threaten the tribunes with death (V. iv). Martius submits to his mother, lifts the siege, and returns to Volscian territory, where Aufidius, Martius's Volscian rival, has him murdered.

It is to be assumed that the uneasy balance of power between the senate and consuls, and the tribunes has been restored. In this case, the revolution has not been carried through. The *status quo ante* has returned, through the pressure of foreign war on the contending classes. Historically, this situation endured in Rome for several centuries, producing continual crises.[42]

VI

L. C. Knights has suggested that with authors like Clarendon and Shakespeare their political wisdom is derived from their moral wisdom. I do not wish to dispute Knights's further contention that politics should be subordinated to ethics.[43] I only wish to suggest that the relations between Shakespeare's moral-psychological insight and his political understanding, at least in the case of *Coriolanus*, can be viewed in another way.

It has long been remarked that in Shakespeare's mature work there tends to be a unity of tone or spirit in each play. In the case of *Coriolanus* it is possible, I suggest, that it was the political situation in Rome that influenced Shakespeare's conception of the three principal characters, Martius, his mother Volumnia, and Aufidius, and their personal relations. More specifically, it was the idea of a totality with a structure of dual power that gave Shakespeare the key to how Martius, Volumnia and Aufidius should be depicted. With this play, then, it was his understanding of the political situation, which he could take over directly from Livy and Plutarch, that deepened Shakespeare's understanding of Martius and his personal relationships, in ways that are not represented in Livy or Plutarch, and which, therefore, must be considered the effects of Shakespeare's own creative imagination.

I suggest that it is not too artificial a claim that Martius's personal relationships with his mother and with Aufidius are also characterised by

---

[42] The conflict between patricians and plebeians, and between senate, consuls and tribunes lasted for as long as Rome was threatened by foreign war. But when Rome had conquered Italy, and subjugated Carthage, the ruling classes no longer needed to make concessions to the plebeians. The conflict came to a head during the tribuneships of the Gracchi, whose measures of land and other reforms conflicted with the interests of the senatorial oligarchy. Both Tiberius Gracchus and Gaius Gracchus were murdered (in 133 and 122 BCE, respectively). The common people, by now a dispossessed proletariat, thereafter gave their support to military dictators in the period of the civil wars. Out of the civil wars emerged the imperial monarchy (still disguised as a republic) of Octavius Caesar, who assumed the name of Augustus. As *princeps*, Augustus absorbed the powers of the tribunate. This allowed him to veto the decisions of all other magistrates, thus making his own power absolute. In this way the conflict between the established order and the tribunate finally came to an end. See Donald Dudley, *Roman Society* (Harmondsworth, Middlesex: Penguin Books Ltd, 1975), Parts II to V; de Ste Croix, *Class Struggle*, Part VI.

[43] Knights, *Further Explorations*, 24-32 ("Shakespeare's Politics"). Aristotle held that ethics was subordinate to politics. But for him, politics concerned the good of the community, both as a whole and as the sum of the individuals composing it. For various reasons we have become so disillusioned with practical politics over the last five hundred years that we can no longer think of politics in this way, and have transferred all thought about the Good into ethics. See Aristotle, *Nichomachean Ethics*, I. ii.

relations of dual power.⁴⁴ In both cases the personal relationship is a power-relation, which lapses into a power struggle, the outcome of which depends on a peculiar weakness in Martius – a weakness that is not depicted in Livy, and only barely suggested in Plutarch, and that therefore may be considered an essential insight that Shakespeare brings to the imagining of these characters. I refer, of course, to Martius's immaturity, his 'boyishness'. This boyishness may also be considered as the key to Martius's behaviour towards the plebeians.⁴⁵

Shakespeare seems to have seen the clue to Martius's immaturity in his intemperance, his lack of self-control when angered. This connection is not made in Livy, and only just hinted in Plutarch. Significantly, Plutarch does not see any immaturity in Martius's relations with his mother, or with Aufidius.⁴⁶ It is Shakespeare who brings all these aspects of Martius's character and relationships together, so that at the end of the play Aufidius can tempt Martius to destruction with the cry "thou boy of tears!" (V. vi. 101).

In his own world Martius is universally regarded as noble, and as the epitome of virtue. *Virtus*, or manliness, is both physical courage, and virtue in general.⁴⁷ But, arguably, Martius is not virtuous. He is not just towards the plebeians. He is certainly not prudent in his general conduct. He is manifestly lacking in self-control.

It is even arguable that his boldness in battle is not, strictly speaking, the virtue of courage. C. S. Lewis distinguishes between natural qualities and dispositions on the one hand, and genuine virtues on the other. A virtue is a choice, and an act of will in opposition to some desire or passion that would seduce one into vice.⁴⁸ Courage as a virtue must involve the overcoming of fear.⁴⁹ It is hard to believe that the kind of man Martius is depicted as in Shakespeare ever feels fear. There is no sign of it. His fighting prowess and natural boldness carry him through. What he feels is exalted pleasure in the exercise of his own powers.

---

⁴⁴ *Coriolanus* was probably written in 1608. In 1607 Shakespeare had written *Antony and Cleopatra*, in which personal relationships are also power relationships: Antony and Octavius; Antony and Cleopatra.

⁴⁵ Martius's boyishness seems to have been first discussed by Wyndham Lewis in his *The Lion and the Fox: the Role of the Hero in the Plays of Shakespeare* (London: G. Richards Ltd, 1927). I have used the 1951 edition, in a 1966 reprint, published by Methuen & Co Ltd. See 202-203, 235-246.

⁴⁶ Plutarch states that Martius lived in his mother's house even after he was married, and had children. But Plutarch sees in this only Martius's respect for his mother, nothing more psychologically interesting. For Shakespeare, doubtless, it was a hint. See Spencer ed., *Shakespeare's Plutarch*, 300; Plutarch, *Lives*, 265.

⁴⁷ Spencer ed., *Shakespeare's Plutarch*, 297; Plutarch, *Lives*, 263.

⁴⁸ C. S. Lewis, *Mere Christianity* (Glasgow: William Collins Sons & Co. Ltd, 1977 [first publ., 1952]), 70-74, 81-84. Lewis's views belong to the tradition of moral philosophy deriving from Aristotle. See *Nichomachean Ethics*, Books III and VI.

⁴⁹ Aristotle held that unruly passions might be permanently moderated; the Stoics held that they might be eliminated altogether. But neither of these paradigms fits Martius.

This lack of genuine virtue, and especially of self-control ('temperance'), seems to have suggested to Shakespeare not just a faulty character, but an immaturity, a failure to grow up. This is undoubtedly paradoxical when affirmed of a man reputed to exemplify *virtus* or manliness, but such paradoxes are common in Shakespeare's tragedies.[50]

It was probably Plutarch's account of Martius's intemperate behaviour towards the plebeians that gave Shakespeare the hint of Martius's immaturity, for in relation to this Plutarch makes a suggestive comment. When the people refuse Martius the consulship, and Martius is "out of all patience", Plutarch remarks:

> So, Martius, being a stout man of nature, that never yielded in any respect, as one thinking that to overcome always and to have the upper hand in all matters was a token of magnanimity and *of no base and faint courage, which spitteth out anger from the most weak and passioned part of the heart*, much like the matter of an impostume, went home to his house full freighted with spite and malice against the people....[51]

Plutarch, however, does not see this "weakness" as immaturity, nor does he relate it to Martius's relations with his mother or with Aufidius.[52] These are Shakespeare's insights.

On the basis of this general sense of Martius's immaturity Shakespeare reconceives Martius's relationship with his mother, so that it becomes the explanation for virtually everything that happens in the play.[53] Martius's immaturity clearly arises from his relationship with his mother. It is an extreme case of emotional dependence. Shakespeare emphasises this by enacting it not once but twice in the play, in III. ii, as well as in V. iii.

But it is also essential that this transformation of the Martius-Volumnia relationship involves conceiving it as a relation of power, as a relation prone to a power struggle, as a relation of dual power, in fact. Like other dual power relations, it is uneasy and unstable, and liable to fall into crises in which one side must defeat the other. In such crises Martius always loses.

---

[50] Hamlet, the thirty year old who regresses to adolescence; Othello, the general of immense self-possession who completely loses self-control; Lear, the majestic king who behaves childishly; Macbeth, the heroic warrior whose moral cowardice must be shored up by his wife; Antony and Cleopatra, the middle-aged lovers who behave like infatuated adolescents.

[51] Spencer ed., *Shakespeare's Plutarch*, 321 (italics added). See also Plutarch, *Lives*, 272.

[52] See footnote 46.

[53] This was noticed by Bradley. See A. C. Bradley, *Coriolanus: British Academy Lecture, 1912* (London: British Academy, 1912). See also Wyndham Lewis, *The Lion and the Fox*, 243; Janet Adelman, *Suffocating Mothers: Fantasies of Maternal Origin in Shakespeare's Plays, Hamlet to the Tempest* (New York: Routledge, 1991), 146-164; Harold Bloom, *Shakespeare: The Invention of the Human* (New York: Riverhead Books, 1998), 577-587.

It should be remembered that Shakespeare has invented all the scenes in which Volumnia appears, prior to V. iii. The crucial scene for our argument is, of course, III. ii, since it is in this scene that Shakespeare exhibits Martius's emotional dependence on his mother, in anticipation of its being exhibited again in V. iii, at the climax of the play.

In III. ii the patricians have returned to Martius's house after the riots. They wish Martius to go to the Forum, and placate the plebeians. But Martius will not give way. He will not even calm down. A senator declares that Martius must be conciliatory, or Rome will split in two and perish. Volumnia reinforces this invocation of the general interest, but Martius still refuses. Volumnia urges that policy is compatible with honour in peace, as well as in war. Martius still stands out. Eventually, he agrees, but as he thinks about it, he works himself up into another furious refusal.

> Well, I must do't.
> Away my disposition, and possess me
> Some harlot's spirit! My throat of war be turn'd,
> Which choired with my drum, into a pipe
> Small as an eunuch, or the virgin voice
> That babies lull asleep! The smiles of knaves
> Tent in my cheeks, and schoolboys' tears take up
> The glasses of my sight! A beggar's tongue
> Make motion through my lips, and my arm'd knees
> Who bow'd but in my stirrup, bend like his
> That hath receiv'd an alms! I will not do't,
> Lest I surcease to honour mine own truth,
> And by my body's action teach my mind
> A most inherent baseness.
> (III. ii. 110-123)

Martius's lack of constancy infuriates Volumnia, who now rages against her son, implicitly casting him off.

> At thy choice then:
> To beg of thee it is my more dishonour
> Than thou of them. Come all to ruin; let
> Thy mother rather feel thy pride than fear
> Thy dangerous stoutness, for I mock at death
> With as big heart as thou. Do as thou list.
> Thy valiantness was mine, thou suck'st it from me,
> But owe thy pride thyself.
> (III. ii. 123-130)

Immediately, when Volumnia rejects him, Martius submits.

> Pray be content.
> Mother, I am going to the market-place:
> Chide me no more. I'll mountebank their loves,
> Cog their hearts from them, and come home belov'd
> Of all the trades in Rome. Look, I am going.
> Commend me to my wife. I'll return consul,
> Or never trust to what my tongue can do
> I'th'way of flattery further.
> (III. ii. 130-137)

But, Volumnia is incensed, and will not stay to speak with him. She storms off, exclaiming, "Do your will." (III. ii. 137)

It is clear from this episode that Martius, the epitome of *virtus*, is still dominated by his mother. He not only wants to please her. He cannot bear her disapproval. In this power-relationship Volumnia will always win.

It is, therefore, a foregone conclusion that, when, in V. iii., Volumnia urges Martius to lift the siege of Rome, and make peace between the Romans and the Volscians, Martius will eventually submit to his mother's wish.

Martius has refused all the embassies from Rome, including that of his friend Menenius. But when his mother, wife and child come to his camp, he finds that he has to struggle with natural affection. But, he does so, and resolves to remain firm.

> I'll never
> Be such a gosling to obey instinct, but stand
> As if a man were author of himself
> And knew no other kin.
> (V. iii. 34-37)

However, Martius greets his family affectionately, and agrees to hear Volumnia's plea. Volumnia first makes a formal, rhetorical speech, appealing to Martius's pity, and ending with her resolution to commit suicide.[54]

Martius feels that he is being emotionally affected, rises from his seat, and turns to leave.

> *Cor.* Not of a woman's tenderness to be,
> Requires nor child nor woman's face to see.
> I have sat too long.
>
> *Vol.* Nay, go not from us thus.
> (V. iii. 129-132)

---

[54] V. iii. 94-125.

Volumnia now speaks more plainly, urging him to accept the pragmatic arguments for making peace between Rome and the Volscians. But Martius remains silent.[55]

To this point Volumnia has controlled herself. But now she is exasperated, and lets loose her anger against her disobedient son.

> There's no man in the world
> More bound to's mother, yet here he lets me prate
> Like one i' th' stocks. *Thou hast never in thy life*
> *Show'd thy dear mother any courtesy,*
> When she, poor hen, fond of no second brood,
> Has cluck'd thee to the wars, and safely home,
> Loaden with honour.
> (V. iii. 158-164; italics added)

The rest of Volumnia's impassioned speech consists of a series of threats, from which Martius turns away, until the very end. She falls to her knees to shame him, but he does not respond. So, at last she breaks her relation to him, and threatens him with her dying disapproval.

> Down ladies: let us shame him with our knees.
> To his surname Coriolanus longs more pride
> Than pity to our prayers. Down! *An end:*
> *This is the last.* So, we will home to Rome
> And die among our neighbours. Nay, behold's,
> This boy that cannot tell what he would have,
> But kneels, and holds up hands for fellowship,
> Does reason our petition with more strength
> Than thou hast to deny't. Come, let us go:
> *This fellow had a Volscian to his mother;*
> *His wife is in Corioles, and his child*
> *Like him by chance.* Yet give us our dispatch:
> *I am husht until our city be afire,*
> *And then I'll speak a little.*
> (V. iii. 169-182; italics added)

Martius "[h]olds her by the hand, silent", and submits. But, submitting, he knows it must end in his death.

> O mother, mother!
> What have you done?...
> ... O my mother, mother! O!
> You have won a happy victory to Rome;

---

[55] V. iii. 131-155.

> But for your son, believe it, O, believe it,
> Most dangerously you have with him prevailed,
> If not most mortal to him.
> (V. iii. 182-3, 185-189)

In this second power struggle with his mother Martius has once again lost.

In Livy there is no account of Martius's mother urging her son to go the Forum to placate the plebeians. And when she comes to the Volscian camp to urge her son to lift the siege, while she does become angry with him, he does not respond. He only relents when embraced by his wife and children, and amidst the general lamentation of all the women.[56]

In Plutarch there is also no account of Volumnia urging her son to go to the Forum. And when she comes to the Volscian camp, she is more sorrowful than angry. Martius relents when his mother flings herself at his feet.[57]

Thus, the psychological dynamics of Martius and his mother are quite different in Livy and Plutarch from what they are in Shakespeare. Neither of the ancient authors shows the mother of Martius in a relation of domination over her son.

Martius's emotional dependence on his mother surely helps to explain his attitude towards the plebeians, as other critics have remarked.[58] Martius projects onto the plebeians his own sense of dependence and weakness. Or, if it seems too implausible to invoke a concept of Freudian psychology, we can say that Martius finds and hates in others what pains him in himself. A creative genius of the seventeenth century could surely intuit that emotional process, even though he had no access to twentieth-century psychological theory.[59]

Finally, the relationship between Martius and Aufidius is clearly a love-hate relation, subject to extreme fluctuations and sudden reversals. They are bound together in a strong but unstable and contradictory relationship, in which their mutual admiration is based in their common pursuit of military glory, and their mutual hatred aroused by the competition that necessarily accompanies it. For most of the play their power struggle is in the external world, a contest for military superiority, but at the end of the play Aufidius turns it into a psychological struggle. On the battlefield Aufidius habitually loses to Martius. But once the struggle has become psychological, Aufidius easily wins, because he discerns Martius's weakness.

---

[56] Livy, *Early History*, 150.
[57] Spencer ed., *Shakespeare's Plutarch*, 356-358; Plutarch, *Lives*, 287-288.
[58] Adelman, *Suffocating Mothers*, 153.
[59] Compare Hamlet's verbal attack on Ophelia in III. i of *Hamlet*. Freud would say that this is *displacement* of his anger from Gertrude to Ophelia, as it undoubtedly is.

In the first half of the play the emphasis is on Martius' and Aufidius' mutual hatred, and the deterioration that this brings about in Aufidius' character. Defeated yet again by Martius in the battle for Corioli, Aufidius, angry and ashamed, feels that he is losing his sense of honour. His envy of Martius overcomes him, and he resolves to kill Martius by any means possible, honourable or dishonourable (I. x.)

The point of these early episodes in Act I is to anticipate the same process of moral deterioration in Aufidius happening all over again at the end of the play.

But before the final resolution of the Martius-Aufidius conflict, there is a sudden and extreme reversal in their unstable relationship. Martius is banished from Rome, and comes to the Volscian city of Antium to offer his services against Rome to Aufidius. Aufidius is overwhelmed by love for his admired rival.

> O, Martius, Martius!
> Each word thou hast spoke hath weeded from my heart
> A root of ancient envy …
>
> … Let me twine
> Mine arms about that body, where against
> My grained ash an hundred times hath broke,
> And scarr'd the moon with splinters. Here I clip
> The anvil of my sword, and do contest
> As hotly and as nobly with thy love
> As ever in ambitious strength I did
> Contend against thy valour. Know thou first,
> I lov'd the maid I married; never man
> Sigh'd truer breath; but that I see thee here,
> Thou noble thing, more dances my rapt heart
> Than when I first my wedded mistress saw
> Bestride my threshold.
> (IV. v. 102-104, 107-119)

Aufidius' feelings are doubtless sincere, but highly unstable, and a prey to the fluctuations of military power in the external world. Even before the siege of Rome Martius has become more popular with the Volscian troops, and his glory has eclipsed that of Aufidius. Aufidius' love turns to hate through envy, and he plans to destroy Martius after the war is over (IV. vii)

Martius's lifting of the siege of Rome gives Aufidius his opportunity. He now has material with which to denounce Martius to the Volscian senators and people, but mere denunciation is not enough. Wanting Martius dead, Aufidius arranges for his followers to kill Martius in the Volscian Forum.[60]

---

[60] V. vi. 1-60.

Martius returns to the Volscian city in triumph. Aufidius denounces him as a traitor. This accusation is in itself enough to provoke Martius. But Aufidius improves on the provocation by accusing Martius of giving up Rome for the sake of the tears of his wife and mother. When Martius angrily protests, Aufidius takes his well-aimed shot.

> *Cor.* Hear'st thou, Mars?
> *Auf.* Name not the god, thou boy of tears!
> (V. vi. 100-101)

Provoked beyond self-control by the accusation, Martius speaks the words that must ensure his death. This time his intemperance is fatal.

> Boy! False hound!
> If you have writ your annals true, 'tis there,
> That like an eagle in a dove-cote, I
> Flutter'd your Volscians in Corioles.
> Alone I did it. Boy!
> (V. vi. 112-116)

Aufidius' followers call for Martius's death. Their call is taken up by the Volscian people, and the conspirators kill him.

Once Martius is dead, Aufidius' highly unstable emotions take another turn, and he grieves for what he has done.

> My rage is gone,
> And I am struck with sorrow.
> (V. vi. 146-147)

One cannot help observing that Aufidius' change of heart is made easier by the fact that Martius is now dead, and no longer a competitor.

None of this is in Livy, who does not know what happened to Martius after he lifted the siege of Rome. He may have died in old age, still in exile.[61] Plutarch reports Aufidius' plot against Martius, and the assassination of Martius by Aufidius' followers. But, Plutarch never mentions the accusation "boy!"[62] It is Shakespeare who has brought the issue of Martius's emotional dependence on his mother to bear on his relationship with Aufidius.

Thus, the notion of Martius's immaturity renders intelligible all Martius's significant relationships – with his mother, with the plebeians, and with Aufidius. It should be emphasised that this notion is not present in Livy or Plutarch. They present Martius as arrogant and insolent, proud and indignant,

---

[61] Livy, *Early History*, 150-151.
[62] Spencer ed., *Shakespeare's Plutarch*, 360-362; Plutarch, *Lives*, 289-290.

and intemperate towards the plebeians, but that is all. There is no centre to their presentation to unify all the character traits. They present Martius's character in a series of conventional moral judgments (although Plutarch makes some acute psychological observations). Shakespeare, by contrast, passes beyond the moral judgments to the "deep springs" of Martius's behaviour.

I wrote "notion" above. I do not suggest that Shakespeare thought this all out. I suppose that he intuited it as he was working on his sources. *Coriolanus* confirms yet again that the poetic imagination can be a cognitive power. We also might say that *Coriolanus* reconfirms Aristotle's dictum that poetry is more philosophic than history, by displaying the patterns of cause and effect in the human world more clearly.[63]

But it was the early history (possibly legendary) of Rome that worked in Shakespeare's imagination to produce this insight into a man's deepest motivation. It was, I suggest, the dual power relation that conjured up the idea of immaturity that finally brought Gaius Martius Coriolanus into focus, and *Coriolanus* into "the sunlight".[64]

Thus, it is not that Shakespeare's political wisdom is derived from his moral wisdom. It is rather that his moral-psychological insight and his political understanding overlap, and reinforce each other. Whether this is due to a Renaissance Neoplatonic idea of correspondence between the different levels of being, or just the effect of the synthetic power of Shakespeare's imagination, we cannot know. But the fact of the interpenetration is surely clear.

As to Trotsky, it is a mark of Shakespeare's "many-sidedness" that we can find in him a resemblance to someone as apparently remote as Trotsky. But this is only possible because Shakespeare already has much in common with Livy and Plutarch.

---

[63] Aristotle, *Poetics*, 5.5.
[64] T. S. Eliot notoriously compared *Hamlet* unfavourably to *Antony and Cleopatra* and *Coriolanus*, both of which he described as "intelligible, self-complete, in the sunlight". See *Selected Essays* (London: Faber and Faber Ltd, 3rd enlarged ed., 1951), 144 (from "Hamlet", 1919).

Milton's *Samson Agonistes:* A Political Reading

Michael Wilding

Samson Agonistes is the only play that Milton wrote. At the beginning of his career he wrote two masques, *Arcades* and *A Masque presented at Ludlow Castle, 1634* [*Comus*], but nothing else for the stage. Indeed he makes a point of telling us in the opening note, "Of that sort of dramatic poem called tragedy", that *Samson Agonistes* "never was intended" for the stage.[1] During the years of the English Revolution, 1640-1659, the theatres had all been closed by official order. Milton, as the foremost propaganda writer for the revolutionary government, might be expected to have agreed with its hostility to the public theatre, something seen as a corrupt institution, identified with royalists, prostitutes and such like. So it is not surprising that *Samson Agonistes* "never was intended" for the stage; nor is it surprising that the model Milton followed was not that of English Shakespearean theatre, but the archaic model of classical Greece.

This was a model rarely seen performed, except in occasional university productions. For most people's experience of it would have been a reading experience. It is a "dramatic poem". And to stress Milton's conscious rejection of theatre, we should notice that the building which Samson demolishes when he pulls down the columns supporting the roof is called a "house" in the Hebrew, in the Greek Old Testament (the Septuagint), in the Vulgate and in the Authorized Version (the "King James" Bible). Milton, however, writes that "the building was a spacious theatre" (1605). His implication is surely that theatres are places of barbaric, pagan performance and it is appropriate that they should be pulled down. This is the supreme gesture of anti-theatre.[2]

So why did Milton write a "dramatic poem"? It may be that he wanted to fulfil the range of major classical and renaissance literary forms, having already written elegies, sonnets, pastoral, epic and formal speeches. But there

---

[1] John Carey and Alastair Fowler, eds., *The Poems of John Milton* (London: Longman, 1968), 345, l. 46. All quotations are from this edition.

[2] David Loewenstein, *Milton and the Drama of History: Historical Vision, Iconoclasm and the Literary Imagination* (Cambridge: Cambridge University Press, 1990), 136-140. David Loewenstein quotes William Prynne's interpretation of Samson's fate as "God's vengeance not onely on their Actors and Spectators ... but likewise on those States and Cities which allow them", and he goes on to explore "the complex sense of theatricality" in *Samson Agonistes*.

are many forms he did not chose – satire, comedy, the erotic fable, prose narrative.

The distinguishing feature of drama is its potential for multiple points of view. Different positions, different value systems, can be expressed by different characters, and there is no single, identifiable authorial voice that resolves their conflict.[3] Drama allows for the possibilities of different interpretations while evading authorial identification with any individual position. And so Samson can be seen as heroic, or as deluded, as self-pitying and paranoid, or as patient and confident of his divine role. A dramatic presentation allows this debate, this argument about Samson's part. The focus is on ambiguity, on questioning. But this does not mean that the reader is not expected to provide an unambiguous answer.

In this, *Samson Agonistes* is in marked contrast with *Paradise Regained*, the poem with which it was published in 1671. *Paradise Regained* is a brief epic and the Son of God is indisputably the hero. He is tested by Satan and there is some debate and argument about what "Son of God" means. But there is no doubt that he is divinely authorized, and there is no doubt that he is in the role of epic hero. He is redefining heroism, certainly: he is not a military warrior but a man of peace. But there is no ambiguity about his role as an appropriate hero.

With Samson, however, instead of epic certainty there is dramatic questioning. Everything is ambiguity and questioning. As John Carey noted in the introductory remarks to his edition, *Samson Agonistes* "is full of questions: all the characters ask them, so does the chorus" (p. 337). Samson's first speech asks:

> Why was my breeding ordered and prescribed
> As of a person separate to God,
> Designed for great exploits; if I must die
> Betrayed, captived, and both my eyes put out,
> Made of my enemies the scorn and gaze…? (30-34)

And even though he corrects himself for questioning God's plan, "divine prediction" (44), it is with a further question that he makes the correction:

> Yet stay; let me not rashly call in doubt
> Divine prediction; what if all foretold
> Had been fulfilled but through mine own default…? (43-45)

What if the prophecies fail to become true because of his own failures?

---

[3] Anne Davidson Ferry, *Milton and the Miltonic Dryden* (Cambridge MA: Harvard University Press, 1968), 128. There is "no narrator … with authority to interpret the drama for the reader".

We are presented with the former heroic warrior, now blind and imprisoned. The Chorus asks its own question:

> Can this be he,
> That heroic, that renowned,
> Irresistible Samson? (124-6)

The Chorus is asking how did this happen, and was Samson perhaps not so marvellous after all? Samson himself goes on to ask:

> tell me, friends,
> Am I not sung and proverbed for a fool
> In every street…? (202-4)

The Chorus rebukes him, as Samson has already rebuked himself, for questioning God's plan:

> Tax not divine disposal, wisest men
> Have erred, and by bad women been deceived;
> And shall again, pretend they ne'er so wise. (210-2)

But then the Chorus goes on to question Samson's own behaviour:

> Yet, truth to say, I oft have heard men wonder
> Why thou shouldst wed Philistian women rather
> Than of thine own tribe fairer, or as fair,
> At least of thy own nation, and as noble. (215-8)

Samson's answer is:

>   they knew not
> That what I motioned was of God; I knew
> From intimate impulse, and therefore urged
> The marriage on; that, by occasion hence
> I might begin Israel's deliverance. (221-5)

But this is the crux of the problem. Was Samson's decision to marry his first and second wife indeed "motioned … of God"? How can anybody but Samson know? Indeed, does he know, or is he simply rationalizing his own impulses? Is he inspired, or is he deluded? As the Chorus sardonically replies: "Yet Israel still serves with all his sons."(240)

For all Samson's sense of his destiny to deliver Israel from domination by the Philistines, he has not yet achieved anything.[4] Is his sense of his chosen destiny a true sense, or is he simply deluded, or so involved in self-justification as to imagine that there is something special about himself?

This pervasive uncertainty about Samson's motivation, about whether or not he was divinely inspired, relates not only to what occurred before the events of the drama, but to Samson's culminating decision and the consequent off-stage action. After having been confronted and provoked by Harapha, Samson initially refuses to appear as a public spectacle at the feast of Dagon. Then, before the second request to attend is delivered, Samson announces:

> I begin to feel
> Some rousing motions in me, which dispose
> To something extraordinary my thoughts.
> I with this messenger will go along,
> Nothing to do, be sure, that may dishonour
> Our Law, or stain my vow of Nazarite.
> If there be aught of presage in the mind,
> This day will be remarkable in my life
> By some great act, or of my days the last. (1381-9)

But is this sense of "something extraordinary" divine inspiration or delusion? There is no way for us, the readers, or for the other characters to tell. When Samson says "if there be aught of presage in the mind" it remains as ambiguous as ever. For Samson has done things that had he been able to foretell their consequences, he surely would not have done – like revealing the secret of his strength to Dalila. The mind may be capable of presage, but is Samson capable of correctly recognizing and interpreting what is foretold? The evidence suggests not. And what he foretells here is expressed with a strange ambiguity:

> This day will be remarkable in my life
> By some great act, or of my days the last. (1388-9)

The day indeed turns out to be remarkable in the "great act" of killing all the Philistine lords, but it is also for Samson "of my days the last" since he kills himself at the same time. Anthony Low interprets this passage as irony: "it is

---

[4] Mary Ann Radzinowicz, *Toward "Samson Agonistes": The Growth of Milton's Mind* (Princeton: Princeton University Press, 1978), 30. Mary Ann Radzinowicz remarks: "Israel's continued servitude cannot be held to disprove the validity of inner light; as Samson was free to attend to the impulse to offer deliverance, so Israel was free to cooperate or not in the difficult task of realizing it". My stress here, however, is that Milton presents Samson's belief in having received the inner light as open to question, and has it explicitly questioned by the Chorus in this response.

more true than Samson realizes: this will be both the last and the greatest day of his life." Ironically or not, Samson has once again failed to see the future clearly. And if he has failed to get this message right, does that mean that he has also failed to get other aspects of the message right, and that his decision to go to the theatre was not divinely inspired? There is another way of looking at Samson's words that might support this interpretation. Samson has expressed his prediction as an alternative – "some great act, or of my days the last." What if we interpret this alternative as meaning that though this was his last day, it was not a "great act"? It was a large scale destructive act, but not great in the sense of good, or heroic, or divinely inspired? A theatrical act rather than an act of God. Mary Ann Radzinowicz takes the "rousing motions" as firm evidence of "divine impulsion;" but Joseph Wittreich interprets Samson's final words in the theatre with the key phrase "of my own accord" as evidence that his final act was not divinely inspired.[5]

> Now of my own accord such other trial
> I mean to show you of my strength, yet greater;
> As with amaze shall strike all who behold. (1643-5)

The polarized critical responses – and such polarized responses could be multiplied from other commentators – are irreconcilable; unless we argue that both have their truth, and that a total response is one that would recognize the ambiguity of the issue.

If we turn to "the argument", the prose summary of the action at the beginning of the dramatic poem, the ambiguity is not resolved but remains as puzzling as ever. Required to attend the feast, Samson "at first refuses, dismissing the public officer with absolute denial to come; at length persuaded inwardly that this was from God, he yields to go along with him, who came now the second time with great threatenings to fetch him." (p. 346, ll. 71-4)

Samson is "persuaded inwardly that this was from God," but was it? The phrase "persuaded inwardly" avoids making it clear whether this was a true persuasion or a personal delusion. The ambiguities are scrupulously maintained.[6]

---

[5] Anthony Low, *The Blaze of Noon: A Reading of* "Samson Agonistes" (New York and London: Columbia University Press, 1974), 81; Radzinowicz, 345, 349; Joseph Wittreich, *Interpreting* Samson Agonistes (Princeton: Princeton University Press, 1986), 355.

[6] I first discussed these issues in Michael Wilding, "Regaining the Radical Milton" in *The Radical Reader,* eds. Stephen Knight and Michael Wilding (Sydney: Wild & Woolley, 1977), 130-141, reprinted in Michael Wilding, *Dragons Teeth: Literature in the English Revolution* (Oxford: Clarendon Press, 1987), 249-257. Joseph Wittreich likewise stresses that "Milton does not allow us to accept this mass slaughter unquestioningly", that it remains unknown whether "Samson really act[s] by divine commission? how does he, how do we, know?" and that "Samson's failure is that, by employing force, he perpetuates the very patterns of history that he would reverse" (79, 139, 284).

Samson Agonistes was published in 1671, eleven years after the collapse of the English republic and the reinstitution of the monarchy. Milton had been one of the foremost propaganda writers for the republic, and was writing political tracts in its defence until the very end – his *Ready and Easy Way to Establish a Free Commonwealth* was published in March 1660. After the restoration there was some chance he might have been brought to trial or assassinated. He spent time in hiding and parliament requested the king to order the burning of his *Eikonoklastes* and *Defence of the People of England*.[7] In part his blindness saved him: the royalists interpreted it as evidence that God had already punished him. When *Samson Agonistes* appeared, it would inevitably have been read in the context of Milton's political past. As William Empson put it, "the poem was calculated to strike the first readers as about Milton himself, and *a fortiori* about current politics; and it drives home its political point very firmly".[8] Anything written by this prominent revolutionary would be read to see what he believed now: the censors would have read it to make sure he was not reasserting radical republicanism.[9] The former revolutionaries who had not changed their beliefs would have read it in the hope he was saying something about politics. Because of the tight censorship controls Milton was not able to write anything explicit. It all had to be done in a hidden way, it all had to be interpreted. But that political context, that political expectation was inevitably there. Did he still believe in the Good Old Cause, or had he seen the error (in Royalist terms) of his ways? Was he writing a reassessment of his political beliefs, a reconsideration of those twenty years of commitment? Or was he reasserting the same beliefs? Or was he reasserting the same beliefs but at the same time reconsidering the past to explain what went wrong?

And of course to have the main character of *Samson Agonistes* a blind man inevitably encouraged the expectation of identification with the poet. When

---

[7] William Riley Parker, *Milton: A Biography*, 2nd rev. ed., ed. Gordon Campbell (Oxford: Clarendon Press, 1996), 1: 570, 2: 1084, n. 19.

[8] William Empson, *Milton's God* (1961; Cambridge: Cambridge University Press, 1981), 217. Other readings taking into account Milton's own political situation include Frank Kermode, "Milton in Old Age", *Southern Review*, 11 (1975), 513-529; Christopher Hill, *Milton and the English Revolution*, 446; and Wittreich, *Interpreting* "Samson Agonistes", xxi: "Any poem about Samson written or published during the years of the Civil War, or in its aftermath, would predictably involve some reflection on a revolution that had found its identity in, and drawn much of its spirit from, the Samson story. A poem about Samson written by John Milton would, just as predictably, involve reflections upon a revolution which Milton had championed and self-reflection by virtue of the fact that Milton himself had been given an identity with Samson and certainly preserves a measure of that identity in his poem".

[9] On censorship see Christopher Hill, "Censorship and English Literature" in *The Collected Essays of Christopher Hill*, volume 1, *Writing and Revolution in Seventeenth Century England* (Brighton: Harvester, 1985), 32-71; Annabel Patterson, *Censorship and Interpretation: The Conditions of Writing and Reading in Early Modern England* (Madison: University of Wisconsin Press, 1984).

he wrote those moving words about Samson's blindness, surely Milton was writing about his own situation:

> O dark, dark, dark, amid the blaze of noon,
> Irrecoverably dark, total eclipse
> Without all hope of day!
> O first-created beam, and thou great word,
> Let there be light, and light was over all;
> Why am I thus bereaved thy prime decree?
> The sun to me is dark
> And silent as the moon,
> When she deserts the night
> Hid in her vacant interlunar cave. (80-9)

Samson's laments about his blindness are some of the most deeply moving passages of English poetry. Equally powerful are his laments about the degradation and humiliation he now suffers:

> Ask for this great deliverer now, and find him
> Eyeless in Gaza at the mill with slaves … (40-1)

Particularly painful is his sense that his suffering is his own fault:

> Whom have I to complain of but myself?
> Who this high gift of strength committed to me,
> In what part lodged, how easily bereft me,
> Under the seal of silence could not keep,
> But weakly to a woman must reveal it,
> O'ercome with importunity and tears.
> O impotence of mind, in body strong!
> But what is strength without a double share
> Of wisdom…? (46-54)

Samson recognizes his error here in having revealed the secret of his strength. But that is all that he recognizes as error. At no point does he consider his belief that he was "designed for great exploits" (32) was mistaken. His sense of being chosen by God remains unchanged. He may speculate that because of his mistakes God will no longer use him, that the prophecies will now not be fulfilled:

> what if all foretold
> Had been fulfilled but through mine own default…? (44-5)

He may complain that God did not make him intelligent enough:

> Immeasurable strength they might behold
> In me, of wisdom nothing more than mean;
> This with the other should, at least, have paired,
> These two proportioned ill, drove me transverse. (206-9)

But he at no point doubts his inner conviction that he was destined to be an instrument of God.

If we are to find a political interpretation of *Samson Agonistes*, if we are to discover a reading that relates the dramatic poem to Milton's own political beliefs, then this unwavering certainty of Samson's, amidst all the ambiguity of critical interpretation of his final act, is its basis. Milton's own suffering in his blindness, his sense of being effectively imprisoned in the restoration society, is given expression in Samson's moving laments. Significantly, what is never lamented is that initial commitment to God's purpose. Samson regrets his mistakes, his marriages, the way things turned out, but he never questions his commitment to the project of freeing his people from bondage. This is Milton's answer to those who would seek a reading of the poem relating to his personal situation and political beliefs: his commitment remains unchanged, unlamented, unambiguous. And unchanged is his belief that his political position, his revolutionary commitment, was in accord with the divine will.

The regrets are all for the way things have turned out. And these regrets dominate the opening of the poem. Time and again it is asked why did everything go wrong? Samson is tormented by his "restless thoughts" (19) that

>   present
> Times past, what once I was, and what am now. (21-2)

The contrast between the good times and the present times is constantly reasserted. The Chorus remarks: "O change beyond report, thought or belief! (117)

Sometimes it is expressed in that traditional wheel of fortune way, how are the mighty fallen. The Chorus declaims:

> By how much from the top of wondrous glory,
> Strongest of mortal men,
> To lowest pitch of abject fortune thou art fallen. (167-9)

Manoah, Samson's father, remarks likewise on the "miserable change" (340):

>   Nay what thing good
> Prayed for, but often proves our woe, our bane? (350-1)

This insistent questioning of why everything has turned out badly is focused specifically on Samson's personal situation. But since Samson sees himself primarily as someone with a public role, as a potential liberator of his people, it is an obvious step of interpretation to see these remarks on the sorry change of things as relating to Milton's attitude to the restoration. But it would have been impossible to write explicitly about the "betrayal of the revolution" in the 1660s or 1670s. The focus in the dramatic poem remains carefully on Samson the individual, not on any wider explicit lament about social change. But Samson in bondage is an emblem of his people in bondage to the Philistines. What has happened to Samson is an image of what has happened to them. Samson's fate is representative – "Samson's tragedy is the tragedy of Israel" as Wittreich remarks.[10] In this regard the laments about tragic change, about decline and fall, are readily interpretable as laments about the fate of the chosen people; and that readily transfers to a lament about the English people who, during the revolutionary years, were consistently presented in radical propaganda as the new chosen people of God, leading forward the completion of the Protestant reformation of the church and state.

Continually the characters stress that God and the divine plan are not to be blamed. The Chorus says: "Tax not divine disposal". (210) Samson says:

> Appoint not heavenly disposition, father,
> Nothing of all these evils hath befall'n me
> But justly.... (373-5)

If God is not to be blamed, who is? Samson readily admits some, at least, of his own errors. But he also points to the political failings of the ruling class. The Chorus says:

> In seeking just occasion to provoke
> The Philistine, thy country's enemy,
> Thou never wast remiss, I bear thee witness:
> Yet Israel still serves with all his sons. (237-240)

Samson replies:

> That fault I take not on me, but transfer
> On Israel's governors, and heads of tribes,
> Who seeing those great acts which God had done
> Singly by me against their conquerors

---

[10] Wittreich 96 n.10. Radzinowicz remarks, "On the political level, Milton uses the figure of Samson to show the way in which an individual may represent a nation and thereby encapsulate a nation's political existence" (113).

Acknowledged not, or not at all considered
Deliverance offered.... (241-6)

Mary Ann Radzinowicz comments on this speech that "Milton expressed through the defeated, tormented words of Samson his bitterest disappointment in his own countrymen". This is true. But it is not simply his, either Samson's or Milton's, own countrymen in general who are indicted here. It is more specifically the ruling class, the "governors, and heads of tribes".[11] The rulers failed to take advantage of Samson's guerrilla war activities. Instead, they handed him over to their enemies in order to protect their own property – "to prevent / The harass of their land...." (256-7) Even at this point, Samson stresses, if some of them had joined with him, the Philistines could have been defeated. Samson was handed over

> Bound with two cords; but cords to me were threads
> Touched with the flame: on their whole host I flew
> Unarmed, and with a trivial weapon felled
> Their choicest youth; they only lived who fled.
> Had Judah that day joined, or one whole tribe,
> They had by this possessed the towers of Gath,
> And lorded over them whom now they serve;
> But what more oft in nations grown corrupt,
> And by their vices brought to servitude,
> Than to love bondage more than liberty,
> Bondage with ease than strenuous liberty;
> And to despise, or envy, or suspect
> Whom God hath of his special favour raised
> As their deliverer; if he aught begin,
> How frequent to desert him, and at last
> To heap ingratitude on worthiest deeds? (261-76)

This is a piece of past history that Samson tells. It is crucial to a political reading of the drama. It relates directly to Milton's view of the English people – that they had been corrupted by the policies of Charles I before the revolution, that they had grown to love their bondage because that was easier than fighting for liberty. Later we are told of some of the specific social corruptions of the Philistine lords when Manoah approaches them about ransoming Samson:

---

[11] A consistent class analysis runs through Milton's presentation of the situation. Empson remarks of Samson's comments to Dalila that the Philistines who recruited her against him are "No more thy country, but an impious crew / Of men conspiring to uphold their state" (891-892) that "the language suggests that the Philistine lords have practically become a wicked political party or ruling class" (*Milton's God*, 214). For issues of class in *Samson Agonistes*, see Thomas N. Corns, "Milton and Class" in *Running Wild: Essays, Fictions and Memoirs Presented to Michael Wilding*, eds. David Brooks and Brian Kiernan (Manohar, New Delhi: Sydney Studies in Society & Culture, 2004), 55ff.

> Some much averse I found and wondrous harsh,
> Contemptuous, proud, set on revenge and spite;
> That part most reverenced Dagon and his priests,
> Others more moderate seeming, but their aim
> Private reward, for which both god and state
> They easily would set to sale, a third
> More generous far and civil, who confessed
> They had enough revenged, having reduced
> Their foe to misery beneath their fears,
> The rest was magnanimity to remit
> If some convenient ransom were proposed. (1461-71)

It is not a totally corrupt public world that is presented. A third of men are reasonable, a third are ideological hard-liners, and a third are corrupt and would sell "both god and state." This is the Philistine society, but we can readily deduce a parallel with English society.

Greed is one motivation. Samson himself as a prisoner is hired out by his owners: "which earns my keeping / With no small profit daily to my owners". (1261-2)

It is a small detail, but the stress on cash and profit serves to connect the Old Testament world with the motivations of seventeenth-century England. And when Samson denounces the Philistines to Dalila, his indictment suggests a parallel with the view of restoration England that a former revolutionary might well hold:

> No more thy country, but an impious crew
> Of men conspiring to uphold their state
> By worse than hostile deeds, violating the ends
> For which our country is a name so dear;
> Not therefore to be obeyed. (891-5)

The Danites and Philistines may differ in religious commitments, but their ruling classes are presented as equally corrupt.

The slaughter of the Philistines in the theatre, Samson's last great act, is something presented off-stage and reported to us. The striking dramatized conflict is the confrontation of Dalila and Samson. It is a very bitter exchange and those writers who want to argue that Milton was a male chauvinist and misogynist have seized on it:

> Out, out hyaena; these are thy wonted arts,
> And arts of every woman false like thee,
> To break all faith, all vows, deceive, betray.... (748-50)

These words are Samson's, but as with everything of Samson's they are open to the possibility that he has got things wrong. He is not a mouthpiece of truth but someone whose utterances have to be assessed. Even more virulent are the words of the Chorus on woman's love:

> Whate'er it be, to wisest men and best
> Seeming at first all heavenly under virgin veil,
> Soft, modest, meek, demure,
> Once joined, the contrary she proves, a thorn
> Intestine, far within defensive arms
> A cleaving mischief, in his way to virtue
> Adverse and turbulent, or by her charms
> Draws him awry enslaved
> With dotage, and his sense depraved
> To folly and shameful deeds which ruin ends. (1034-43)

But the Chorus is not the embodiment of truth; the Chorus is not an objective summing up of actions and opinion. It is, as the list of "The Persons" at the beginning of the drama makes clear, a "Chorus of Danites." The Chorus consists of members of Samson's own tribe of Dan, "certain friends and equals of his tribe, which make the Chorus" it is spelled out in "The Argument" (p. 346; ll. 61-2). So anything that the Chorus says is partial, one-sided, in this dispute. As Empson puts it, "...the Chorus are Israelite patriots". [12] The Danites of the Chorus are the enemy of Dalila and her people, the Philistines. We need to assess what they say, not simply accept it. And their final summing up on women certainly needs assessment:

> Therefore God's universal law
> Gave to the man despotic power
> Over his female in due awe,
> Nor from that right to part an hour,
> Smile she or lour:
> So shall he least confusion draw
> On his whole life, not swayed
> By female usurpation, nor dismayed. (1053-60)

Milton's entire political writing was against "despotic power". Despotism, tyranny, was what he always, consistently opposed. It is inconceivable that he

---

[12] Empson, *Milton's God*, 222. The Danites, who comprise the Chorus, and their values, are certainly open to question. "In the Book of Judges, the account of Samson is immediately followed by another story about the Danites in which, after appearing in a most contemptible light as idolaters, thieves, and murderers, they vanish from history. In Jacob's prophecy of the twelve tribes at the end of Genesis, Dan is described as a treacherous 'serpent in the way', and in the list of twelve tribes in the Book of Revelation the name of Dan is omitted. For Milton this would practically mean being erased from the book of life". Northrop Frye, *Spiritu Mundi: Essays on Literature, Myth and Society* (1976; Bloomington: Indiana University Press, 1983), 222.

would have endorsed the exercise of "despotic power" in any context. It is a deliberately excessive statement. It expresses the value system of the Old Testament tribe of Dan, to which Samson belongs, and indicates some of the problems of Samson.

Samson is an Old Testament hero, a man of brute violence. His final "great act" is a massacre of horrific dimensions.[13] As soon as the Messenger has described the slaughter, the Chorus responds ecstatically:

> O dearly-bought revenge, yet glorious!
> Living or dying thou hast fulfilled
> The work for which thou wast foretold
> To Israel, and now li'st victorious
> Among thy slain self-killed
> Not willingly, but tangled in the fold,
> Of dire necessity, whose law in death conjoined
> Thee with thy slaughtered foes in number more
> Than all thy life had slain before. (1660-1668)

That line "than all thy life had slain before" is a chilling way to sum up a career, a "life" measured in terms of those it has "slain". And the language of the Chorus here – "dearly bought revenge, yet glorious" and "dire necessity" – is the language with which Satan is identified in *Paradise Lost*, where it is in marked contrast to the language of the Son of God.[14] In Christian terms revenge is not glorious but barbaric – Christ's message was to turn the other cheek, not seek revenge. And "necessity" was the world view of the pagan world, of classical Greece – inevitability, fate. The Christian view was a world of "providence", of divine aid. The contrast of these two world views is especially marked in the collocation of *Samson Agonistes* and *Paradise Regained* in the same volume at their first publication.[15]

Samson's values are of the primitive, revenge oriented, violent heroic world, a pre-Christian world. His father, Manoah, concludes

> Samson hath quit himself
> Like Samson, and heroicly hath finished
> A life heroic, on his enemies
> Fully revenged, hath left them years of mourning.... (1709-12)

---

[13] David Loewenstein, however, argues that "Milton is dramatizing in Samson's terrifying act a poetics of regenerative iconoclasm" (147).
[14] See Dennis H. Burden, *The Logical Epic* (London: Routledge & Kegan Paul, 1967), 65, and Alastair Fowler ed., *The Poems of John Milton*, 636n.
[15] I explored the parallelism of *Paradise Regained* and *Samson Agonistes* and its political implications in "Regaining the Radical Milton" in *The Radical Reader*, 130-141, reprinted in *Dragons Teeth*, 249-257. The issue is further examined by Joseph Wittreich, *Interpreting Samson Agonistes*, 329-385.

It is a limited, primitive world view. It is the world of the Old Testament, before Christ's new dispensation. The ambiguity as to whether Samson was divinely inspired or not can be explained in this context. Perhaps inspiration in the Old Testament did lead to mass slaughter; there are enough barbarous episodes to suggest so. Perhaps that was the best that could be done at that historic stage of world development, before Christ's coming. Milton can afford to leave the issue ambiguous; it may have been strategic to leave it so. What he is unambiguous about is that such military values are superseded by the new dispensation. As the narrator of *Paradise Lost* makes clear, the old brutal, military heroic ethic is replaced by Christianity's "better fortitude / Of patience and heroic martyrdom" (9: 31-2).[16] Similarly, the message of *Paradise Regained*, published in the same volume as *Samson Agonistes*, is that the revolution must be internal. Imposing a new social order by violent means is not the answer.[17]

It may, of course, be objected that the revolution to which Milton had committed himself was brought about by military means. Jackie Di Salvo has usefully explored the concept of "divinely inspired military vocation" in Samson and the New Model Army.[18] But by 1660 that revolution had failed. And any analysis of the causes of the failure would have to consider whether military means had been the appropriate ones to effect a change in social consciousness. It is my argument that Milton's view was that the military solution had been a bad idea.[19]

If we turn back to the confrontation with Dalila, we can see a comparable limitedness of perception in Samson's attitude to her. For what he cannot forgive in Dalila is the way she acted from the same political and nationalist convictions as his; the same, that is, in principle, the difference being that she was on the other side. As Dalila tells Samson:

> thou know'st the magistrates
> And princes of my country came in person,
> Solicited, commanded, threatened, urged
> Adjured by all the bonds of civil duty
> And of religion, pressed how just it was,

---

[16] G. A. Wilkes, "The Interpretation of *Samson Agonistes*", *Huntington Library Quarterly*, 26 (1963), 175. Wilkes, citing lines 1268-1291, has pointed out that "the chorus at the end presents two different roles that a deliverer may play. First is the role of force (in which Samson has hitherto cast himself) ... and then the contrasting role of patience, the lot of the martyr".

[17] I discuss the message of *Paradise Regained* in Michael Wilding, "Something Better: Reflections on Fundamentalism, Revolution, Loss of Faith and the Future", *Griffith Review*, 7 (2005).

[18] Jackie Di Salvo, "'The Lord's Battells': *Samson Agonistes* and the Puritan Revolution", in *Milton Studies IV*, ed. James D. Simmonds (Pittsburgh: University of Pittsburgh Press, 1972), 54.

[19] In arguing that Milton presents Samson's military role as a model to be rejected, I am for once in marked disagreement with Christopher Hill. See his *Milton and the English Revolution*, 440-445, and "Samson Agonistes Again", *Literature and History*, (2nd series) 1 (1990).

> How honourable, how glorious to entrap
> A common enemy, who had destroyed
> Such numbers of our nation: and the priest
> Was not behind, but ever at my ear,
> Preaching how meritorious with the gods
> It would be to ensnare an irreligious
> Dishonourer of Dagon: what had I
> To oppose against such powerful arguments? (850-62)

There is no difference in their roles.[20] Both Samson and Dalila are committed to the causes of their own peoples. What Milton presents here is the irreconcilability of opposed nationalist and religious politics. It is a barbarous confrontation: one people set against another, one religion set against another.

Samson's problem was that he wanted to separate his own brand of heroic activity – mass slaughter – from the rest of his life. His existence as a killing machine was political: but his sexual and marital relationships he saw as private. What he finds unacceptable is that Dalila becomes equally political. This can be interpreted as a sexism – the man's role is political, the woman's is not. But it is also a sexism markedly out of touch with realities. Dalila herself cites the Old Testament precedent of the Israelite Jael (989) – "a telling stroke" as Empson remarks.[21] We can safely assume Samson could have been aware of it, had he chosen. At the time that *Samson Agonistes* was published, Aphra Behn had already launched on her role as a political agent, a spy.[22] This was the contemporary world and there is no reason to think that Milton was unaware of it. We should be careful in identifying Samson's attitudes with Milton and so ascribing sexism to Milton here. But sexism is certainly a quality that Milton shows in Samson's attitudes – the old-style

---

[20] But cf. Stanley Fish, "Question and Answer in *Samson Agonistes*", *Critical Quarterly*, 2 (1969) 237-264, reprinted in *Milton: Comus and Samson Agonistes: A Casebook*, ed. Julian Lovelock (London: Macmillan, 1975), 209-245. Fish paraphrases Dalila's speech: "In other words: what I did looks exactly like what was done by one of your reverend heroines. Where is the difference between us? And of course there is none, if we attend only to the appearances surrounding the two actions". But he goes on to find differences. "By taking a *series* of stances (some of them contradictory) in relation to her act, Dalila betrays the quality of her moral life. She is not prompted within her, by her 'conscience and internal peace', but by some abstract formula behaviour (like the Law) which is imposed from without and relieves her of the burden of making moral decisions; in a word, she is insincere. What Dalila does not see is that two persons may engage in superficially similar activities, yet still be distinguished on the basis of their respective *intentions;* in fact no other basis for distinguishing between them is reliable". (240-241) However, Fish's distinctions do not seem relevant to, and indeed blur, the political point. For more positive interpretations of the presentation of Dalila, see Empson, *Milton's God*, 211-228; Heather Asals, "In Defense of Dalila: *Samson Agonistes* and the Reformation Theology of the Word", *Journal of English and Germanic Philology*, 74 (1975) 183-194; and Joyce Colony, "An Argument for Milton's Dalila", *Yale Review*, 66 (1977) 562-575.
[21] Empson, *Milton's God*, 221.
[22] In 1666. See Frederick M. Link, *Aphra Behn* (New York: Twayne, 1968), 20-21.

warrior of limited political vision who believes that the conflict should be kept to old-style massacres and is totally unable to accept the fact that the conflict, the nationalist politics, spread into every area of life and destroy the private, intimate, personal existence.

Of course, it needs to be stressed that Milton is not endorsing or supporting this spread of the political and this destruction of the domestic, intimate and sexual. We are not expected to agree when Dalila says:

> at length that grounded maxim
> So rife and celebrated in the mouths
> Of wisest men; that to the public good
> Private respects must yield; with grave authority
> Took full possession of me and prevailed;
> Virtue, as I thought, truth, duty, so enjoining. (865-70)

When any of Milton's characters talk about public good we need to be careful; they are usually politicians justifying some evil, like Satan in *Paradise Lost* using the concept of "public reason" to justify the destruction of Adam and Eve. (4: 389) Annotating that passage, Alastair Fowler cites Dalila's words as a comparable example of political talk to Satan's speech: "Satan is here cast in the role of a contemporary Machiavellian politician, excusing the evil means he resorts to by appeals to such values as 'the common weal', 'the good of the state', 'policy', and 'necessity' (l 393). Cp. Dalila's excuse that she had finally been persuaded to betray Samson by 'that grounded maxim' [l. 865]".[23]

Samson's shock that the political conflict takes place not only in military situations but also in male-female relations is a mark of his naivety and political unawareness. And equally naively he is unable to see that Dalila's political position is no less valid than his. Anything that can be used to justify Samson's "heroic acts" can be used to justify Dalila's. What is the difference here between Danites and Philistines? The drama never tells us. And it is crucially significant that we are never told. We are presented with one ethnic faction,[24] one religious group, against another. Samson believes he is divinely inspired and destined to become a national hero. After his death Manoah promises to "build him/A monument" (1733-4):

> Thither shall all the valiant youth resort
> And from his memory inflame their breasts
> To matchless valour, and adventures high;
> The virgins also shall on feastful days
> Visit his tomb with flowers ... (1738-42)

---

[23] *Poems of John Milton*, 636n.
[24] Empson, *Milton's God*, 213. William Empson points out that "Milton goes out of his way to suggest that Samson acts for an underprivileged class or minority group rather than a separate nation".

But Dalila, too, looks forward to a similar recognition:

> I shall be named among the famousest
> Of women, sung at solemn festivals,
> Living and dead recorded, who to save
> Her country from a fierce destroyer, chose
> Above the faith of wedlock-bands, my tomb
> With odours visited and annual flowers. (982-7)

"It is one of the noblest speeches in Milton", Empson writes of these lines, making the point that Dalila's patriotic politics are presented as on a par with Samson's.[25] But the consequence of these patriotic political commitments is that "wedlock-bands", the private life, the domestic life and intimate life, are politicized and destroyed.

So this seeming celebration of an Old Testament heroic warrior becomes a questioning of the values of military solutions. They are not *solutions*. And if we then apply this to Milton's seventeenth-century political world – as his contemporary readers would inevitably have applied it – we can see a whole questioning of the revolution in which he had participated. Not a questioning of the values of the revolution – the challenge to despotic power, the attempts to achieve individual liberty, the moves towards social justice – but a questioning of the methods used. What is questioned is the military method, the attempts to achieve liberty by warfare. This was something Milton always questioned, from his sonnets to Cromwell and Fairfax, through *Paradise Lost* to *Paradise Regained*. In the end Samson's "great act", his massacre of the Philistines, is deeply ambiguous, at the least, in moral terms, and fails to resolve anything. *Samson Agonistes* is a questioning rather than a celebration of its Old Testament hero, a questioning of military intervention in political situations.

---

[25] Empson, *Milton's God*, 221.

Reading Aloud

Bruce Dawe

'Reading aloud recognises that poets want their works to be heard.'
Barry Spurr, *Studying Poetry*

On the printed page we've pondered many a poem;
Some mortal works we're destined to dissect,
If read aloud, what seemingly was lifeless,
We may after all, more readily resurrect.

Rhythms which, on the page, sound practically static,
Their variables invisible to the eye,
Spoken, may reveal their true musculature,
A pleasure which few listeners would deny.

Variations in metre the inner ear
Has seized upon, those stresses in the sound,
Often benefit the speaking voice which offers
A personal harvest from impersonal ground.

Meanings inherent in the poet's thinking
(And heart) become more personal too, when heard,
As the musical notations of a composer
Cannot compare with the song of an actual bird.

A poem is heard first in the inward ear,
Where the poet's personal history lies in wait;
Intelligently read, the poet's experience
Will in the *hearer's* senses resonate.

To be heard as well as read ... Ah, that's the secret:
A poem's voice will bless what it bestows,
Since many a poem which, on the page, lacks lustre,
Polished by performance once more *glows*.

Many poems in audible reading are enlivened;
They speak and the poet, too, has once more spoken,
While the listener who (for hours, or days, or weeks)
May have heard little, has once more awoken ....

The Legacy of T. S. Eliot to Milton Studies

Beverley Sherry [1]

Considering that T.S. Eliot made more negative pronouncements on Milton than on any other individual writer, it is ironic that he provoked a valuable legacy to Milton studies. This chapter propounds and explores that legacy as twofold: the significance of Eliot's criticism to Milton studies in the twentieth century and the timely challenge his criticism offers to Milton studies today.

Eliot's earliest comments on Milton are in his essays on Marlowe (1919) and on the Metaphysical poets, Marvell, and Dryden (all 1921).[2] The essay on Marlowe applies the notorious appellation of a "Chinese Wall" to Milton's verse, a wall from which "blank verse has suffered not only arrest but retrogression".[3] "The Metaphysical Poets" was a widely influential essay, the most important single piece of criticism in creating the eminence which these poets enjoyed for the next forty years. Eliot defined their characteristic strength as a unified sensibility, which was manifested in "a direct sensuous apprehension of thought"; Donne was the exemplar, for he felt his thought "as immediately as the odour of a rose". Claiming that these strengths disappeared from English poetry after the Metaphysical poets, Eliot announces his theory of the "dissociation of sensibility", the idea that a dislocation of thought and feeling occurred in "the mind of England" in the seventeenth century, for which he held Milton and Dryden mainly responsible.[4] The Cambridge scholar E.M.W. Tillyard responded in what was the first of recurring rebuttals by scholar-critics of Eliot, the poet-critic. In his book, *Milton* (1930), Tillyard acknowledges Eliot's questioning of Milton's eminence as "extremely salutary", and in the book's "Epilogue: Milton Today", evaluates Eliot's theory of the dissociation of sensibility, finds it lacking in credibility in relation to Milton, and explains the fundamental difference in temperament between Milton and Donne.[5]

---

[1] This essay was first published as an article in *The Legacy of T.S. Eliot*, ed. Barry Spurr, a special issue of *Literature & Aesthetics* 18.1 (June 2008): 135-151, and reprinted in *Versification* 5 (2010): 27-38.
[2] "Christopher Marlowe", "The Metaphysical Poets", "Andrew Marvell", "John Dryden", in T.S. Eliot, *Selected Essays* (London: Faber and Faber, 1932).
[3] *Ibid.*, 118.
[4] *Ibid.*, 286-288.
[5] E.M.W. Tillyard, *Milton* (1930; repr. Harmondsworth: Penguin, 1968), 302, 302-312.

Eliot's most substantial Milton criticism, however, was after this: his 1936 essay, "A Note on Milton's Verse", published in *Essays and Studies*, and his 1947 lecture on Milton to the British Academy, the Annual Lecture on a Master Mind, which was delivered also at the Frick Museum in New York two months later. The essay and the lecture were titled respectively "Milton I" and "Milton II" when published in Eliot's collection, *On Poetry and Poets* (1957), "Milton II" a somewhat shortened version of the lecture.[6]

The 1936 essay is succinct and trenchant. Eliot begins by acknowledging that "Milton is a very great poet indeed" and that "what he could do well he did better than anyone else", but follows immediately with: "the marks against him appear as both more numerous and more significant than the marks to his credit". Apart from being a thoroughly unlikeable person, he was not a man of keen senses, a result of his blindness, and his auditory imagination was over-exercised "at the expense of the visual and tactile". Eliot admits that his own literary criticism is that of a practising poet interested to learn from poets of the past, and he considers Milton an exceptionally bad influence. Dryden is a healthier influence because he preserved "the tradition of conversational language in poetry".[7] This was Eliot's view of Milton in 1936. His British Academy lecture of 1947 is longer, more considered, and more knowledgeable. Eliot now has fundamental reservations about his theory of the dissociation of sensibility. He also has some positive things to say about Milton's visual imagination, specifically the images of light and darkness and of vast space in *Paradise Lost*. Further, he makes an about-turn on the question of Milton's influence. (And "no one", he declares, "can correct an error with better authority than the person who has been held responsible for it".) The gist of the lecture is that Milton is no longer a bad influence, and while his poetry is still considered "at the farthest possible remove from prose", this is now a mark of his peculiar greatness. Practising poets might, in 1947, actually profit from the study of Milton.[8] Despite this recantation, "Milton I" and "Milton II" are essentially similar in their formalist approach, focusing upon Milton's style, and in their emphasis on Milton's blindness and his auditory imagination.

---

[6] T.S. Eliot, *On Poetry and Poets* (London: Faber and Faber, 1957). The complete version of the 1947 lecture, delivered before the British Academy on 26 March and 3 May at the Frick Museum, is printed in James Thorpe, ed. *Milton Criticism: Selections from Four Centuries* (London: Routledge & Kegan Paul, 1951), 310-332. In the sections of the lecture deleted for "Milton II", Eliot quotes these lines from *Paradise Lost* and comments approvingly upon them: 3.1-12; 1.192-210, 286-294; 2.51-57; 5.781-784, 778 (Thorpe, *Milton Criticism*, 326-329).

[7] Eliot, *On Poetry and Poets*, 138-145; 138, 143, 142. Eliot considered Dante a particularly beneficial influence because his language was "the perfection of a common language" ("Dante" [1929], *Selected Essays*, 252) and "Dante" (1950), T.S. Eliot, *Selected Prose*, ed. John Hayward (Harmondsworth: Penguin, 1953), 99-101.

[8] Eliot, *On Poetry and Poets*, 146-161; 146, 154.

Of the two pieces, the 1936 essay is clearly the more strenuous denunciation. In 1938 Tillyard, adding his protest to Sir Herbert Grierson's, was provoked to respond again to Eliot because of "Mr Eliot's great influence as a critic", and in *The Miltonic Setting* dealt cogently with Milton's style, particularly in relation to Eliot's comments on Milton's visual imagination.[9] Then, in 1940, the poet, novelist, and critic Charles Williams opened the Introduction to the World Classics edition of *The English Poems of John Milton* with the observation: "We have been fortunate enough to live at a time when the reputation of John Milton has been seriously attacked". He expressed a debt of gratitude to Eliot, and suggested that the effect of his attack was "to compel the reconsideration everywhere of [Milton's] power as a poet". Williams proceeded to do that in his Introduction and, even if briefly, refuted Eliot's imputation that thought and feeling are severed in Milton's poetry.[10]

The twentieth-century attack upon and defence of Milton became known as "the Milton controversy" and has been called "a unique phenomenon in the history of literary criticism".[11] Initiated by Eliot, the attack was aided and abetted by Ezra Pound and Sir Herbert Read, encouraged somewhat by Lord David Cecil, influenced strongly by John Middleton Murry, and lent academic force by the University of Sydney scholar A.J.A. Waldock and especially by the deeply influential Cambridge critic F.R. Leavis, who claimed not to be a scholar and, like Eliot and also many New Critics, insisted on a division between scholarship and criticism.[12] In his essay, "Milton's Verse", published in *Scrutiny* in 1933 and reprinted in his book *Revaluation* in 1936, Leavis announces: "Milton's dislodgement, in the past decade, after his two centuries of predominance, was effected with remarkably little fuss." He then acknowledges this as "Mr Eliot's creative achievement".[13]

There was undoubtedly an eclipsing of Milton. From the 1920s to the 1960s, the popularity of the Metaphysical poets in university teaching and research, "the cult of Donne," as Douglas Bush put it, went hand-in-hand

---

[9] E.M.W. Tillyard, *The Miltonic Setting: Past and Present* (1938; repr. London: Chatto & Windus, 1961), 90; 90-104. Grierson's protest is a lengthy Note in his book, *Milton and Wordsworth: Poets and Prophets* (London: Chatto & Windus, 1937), 125 n.1.

[10] Charles Williams, "An Introduction to Milton's Poems (1940)", Thorpe, *Milton Criticism*, 252; 252-266.

[11] Thorpe, "Introduction," *Milton Criticism*, 19.

[12] See Todd H. Sammons, "A Periplum of Pound's Pronouncements on John Milton", *Paedeuma* 19-20 (1990-1991): 147-161; Herbert Read, *Phases of English Poetry* (1928; repr. Norfolk [Conn]: New Directions Books, 1951), 122-124; David Cecil, ed. *Oxford Book of Christian Verse* (Oxford: Clarendon Press, 1940), xxi-xxii; John Middleton Murry, *The Problem of Style* (London: Oxford University Press, 1922) and *Heaven–and Earth* (London: Jonathan Cape, 1938), 150, 158, 165; A.J.A.Waldock, *Paradise Lost and Its Critics* (Cambridge: Cambridge University Press, 1966); F.R. Leavis, *Revaluation: Tradition and Development in English Poetry* (1936; repr. Harmondsworth: Penguin, 1964) and *The Common Pursuit* (1952; repr. London: Chatto & Windus, 1962). On Leavis's and Eliot's separation of scholar and critic, see Leavis, *The Common Pursuit*, 10 and Eliot, "Milton II", *On Poetry and Poets*, 146-147.

[13] Leavis, *Revaluation*, 42.

with Eliot's and Leavis's promotion of the Metaphysical poets and demotion of Milton; the "dethronement of Milton was necessary to the enthronement of Donne".[14] This was also the period of the New Criticism, to which Milton's poetry was generally thought not to be amenable. In 1942 abuse of Milton even reached the depths of Robert Graves's novel *Wife to Mr Milton*, presented as the diary of Milton's first wife, Mary Powell, who portrays her husband as thoroughly odious. To some extent, and depending on the institution, the history of English poetry was skewed during these years. My experience as an undergraduate in Australia in the 1950s is paralleled by that of C.K. Stead in New Zealand, who recalls that the English literary history he learned at university was Eliot's version.[15] In 1962 B.A. Wright, Professor of English at the University of Southampton, deplored the effect that Milton's "exploded reputation" had had in universities in Britain for more than forty years, the result of the "revolt against Milton by T.S. Eliot and his school".[16] In America, Stanley Fish surveyed the fortunes of *Paradise Lost* from 1942 to 1979, noted a generation which suffered from the eclipsing of Milton, and connected Milton's decline with Eliot, the ascendancy of Donne and the Metaphysicals, and the New Criticism.[17] Meanwhile, Eliot's own poetry, which was sometimes written with the Metaphysical poets in his bones, commanded great respect from the 1920s to the 1970s.[18]

Despite the revolt against Milton by Eliot and his cohorts, Milton was not "dislodged". In 1967, the tercentenary of the publication of *Paradise Lost*, C.A. Patrides, referring to Leavis's notorious "dislodgement" statement, observed that "Milton's consignment to oblivion has not, after all, been

---

[14] Douglas Bush, Paradise Lost *in Our Time: Some Comments* (Ithaca [NY]: Cornell University Press, 1945), 5, 3. The first chapter of this book, "The Modern Reaction Against Milton," consists mainly of an impassioned and systematic refutation of Eliot's 1936 essay.

[15] C.K.Stead, "Eliot, Arnold, and the English Poetic Tradition", *The Literary Criticism of T.S. Eliot*, ed. David Newton-De Molina (London: Athlone Press, 1977), 185.

[16] B.A.Wright, *Milton's "Paradise Lost"* (London: Methuen, 1962) 9, 63. Wright's book opens with this statement: "Since the first war Milton has indeed 'fall'n on evil days, and evil tongues' in his own country. Young men and women go up to the universities to read Honours English without having read a line of him, for their teachers have told them that they need not bother with a poet of exploded reputation. *Paradise Lost* accordingly is not nowadays widely read or highly regarded" (9).

[17] Stanley Fish, "Transmuting the Lump: *Paradise* Lost, 1942-1979", *Doing What Comes Naturally: Change, Rhetoric, and the Practice of Theory in Literary and Legal Studies* (Durham and London: Duke University Press, 1989), 247-293.

[18] At the University of Queensland in the 1950s, Milton was taught briefly in second year, my fourth-year English Honours class made a special study of the Metaphysical poets and of Leavis's *Revaluation*, and I wrote my fourth-year thesis on Eliot's *Four Quartets*. In 1960, as a Junior Lecturer, I tutored second-year students mainly on the Metaphysical poets and applied the New Criticism rigorously in first-year tutorials. To prepare for the latter, staff members met in the lunch hour and together dissected an "unseen" poem in preparation for the tutorial. One of my first publications, signed under my maiden name, "B[everley] C[hadwick]," was "T.S. Eliot: His Poetry and Theories", *The Makar* (University of Queensland) 2.1 (1962): 21-23.

accomplished".[19] The reassessment of his power as a poet, begun by Tillyard and Charles Williams, expanded exponentially from 1940 to 1970. Eliot's attack on Milton goaded B.A. Wright, for example, not just to lament Milton's "exploded reputation" but to produce the Everyman edition of *Milton's Poems* in 1956 and a book on *Paradise Lost* in 1962.[20] Even while the eclipsing was occurring, partly because it was occurring, a rich burgeoning of Milton scholarship was under way, especially in North America. This was manifested in monumental editorial work, biographical and historical research, the establishment of *Milton Quarterly* (originally *Milton Newsletter*) in 1967 and the annual *Milton Studies* in 1969, and the publication of major books by, among others, C.S. Lewis, Rosemond Tuve, Isabel MacCaffrey, J.B. Broadbent, Frank Kermode, Joseph Summers, Northrop Frye, Helen Gardner, and – most pertinent to the attack on Milton – Arnold Stein, Balachandra Rajan, Stanley Fish, and Christopher Ricks.[21] In *Milton's Grand Style* (1963), Ricks aimed to deal once and for all with the Milton controversy and with Eliot and Leavis as "the foremost … anti-Miltonists"; his book-length study of *Paradise Lost* demonstrated, by close analysis, that Milton's poetry is a remarkably flexible medium which does respond to the New Criticism.[22]

Since the 1970s, the New Criticism has declined, and with it the subject of Milton's style and the Milton controversy. By 2001 Richard Bradford could reasonably ask whether Eliot's criticism of Milton "would have been taken seriously had it not been promoted by a man who, in 1936 and thereafter, was the dominant presence in contemporary English verse".[23]

---

[19] C.A. Patrides, "*Paradise Lost* and the Language of Theology," in *Language and Style in Milton: A Symposium in Honor of the Tercentenary of* Paradise Lost, eds. Ronald David Emma and John T. Shawcross (New York: Frederick Ungar, 1967), 102. The same year saw the publication of Patrick Murray's *Milton: The Modern Phase: A Study of Twentieth-century Criticism* (London: Longman, 1967), which included a survey of the attack on Milton.

[20] *Milton's Poems*, ed. B.A. Wright (London: Everyman, 1956; revised 1962, reprinted 1969) and Milton's "*Paradise Lost*".

[21] C.S. Lewis, *A Preface to* Paradise Lost (London: Oxford University Press, 1942); Rosemond Tuve, *Images and Themes in Five Poems by Milton* (Cambridge MA: Harvard University Press, 1957); Isabel Gamble MacCaffrey, Paradise Lost *as "Myth"* (Cambridge MA: Harvard University Press, 1959); J.B. Broadbent, *Some Graver Subject: An Essay on* Paradise Lost (London: Chatto & Windus, 1960); Frank Kermode, ed. *The Living Milton: Essays by Various Hands* (London: Routledge & Kegan Paul, 1960); Joseph Summers, *The Muse's Method: an Introduction to* Paradise Lost (London: Chatto & Windus, 1962); Northrop Frye, *The Return of Eden: Five Essays on Milton's Epics* (Toronto: University of Toronto Press, 1965); Helen Gardner, *A Reading of* Paradise Lost (Oxford: Clarendon Press, 1965); Arnold Stein, *Answerable Style: Essays on* Paradise Lost (Minneapolis: University of Minnesota Press, 1953); Balachandra Rajan, *The Lofty Rhyme: A study of Milton's major poetry* (London: Routledge & Kegan Paul, 1970); Stanley Fish, *Surprised by Sin: the Reader in* Paradise Lost (London: Macmillan, 1967); Christopher Ricks, *Milton's Grand Style* (Oxford: Clarendon Press, 1963).

[22] Ricks, *Milton's Grand Style*, 2. Ricks's opening chapter is "The Milton Controversy". Cleanth Brooks had earlier argued that Milton"s poetry is amenable to New Critical methods – "Milton and the New Criticism", *Sewanee Review* 59 (1951): 1-22.

[23] Richard Bradford, *The Complete Critical Guide to John Milton* (London: Routledge, 2001), 155.

However that may be, Charles Williams's observation that "no critic of Milton ought to be uninformed" of Eliot's criticism, remains valid.[24] Milton scholars continue to refer to him with respect, and in 2003 Neil Forsyth bracketed him as a "great critic" with Samuel Johnson and Stanley Fish.[25] In 2005 Christopher Ricks, then Professor of Poetry at Oxford, spoke of Eliot as "an astonishing poet and critic and phenomenon".[26]

The fruitful and prolific reassessment of Milton from 1940 to 1970 was the positive legacy of the Milton controversy ignited by Eliot. But there is another legacy, I want to suggest, for Milton studies today. It lies in Eliot's emphasis on the sound of Milton's poetry. For a variety of reasons, formal elements of Milton's poetry, including its oral and aural properties, have been neglected since the 1970s; there is not even an entry on "style" planned for the gargantuan *Milton Encyclopedia* forthcoming from Yale University Press. Over the past forty years Milton studies have focused more and more upon Milton's thought and politics, with massive research on his prose writings, and an imbalance has developed, noted in 2005 by Stanley Fish.[27] As for the oral and aural elements of Milton's poetry, while the practice of "Milton marathons" – the public reading aloud of *Paradise Lost* – continues to be widespread, the purpose of these events has been avowedly heuristic and they have tended to remain in the popular culture of academic communities; the knowledge gained from them has scarcely been channelled into Milton scholarship.[28] Generally speaking, in the last forty years Milton scholars have neglected the central importance of sound in Milton's poetry, the importance, that is, of sound to meaning.[29] Eliot's repeated emphasis on Milton's auditory

---

[24] Thorpe, *Milton Criticism*, 254.
[25] Neil Forsyth, *The Satanic Epic* (Princeton: Princeton University Press, 2003), 115. See also Roy Flannagan, "'The world all before [us]': More than Three Hundred Years of Criticism", in *A Concise Companion to Milton*, ed. Angelica Duran (Oxford: Blackwell, 2007), 52-53.
[26] Report by Nicholas Wroe, Saturday 29 January 2005, *The Guardian*.
[27] Stanley Fish, "Why Milton Matters; or, Against Historicism", in *Milton Studies* 44, ed. Albert C. Labriola (Pittsburgh: Pittsburgh University Press, 2005): 1-12.
[28] John Hale at the University of Otago is probably the most experienced in organizing Milton marathons. For an account of his work, see Beverley Sherry, "*Paradise Lost* 'Made vocal'", *Milton Quarterly* 34 (2000): 128-129 and Beverley Sherry, "Introduction" to John K. Hale, *Milton as Multilingual: Selected Essays* (Dunedin: Department of English, University of Otago, 2005), xv-xvii. My entry on "Marathon Readings of Miltonic Works" is forthcoming in the *Milton Encyclopedia* from Yale University Press.
[29] The notable exception is John Creaser, who has written variously on rhythm and in 2007 published a ground-breaking and persuasive study, "'Service is Perfect Freedom': Paradox and Prosodic Style in *Paradise Lost*", *RES* 58 (2007): 268-315. Other exceptions are Diane McColley, "'The Copious Matter of My Song'", *Literary Milton: Text, Pretext, Context*, eds. Diana Trevino Benet and Michael Lieb (Pittsburgh: Duquesne University Press, 1994), 67-90 and *Poetry and Music in Seventeenth-Century England* (Cambridge: Cambridge University Press, 1997), chapter 5; Archie Burnett, "'Sense Variously Drawn Out': The Line in *Paradise Lost*", *Literary Imagination* 5 (2003): 69-92; and William Walker, "Sounds of Elevation: God's Commendation of Abdiel (*Paradise Lost* VI, 29-37)", forthcoming.

imagination might provide a challenge and a wake-up call to Miltonists, especially to their understanding of *Paradise Lost*.

In the long reception history of *Paradise Lost*, the sound of the poem was admired, particularly in the nineteenth century, and Eliot's response falls within this tradition and links him with other poets. Francis Berry (himself a poet), in his book, *Poetry and the Physical Voice*, claims that poets have "a peculiarly physical ... awareness of vocal sound".[30] The responses of Wordsworth and Tennyson to Milton's poetry – "a voice whose sound was like the sea", "organ-voice of England" – bear this out.[31] Eliot likewise responds to the auditory power of Milton's poetry. In "Milton I", he writes that Milton's "gifts were naturally aural", the sensuous effect of his verse "is entirely on the ear", his verse "is dictated by a demand of verbal music". Eliot is overwhelmed by the "mazes of sound" and concludes that Milton's work "realizes superbly" the auditory element.[32] In 1942, between "Milton I" and "Milton II", Eliot gave two lectures – "The Music of Poetry" at Glasgow University and "The Classics and the Man of Letters" at the Classical Association in Cambridge – in which he commends Milton's exploration of "the orchestral music of language", considers his poetry "among the great triumphs of English versification", and emphasizes how Latin entered into the "complete music of his verse".[33] Also between "Milton I" and "Milton II" came the later *Quartets*, by which time the music of Milton has entered Eliot's own verse, the powerful opening of *East Coker* III, "O dark dark dark..." echoing Milton's Samson.[34] Then in "Milton II", Eliot states emphatically that, in reading *Paradise Lost*, "our sense of sight must be blurred, so that our *hearing* may become more acute". Especially interesting are his observations on Milton's handling of verse paragraphs. Declaring Milton "the greatest master of free verse in our language", "of freedom within form", Eliot offers the insight that Milton works in "larger musical units" than any other poet, that his verse paragraphs have their own "wave-length" and

---

[30] Francis Berry, *Poetry and the Physical Voice* (New York: Oxford University Press, 1962), 5; the book includes an interesting chapter on "The Voice of Milton" (83-113).

[31] See Wordsworth's sonnet, "Milton! Thou shouldst be living at this hour" ("Thou hadst a voice whose sound was like the sea: / Pure as the naked heavens, majestic, free,") and Tennyson's "Milton" ("*O mighty-mouth'd* inventor of harmonies, / O skill'd to sing of Time or Eternity, /God-gifted organ-voice of England").

[32] Eliot, *On Poetry and Poets*, 139, 140, 141, 144, 145.

[33] *Ibid*, 36, 29 and T.S. Eliot, *To Criticize the Critic and other writings* (London: Faber and Faber, 1965), 149

[34] *Samson Agonistes* 80 ff. *Little Gidding* III presumably acknowledges Milton as "one who died blind and quiet". On Milton's influence upon Eliot, see Mother M. Christopher Pecheux, "Milton and Eliot: Touched by a Common Genius", *Greyfriar: Siena Studies in Literature* 18 (1977): 29-44; B. Rajan, "Milton and Eliot: A Twentieth-Century Acknowledgment", in *Milton Studies 11: The Presence of Milton*, ed. B. Rajan (Pittsburgh: Pittsburgh University Press,1978): 115-29; and Harry Blamires, "Influence on Twentieth-Century Literature, Milton's, in *A Milton Encyclopedia*, gen. ed. William B. Hunter (Lewisburg: Bucknell University Press, 1978), vol. 4: 145-146.

communicate a "peculiar feeling, almost a physical sensation of a breathless leap".[35] This is possibly the most revealing brief comment ever made on the way *Paradise Lost* moves. Its verse paragraphs are athletic, whether in narration, description, or speeches, varying in manner – at times stately, flowing, twisting, surging – but never inhibited by the unit of the line.[36]

Eliot's response to the physicality of Milton's verse connects interestingly with the mode of composition of *Paradise Lost*. Milton had to *speak* every word of the poem. His early biographers record that he dictated the poem on waking in the morning and that, if a scribe was late, would complain that "*hee wanted to bee milkd*".[37] We would literally not have *Paradise Lost* but for its being physically "milked" out of him via his voice, a voice that, he reminds us, was not "hoarse or mute" even by Book 7 (7.24-25).[38] He would dictate "a Parcel of Ten, Twenty, or Thirty Verses at a Time" or deliver "perhaps 40 Lines as it were in a Breath", significant details in relation both to Milton's prefatory note on "The Verse" and to Eliot's insight into the "breathless leap" of the verse paragraphs.[39]

Eliot had especially keen instincts, then, for Milton's auditory imagination. But there is a sting-in-the-tail, which nevertheless might serve a purpose of goading Miltonists to further reassess Milton's powers. The sting is Eliot's damning criticism of a gulf between sound and sense. This censure is pronounced in "Milton I" and is not really retracted in "Milton II".[40] Because of "the hypertrophy of the auditory imagination the inner meaning is separated from the surface", so that, "[t]o extract everything possible from *Paradise Lost*, it would seem necessary to read it in two different ways, first solely for the sound, and second for the sense".[41] With all poetry of any difficulty this is necessary to some extent, but Eliot's statement, in its context, comes out as an accusation of a division between sound and sense in Milton, and is a bludgeoning which cries out to be rebuffed. In fact, when it comes to exploring the interface of sound and sense, commentary has been relatively

---

[35] Eliot, *On Poetry and Poets*, 157, 158, 160, 157-158.
[36] For statistics on the unprecedented freedom of Milton's use of enjambement, see Creaser, "'Service is Perfect Freedom'", 308-311.
[37] "The Life of Mr John Milton" (attributed to Milton's friend and amanuensis Cyriack Skinner), *The Riverside Milton*, ed. Roy Flannagan (Boston and New York: Houghton Mifflin, 1998). 12.
[38] Citations of Milton are from *The Riverside Milton*.
[39] Edward Phillips, *The Life of Mr. John Milton* (1694), *The Riverside Milton*, 26; Jonathan Richardson, *The Life of Milton and a Discourse on* Paradise Lost (1734), *The Early Lives of Milton*, ed. Helen Darbishire (London: Constable, 1932), 291. In his prefatory note on "The Verse" of *Paradise Lost*, Milton defines "true musical delight" as consisting of "apt Numbers, fit quantity of Syllables, and the sense variously drawn out from one Verse into another, not in the jingling sound of like endings".
[40] There is a suggestion of a retraction in "Milton II" in Eliot's consideration that one of the positive lessons that might be learnt from Milton is "that the music of verse is strongest in poetry which has a definite meaning expressed in the properest words" (*On Poetry and Poets*, 160).
[41] Eliot, "Milton I", *On Poetry and Poets*, 143.

sparse. The New Criticism of the 1950s and '60s did produce some good work which specifically responded to Eliot's attack. The most concerted effort was that of Arnold Stein in his book *Answerable Style* (1953). He confronted Eliot's complaint, made in "Milton II", that in *Paradise Lost* "[t]he emphasis is on the sound, not the vision, upon the word, not the idea", and argued, through textual analysis, that patterns of sound in *Paradise Lost* help shape and modulate meaning.[42] In 1964 Balachandra Rajan also analyzed passages of *Paradise Lost* in order to refute Eliot's accusation, in "Milton I", that Milton's syntax is for musical significance rather than the development of thought.[43] In 1963, however, the doyen of critics of Milton's style, Christopher Ricks, while acknowledging that auditory effects are "indisputably important" to Milton's grand style, did not attempt to deal with them because of the danger of merely imagining that sound was echoing sense, a danger pointed out by Dr Johnson and known today as the "the enactment fallacy".[44] Ricks considered that skilled critics, including Stein, fell into this fallacy, and "[i]f critics as intelligent as these can sink, it may be best to conclude that the close analysis of Milton's rhythms and music is 'a gulf profound as that Serbonian Bog … Where Armies whole have sunk'".[45]

Nevertheless, in attempting to refute Eliot's damning indictment of a breach between sound and sense, I must venture into the "Bog". In doing so, I will draw upon an analogy to aid my argument. There is an analogy, I believe, between the philosophy of materialist monism that pervades *Paradise Lost* and the poem itself considered as a created thing. In the Milton industry today, a great deal of research has been expended on the materialist monism of *Paradise Lost*, but the phenomenon of the poem itself has not been related to this ontology.[46] In the cosmos of the poem, all things – from the lowest

---

[42] Eliot, "Milton II", *On Poetry and Poets*, 157 and Stein, *Answerable Style*, 139-153.
[43] B. Rajan, "The Style of *Paradise Lost*", in *Milton's epic Poetry: Essays on* Paradise Lost *and* Paradise Regained, ed. C.A. Patrides (Harmondsworth: Penguin, 1967), 287-97. Rajan's essay is taken from his "Introduction to *Paradise Lost, Books I and II*" (London: Asia Publishing House, 1964). Another (not highly successful) attempt from the period of the New Criticism to deal with the interconnection of sound and sense is Wayne Shumaker, *Unpremeditated Verse: Feeling and Perception in* Paradise Lost (Princeton: Princeton University Press, 1967), chapter 7 ("Auditory Perception").
[44] Ricks, *Milton's Grand Style*, 23; Samuel Johnson, *The Rambler* 86, 88, 89, 90, 94 and his *Life of Pope*; Peter Barry, "The Enactment Fallacy", *Essays in Criticism* 30 (1980): 95-104. Terry Eagleton terms it the "Incarnational Fallacy" in *How To Read a Poem* (Oxford: Blackwell, 2007), 59-64. In a later lecture on "Sound and Sense in *Paradise Lost*", Ricks persuasively shows Milton's use of interlacing sounds, and occasional rhymes, to reinforce sense; the lecture is printed in Christopher Ricks, *The Force of Poetry* (Oxford: Clarendon Press, 1984), 60-79.
[45] Ricks, *Milton's Grand Style*, 26. The quote is from *Paradise Lost* 2. 592-594.
[46] On the materialist monism of *Paradise Lost*, see William Kerrigan, *The Sacred Complex: On the Psychogenesis of* Paradise Lost (Cambridge MA: Harvard University Press, 1983), 193-262; Stephen M. Fallon, *Milton Among the Philosophers: Poetry and Materialism in Seventeenth-Century England* (London and Ithaca: Cornell University Press, 1991); John Rumrich, "Milton's God and the Matter of Chaos", *PMLA* 110 (1995): 1035-1046; D. Bentley Hart, "Matter, Monism, and Narrative: an Essay on

stone up through plants, perfumes, sounds, mind (of human beings and angels) to God – are both spiritual and material. Meanwhile the poem itself is, analogously, a thing at once spiritual and physical: the thoughts, feelings, elaborate structure of ideas, characters, shaping of the plot, images (mental sense impressions), allusions, down to the minutest associations of words – all these are abstract, existing in the mind of the author and the reader. But they only exist, are only brought into being, by the physical properties of the poem, that is, the visual appearance of the words on the page (lexical, syntactic, linear) and the auditory effects. In *Paradise Lost*, these auditory effects, the materiality of sound, is of central importance, as Eliot's instincts so strongly registered and as eighteenth- and especially nineteenth-century critics also recognized. Milton's materialist monism is best demonstrated, I want to suggest, in the living poem itself as it was "milked" out of his body in his voice and continues to be read aloud by those who "[will] not willingly let it die".[47]

This requires explanation by textual analysis, and I take a passage from Book 1. Satan, having heaved himself off the lake of fire and conferred with Beelzebub, moves towards his followers in order to rouse them:

He scarce had ceas't when the superior Fiend	
Was moving toward the shoar; his ponderous shield	
Ethereal temper, massy, large, and round,	285
Behind him cast; the broad circumferance	
Hung on his shoulders like the Moon, whose Orb	
Through Optic Glass the *Tuscan* Artist views	
At Ev'ning from the top of *Fesole*,	
Or in *Valdarno*, to descry new Lands,	290
Rivers or Mountains in her spotty Globe.	
His Spear, to equal which the tallest Pine	
Hewn on *Norwegian* hills, to be the Mast	
Of some great Ammiral, were but a wand,	
He walkd with to support uneasie steps	295
Over the burning Marle, not like those steps	
On Heavns Azure, and the torrid Clime	
Smote on him sore besides, vaulted with Fire;	
Nathless he so endur'd, till on the Beach	
Of that inflamed Sea, he stood and call'd	300

---

the Metaphysics of *Paradise Lost*", *Milton Quarterly* 30 (1996): 16-27; Phillip J. Donnelly, "'Matter' versus Body: The Character of Milton's Monism", *Milton Quarterly* 33 (1999): 79-85; and Juliet Cummins, "Milton's Gods and the Matter of Creation", in *Milton Studies 40*, ed. Albert C. Labriola (Pittsburgh: University of Pittsburgh Press, 2001), 81-105.

[47] Describing his literary aspirations in an autobiographical passage of *The Reason of Church Government* (1642), Milton expresses a hope that he "might leave something so written to aftertimes, as they should not willingly let it die"–*Riverside Milton*, 922.

> His Legions, angel Forms, who lay intrans't
> Thick as Autumnal Leaves that strow the Brooks
> In *Vallombrosa*, where th'*Etrurian* shades
> High overarcht imbowr; ... (ll. 283-304)

This passage exemplifies some of the positive things Eliot observed about Milton's handling of blank verse. The peculiar wave-length is heard, especially in the way the similes advance confidently, disdaining the line endings: "in comparison with Milton," Eliot declares, "hardly any subsequent writer of blank verse appears to exercise any freedom at all".[48] In addition, Eliot quoted these particular similes and commented favourably upon them in his 1947 British Academy lecture. Unfortunately that part of the lecture was deleted for "Milton II". He regarded them, as also the Leviathan simile (1.200-07), as evidence of "a mark of the first rank of genius" and related them to "the absorbed attention which ... any poetry lover today ought to be able to give the poem from end to end" because of the "perpetual variety" of its "extraordinary style".[49] However, Eliot's heresy of a gulf between sound and sense still demands to be confronted and refuted. For this, I want to look particularly at the last five lines of the passage, mentioned by Leigh Hunt in 1825 as exemplifying Milton's "harmonious" sound effects,[50] although Hunt made no attempt to explain how these effects work:

> ... he stood and call'd   300
> His Legions, angel Forms, who lay intrans't
> Thick as Autumnal Leaves that strow the Brooks
> In *Vallombrosa*, where th'*Etrurian* shades
> High overarcht imbowr; ...   (ll. 300-304)

A recent interpretation of these lines struck me as a blatant example of how ignoring the aural properties of Milton's poetry can result in totally inept interpretations. In his book *Destabilizing Milton: "Paradise Lost" and the Poetics of Incertitude* (2005), Peter Herman argues, by a long and circuitous route, that these lines are about both republicanism and monarchy and therefore betray Milton's incertitude about the seventeenth-century Revolution; Herman's book focuses on Milton's politics and completely ignores the sound of *Paradise Lost*.[51] If he had listened to the lines, he might have offered a more credible interpretation.

---

[48] Eliot, "Milton II", *On Poetry and Poets*, 161.
[49] Thorpe, *Milton Criticism*, 328.
[50] Leigh Hunt, "Originality of Milton's Harmonious Use of Proper Names", in *The Romantics on Milton: Formal Essays and Critical Asides*, ed. Joseph Anthony Wittreich, Jr. (Cleveland / London: Case Western Reserve University Press, 1970), 438.
[51] Peter C. Herman, *Destabilizing Milton: "Paradise Lost" and the Poetics of Incertitude* (New York: Palgrave Macmillan, 2005), 31-32. I have reviewed this book in *Milton Quarterly* 41 (2007): 43-46.

How, then, do they sound and how does the sound relate to sense? First, the angels are stunned, "intrans't", and there is an appropriate sense of stillness in the lines. They move fairly slowly because of a predominance of long vowels and a number of pauses, two in line 301, one each in lines 303 and 304. And there is an extra pause at the end of line 301, on "intrans't". This is because of the long vowel of "intrans't", but also because the cluster of unvoiced consonants at the end of line 301 and the beginning of line 302 – "intrans't", "Thick" – together with the plosive "t"s, requires meticulous articulation, making it impossible to slide over easily from "intrans't" to "Thick". The pause on "intrans't" is the only end-line pause in these five lines and helps to evoke the sense of the word. In addition to slowing the pace, the long vowels of the lines produce that fullness of sound or sonority for which Milton is famous. This is increased by the harmony of consonance ("Legions / Angels"), by liquid and voiced consonants, and especially by assonance, that is, the repetition of like vowels and diphthongs ("sore ... vaulted ... stood ... call'd ... Form ... Autumnal ... Brooks" and "strow ... *brosa* ... over"). Milton scorned the use of rhyme but, by these means, he creates more subtle interlinking of sounds. What is happening is not onomatopoeia but a mutual reverberation of sounds which has an expressive effect: as one word resonates with another, the sense of each is intensified. The sonorousness is epitomized in the word "*Vallombrosa*" with its open vowels and liquid and voiced consonants. It is an Italian word and the double "l" is sounded. Milton loved the Italian language, its musicality and open vowels, which result in sonorousness; he composed sonnets in Italian and, a few lines earlier in this passage, uses other Tuscan place names, "*Fesole*" and "*Valdarno*" (11.289-90). Vallombrosa is a place outside Florence. It means "shaded valley," in this context with a hint of "the valley of the shadow of death". But Milton does not say "shaded valley," although that would fit metrically – he says "*Vallombrosa*." What I suggest is: the aural effects of these lines combined with the associations of words and images, and especially the union of the semantic and phonetic properties of the word "*Vallombrosa*", evoke a melancholy sonority which is inescapably part of the meaning of the passage, part of the sense of loss and devastation. There is no gulf, that is, between sound and sense.

The modern critic and theorist Derek Attridge, writing of aural effects in James Joyce's *Ulysses*, speaks of "a reciprocal relationship ... between phonetic and semantic properties" and of "the materiality of language *as it does its work of bringing meaning into being*".[52] This is what is happening in the Vallombrosa passage through the materiality of sound. And it is happening everywhere in *Paradise Lost* in countless ways, but always according to Milton's

---

[52] Derek Attridge, *Peculiar Language: Literature as Difference from the Renaissance to James Joyce* (London: Methuen, 1988), 151, 154.

deeply imaginative, elastic, even imperious handling of decorum, which he considered "the grand master peece to observe".⁵³ The very opening lines of the epic would have thrown his contemporary readers: not only are they unrhymed but they surge forward in a long suspended sentence – a "breathless leap" – and the first line is quite out of kilter metrically, with full stresses on the second, third, and fourth syllables: "Of MANS FIRST DIS-o-BED-ience AND the FRUIT".⁵⁴ Yet this strange rhythm, in its sublime weightiness, is right for the astonishing announcement the bard is making. It is *appropriate* rhythm, or what Milton calls "apt numbers", which, through their aptness, help bring meaning into being.⁵⁵ Rhythm varies continually in *Paradise Lost* for expressive purposes. It works quite differently, for example, where Milton narrates how the fallen angels spread among the sons of Eve: a long sentence (1. 364-73) – another "breathless leap" – resolves in the line, "And DE-vils TO a-DORE for DE-i-TIES". The rhythm is bizarre. Dr Johnson would have considered this a "vicious" line, hopelessly impure.⁵⁶ It has only three full stresses, and alliteration falls on all three. The result is a jolting effect, especially after the metrically regular preceding line ("With gay Religions full of Pomp and Gold"), and these aural effects, reciprocating the startling effect of the semantic content ("Devils to adore for Deities"), help bring meaning into being, specifically, the narrator's concentrated outburst of incredulity and disgust as he concludes his long sentence. A different meaning again is created in the rhythm of the last two lines of *Paradise Lost* (12.648-49): "They hand in hand with wandring steps and slow, / Through *Eden* took thir solitarie way" (12.648-49). The lines move with an even iambic pulse which contributes to the subdued and chastened feeling of the departure from paradise, and the two beats on "SO-li-TAR-rie" slow down the closing line appropriately and emphasize the sense of "solitarie".

Returning, then, to my analogy drawn from Milton's metaphysics, I would claim, strongly against Eliot, that *Paradise Lost* is "monist" poetry: just as there is no duality of body and spirit in the cosmos of *Paradise Lost*, so there is no gulf between sound and sense in this supremely oral and aural epic. This view has been provoked by Eliot's complaint that, because of "the hypertrophy of the auditory imagination the inner meaning is separated from the surface", so that one must read *Paradise Lost* once for the sound and once

---

⁵³ *Of Education, Riverside Milton*, 984. See my entry on "decorum" in the *Milton Encyclopedia* forthcoming from Yale University Press.
⁵⁴ I follow John Creaser's method of scansion in "'Service is Perfect Freedom'". Capitals indicate stresses; small capitals are used for a "promoted" syllable, that is, a syllable such as a pronoun or preposition naturally given light emphasis but which, because of its place in the line, is felt as a metrical beat. See Creaser, "'Service is Perfect Freedom'", 275.
⁵⁵ See Milton's note on "The Verse"; also, on this line, Creaser, "'Service is Perfect Freedom'", 300.
⁵⁶ Samuel Johnson, *The Rambler* No.86 (1751), *Milton 1732-1801: The Critical Heritage*, ed. John T. Shawcross (London and Boston: Routledge & Kegan Paul, 1972), 203, 202.

for the sense. It has been provoked also by Eliot's accusation of a "dissociation of sensibility" in Milton: the "fidelity to thought and feeling" which he so admired in the Metaphysical poets' handling of syntax is matched and surpassed by the fidelity of Milton's (very different) music to the thought and feeling he expresses in *Paradise Lost*.[57]

To conclude then, it seems to me that Eliot has left a mixed but rich legacy to Milton studies. In the twentieth century, he stirred up a unique storm which shook Milton's eminence for approximately forty years but also provoked a reassessment of his power as a poet, which flowed into a resurgence of Milton studies from 1940 to 1970. During those years, the peculiar value of a poet-critic is manifest in the repeated argued reactions of scholar-critics to Eliot's criticism of Milton. For the twenty-first century, we need a great poet-critic and quite possibly Eliot will be the last. For Milton scholarship such as it is today, largely neglectful of Milton's auditory imagination, Eliot's value is as a poet-critic who *heard* Milton's poetry, placed the highest priority on the sound of *Paradise Lost*, and challenges us to explore the interconnection of sound and sense.

---

[57] "The Metaphysical Poets", *Selected Essays*, 287-288, 285

Why Study the Humanities?

Stephen Prickett

The quick answer to that question is because you cannot do without them. Once upon a time, long, long ago in the 1960s, when all the world was young, I taught at the University of Sussex, in the South of England, which then prided itself on its bold thinking – naturally, "outside" every possible box – and on its sweeping ability to re-imagine and reconstruct the curriculum according to the needs of the modern world. A problem area for the most vocal modernists, however, was Religious Studies, which seemed to smack of the very outmoded ways of thinking they were trying to transcend. It was a small "subject group" – we had nothing so traditional as "Departments" – with only three members. Unfortunately, it was popular with a surprisingly large number of students. But there came a time when the Muslim had study leave in Cairo to complete an important book; the Buddhist had retreated in mystic contemplation at the top of a Himalayan pass; and there remained only the Christian to try and carry on with the classes of all three. Quite predictably, he complained to the Dean about his extra workload. Quite predictably, the Dean expressed his most profound sympathy, and did nothing at all. The overworked Christian then pulled out his ace card: "Since you are not prepared to address this crisis constructively, you leave me no choice but to accept the offer of a fellowship in Cambridge, which Sidney Sussex has been holding open for me for the past three months". And, to the consternation of what was left of his subject group, and many outside it, he departed for the fens of East Anglia.

A general meeting of the Humanities was called to consider this totally unforeseen crisis. A motion was put forward to abolish Religious Studies forthwith. Then one of the more outspoken atheists rose to speak. "Beware of abolishing Religious Studies", he warned. "If you do that and remove what is left of the current group, who by common consent, are experts in their respective fields, then you will find it being taught by amateurs – even (God help us!) by the English lecturers – who do not know their religious history anything like as well as the original Religious Studies group. But, don't kid yourselves that no religious studies will be taught in this university. Religion is far too important a study for it to be ignored by any of the Humanities. But instead of having it centred officially in one place, you will find it spreading unofficially like a rash all over the Arts Faculty. Though I may regret this, Religion is an inescapable and active part of human life. So I would rather it were taught well by genuine scholars, than badly by self-opinionated amateurs".[1]

My former colleague's point still stands – as shown by an interesting sequel. Some twenty years after my atheist friend had issued his dire prophetic warning, the very traditional English Department of the University of Glasgow, of which I was then a member, was so appalled by the sheer scriptural ignorance of its undergraduates, that it decided to introduce a series of lectures on the Bible. Though individually Department members ranged from fundamentalist Christian through all shades of agnosticism to atheism, all were unanimous that you could not begin to study English literature without some acquaintance with the English Bible. The lectures, I should add, were overwhelmingly well attended. Though those giving these lectures were careful to talk about the English Bible simply as a book, and to avoid, where possible, doctrinal disputes, this was not always possible. How, for instance, does one start to talk about the Reformation? Nor do I have any doubt that though my friend's conviction that it would have been better done by biblical professionals was absolutely correct, it was, as he prophesied Cassandra-like, the English Department that in the end picked up the baton.

As my atheist friend gloomily foresaw, the Humanities are not avoidable options that can be excised at will from human scholarship. No branch of human learning is an island. To the old cliché that those who ignore history are condemned to repeat it, one can add that those who try to abolish it will simply find that some other discipline has – consciously or unconsciously – annexed it. As Horace was probably not the first to observe, "though you expel nature with a pitchfork, yet she will always come back". We need to articulate our collective past as much as our individual ones. Memory, individual or collective, is not a matter of choice. Every society needs its past. Similarly, if you are rash enough to abolish the study of art, history, literature, music, philosophy or religion you will simply get it returning in another guise – very often either as wildly prejudiced opinion or as closed dogmatic authoritarian systems of propaganda, reducing real choice or understanding in favour of some second-hand pap. As with all the humanities, the adage, "bad money drives out good" may often work in the short term; in the long run the real thing usually proves much more attractive than its substitutes. At their best, such subjects involve the study and discussion of the flowers of civilization. The attraction is in themselves. Their interest is intrinsic, of no more practical use than pure mathematics, astronomy, or the search for extra-terrestrial life. In contrast, such subjects as business studies, economics, medicine, or technology, important as they are, and however sophisticated,

---

[1] Religious Studies was saved on that occasion. The relevant website suggests it is still active.

are merely means to an end; they are not ends in themselves.

Which is not to say that the Humanities are devoid of practical use. Far from it. To put it very simply, art, literature, philosophy, and above all, religion help us to understand and define our values. There are few activities more valuable. In a post-Nazi world, where we have become uncomfortably aware of concentration camp mass-murderers who enjoyed listening to Beethoven in the evenings, we have become a little too shy of making this point. We also need to recall that these music-loving monsters were, at least partly, products of Heinrich Himmler's propaganda machine. But no one sophisticated enough to have read their New Testament, has ever supposed that the wheat could easily be separated from the tares. We only have to look at the Sistine Chapel to remember that renaissance Popes really did sponsor great art. That they did so does not in any way devalue the art, nor does it excuse their other crimes. Similarly Caravaggio was a great artist, *and* a violent thug, and these are *not* contradictions. Humans are human. Which is where the cross-check of the other Humanities is invaluable. Whereas, as we have seen, there have been value-systems such as Communism, Nazism, and Islamism, and, indeed, some historical forms of Christianity, that have condoned torture, violence, and the suppression of free thought, in pursuit of their aims, the overwhelming consensus of philosophical thought since New Testament times has been to reject such leanings well before their tipping-point. Certainly the study of their history has not given such theories a good run. But, contrariwise, even in the case of biblical studies, the Humanities have never been a *source* of unequivocal values – nor can they be. If they had, there would presumably have never been the Reformation. In their various ways they mirror the conflict and disagreement that attends any real intellectual or aesthetic endeavour. As I wrote earlier, they do not *give* us our values – which, though perhaps "given" in another sense, are never capable of demonstrable proof – they help us define and understand them. They are aids to reflection, not sources of revelation.

Thus the study of history is the study of our civilization's past – it is always worth looking closely at what Voltaire called "the crimes, follies, and misfortunes" of mankind in at least the hope that we do not repeat them too blatantly. But history is more than simply a record of the past. We have a word for such a simple list of events. It is called a "chronicle" of which perhaps the most famous example is *The Anglo-Saxon Chronicle*. But "history" is something more than such a list, it involves the discovery of *meaning* in those events, and that involves interpretation, which also implies selection. Thus once we begin tracing meaning, some events become more significant than others in our narrative – and any interpretation inevitably suggests other interpretations. There is always more to be said. So far from being a weakness, however, that process of evidence, debate, and interpretation is, in effect, what the study of history is about. There are many histories. The story of our past is not univocal, but manifold.

Such pluralism can only too easily be threatened by unequivocal or selective narratives of the past, driven by personal prejudice, political or religious dogma, nationalism, or concealed economic interest. Put simply, an un-conflicted history, where a single uncontested version of the past is allowed to reign unchallenged, is almost certainly "bad history". Just as any insight, like sight itself, can only create a picture from a particular stance or viewpoint, there is no such thing as perspectiveless knowledge. To perceive, is to be located "somewhere" – and if the location is not acknowledged, it will still be there, lurking and distorting any assumptions of objectivity.

This is not to say that, for instance, national myths are invariably bad history, but they must be constantly subject to new evidence. The cherished British myth of the Battle of Britain has recently been revised with significant new information. The fact of the victory of the RAF over the Luftwaffe is not in doubt, nor the heroism of its pilots – that is, as it were, the "chronicle" – but only recently have historians working through German records uncovered the fact that the real victory lay less in the destruction of some 1,800 German planes, but in the loss of as many pilots. The British lost nearly as many planes (some 1,500) but because the battle itself took place over England and the Channel, more than 1,000 of the RAF pilots survived to fly again, whereas even if German pilots survived, their immediate future lay in British prison camps, not in the air. The British ended the battle with more planes and pilots than when they started. The Luftwaffe never recovered from the loss of flying skills inflicted in 1940. Few realised at the time, and it was never publicised for obvious reasons, that a pilot's training takes far longer, and is much more expensive, than building an aircraft.

C.P. Fitzgerald, the distinguished Australian Sinologist and historian, tells of the problem of the guardian of the "dynastic gate" of Beijing at the foundation of the Republic in 1912. His immediate difficulty was the order to replace the inscription hanging over the gateway which read, the "Great Qing Gate" – the dynasty overthrown by the republican revolution – with a new inscription for the new republic, reading the "Gate of China". Suspecting – probably rightly – that this would not endear him to the Manchus if the Qing Dynasty were ever restored, he unhooked the notice and decided to hide it, rather than destroy it. The only convenient place immediately available seemed to be an attic, which was difficult to access, and which he had consequently never been in, but which, simply by its inaccessibility, would provide a safe hiding place for the now-dangerous notice. When he entered it, the first thing he saw was an identically-sized notice reading the "Great Ming Gate" – as his predecessor, nearly three centuries earlier at the fall of the Ming to the Qing, had sought the easiest way of both disposing of the embarrassing display of outmoded loyalty, and of holding an insurance against punishment in the event of a restoration. What had been taken as a public record and display of stability was, in fact, an unrivalled record of political transience – each carrying its own politically ordained version of the meaning of history.

Less consciously, but for that reason more pervasive, is that a view of history is also dependent on the metaphors by which it is described. Whereas the English-speaking world is used to, indeed bored by, the endless clichés of politicians who "look forward to the future", the Chinese do no such thing. For them, as for the oarsmen in a boat, they look backwards on the past which for that reason is ever in front of them, because that is known. They have their backs to the future, because that is totally unknown. One position is as logical as the other, but it is fairly obvious that such metaphors betray much deeper and more radical differences in "outlook" than mere questions of how to dispose of obsolete signs of dynastic self-glorification.

In other cases, as might be expected, national myths are in direct conflict. We all know the Australian narrative that the continent was *terra nullius*, allowing for its occupation by European settlers – as it happens to start with, mostly convicts. The Aborigines' story is naturally rather different. On the other hand, there is, or used to be, a sour joke in Argentina that their greatest defeat was what is now celebrated as their greatest victory, when in 1812, a British landing was decisively repelled by the patriotic citizens (especially women) of Buenos Aires. Had the British succeeded, so the new narrative runs, Argentina would now be a proud, democratic and wealthy Commonwealth Dominion, the equal of Australia or Canada, instead of being a chaotic South American banana republic. Even more stark and ironic, of course, is the Chinese and British versions of the founding of Hong Kong – with the added twist that a colony founded on a blatantly unjust war to further the opium trade went on to achieve a level of prosperity – and even of freedom – rare elsewhere in S.E. Asia.

The study of literature may well also involve many similar assumptions, questioned or unquestioned, but, more important, it is also the story of our collective inner world, our "inner space". From it comes what little self-understanding we may possess of our aesthetics and our social values. As, among other things, chairman of our local branch of the English Speaking Union, I agree with the Argentinians that it is no accident that the English-speaking world, with one of the richest and most varied literatures of any language, also has produced unusually free, peaceful, and well-organized societies. But that, of course, is more a declaration of interest – my personal prejudice, my individual value system – than any objectively demonstrable historical judgement. Yet that judgement is *not just* a display of personal prejudice (I just "know" that Australia/England/the USA is the "best country in the world"), it is also the result of a lifetime's observation, experience, and reading. It did not arise without some exercise of evidence and judgement. As Cardinal Newman once wrote: "We are what we are; we do not negotiate with ourselves".

Though our personal "inner space", housing the private narrative that all modern people carry within themselves, may be – and usually is – in a constant state of reconstruction, it is nevertheless what makes us distinctive individuals, and gives us a sense of our own identities. But if literature plays a major part in that process, it is also much more than that. Thus *Pride and Prejudice*, for instance, is not just a personal possession, it is part of our collective psyche – hence our outrage at a film that violates the pictures of it that adorn our inner worlds. In some strange way, the more we personalize our reading of literature, the more we share it, and consolidate our cultural community with people – from all over the world – who are part of our reading community. One thinks of the extraordinary moment when Patrick Leigh-Fermor, who had kidnapped the German General, Heinrich Kreipe, on Crete, was watching the sunrise on the coast while awaiting the Royal Navy launch that was to take Kreipe off into captivity. Kreipe, half to himself, quoted lines from Homer about the rising sun in Greek and was astonished to hear Leigh Fermor complete the quotation. Still at war they may have been, but, for better or worse, they remained members of the same cultural community. One common feature of Islamic terrorists, so far, is that though they tend to be literate, and even occasionally highly educated, they come either from an Islamic tradition that brooks no debate over meanings of texts, or, if educated in a Western university, they tend to come from the technologies rather than from the Humanities. So far we have had no attacks from English Literature graduates!

And yet ... and yet.... In the end my distinction between the Humanities and technology may turn out to be a false one. No branch of human learning is an island. Business studies, economics, engineering, technology have themselves unavoidably moral, even philosophic implications. They can be used either to free or to enslave – and that is true not merely of the external consequences of their work, but also of the *internal* consequences to the personalities of their practitioners. The criminal activities of bankers have become only too familiar in the last five years; fewer people have commented on what those activities have done to the bankers themselves, whether or not they have been arrested and charged. The classic statement of this, of course, is from literature – by one of the masters of the English language:

"But you were always a good man of business, Jacob", faltered Scrooge....

"Business!" cried the Ghost, wringing his hands again. "Mankind was my business. The common welfare was my business; charity, mercy, forbearance, and benevolence were, all, my business. The dealings of my trade were but a drop of water in the comprehensive ocean of my business!"

Dickens was never afraid of preaching, but rarely, if ever, does he do it so effectively as in *Christmas Carol*. However, I doubt if it appears on the reading list for many MBAs.

This internalisation of the Humanities was taken to a new level with Iain McGilchrist's astonishing book, *The Master and his Emissary* (2009). McGilchrist has the rare (possibly unique) distinction of having been a psychiatrist, a brain-surgeon, and a teacher of English at Oxford. For him the "master" is the right-hand lobe of the brain, which makes long-term judgements, and seems also to be responsible for moral decisions. It also, of course, controls the left side of the body, including the left hand itself. The left lobe (which controls the right hand) is the practical, instrumental, side of the brain, responsible for physical skills and actions. It is part of McGilchrist's thesis that one of the problems of our civilization – perhaps *all* civilizations in the last few thousand years – is that the "emissary", the left-hand lobe of the brain, has come to usurp many of the functions that properly belong to the right-hand lobe. He stops short of suggesting that this is the root cause of human dysfunction ("original sin"?) but that is a conclusion that could easily be drawn from his overall thesis. Perhaps more immediately relevant is the fact that our art, music, and literature – our highest and most subtle perceptions and aspirations – originate in the realm of the "master", the right-hand lobe. Put crudely, the Humanities are the products of the right lobe, the instrumental sciences to the left. He does not, however, come much nearer to cracking the further problem of brain science: the problem of consciousness itself.

Yet the interrelatedness of our inner and outer worlds means that each constantly affects the other. Just as the boundaries between what we call academic "disciplines" are porous constructs, always subject to revision and modification, so also a society that turns inward to understand only itself will fail even in that. Just as the study of history is always the study of *histories*, so, likewise, the study of any particular literature, is the study of *literatures*. Here I salute Axel Clark, son of Manning Clark, one of my more brilliant colleagues at the ANU, who embarked on a course of teaching Australian literature – a subject few knew more about than he did – by making his students read *Anna Karenina*. As he cheerfully explained to me, there was no point in trying to read Australian literature without having some acquaintance with the nineteenth-century European literature out of which it had grown.

Every so-called "national" literature has developed through the constant influx of foreign writings of all kinds. Some years ago it was my privilege to chair a conference on European Romanticism, out of which eventually emerged the 1,000-page *Reader in European Romanticism*.[2] This was in fourteen languages arranged in parallel text, with the original language on the left hand

---

[2] Stephen Prickett and Simon Haines, eds., *European Romanticism: A Reader* (London: Continuum, 2010).

page, the English translation on the right, corresponding line by line, so that anyone unsure of the translation might immediately cross-check with the original – and *vice versa*. Two things stand out from this experience. The first is how densely woven and inter-connected all European literature was – essays on Shakespeare, for instance, or Byron, appear in almost every language. Indeed, it became clear that what we now call Romanticism is first and foremost a phenomenon of translation. The second is how much the history of such translation is a history of creative misunderstanding. Thus Byron, by far the most widely-read English poet of the day, was hailed across Europe as everything from a left-wing bogeyman to a liberal martyr, according to the needs and conditions of the recipient country, not to mention the politics of the translator.[3]

Even the language in which I am now writing this essay has multicultural origins. If we accept Robert McCrum's thesis in *The Story of English*, the origins of what is now the world language lie not in the speech of a specific people, but in a hybrid patois enabling crude communication between Anglo-Saxon speakers and their Norse neighbours. In *After Babel* George Steiner takes the necessity of translation one step further by suggesting that not merely do we need translation between cultures, but that we need translation in understanding the past of our own culture. It lies at the heart, he claims, of all the other Humanities – art, history, literature, philosophy, even religion. Without it, we might add, we are prisoners of our own time and place – and impoverished prisoners at that, who like Plato's cave dwellers, are unaware of what lies outside our own dark little world.

Perhaps we should conclude with another metaphor from Plato. There is a very real sense in which the Humanities offer us not so much a course in knowledge, but a course in *recognition*, in discovering what we already are and only through that discovery, do we find the power further to grow and develop. I mean this also as a *collective* statement. The value of the Humanities for a society may even be greater than for any individuals within that society. Much has been written recently about "crowd-judgement" (the principal, of course, behind the jury system). Societies or states that have concentrated on technical education at the expense of the Humanities – Russia would be a good example – tend to have less sophisticated electorates and much weaker records on liberty. In that sense Civil Society ultimately rests on the Humanities. This does not necessarily imply consistently sound judgement by individuals – though no doubt that helps – but a more consistent collective judgement in a free society. Injustice is less something that can be proven in a legal sense, more a matter of *recognition*. We know it when we see it.

---

[3] *Ibid.*, 10.

On Professing Poetry in Australia in the 21st Century

Simon Haines

Why would an institution calling itself a university still, in the 21st century, be employing a "professor of poetry"? Surely no-one of the millennial generation would want to spend a lot of money which could have been spent on more professional training, just to be able to talk or write about Les Murray, T.S. Eliot or John Donne? Who are, in any case, all reactionary and/or misogynist. Borderline racist, even. Certainly all white; all men. How about Emily Dickinson, then? Sylvia Plath, Maya Angelou? But surely those who want to will read these poets in their own time? Only the wealthy, or the terminally pretentious, could afford to waste these precious years of education chattering about "Hope is the thing with feathers" or "Phenomenal Woman" or "a country far away as health". Nor is this only a matter of private expense. A good deal of the financial burden of this professorship is born by the public purse. What could the public utility of such a role possibly be?

These are not typically questions asked by sports editors, say, or hedge fund managers, or postal workers, who understandably have no interest in them at all – unless their daughters or (less likely) their sons unaccountably declare an intention to major in English. (Besides, anyone so disposed will probably opt for Cultural, Media or Gender Studies, since those are more widely available. Perhaps the latest Rihanna offering will open their minds.) Instead, those who *do* ask such questions, and ask them most urgently, are university presidents, deans of Arts, tertiary funding agencies and research grant panellists. Politicians too, of course: but wasting public money is something they are almost as good at drawing attention to when others allegedly do it on a small scale as they are at concealing it when they do it themselves on a large one. No surprise there, then. Nor, on the other hand, should it be disconcerting if a conscientious civil servant asks whether being a professor of poetry is a serious occupation for an intelligent grown-up person with a proper sense of public responsibility. A good question deserving a thoughtful answer. The surprise, rather, is that the universities themselves are often so indifferent, or even hostile – and not just the cadres of financial managers, strategic planners and human resources experts who constitute the officer class in these huge corporations now (yes, yes, a lot of them are good people who want their institutions to prosper): but many research-income-generating academic subalterns as well.

"Hostile" isn't really an exaggeration. Most humanities scholars have had some experience of scientist or engineer colleagues (disciplines which often provide the leadership cadres) expressing incredulity that any money at all is spent on such nonsense. Humanities departments are cheap, admittedly, but why waste this precious money when overall resources are shrinking? Besides, their return on investment is absurdly low. Yet even this "two cultures" hostility is to be expected, is of long standing, and is still far from universal. What has been hardest of all to fathom is the decades-long war of attrition carried out against the study of poetry and other literary genres, especially the English poetry and literature of the past, by other academics in the humanities – most of all, incredibly, within English departments themselves. One of my most vivid conference memories is from the later 90s, of Stephen Greenblatt and Catherine Belsey, leading representatives respectively of the "new historicist" and "post-structuralist" movements in literary studies (roughly, the schools of Foucault and Derrida), agreeing in a public forum in Ghent that the most important institutional goal shared, in fact the only goal shared, by these two implacably opposed intellectual positions, which between them have dominated literary studies since the 1970s, was "to destroy departments of English". By and large, this has in fact happened. There aren't many clusters of scholars left in Australia, to take our local example, whose business is with the poetry or prose of the past. (The distinction between poetry and prose isn't as clear-cut as we tend to assume nowadays. What about the King James Bible, for example? Very roughly, what we call "literature" is what Aristotle and the long critical tradition following him would have called "poetry" – and we should also bear in mind that literary criticism itself goes back to Socrates and Plato.) And even when it is, that business is often really with the past, not the poetry – with history, in short, and furthermore with a certain progressive, politicised, materialist view of history, in which the poetry is enlisted as a store of case studies to illustrate modern, identity-politics theses about gender, race, class, colony or language, which can thus be read back into the culture of the past.

I'm over-dramatising and over-simplifying, certainly, and in a cross sort of way. But not all that much, and with some reason. The conviction that poetry is an utterly distinctive, powerful and indispensable form of humane thought is foundational in the teaching and writing of all too few of the scholars whose profession it is to explain and advocate for literature, let alone the wider humanities. And if few such are to be found even in that group, no wonder that the broader academic and general community is uninterested or hostile. What those few have faced is an unwinnable war on two fronts. (I'm not talking about the "old quarrel" between poetry and philosophy, which also goes back to Socrates, but is a hugely enlightening if somewhat one-sided argument between these two contrary but complementary disciplines of thought.)

Two fronts, then. The forces of public or social utility "outside the gates" have been with us since the nineteenth century. They retreat a little during periods of prosperity such as the 1960s and 70s, but the years since 2008 have not been such a period; while since the 90s the post-Dawkins deployment of universities as weapons of mass instruction has made utility their only guiding principle. The forces of *ressentiment* "inside the gates", meanwhile, have gained strength since those very same 1960s and 70s. (It's no coincidence that public and political opinion has turned against the humanities during this same period.) The project of destroying English departments, rather than just promoting alternative groupings such as Cultural Studies, *is* in large part the determination to destroy the study of poetry, or literature more widely, and replace it with something else. Above all, it is the determination to destroy the study of English and European poetry *of the past*. After all (the propaganda goes) this was written mostly by men, and by men who oppressed women; by colonialists and imperialists; by white people; and by racists. The study of it was promoted and shaped by hegemonic, patriarchal elites who used it to oppress and brainwash minorities and/or the masses. And English, above all, is *the* language of oppressive racist sexist patriarchal misogynist hegemonic colonialism. Any text at all in that language, but especially any text from the unreconstructed past, and even more especially any "canonical" text (that is, one considered of exceptional value by many readers over long periods), has to be treated with the utmost suspicion. Prizes are to be awarded for ingenuity in discovering any traces of these contaminating sins, even when unintentionally committed: in fact the lack of intention *proves* the sin. We are all in bad faith except for those who tell us we are in bad faith, so the safest way to avoid being accused of being in bad faith is to accuse someone else of it (this is a favourite device in totalitarian societies). So successful has this fifty-year project been that a third generation, especially but not only in the United States, is now threatening the complacencies of the older tenured radicals themselves, many of them now retiring. How can you enjoy holding up Donne as a misogynist or heterosexist to students who might feel that he was therefore a potential rapist? Or that you might in merely talking about misogyny (thus rape) be unwittingly condoning these awful things yourself – at the very least making too many students "uncomfortable"? On the other hand, how can you piously hold up Eliot as anti-semitic to students who are themselves implacably anti-Zionist?

These zealotries would have sounded hilariously far-fetched a generation ago, but in many American colleges and universities they are now an intimidating reality for administrators anxious to avoid offending the concept-fanatics, and lacking richer and more extensive moral assurances of their own. Australia's campuses are not so far behind: nor are Britain's, if the Tim Hunt affair is anything to go by.[1] In both the United States and Australia, as well as Scotland and Ireland, the word "English" itself carries for many people an overtone of post-colonial and anti-imperialist resentment. You might expect all that in China, say, or even India, where there are many whose resentment of the power of "English" encodes authentic national memories of past humiliations – although there are many more who pragmatically acknowledge the advantages of speaking it well. But it's just absurd in native speakers. "That subject people stuff is a cod's game, infantile", as James Joyce (the Virgil figure) tells Seamus Heaney (the Dante pilgrim figure) in Heaney's "Station Island" poem sequence. "The English language belongs to us". To *us*, the Irish. No nation has more reason to resent the English. And yet here is the greatest of (near) contemporary Irish poets proudly taking possession of the English *language* just as his even greater countryman and forebear had done. What a man! Talk about forging in your soul the uncreated conscience of your race. In just this way did the greatest and most original of all vernacular poets throw off the imperial shackles of Rome, forging them into the sinews of a new race of Italian speakers. The Hong Kong Chinese students I teach understand all this at once (there's an old Chinese view that speaking a language is a form of conquest or assimilated ownership); whereas

[1] After an allegedly sexist comment made by Sir Tim Hunt, FRS and Nobel laureate, at a conference in June, 2015 was reported by science writer, Connie St Louis, Hunt came under global attack on social media. University College London, where he held an honorary professorship, said he had to resign to protect its reputation. [Editor's note]

we Australians, already blessed from birth with this formidable capacity as with so many other natural advantages – coal, minerals, sheep, the Barrier Reef – are often oblivious to it: dismissive, cynical, complacent. It's a native intelligence-enhancement app. A clever country would make the most of it.

This is a matter of owning your own language, which is the most important constituting agency in any civilisation (as those who set out to destroy "English" know perfectly well). The language, the whole of it, not just selected highlights, is our free pass to stores of value literally unimaginable for any of us alone, in the thin, shallow moment of the present – value, moral life, as imagined *for* us already, by generations of legendary language builders. A world of life in language. And as Heaney implies, it's a Eurail pass. English leads out into German, but also, perhaps more significantly, into both French and that same Latin which Dante owned and then renovated (the English too were once a Roman colony). Let's not be so chippy about this: it's European civilisation we're talking about, the one we and our political and cultural institutions and practices inevitably belong to, no matter how we are situated geographically, no matter what crimes it may also have committed. This civilisation is almost despised, certainly marginalised, in many Australian universities. As if there's an unspoken consensus that it's just the chatter of cultured apes, in A. D. Hope's deeply ironical words. Asian studies, indigenous studies: yes, of course. We can use that same European Enlightenment heritage to our advantage in those fields. European studies: now that's a different matter. There's the awful risk of being seen as a monotonous tribe of second-hand Europeans, to stay with Hope. (But Asians laugh at us when we try too hard to be one of them.)

Professing poetry means constantly re-opening the linguistic territory which is always our birthright, a *terra incognita* to be re-cognized by each generation. *Writing* poetry, by contrast, is an altogether riskier and lonelier business. You just never know whether that new stretch of land, your own language farm at the edge of the known territory, will support life. Farming this *terra nullius* certainly won't be profitable. And when the existing lands are so vast, it requires genius to make much of a difference to the map. On the other hand, this is a way of life that makes better sense of life than most other ways. It isn't for everyone; but those who pursue it in its various forms deserve our respect and support. Meanwhile, however, the academic study of good poetry allows anyone of intelligence and judgement to inherit and inhabit a language world extending back at least to the fifteenth century or even (with a little more effort) to the tenth and before; as well as (with a little more effort still) to neighbouring and older worlds. Language is an entailment for all its speakers.

The inheritance is of course historical, since no study of tripods or ruins will tell you as much about Homeric Greece as the *Iliad*; while in Shakespeare you are hearing Elizabethans and Jacobeans speak as clearly as if you had them on tape. But the interest isn't essentially antiquarian. This isn't so much about understanding the past in itself as about understanding *our*selves better. It's a terrible but very common and easy mistake to think of the study of poetry and literature as a branch of history. When students are told – as they often are now, perhaps especially in Australia – that a text is just a text; that the playbills advertising early modern dramas (for example) have just as much historical value and *just as much right to be called literature* as the plays they promote; that there is only "cultural production" in which poets are products as much as they are producers, and in which all producers and products are of equal value and interest: when impressionable younger people, who often go on to become teachers or (alas) school syllabus authorities, are told all this, then an incalculably great but intangible loss is being sustained. (We are seeing some of the effects of this loss in what has been done to the New South Wales HSC English syllabus, with its deadening and narrowing insistence, disliked by many teachers, on key concepts and ideologies superimposed like schematic diagrams onto even the richest literary texts.)

The currency in which this loss is realised is language. And it happens in two ways, two linguistic dimensions. One is conceptual. Some philosophers – Elizabeth Anscombe, Alasdair MacIntyre, Iris Murdoch – have argued recently that European civilisation has suffered a loss of value-concepts since the Enlightenment, and that this has gone hand in hand with a changed conception of the self, such that the human being now seems like a disengaged centre of will or reason set over against a world of physical fact. This is a scientistic picture, they say. Honour, humility, duty, pride, faith, conscience, envy, sloth and so on and on (the seven deadly sins and their corresponding virtues, with their classical analogues, are the tip of a vast iceberg of hundreds of terms) no longer resonate, are not embodied, within a rich experiential and cultural fabric. We have tended to slip into a stark, black-and-white, essentially Nietzschean picture of moral life in which power and will are the only agents, and a small handful of master concepts, ultimately just "good" and "bad", dominate moral thought ("four legs good, two legs bad", in Orwell's parody). Complex moral ecosystems once inhabited by multiple species or shadings of approbation and disapprobation are now evacuated, their biodiversity degraded into a few hardy mutant strains surviving in a desert. Racism, sexism and oppression of all kinds are bad and cause justifiable outrage; "human rights", liberation and self-expression are good and must never be impeded. And freedom of speech becomes the right, or rather obligation, to deploy these concepts wherever possible, and impede the expression of any other form of language, particularly if it calls their primary status into question.

If all this is so, and if we want to recover or renew our ancient richer sense of life-with-concepts, which after all is what makes us at least *capable* of being civilised and not barbaric ("don't do that it's dishonourable … cruel … selfish … malicious"; "do that because it's generous … courteous … decent" etc), then the literature of the past is more or less the only way to do it. And here it is critical that "literature" include philosophy. The history of philosophy is part of the terrain in which we can rediscover our lost concepts; but it too is being taught less and less.

Now for the second dimension of the loss. Poetry, which is literature at its most high-tech and specialised, the Lamborghini of literature, is not fundamentally conceptual, as philosophy is. It is fundamentally metaphorical. As Aristotle said, the most distinctive mark of poetry is metaphor, and a mastery of metaphor is a sign of genius; it can't be learned. To blur or erase the distinctions between poetry and other forms of cultural production is to lose sight of this "sign of genius" and to become desensitized to its power. Of course it's simply everywhere in our language life, in all sorts of forms, vital or ossified, shallow or profound, manipulative or revelatory. But this is the workshop, the source. Here in good poetry we see metaphor being used not sloppily or tiredly but as real original thought (this is how you *tell* if poetry is any good): a mode of thought complementary with but utterly distinct from the concept-thought we tend to see as normative and legitimate (there's the old "quarrel" between poetry and philosophy). Jealousy is a green-eyed monster. Perseverance keeps honour bright. The quality of mercy is not strained. Pity is a naked new-born babe. Let slip the dogs of war. Life's but a walking shadow. Conscience doth make cowards of us all. Thou art a soul in bliss but I am bound upon a wheel of fire. (The best lack all conviction, I'm tempted to add, sliding over to Yeats.) This is the high-octane version of how we all talk and think. We use concepts, all right, but we tend to metaphorize them, mutate them, cross-breed them. A metaphorized concept, a poetry-philosophy hybrid, is about as powerful and self-formative as thought can be. Overwhelmingly, our life together, our inter-personal, communicative life, is lived in language; and in poetry, especially in really good poetry, we can see this happening at the most fine-grained levels of representation. In this hybrid medium, language becomes life-moral rather than concept-moral. In Cleopatra or Portia or Antigone or Medea or Catherine Earnshaw or "Emily Dickinson" we see human beings not as more or less "good" but as more or less rich, elemental, variegated, concentrated. They aren't exactly our next-door neighbours, because they are made entirely of language, and the language of genius at that; but they are for that reason more intensely themselves than any of us can ever be, and thus archetypes in which we can recognise both our neighbours and ourselves.

Philosophy and poetry together are the linguistic core of the European humanities, the double helix which is its DNA, the two disciplines of thought, conceptual and metaphorical, where we are most deeply and essentially ourselves as beings who think, communicate and live in language. (Of course we also think in music and plastic art; in mathematical forms; and in empirical ways, both scientific and historical. But *live*? Communicate every minute, including with ourselves? A rare few do: not most of us.) Reading the philosophy and poetry of the past, but perhaps especially the complex poetry, shows us ourselves over time, which is to say our whole selves, as no other discipline can. And it's simply ludicrous, by the way, to claim that all those dead poets were apologists for empires and elites. Usually they were exactly the opposite. The very attitude of hostility to power and entrenched complacencies is one we have learned from Antigone, Aristophanes, Juvenal, the Wife of Bath, Swift, Byron…. Homer, a Greek, initiated Western poetry by writing a poem marked by compassion for the Trojans rather than for the Greeks. He also wrote one whose heroine is entirely as strong and admirable as its hero.

But anyone saying all this sounds increasingly like some sort of quaint Jeremiah: a Cassandra figure on a hilltop in a gale. From far off she can be seen pointing and shouting something, but no-one can hear what, and in the end it's just too boring to try. This is the infuriating experience anyone will have had in the last generation or so advocating for the humanities within their own institutions and societies. From the hilltop you can see the whole road, and then the eventual slow-motion crash. Universities ought to be, and once were, precisely the places, the *only* places, where a professor of poetry could be heard, and through him or her the voices of all the Dickinsons and Plaths and Donnes and Eliots (T.S. or George) and Miltons and Dantes and Virgils and Homers. Not the voices of *The Wire* or *Breaking Bad*, powerful and compelling as those are – let alone the Rihannas and Gagas. You don't need much help hearing these. Access to those other voices of the past, that linguistic bank and capital of our entire civilisation, is on the other hand a precious and fragile social asset. Use it or lose it: and to lose it would be a cultural devastation – no, *will* be. Reading the great poetry (and philosophy) of the past is not even like going to a museum or art gallery or concert, important as that also is. We still use the same language, the same medium, as those writers; they aren't exhibits but interlocutors; they are the best guides to their own work. Responding to them is in a deep sense interactive, and requires great teachers more than it does researchers. If universities and their contemporary managers do not understand that they have a critical role as cultural institutions in fostering such an interactivity, then they are abnegating their responsibility to preserve, to keep alive, some of what is best in our *own* civilisation, and perhaps to redeem some of what is worst. Without this our very language itself will become threadbare; indeed, this is exactly what's happening.

Never having developed anything like the wonderful American liberal-arts college system (itself now showing signs of wear and tear), we in Australia are now also marginalising the once-central humanities function within the broadly Scottish Enlightenment university model we did inherit. Professional training schools, social policy think tanks, research institutes in the sciences and social sciences: all these important institutions, driven as they are primarily by research investment and by research-driven rankings, and essential as of course they are to our growth and prosperity, were still never intended to reconnect their students with vital legacies of humane thought, and thus remind them of the values we have lived or failed to live by, or the habits of thought and disposition we would do well to avoid. This was once an essential, indeed the definitive, function of a university. Since the 1960s immense damage has been done to our civilisation from within, not least from the faculties of humanities and (to a lesser extent) social sciences within its universities, which have increasingly tended to see themselves purely as sceptical or adversarial towards it and its discontents: less often as illuminative or in the best sense educational. This has left the humanities, especially, with fewer friends in the wider society; but also without much to fall back on when faced by a callow second- or third-generation outrage culture with the most primitive of moral reflexes – the most threadbare of concept-sets. Let's hope the University of Sydney doesn't waste any time appointing its next Professor of Poetry: she or he will and should have a lot to do. And as long as there are courses for such a professor to teach, there will always (or so we must hope) be appreciative and thoughtful students to respond to this sort of humane education, perhaps even more so as it becomes a novelty: for they certainly aren't finding it any more in the HSC syllabus, and more and more rarely in their universities. There needn't be many of them; in fact there never were, relative to the population. But without any, ours will be a diminished culture.

I'd like to end with some less abstract observations about poetry of the late sixteenth to mid-seventeenth centuries, since this is a period of special interest to Sydney's retiring Professor. Our two greatest poets are Shakespeare and Milton; the observations concern their treatments or representations of *evil*, a concept and a principle which we seem to have trouble nowadays accepting or articulating, except in the crudest terms – and hence counteracting or neutralising. Specifically, I am interested in Milton's Satan, on the one hand, and a gallery of Shakespearean villains on the other.[2]

The Satan of *Paradise Lost* was developed by Milton out of minimal existing source material (much of it pre-Biblical and non-Christian) into the modern paradigm of that Great Adversary: a figure of enormous secular but *not* religious influence; a prototype for hundreds of Romantic and post-Romantic figurings of the lonely and obsessive anti-hero, from Frankenstein's monster to Darth Vader, Byron to bin Laden, Heathcliff to Heath Ledger, Stavrogin to Sauron (cultural studies, anyone?). Above all, however, for that definitive figure of modernity referred to by Iris Murdoch as "Kantian Man", and traced by her explicitly to Milton's Satan: "free, independent, lonely, powerful, rational, responsible, brave".[3] The principal concepts explicitly constituting Satan in the poem, the ones Milton uses all the time to define him, include disdain, impairment, shame, a will both free and fixed, remorse, conscience, despair, ingratitude, rage, malice, spite, revenge, envy, ambition, self-creation, choice, pride, and obsession with equal rights. The character is utterly conceptual from the ground up: represented very largely in terms of this list. Fascinatingly, this portrait has supplied a blueprint for a great deal of *terrorist* literature, both primary and secondary, in the social sciences – at least until very recently.[4] Satan is a concept-driven fanatic, a resentful dispossessed

---

[2] What follows is something like an "executive summary" of two unpublished lectures delivered at the Lowy Institute for International Affairs in Sydney in 2006 and 2008. The full texts can be found on the Lowy website.
[3] Iris Murdoch, *The Sovereignty of Good* (London: Routledge, 1970), 78.
[4] The work of Robert A. Pape, Marc Sageman and Louise Richardson, for example, has changed and humanised the way in which social scientists think of "the terrorist".

outsider, a fundamentalist, a Zealot, an Assassin, a Russian Nihilist, a kind of Universal Soldier ("without him all this killing can't go on"). Milton's own experience and circumstances, including as an apologist for regicide, may have contributed to this creation of an enduring, influential portrait of extremist, terrorist pathology. And yet at the same time this figure is a precursor of the even more influential Kantian Man: self-created, self-legislating, isolated, brave, answering only to his own will and reason, but obedient to the moral law as delivered to him by them. What we see in "the terrorist" is partly a distorted mirror-glimpse of this hero (the good and bad Terminators – Milton as meme-pool).

But in remembering and seeking to emulate Milton's humanized-alien concept-hero we suppress or underestimate two critical contexts, and thus read him against the grain, as if he too were "in bad faith". First, we dismiss his very human, sensual and affective hero and heroine, their plight so exquisitely tragic (created to seek *and* suffer knowledge, to know *and* lose paradise, to accommodate themselves to the arrival of evil in the world), as if they were merely sexist, doctrinalized puppets ("He for God only, she for God in him"). And yet their disobedience, not Satan's, is the subject of the poem (but we don't like hearing about "disobedience", do we?). Secondly, Milton offers us a devastating implicit elaboration and hence critique of his concept set, itself rich and extensive, deeply grounded in value and language systems which have both Christian and classical roots, including at the level of etymology, and which have almost entirely lost their hold on us. "Envy" means "looking maliciously in upon"; "gratitude" is more an action than a feeling ("thanks" are something you *do*); "rage" is from the Latin word *rabies*; "revenge" means "speaking force back against"; "ambition", the politician's vice, means "walking around, circulating" – networking. Milton's Latin, Greek, Hebrew and Italian were as fluent as his English, and for him moral concepts were a European inheritance, to be understood historically and deployed above all in understanding our fallen but not irredeemable condition – and in defending our liberties (he wrote the most powerful defence of free speech in our language). But without that kind of sophistication, that rich inherited linguistic context, we tend to reify our concepts, turn them into *things*. So racism and sexism are *evil things*, frightening monsters.

Now if we turn to Richard III, Edmund, Iago, Brutus, the Macbeths, or a host of minor Shakespearean villains, we find no list at all of defining "evil" concepts. Richard is the prime pre-Tudor Machiavellian bogeyman, so he duly and disarmingly tells us that he is "subtle false and treacherous" and "determined to prove a villain". Edmund is a bastard and therefore immediately suspect to an early modern audience; but his cold-hearted ambition is not easily conceptualised. The Macbeths' "black and deep desires" are offset by their haunted guilt. Iago like Richard and Edmund cheerfully admits his villainy, but his malignity is notoriously motiveless (it isn't really, but we have to conceptualise it for ourselves). Several of them are likeable multiple murderers. As for Brutus, he murders his dear friend, but is still the noblest Roman of them all. It's the vengeful politician Antony who is really chilling: "mothers shall but smile when they behold / Their infants quartered with the hands of war". What concept will capture *that* vision? Ambition, justice, honour or jealousy in any of them, malice or conscience in Claudio and Hamlet, even mercy in Isabella and Portia, all of them concepts occasionally foregrounded by the thought, are still only ever explored by it, rather than being what it rests on. Shakespeare is instinctively anti-ideological; founding concepts don't long survive the solvent scrutiny of his metaphorical, character-driven poetry. Instead we have a vast, rich array of second-order, often semi-metaphorical, moral and emotional terms – far too many to quote, as they are embedded everywhere in the poetry. And there are no evil monsters: there are evil *people*, human beings. Shakespeare is not apocalyptic. For him time is not an arrow as it is for Milton, speeding on its way towards the last days and a final Judgement (this too is a model modernity has internalised in a secular form). It is an endless cycle, forever renewed but with the same instructively recurrent patterns. Ideological fanatics are not his stock in trade. Iago is a resentful middle-management sociopath: Brutus, a high-minded republican. They are both still murderers. But in Shakespeare even the awful gallery of modern mass-murderers, bin Laden or Milosevic, Assad or Mao, Pinochet or Mugabe, Hitler or Stalin, Pol Pot or Abu Bakr, all of them only too ready to quarter all the infants, would still have been seen as *people*, not monsters.

A professor of poetry might well suggest to his or her students that one kind of poetry offers us concepts as *prior to* experience; the other kind offers them as *derived from* it (it's arguable that philosophy also comes in these two forms: one Platonist, one Aristotelian). One kind of thinking is deductive, or perhaps proto-rationalist; the other inductive, or perhaps experientialist (not really empiricist, since the material is not only sensory but also emotional and moral). Each proposes a way of making sense of the chaos of life experience, but in one *we* have to do the conceptual work, engaging with the quasi-metaphorical material of character; in the other, it seems to have been done for us before we ever get near the character. One says, rather in the style of the old morality plays, "what might despair or envy look like if it were a real person?" (but this can lead to some powerful thought about what the concepts mean in practice); the other, "how might real persons behave in such and such circumstances?" – leaving it to us to conceptualise their behaviour in terms of despair or envy or whatever concepts we might find for ourselves. This is how we also think about people we know. The third-generation outrage culture mentioned above is a direct but brutally debased consequence of the first kind of thinking, an *a priori* conceptualism without the conceptual richness, groundedness or analysis. But we can turn to either kind to counteract that shrill outrage, or more generally to get back in touch with our deeper moral assurances. What folly it would be *not* to make this kind of education available for each new generation.

'Pour forth thy fervours for a healthful mind': Pagan and Christian Views of Courage

David Daintree

It is a sad truth about the human condition that good men and women can fall victim to the destructive spite and malice of others and suffer terribly as a result. Some would list such miseries among the consequences of Original Sin, while others of a more secular bent would simply shrug and say that life was never meant to be easy. But regardless of the explanation offered, human cruelty has to be borne, and if possible with equanimity.

Many resources are available to fortify the heart. In our own Western tradition there has been a shift in focus from that passive *apatheia* or *ataraxia*, that is so characteristic of both stoicism and epicureanism, to a more active faith in the Christian God. For the stoic *apatheia*, freedom from passion of every kind, was a virtue of the highest order; for the epicurean it was actually identifiable with *eudaimonia*, of which the usual English translation is "happiness", or the more accurate but rather insipid "well-being".

Christianity too is arguably a eudaimonistic religion, but the *eudaimonia* of Christianity has a very different character from that of classical paganism.[1] The aim of this paper is to illustrate the progression from one to the other, from the intellectual and emotional comfort zone of certain Roman poets to the faith-based assurance of orthodox Christianity in the Middle Ages and up to our own times.

The Roman poet Horace[2] is always a good place to start if one wants to experience practical epicureanism expressed in language of incomparable beauty and elegance:

> Iustum et tenacem propositi uirum
> non ciuium ardor praua iubentium,
>   non uoltus instantis tyranni
>   mente quatit solida neque Auster,
> dux inquieti turbidus Hadriae,   5

---

[1] So the Westminster Confession says that "Man's chief end is to glorify God, and to enjoy him for ever". The second element of that might justly be called *eudaimonistic*, though its character is much modified by the first.
[2] Quintus Horatius Flaccus, 65 BC – 27 AD.

> nec fulminantis magna manus Iouis:
>   si fractus inlabatur orbis,
>   inpauidum ferient ruinae.[3]

> "Neither the passionate bigotry of his fellow citizens,
> nor the face of the threatening tyrant,
> nor the boisterous South Wind, lord of the Adriatic,
> nor the loud thundering that Jove sends
> can unseat the mind of the man who is just and firm of intent;
> the collapse of a broken world,
> though it may wound him, will find him fearless".[4]

And again:

> Aequam memento rebus in arduis
> servare mentem, non secus in bonis
>   ab insolenti temperatam
>   laetitia, moriture Delli,
> seu maestus omni tempore vixeris   5
> seu te in remoto gramine per dies
>   festos reclinatum bearis
>   interiore nota Falerni.[5]

> "Dear Dellius, though bound to die,
> remember to keep your mind tranquil in suffering:
> in good times free from overweening happiness;
> or when your life is filled with sadness;
> or when you relax your tired limbs,
> reclining on some sheltered sward,
> with a glass of excellent wine".

But the same poem leads on to a bitter pagan conclusion, the inevitable ending of all things in nothingness:

> … omnes eodem cogimur, omnium   25
> versatur urna serius ocius
>   sors exitura et nos in aeternum
>   exilium impositura cumbae.

> "… we are all driven to the same end:
> our lots are cast from the same urn.
> Sooner or later our number will come up
> and we'll set sail for eternal exile".

---

[3] Odes III, iii.
[4] This and the following translations are my own.
[5] Odes II, 3.

Horace famously called himself "a pig from Epicurus's sty".[6] As a young man he had studied in Athens at the Academy, founded by Plato, where he could hardly have failed to imbibe the principles of both the stoic and epicurean philosophies which then dominated that venerable institution. But Horace was a lyric poet, not a critical thinker, and more temperamentally in tune with the epicurean mentality – if we are to believe not only his self-assessment quoted above but the worldly and sweetly-sad evidence of his poetry.

Decades later, Seneca the Younger,[7] tutor and afterwards minister to Nero, tough-minded (he would have to be!), if perhaps also devious and smarmy,[8] found his solace in the sterner discipline of stoicism. Popular thinking often associates epicureanism with mere hedonism, a judgement that is superficial and unfair, but it would be reasonable to say that the epicurean approach to the problems of living were comparatively light-hearted. Seneca, at least in his published writings, reveals a very different cast of mind from Horace's, harder, more resolute, more active in pursuit of virtue, yet impassive in the face of adventitious suffering. It was a commonplace of stoicism that the truly virtuous man could be happy even on the rack. Aristotle thought that absurd, as does almost everybody else, especially, one supposes, those who have actually had the experience. A stoic could sometimes sound like a prig:

> nullus hunc terror nec impotentis
> procella Fortunae mouet aut iniqui
>   flamma Tonantis.   595
> pax alta nullos ciuium coetus
> timet aut minaces uictoris iras....[9]

"No kind of terror disturbs this man:
neither the raging tempest of luck turned against him,
nor the thunderbolt of a hostile Jove.
His profound peace fears neither the rioting mob
nor the arrogant menace of his vanquisher".

Juvenal the satirist[10] was an angry writer whose impatience with feeble humanity is never far beneath the surface. We know so little about him; how

---

[6] "Epicuri de grege porcus", Epist. I,4.
[7] Lucius Annaeus Seneca, 4 BC – 6 AD.
[8] The great H.J. Rose, in his *Handbook of Latin Literature* (1954), says of Seneca: "of [his] works the writer finds it hard to judge fairly, owing to the loathing which his personality excites"! Not everybody would make so severe a judgement, but Rose's is worth quoting as much for his learning as his trenchant wit.
[9] Agamemnon, 593-603.
[10] Decimus Iunius Iuvenalis, fl. late first and early second centuries AD. No firmer dates are known.

one wishes it might be otherwise! Amidst his bitter and resentful grumbling we find passages of great serenity, such as –

> orandum est ut sit mens sana in corpore sano.
> fortem posce animum mortis terrore carentem,
> qui spatium uitae extremum inter munera ponat
> naturae, qui ferre queat quoscumque labores,
> nesciat irasci, cupiat nihil et potiores   360
> Herculis aerumnas credat saeuosque labores
> et uenere et cenis et pluma Sardanapalli.[11]

> "Pray for a sound mind in a sound body;
> for a brave heart that has no fear of death,
> and counts length of days among the least of Nature's gifts;
> that can bear any kind of suffering;
> that knows neither wrath nor desire,
> and thinks the trials and hard labours of Hercules preferable
> to love affairs and banquets and the cosy bedding of an eastern princeling".

The influence of Christianity on Western thought and Western spirituality was revolutionary. The greatness of its triumph has paradoxically led to its invisibility: in this post-Christian age everybody accepts the basic principles of Christian morality (apart from the sexual ones), though forgetful of the theology that spawned them. Justice, mercy, humility, brotherly love, the equitable distribution of goods were, in general, not understood to be virtues in the pagan world. Their elevation has not been exclusive to Christianity, but Christianity made them obligatory, part of the air we breathe. It is achronological but apt to quote at this point Dr Johnson's transmutation (it can scarcely be called a *translation*) of Juvenal's tenth satire:

> Pour forth thy fervours for a healthful mind,
> Obedient passions, and a will resign'd;   360
> For love, which scarce collective man can fill;
> For patience, sovereign o'er transmuted ill;
> For faith, that, panting for a happier seat,
> Counts death kind Nature's signal of retreat:
> These goods for man the laws of Heaven ordain,
> These goods He grants, who grants the power to gain;
> With these celestial Wisdom calms the mind,
> And makes the happiness she does not find.[12]

---

[11] Satire 10.
[12] *The Vanity of Human Wishes.*

Rejoining the time-line, Prudentius[13] was a Christian writer capable of producing on occasions very powerful and affecting poetry. The following piece, in the sapphic metre, may not be among his finest but it neatly illustrates that shift in focus from the undeserved and inexplicable suffering of the proud to the undeserved but not quite inexplicable suffering of the humble soul who considers all things subject to providence, even if he cannot grasp their purpose:

Plena magnorum domus angelorum
non timet mundi fragilis ruinam
tot sinu gestans simul offerenda
munera Christo.

Cum deus dextram quatiens coruscam
nube subnixus ueniet rubente
gentibus iustam positurus aequo
pondere libram … [14]

"The house that's filled with mighty angels
fears not the ruin of a fragile world,
for it bears within its hearth
   so many gifts for Christ.
When God waves his dazzling arm,
riding upon the rosy clouds,
with just measure will he set the scales
   to judge the nations…".

There is nowadays some doubt whether Boethius[15] was a Christian, for his greatest work never mentions Christ by name. He has throughout the ages been regarded as a Christian writer of the very first rank, doubts about his beliefs only emerging during the last two centuries, and predictably among non-believers who liked what he said but preferred to have him to themselves. The fact that some orthodox theological treatises are also traditionally ascribed to his authorship is easily dismissed by those who prefer him to be a non-Christian. The following passage, thoroughly stoic in tone, seems to confirm their opinion:

Quisquis composito serenus aevo
Fatum sub pedibus egit superbum
Fortunamque tuens utramque rectus

---

[13] Aurelius Prudentius Clemens, 348 – c. 413 AD.
[14] Peristephanon 4.5-xii.
[15] Anicius Manlius Severinus Boethius, c. 480 – 524 AD.

> Invictum potuit tenere vultum,
> Non illum rabies minaeque ponti
> Versum funditus exagitantis aestum
> Nec ruptis quotiens vagus caminis
> Torquet fumificos Vesaevus ignes
> Aut celsas soliti ferire turres
> Ardentis via fulminis movebit.[16]

> "Whosoever, placid in mature age,
> unmoved by fortune, good or bad,
> has trodden haughty fate beneath his feet
> and held his head unconquerably high:
> that man the sea's mad raging will not topple,
> nor the volcano's smoke and flame
> as often as it bursts forth from its forge,
> nor the stroke of lightning
> wont to bring down lofty towers".

But if a man chooses to write a manual of philosophy why should he, any more than a plumber writing about plumbing, mention Christ? That has always been the argument of those who accepted the tradition that Boethius was a Christian. Moreover that tradition was a particularly powerful one: the *Consolatio* was one of the most widely read books in Christian Europe, nobody apparently feeling uncomfortable about what we now consider a rather glaring omission. King Alfred thought it one of the most important books in his educational curriculum.

Now back to Horace, but only as a means to introduce another, much later writer, Metellus of Tegernsee.[17] Here is an extract from one of Horace's favourite odes, in the alcaic metre:

> Dissolue frigus ligna super foco   5
> large reponens atque benignius
>   deprome quadrimum Sabina,
>   Thaliarche, merum diota ...
>
> ... permitte diuis cetera, qui simul
> strauere uentos aequore feruido   10
>   deproeliantis, nec cupressi
>   nec ueteres agitantur orni.[18]

---

[16] De Consolatione Philosophiae I, 4.
[17] The years of his birth and death are not known, but from internal evidence we know that he was engaged in writing in 1167.
[18] Odes I, ix.

> "Friend, heap logs lavishly on your hearth
> to drive away the cold,
> decant your best vintage Sabine wine....
> Leave all else to the gods
> who scatter their violent, feuding winds,
> though the old cypress and the mountain ash stand firm".

Metellus wrote a number of adaptations of Horace's poems, in matching metres, using as much of Horace's diction as was compatible with his greater goal of "converting" noble pagan hopelessness to Christian faith. This is his version of the previous poem:

> Dissolve frigus pectoris, ut loco   5
> Sacro reponam digna tibi, Pater,
> Ode canens laetus pedestri
> Carmina laude tua referta ...
>
> ... Deo pius des omnia nunc tua
> Qui stravit aequor turbinibus grave,
> Ut pace te prompti serena   15
> Magnificent famuli patronum.[19]

> "Father, drive away the cold of the heart,
> that I may repay thee fitly in thy holy place,
> happily singing thy praise
> though my songs be poor ...
> In your devotion give all you possess
> to God, whose gales lay low the angry sea,
> that in calm and peace thy servants
> may readily proclaim thy power".

With the kindest of intentions one cannot describe it as a great poem; its metre is sound, but the sense of the second stanza is muddled. But it does do two things: it demonstrates Metellus's esteem for the old pagan Horace and his desire, perhaps even his longing, to *christianize* a poet who has always seemed like a friend to the many who love him; and it illustrates the extent of the transformation in human thinking that Christianity wrought.

Is fortitude in the face of persecution a virtue? Some argued that it is not. St Thomas Aquinas,[20] in accordance with scholastic practice, always summarises the opposing arguments before coming to his own conclusions, so he quotes St Paul's remark that virtue is perfected in infirmity[21] and

---

[19] Quirinalia 10.
[20] 1225-1274.
[21] 2 Corinthians XII, 9.

concludes that fortitude is *contrary* to infirmity, and therefore *not* a virtue. He then calls on his favourite Aristotle to posit a similar conclusion. Bravery or fortitude arise from (a) ignorance of possible consequences, (b) expertise and training and pride in one's own skills, or (c) passions such as anger, love or a desire for revenge. But virtue is a matter of choice. Therefore fortitude is not a virtue!

So having set the reasons for denying that fortitude is a virtue, he finally concludes that it *is*, for it arises from a rational assessment of the situation in which one finds oneself:

> Unde manifestum est quod fortitudo est virtus, inquantum facit hominem secundum rationem esse.[22]
>
> "Whence it is evident that fortitude is a virtue, insofar as it conforms man to reason".

The virtue of courage or fortitude has come a long way. To the ancient pagan it was a kind of tool or device to help a proud and upright man stand firm in his own self-containment against undeserved pain and suffering.

To the modern post-Christian pagan it is transmogrified and its manifestations are legion: dieting, physical fitness, meditation are all activities by which the modern egotist hopes to hold time and fortune at bay.

To the orthodox believer it is a means of conforming the whole person to God.

---

[22] Summa II.IIae, q. 123.

State of the Arts

Jonathan Mills [1]

I wish to explore the basis upon which we think about, plan and act on behalf of our culture. I wish to understand what motivates our intentions as well as our actions; what assumptions, premises even prejudices shape the way we think about the arts and the role they play in our lives.

A lecture entitled "State of the Arts" would seem to be asking for trouble or at the very least a modicum of controversy. Hyperbole aside, I would like to suggest that any consideration of the arts, should reveal something more akin to a state of mind, a way of being, or a concept of existence to which the arts can contribute. In the process, I hope to allude to a role for the arts as an indivisible, intrinsic part of our lives rather than as some kind of desirable extravagance. I believe that the arts are necessary, not peripheral. And as I hope to use the occasion of this lecture to probe, they should not be easily segregated or hived-off from other fields of human endeavour. In fact, I would contend that the very process that encourages an extrinsic approach to different facets of human existence, is itself part of the challenge we all face in our attempts to make better sense of the world around us.

In this lecture I investigate several areas in which the arts conspire with some of our intellectual and sensory faculties and, in both straightforward and unorthodox ways, to create and shape our future. I am searching for ideas which place the arts within a central if not exactly conventional position within society. What you are about to hear is in two parts; the first asks some questions about the ways in which we choose to define, measure and ultimately value the worth of any individual in our midst; it is a discourse about evolving definitions of intelligence, creativity and human capacity. The second part of this lecture relates to some basic assumptions we make about the nature and composition, the very fabric of our society; it seeks to draw connections between those designations of intelligence and creativity and society itself; how our concept of individual capacity is reflected, nurtured and supported in and by the institutions and organisations through which we express our collective values and ambitions.

---

[1] This essay is based on the Inaugural Harold Mitchell Lecture, delivered in The Great Hall, National Gallery of Victoria, 3 August 2010.

For sheer technological accomplishment alone, the achievements of European civilisation have been staggering. Yet I am not the only one urging a modicum of caution and humility. Consider the words of the philosopher and critic George Steiner in his book *In Bluebeard's Castle* (1971):

> Technical advances, superb in themselves, are operative in the ruin of primary living systems and ecologies. Our sense of historical motion is no longer linear, but as of a spiral. We can now conceive of a technocratic, hygienic utopia functioning in the void of human possibilities.

Our planet is shrinking – ecologically and metaphorically. The march of humankind is causing vast tracts of natural landscape, ecosystems teeming with diverse species, some of which we may never know, to disappear. Is it not the simultaneous tragedy of our times that every city, European, Australasian, American, is becoming a carbon copy of every other city? Polluted, congested, unsustainable. When a rainforest is torn down, it is not just the ecology that is affected, the oxygen that is depleted; it is most particularly, the human relationships with specific environments and places that are destroyed; the poetry and songs, the stories and rituals, the intimate knowledge alongside the memory of unique locations that vanish too. We are both the beneficiaries and the victims of our actions and most especially our modes of thinking.

I want to get beneath the surface of this conundrum. I want to explore some of the ways in which we construct a shared sense of reality; to engage with the patterns of thinking, the very processes of our own minds; to delve into the ways we conceive of intelligence itself. I suspect that if I asked everyone in this room for their immediate reaction to the word "intelligence" most of us would conjure up memories of psychologists and IQ tests – tests which focus exclusively on linguistic and logical, that is to say, mathematical and analytical forms of intelligence; definitions which themselves reveal as much about the aptitudes of those in control of the process or experiment, those creating the models or asking the questions, as those being assessed.

It is said that the medical discoveries of the next decades will focus upon a greater understanding of the brain, with the field of neuroscience set to be an exciting, expanding, new frontier for medical research. By far the most interesting and provocative ideas I have encountered recently on the broad subject of neuroscience come from a psychiatrist and former literary scholar, Iain McGilchrist. He has written a book with the rather forbidding title of *The Master and His Emissary: the Divided Brain and the Making of the Western World*.

Dr McGilchrist has some pretty startling things to say about the human brain. He begins his *magnum opus* with a description of the difference between its right and left hemispheres; between the areas of this complex organ that to some extent control emotion and imagination, that is the right hemisphere, and the location of reason or rational thought, that is the left hemisphere.

Yet he goes to considerable lengths to assert that:

> ... every single brain function is carried out by both hemispheres. Reason and emotion and imagination depend on the coming together of what both hemispheres contribute.

Dr McGilchrist develops a powerful narrative about how each hemisphere of the brain produces a different "version" or "take" on the world. *The Master and His Emissary* offers some powerful paradigms for how we might better begin to understand aspects of the most basic functions of the human brain.

It is also relevant to the purpose of this lecture; for the first time in my limited experience, here is evidence from a leading medical scientist about the various ways in which we construct a mental image of the world and why it seems vital to achieve an equilibrium within the different components and great capacities of the brain that modern neuroscience is just beginning to understand as vastly more "plastic" than we ever imagined it to be.

In a world so dominated by scientific and technological innovation, it is important to assert that there is likely to be no single way of thinking that alone encapsulates the essence of human intelligence. Beyond the world of medicine, the work of the educationalist Howard Gardner is especially illuminating. In his ground-breaking book, *Frames of Mind* (1983), Gardner describes multiple forms of human intelligence, not just linguistic and logical, but spatial, bodily-kinaesthetic, musical, interpersonal and intrapersonal; forms of intelligence demonstrated by architects and sculptors, dancers, athletes and gymnasts, violinists, actors, business leaders and even politicians.

Courtesy of the work of Professor Gardner, the definitions of intelligence became vastly expanded. He argues persuasively that intelligence is not single-minded but multi-faceted. He describes the need for "multiple intelligences" to navigate the complex challenges of the world around us. Gardner's work has articulated the crucial importance of sensory stimulation and engagement as part of the development of neural pathways in early childhood.

What lies at the core of these remarks is a search for an understanding of intelligence as a crucible to unlock resources of human potential and insight. It helps explain why I am an artist; and to propose a narrative, which I hope is a potent alternative to a prevailing wisdom, which relegates the arts, far too readily, to a subsidiary role in society.

I am a composer. Sound and music is the prism through which I experience and make meaning of the world. I am attempting to do so at a moment in history when one is overwhelmed by information; in an era where one's senses are deluged by an overload of visual and aural stimulation. As an artist, my relationships are experiential rather than theoretical. I certainly share with scientists and philosophers a desire to make sense of my existence. My approach is poles apart from theirs. It is a fragile, highly intuitive process, in which sensory acuity and memory are subtly intertwined.

In his book, *Material Thinking* (2004), historian and artist Paul Carter explores the thought processes that he has observed, both as a critic and a collaborator as part of the practice of making art. He describes his ideas as follows:

> Material thinking occurs in the making of works of art. It happens when an artist dares to ask the simple but far-reaching questions; what matters? What is the material of thought? To ask these questions is to embark upon an intellectual adventure peculiar to the making process. Critics and theorists interested in communicating ideas about things cannot emulate it. They remain outsiders.

My experiences as a composer closely resemble Paul Carter's thesis. When I write music, my mind is constantly searching for sonic shapes, rhythmic fragments and melodic phrases, which begin to be conceived in isolation and then in ever-increasing combinations and permutations, until textures and patterns emerge and evolve.

In my quest for ideas that bring the acoustic into some sort of equilibrium with the visual, the works of anthropologists Edmund Carpenter and Steve Feld have been a huge influence. Carpenter and Feld undertake research in completely different places with one crucial similarity: the role of sound as the primary way of sensing and responding to their environments.

Edmund Carpenter is a Canadian anthropologist who has worked closely for many years with the Inuit peoples, the indigenous populations to be found across the Arctic Circle from Greenland to the far-northern parts of Canada. For most of the year, this environment is snow-bound. Navigating across this isolated landscape, the horizon barely discernible requires a completely different set of skills to taking a stroll along Swanston Street. A highly-developed sense of sound and touch are more important than sight. To the uninitiated, this environment looks like a confusing, white canvas. Only an acute sensitivity to the sound of the ever-changing direction of the wind, the constantly-shifting texture of snow, offers any hope of accurate navigation.

Steve Feld is an ethnomusicologist who has lived amongst, recorded and written about the poetry and music of the Kaluli people, from Mt Bosavi in the central highlands of Papua New Guinea. The dense equatorial rainforest of this remote region of PNG does not reveal a horizon. One navigates through the landscape relying on other senses, especially sound. In describing the way in which the Kaluli people relate to their world, Steve Feld invented a new word – "acoustemology", meaning "knowledge of the world through sound".

I make these observations, partly out of a deep concern that urban environments, increasingly indistinguishable one from another, are proscribing our potential and even our ambitions and creativity. I fear that for reasons of information overload our ability to sense the world around us is somehow diminished. Indeed there is some emerging research that points to a relationship between certain types of physical and sensual stimuli, which would suggest that our habits and behaviour can exert an influence on our neural pathways. Such claims are to some extent still speculations. Were they to be true, they would radically shift our understanding of the importance of environmental factors in relation to our cognitive existence.

The most enlightened attitude we can adopt in relation to a definition of intelligence is to treat it as an evolving entity.

I make the case for the arts, not merely as a reinforcement of a status quo, but a potential and ultimately essential enlargement of the circumstances in which we imagine our lives. Our artistic capacity is unique to our species. To ignore or diminish its development undermines our whole being.

We live in a world that faces huge challenges: exploding population growth, diminishing natural resources, vanishing indigenous cultures, increasing tribalism and bitter localised feuds, human dislocation of unprecedented dimensions, of large-scale suffering from easily preventable or treatable diseases. When the former Prime Minister Kevin Rudd stated a strongly-held view that Australia should expand its population; to become a "big Australia", a nation of approximately thirty-five million people by 2050, he let the genie out of the bottle.

While I have no desire, particularly in the middle of a Federal election campaign, to wade into this particular debate about population and immigration, I do believe that the heat being generated by such issues at the moment needs light, a certain amount of perspective and clarity. Australia is likely to achieve something close to a population of thirty-five million without too much change to prevailing conditions. So various statements by former, current or indeed future Prime Ministers will not change the fact that, short of a rather radical and highly contentious reversal of the broad thrust of fifty years of immigration policies, a "bigger" Australia, if not a truly "big" Australia, will become a reality of some sort by the middle of the century.

This position is not without controversy. Critics rightly point to the fragility of our environment. Australia is the driest continent on earth; and Australians, it would seem, among the thirstiest. Notwithstanding one's political affiliations, the language used by all of our political leaders has been almost exclusively utilitarian. It has become a statistical narrative of GDP and CPIs, of economics and markets, of ageing and life expectancy, of productivity and competition. To be fair it recognises a series of challenges with descriptions of "urban congestion", the "adequacy of infrastructure", and the impact on "housing supply".

But in preparing this lecture I read a number of official documents, as well as speeches, comments and interviews with a variety of Government Ministers and I struggled to find the slightest mention of culture. So let's attempt to come to terms with a set of implications and effects that will not only be felt in politics or the economy; but in every other aspect of our life, including our culture and its artistic expression.

How does one begin to describe a role for the arts in the light of these circumstances? What will be the influence of these likely demographic shifts on our cultural institutions? To what extent will they need to be recast to represent or reflect the evolving interests or aspirations of citizens? While English will remain the official language of the country, in what ways will we communicate with each other? What music will we play? What kinds of films or books will we create to describe or define ourselves? Where will we be able to find common cause?

That all of this will be negotiated in an environment of rapidly expanding digital communications will only add to its layers of complexity and dislocation.

Let's take a moment to test some fairly basic assumptions.

Australia's cultural institutions, our orchestras, theatre companies, art galleries, libraries and museums, opera and dance ensembles, are all modelled upon mainly British prototypes that have evolved over the past several centuries. I have no wish to criticize these institutions or what they have achieved. I would not be the person I am today without decisions and sacrifices taken decades ago to assemble an orchestra in Sydney, found a festival in Adelaide, gather a gallery in Melbourne or open a library in Canberra.

I do however want to point out that every single one of these cultural institutions is a bequest from a European inheritance; a rich, extraordinary legacy, which deserves to be built upon and further enhanced and developed. Even as I proudly proclaim the advantages of these cultural opportunities, I foresee some immense challenges. Without question, institutions which remain static are in danger of becoming decreasingly relevant. And no doubt, many of our long-standing cultural bodies have adapted with the times. It is just that in light of some of the truly enormous shifts now being contemplated, a more far-reaching shift might be appropriate.

Let me explain why.

The past millennium has been dominated by European science and technology, culture and philosophy. There is some plausible speculation that an era of European hegemony might possibly be drawing to a close. We have already begun to enter a period in history where no single culture, ideology, theocracy or politics will be all-pervasive or dominant. We are now living in world in which knowledge comes simultaneously from various, divergent, technological, ethical, cultural and philosophical sources and locations.

I am not alone in detecting an unusual alignment of forces at work in the world at the moment, which has the capacity to disrupt and dislodge many of our perceptions and preconceptions. What troubles me most about such a potentially radical recasting of society is the widespread myopia accompanying it.

If we are prepared to acknowledge the enormous impact of the economies of countries like China and India in the next decades, why are we so tentative and unconfident about discussing and engaging with their potential cultural influence? I believe that it comes down to a reticence about that much abused concept, multiculturalism.

Most of us listening to this lecture would assume that we espoused the values of a pluralist, liberal democracy. I find it hard not to become cynical about the way in which so much of the discourse on immigration and multiculturalism is framed. Quite frankly this particular multi-syllabic label is used to cover and cover up a multitude of shortcomings. For I think we are incredibly loose and lazy in the ways in which we define and apply this particular word.

Please do not misunderstand me. I am not arguing against multiculturalism. In its current usage I simply don't think it goes far enough to connect to the present or future requirements of our society. My concerns about the assumptions and generalisations of multiculturalism are echoed by the sociologist Ulrich Beck:

> For a long time now, we have been hearing a lot about cultural relativism, multiculturalism, tolerance, internationalism – and ad nauseum – globalisation….

> … All of the above ideas are based on the premise of difference, of alienation, of the strangeness of the Other. Multiculturalism, for example, means that various ethnic groups live side by side within a single state. While tolerance means acceptance, even when it goes against the grain, putting up with difference is an unavoidable burden. Cosmopolitan tolerance on the other hand, is more than that. It is neither defensive nor passive, but instead active: it means opening oneself up to the world of the Other, perceiving difference as an enrichment, regarding the Other as fundamentally equal….

> …Cosmopolitanism, then, absolutely does not mean uniformity or homogenisation. Individuals, groups, communities, political organisations, cultures and civilisations wish to and should remain diverse, perhaps even unique. But to put it metaphorically: the walls between them must be replaced by bridges.

Here is a very direct challenge to which all facets of society should listen. A call to action, which, if accepted, requires a considerable shift in emphasis throughout our community; in political language and government policy; in the ways we chose to educate ourselves; in the shape and design of both our physical realities – our cities, suburbs, dwellings and public spaces – as well as our patterns of thought: our customs, belief systems and personal behaviour; and perhaps not least in the way individual artists and arts organisations perceive and define their roles in the future.

I would like to take a moment to consider carefully a course of action which Ulrick Beck urges – to take up his challenge to build bridges between "minds, mentalities and imaginations", but also within "nations, localities … and institutions"; to contemplate how the cosmopolitanism which Professor Beck describes might find its way to influencing the shape of a discourse on the arts in Australia today.

I am going to be quite deliberately provocative and draw an example from an art form that many in this room would identify exclusively with a European heritage; an art form that has the additional difficulty of being elaborate and expensive. I am going to illustrate my point with specific reference to opera. Furthermore I want to continue this provocation by referring to the ideas of two giants of European culture, Richard Wagner and Claudio Monteverdi.

In his famous essay *Die Kunst und die Revolution* (1849), Richard Wagner's use of the word *Gesamtkunstwerk* – the idea of a total, all-embracing artwork – is a restatement of an ancient idea. He was exploring not only relationships between words and music, dance and theatre, but much else besides, an intrinsic concept whereby the combination of various art forms were to be fused inextricably within a ceremony or ritual, language, custom, folklore and allegory, thus making a complete entity, an undilutable whole. He was, of course, attempting to define the genre of opera itself.

Similar thoughts occupied the mind of Claudio Monteverdi almost two hundred and fifty years earlier as he composed his very first opera, *Orfeo*, a work he described as a *favola in musica*.

Whereas Monteverdi's or Wagner's investigations lay in the crevices of their own European traditions, I would strongly suggest that in some form or other, opera is a universal phenomenon. There are very few cultures in which the most fundamental concept of *Gesamtkunstwerk* does not exist. The various forms of Chinese opera, Japanese Kabuki and Noh drama to *Taziyeh*, the musical and dramatic pageants of ancient Persia, or the Sufi devotional ceremonies of the Whirling Dervishes from Turkey, the Voodoo rituals of Haiti or indeed the great Sanskrit epics of India, all encompass the attributes of the *Gesamtkunstwerk*. Closer to home, the elaborate ceremonies transacted through poetry and song of the Aranda people of the desert of Central Australia are in every way a total, all-encompassing art work. I could go on.

What is the point of all this?

Beyond offering a very tangible way of connecting to an artistic genre that is often seen as elitist or remote, I am trying to honour the very notion of history and tradition, wherever it may be found; to acknowledge the presence of virtuosic skill and artistic rigour in a wide variety of cultures; and in the process to urge us all to consider through the remarkable artistic achievements of an array of cultures, beyond those of Europe, in order to insist on a level of respect and care for ideas and values that are very different from our own. And to suggest that the benefits of any expression of respect will be reciprocal; that they will enhance every side of any perceived cultural divide. I would suggest that it is in such places and through such experiences that one might find the building blocks, the arched contours and centre-stones of the bridges we must build for our future.

I would also suggest that this argument is not arbitrary or optional. Without a proper engagement with the specific processes that I have just described, we will not achieve the kind of respect or understanding so necessary for a cosmopolitan society. None of this is easy or straightforward and it cannot be achieved if culture is considered or treated in isolation; as nothing more than entertainment, an optional extra or a frivolous luxury.

To a great extent these ideas cannot take hold unless they are carefully and powerfully embedded in our learning or through our earliest contacts and experiences of one another. This is an elaborate, iterative process that requires patience and perseverance and a course of both thought and action that should begin at school.

Alas, where there might be potential for learning about the *Mahabharata* or understanding the subtleties of *kun* opera or appreciating Shia religious ceremonies through exposure to a *Taziyeh* performance alongside the symphonies of Beethoven or cantatas of Bach, we rely instead on a diet which is exclusively comprised of adolescent, self-expressive rock eisteddfods. There is nothing wrong with fun and frivolity, unless it becomes an overwhelming controlling metaphor for absolutely everything that occurs in a classroom.

I have a deep-seated concern about the superficiality of the education of our children, especially, though not exclusively, in the arts. We have regressed considerably in the level of achievement we demand of music teachers today, compared with a century ago. Various distinguished Australian educationalists such as Margaret Sears and Richard Gill have told me that "the average university graduate today would have enormous difficulty coping with the most basic prerequisites to gain a music teaching certificate in 1902".

The situation in Australia has deteriorated in other ways. Compared to the 1960s and 70s, the range and nature of courses offered by Australian universities has been reduced to a point of absurdity. In addition to institutions offering a syllabus whose focus was European music, there were numerous departments that worked, taught and undertook research in the general area of ethnomusicology, and, specifically, the music of Japan, China, India, Indonesia, Vietnam and Papua New Guinea. We have now reverted or regressed to a "one size fits all", corporatised mind-set that seems to be so pervasive in Australia's institutions of higher education. To lose these centres of diverse excellence at a time of continuing population change and ever-increasing diversity in the broader Australian community seems unrepresentative, wasteful – and absurd.

To restate the obvious, any expansion of Australia's population will continue to enhance the extremely varied ethnicity of our society. Let's acknowledge the importance of the word culture in that misused term "multiculturalism". And let's expand our creative horizons to insist that any definition of multiculturalism becomes exactly what the word means; a curiosity kindled by and genuine support for the many different cultures that comprise a secular, liberal democracy and that are continuously reinforced throughout our education system.

Unless we urgently consider new ways to articulate, calibrate and modulate the *mores* of a rapidly shifting set of social conditions so as to be mindful of the need to remain open, generous-spirited, respectful and most of all inclusive, they could all so easily spin out of control.

To revisit the work of Iain McGilchrist for a moment: he makes a powerful point in describing those moments in our history when "the flowering of the best of the right hemisphere and the best of the left hemisphere working together" converge for the immeasurable benefit and prosperity of humankind: as witnessed in Athens in the sixth century by activity in the humanities and in science working together, and in ancient Rome during the Augustan era; or through an openness and energy that was regained during the Renaissance a thousand years later which brought "sudden efflorescence of creative life in the sciences and the arts". To Dr McGilchrist's examples, I would add two of my own – that period of remarkable prosperity that existed during the height of the Caliphate of Cordoba in tenth- and eleventh-century Spain in which Islam, Judaism and Christianity co-operated and collaborated so harmoniously; and the extraordinary period of science, art and technology that flourished in China during the Song or Ming dynasties.

However, McGilchrist reminds us that these are sadly the exceptions rather than the norms and that as time passes, so the left hemisphere once again comes to dominate affairs and things slide back into "a more theoretical and conceptualised abstracted bureaucratic sort of view of the world." That kind of banal mindset, I would suggest, too often dominates the way we frame agendas and priorities to this day.

I believe that the place occupied by the arts is a prism through which to perceive the equilibrium of any society. The fullness of our understanding of the value of the arts will have an inestimable impact on the world we will create.

So, in a sense this lecture is not really about the State of the Arts at all – it's about the state of our world and the role that the arts can play in it and how imaginative and open-minded we wish that world to be. If I might be so bold as to urge any kind of outcome from this presentation, I have a couple of simple suggestions.

Let's not opt for the usual, expensive but ultimately easy solutions of proposing to build another edifice. Instead let's evaluate our existing institutions and insist that they become much more ambitious and better prepared to face some of the opportunities and challenges that I have been describing.

We could start by undertaking a comprehensive, creative audit of the multitude of organisations through which the arts might discover new opportunities and lines of influence – quite literally the synapses and cortex of society itself. Such a process would, I am sure, be an inspiring revelation. Neuroscience and its relationship to the arts is, as I have indicated in this lecture, an obvious target for this treatment.

To be genuinely effective, government must be much more aware of its own potential. We must insist on a greater level of ingenuity and entrepreneurship in our public institutions. And we must properly co-ordinate these efforts through the mechanisms of a cultural policy that relates directly to other aspects of government activity. Integrating and assimilating the work of schools and universities with that of professional ensembles is only the first step. Sadly it is a step Australian governments have yet to take.

To do some of the work I envisage, it is not necessary to build another theatre, classroom or arts centre; nor to invent another quango or piece of bureaucracy. I work in a city which, for the month of August each year, becomes an extraordinary centre for the arts without ever having given the slightest thought to constructing an arts centre. A "State of the Arts" should be a matter of encouraging or reinvigorating extremely powerful alliances, wherever they might exist, in order to assert with confidence and compassion our own commitment to the ideals that will foster a continuum of imagination in and to which our children and our community can all aspire and share.

Four Sonnets

Stephen McInerney

I

The Back Window, Kiama

A morning soaking in the windowpane
like a photograph; dripping with ablution
from its last bath, and lifted to the line;
details drying in their resolution –
wattle; mountain sloping to the ocean;
six lorikeets who've drifted off the plain.
The scene emerges after early rain
fresh in wintry sunshine.

These are the mornings that I love the most:
to watch all this, warm coffee in the palm,
a pile of books, the plump, unopened post,
content with what has been and what's to come,
old neighbours with their grandkids idling past,
as if they'll never come to any harm.

II

How Calm The Harbour

How calm the harbour from the hotel:
docked boats, sails like scrolls of parchment
wait to be deciphered by tomorrow's storm;
the lighthouse among slack ropes, frayed manuscripts,
the nightwatchman in this museum;
as the swell, like a palette in the palm, lifts
to receive the moon on the horizon,
its blacks and blues and ivories newly mixed.

And a gull, like an envoy from that city,
skims and rests on the surface of Storm Bay,
feet beneath the surface working furiously;
so the painter touches and retouches
the canvas, all night in her studio,
working to keep the harbour just so.

III

A Short Walk At Dusk, Forest of Dean

Looking over the distance he has come
to where he first set out from Freeman's farm,
a distance which the farm's unravelling smoke
traverses, as it searches for the dark,
the day is shrunk to vast particulars –
the moon and stars, the silence after tractors –
as wind drags to cinders the warm note
this morning's lamb found kindling in her throat.

He keeps on through the snow as horses' hooves
seal his rambling thoughts with omegas. Calves
resume life at the teat. Reflections die
in the trough – and the tall, uprooted sky
loses itself, wandering without plans
across the hills, in search of its dimensions.

IV

Were The Window Frosted

Could I, were the window frosted here, contain
the spirit of that tree, the kind I've seen
in sunrooms when I've stepped in from the snow
(iced-windows like a Chinese folding screen
on which was spread a sapling's pure shadow),
glancing up and down, I'd note the stages
of the shadow's sun-backed movement on the pane,
pencilling its form on porous pages.

An aching thing that yet could not be broken,
that form would be the paradox of winter
brushing against the window's fragile ice –
like one who'd brush the sleep from dreaming eyes
when I was young, until I'd reach for her
who now, from her long sleep, will not be woken.

Eliot's Rose-Garden: Some Phenomenology and Theology in "Burnt Norton"

Kevin Hart [1]

I wish to read the opening passage of T. S. Eliot's "Burnt Norton," the first of *Four Quartets* (1944), because I find it the most difficult part of the poem as well as one of the richest sections of it. Its difficulty and its richness are co-ordinate in ways that need to be specified, and while *Four Quartets* as a whole continually interprets the opening passage while further enriching it, it is also true that this passage establishes the lines along which we interpret the whole of the *Quartets*, including what we understand to be the character of its wholeness. "Burnt Norton" was written in the autumn of 1935 and published before the idea of the further three poems came to Eliot.[2] That *Four Quartets* is a whole can scarcely be denied – its unity is thematically and formally insisted upon in "East Coker", "The Dry Salvages" and especially "Little Gidding". And yet "Burnt Norton" also exists as a poem in its own right. More exactly, one might say that it once existed simply by itself but now does not. It was progressively taken up into a greater unity, and now the later three sections permeate the first, ramifying and deepening some if not all of its lines. This first poem, section or movement of *Four Quartets* has two epigraphs taken from Heraclitus, which frame the whole. Let us begin with these.

The first epigraph is the second of Heraclitus's fragments: τοῦ λόγου δὲ ἐόντος ξυνοῦ ζώουσιν οἱ πολλοὶ ὡς ἰδίαν ἔχοντες φρόνησιν. In English: "Though wisdom [λόγος] is common, yet the many live as if they had a wisdom of their own". And the second epigraph is the sixtieth of the fragments: ὁδὸς ἄνω κάτω μία καὶ ὡυτή. In English: "The way up and the way down are one and the same". Puzzled as one might be by the title, "Burnt Norton", one is not likely to be entirely bewildered by the epigraphs, for we are told that they are from Heraclitus's fragments, indeed from Hermann

---

[1] This article was originally published in *Christianity & Literature*, June 2015, vol. 64 no. 3 243-265. doi: 10.1177/0148333115577900

[2] "Burnt Norton" was first published in *Collected Poems, 1909-1935* (London: Faber and Faber, 1936), and was reproduced as a pamphlet in 1941 before appearing in *Four Quartets* (London: Faber and Faber, 1944). See also, John Lehmann, "T. S. Eliot Talks about Himself and the Drive to Create", *The New York Times Book Review*, Nov. 29, 1953, 5.

Diels' edition, *Die Fragmente der Vorsokratiker* (1903).³ One might not frequent the redoubtable Greek scholarship of the Germans or even be able to read pre-Socratic Greek, yet one knows that these remarks are *philosophy*, taken from the very fount of Western thought. Eliot's audience is expected to construe Greek, it would seem, or at the very least be able and willing to read poetry with philosophical resonance. Doubtless too Eliot's intended audience in 1935 is educated and Christian for the most part, and would be quite capable of performing the hermeneutical task of adjusting pagan Greek insights to Christian teachings, of giving λόγος a Johannine spin – Ἐν ἀρχῇ ἦν ὁ λόγος, καὶ ὁ λόγος ἦν πρὸς τὸν θεόν, καὶ θεὸς ἦν ὁ λόγος ("In the beginning was the Word, and the Word was with God, and the Word was God") – perhaps by way of early *Logos*-theology. Diels encourages his readers in this enterprise by translating λόγος as *Wort*.⁴ Certainly the poem is often taken to bring philosophical fragments into the field of theological remarks.⁵ When read in the context of "Burnt Norton", the first epigraph would thereby come to mean something like, "The Christian revelation is given to all, though many persist in following their own minds", and the second, "One transcends one's sinful state only through humility, by becoming *alter Christus*". Thus readers of "Ash-Wednesday" (1930) or people who had seen *Murder in the Cathedral* (1935) might think as they come across "Burnt Norton", knowing very well that Eliot converted to Anglo-Catholicism in 1927. Yet by the time they complete the poem they may wonder if the translation is simply and fully from pagan philosophy to Christian doctrine or a Christian theology. That wonder may well persist if they read the whole of *Four Quartets*, though that is an issue I cannot consider in any detail here.

Even before one has construed, let alone interpreted, the epigraphs, the reader will have pondered the title, "Burnt Norton", which names the remains of a seventeenth-century manor house not far from Chipping Camden in Gloucestershire. Over Norton House was set alight by its owner, Sir William Keyte, one night in 1741 when in a drunken rage, and he was burned alive. Eliot and his friend Emily Hale visited the deserted gardens of the house in the summer of 1934. Of course, those who read the poem at the start of *Four Quartets* meet it after encountering a metaphor drawn from music: the overall title suborns the title of the first poem. Eliot had listened to Beethoven's "String Quartet in A Minor" (Op. 132) in 1931, and in a letter had written to Stephen Spender saying, "There is a sort of heavenly, or at least more than

---

[3] Eliot also alludes to Fragments 25 and 68 in the second movement of "Little Gidding".
[4] John Burnett translates λόγος as "Word" in his *Early Greek Philosophy* (London: A. and C. Black, 1892). The French translation of Eliot's poem follows suit: "le Verbe". See Eliot, *Quatre Quatuors*, trans. Claude Vigée (London: Menard Press, 1992), 7.
[5] See, for example, Peter Milward, *A Commentary on T. S. Eliot's "Four Quartets"* (Tokyo: The Hokuseido Press, 1968).

human, gaiety about some of his later things ... which one imagines might come to oneself as the fruits of reconciliation and relief after immense suffering; I should like to get something of that into verse before I die".[6] For the reader of *Four Quartets*, music and philosophy are guiding figures for engaging the poem, each of which lends itself to be translated or transposed into Christian motifs – or perhaps it would be more judicious to say religious or spiritual motifs – without quite erasing themselves.[7] Naturally, the reader who begins "Burnt Norton" as the first of *Four Quartets* will ask himself or herself what makes it a "quartet," and the best answer likely to come is that it involves four themes – the garden, the tube, the still point, and the limits of language when faced with the ineffable. These interplay to form a complex whole. Successive embodiments of the four elements (air, earth, water, fire) and the four seasons also mark *Four Quartets*, though as a structural feature of each quartet rather than as a way of justifying the choice of "quartet" in the first place.

Already we have been doing a little phenomenology, for "Burnt Norton" offers itself as a choice instance of the distinction between independent piece and non-independent moment, as discussed by Husserl in his *Logical Investigations* (1900-01), and *Four Quartets* is an example of a group or combination, something with both objective and subjective aspects, a phenomenon that interested Husserl as early as his *Philosophy of Arithmetic* (1891).[8] Of "Burnt Norton" we might ask if it is detachable from the whole or inseparable from it, a delicate question that has no clear-cut answer so far as I can see.[9] We have also touched upon secondary passivity in reflecting on the epigraphs from Heraclitus: Eliot writes not only as an individual but also as a member of a literary and philosophical community, and his words silently appropriate history and tradition as he writes. These associations are not necessarily restricted to his evocation of Heraclitus, even to a Christian absorption of the fragments, for the poem does not state the one

---

[6] Quoted in John Sutherland, *Stephen Spender: A Literary Life* (Oxford: Oxford University Press, 2005), 125-126. According to M. J. C. Hodgart, Eliot was also listening to Bartok's Quartets. See Hugh Kenner, "Into our First World", in *T. S. Eliot, "Four Quartets": A Casebook*, ed. Bernard Bergonzi (London: Macmillan, 1969), 182.

[7] On this issue, see Eliot, "The Music of Poetry", written in 1942, during the composition of *Four Quartets*, in *On Poetry and Poets* (London: Faber and Faber, 1957), 38.

[8] See Edmund Husserl, *Logical Investigations*, 2 vols, trans. J. N. Findlay (London: Routledge and Kegan Paul, 1970), I, 408-410, 427, among other places. Also see Husserl, *Philosophy of Arithmetic: Psychological and Logical Investigations with Supplementary Texts from 1887-1901*, trans. Dallas Willard (Dordrecht: Kluwer Academic Publishers, 2003), 19-20. It is worth noting that Eliot had some acquaintance with Husserl's writings, though one should not presume any endorsement of phenomenology on his part. See Kristian Smidt, *Poetry and Belief in the Work of T. S. Eliot* (London: Routledge and Kegan Paul, 1949), 20.

[9] Such is the view, for example, of Staffan Bergsten, *Time and Eternity: A Study of the Structure and Symbolism of T. S. Eliot's "Four Quartets"* (New York: Humanities Press, 1973), 75.

philosophical position or even develop into the one philosophical mode. Part of the poem is phenomenological in procedure, as we shall see, while another part reads more like moments in a lecture in the philosophy of internal time consciousness. To be sure, the motifs of time and ecstasy are developed in the later three quartets, though they are fully, if elusively, introduced in the first section of "Burnt Norton," and I shall limit myself to it with occasional references to the complications and embellishments of the larger poem. Needless to say, the phenomenology of composition presents us with all manner of questions about the poem, as does the phenomenology of reception, but I shall set these aside and focus instead on what is given to us in the first part of the poem itself.

"Burnt Norton" begins with a passage that, as we know, is revised from a speech culled from *Murder in the Cathedral* (1935). Originally to be spoken by the Second Priest, the lines were dropped before the first performance of the play when the Director, E. Martin Browne, decided that improving suggestions he had made to Eliot, which prompted the composition of the lines just mentioned, were in fact unnecessary.[10] Whatever the theatrical virtues of Eliot's third play (counting the fragmentary *Sweeney Agonistes* as his first), these lines contribute little or no drama to the poem. They serve to announce the main theme of a meditative poem. Let us take them slowly since they have been read all too cursorily. It is an attitude that is understandable when faced with a highly abstract introduction to an exquisite lyrical passage about a rose-garden. But in reading poetry all haste is regrettable, even when over unwelcoming ground:

> Time present and time past
> Are both perhaps present in time future,
> And time future contained in time past.
> If all time is eternally present
> All time is unredeemable.
> What might have been is an abstraction
> Remaining a perpetual possibility
> Only in a world of speculation.
> What might have been and what has been
> Point to one end, which is always present. (ll. 1-10)

It is, as critics say, a "philosophical meditation on time", though we should be careful not to take this description too narrowly.[11] Nor should we allow

---

[10] See Donald Hall, "The Art of Poetry 1: T. S. Eliot", *Paris Review*, 21 (1959), 57. See also E. Martin Browne, *The Making of T. S. Eliot's Plays*, 2nd ed. (Cambridge: Cambridge UP, 1970), 345-352, and Helen Gardner, *The Composition of "Four Quartets"* (New York: Oxford University Press, 1978), 16.
[11] Kenneth Paul Kramer, *Redeeming Time: T. S. Eliot's "Four Quartets"* (Lanham: MD, Cowley Publications, 2007), 33.

Eliot's distinction between "philosophical *belief*" and "poetic *assent*" to turn the task of reading a demanding poem into an opportunity merely to appreciate its poetry.[12] One of Eliot's less well-known distinctions, drawn in a paper given in French in 1952, is more apt. There are two senses to the expression "la philosophie d'un poète", he says: "Une 'philosophie' qu'il a empruntée ou qu'il a cherchée à construitre lui-même *dans le langage de la philosophie*" and "Une 'philosophie' qui ne peut s'exprimer que *dans le langage de la poésie*".[13] Clearly, with the lines quoted we are in the orbit of the second sense.

I would like to draw attention to several things in these opening lines. First, the speaker's prudence: the present and past are *perhaps* present in the future, a doxic modification of a philosophical belief in a τέλος of time – a final cause, perhaps – or merely a protention of the past into the future; the same sort of modesty applies to the claim about the future being retained by the past. For all the philosophical framing of the poem, we are not given definite philosophical theses but two plausible, provisional statements that could readily be revised. Second, while the lines have a flat donnish tone, they are not philosophical in the sense of the academic discipline of western philosophy, not even the philosophy current when Eliot studied it when a young man (Henri Bergson and F. H. Bradley, above all). It seems likely that Eliot has in mind an Indian philosophical tradition, one coming from Nāgārjuna's verses on the "middle way", the *Mūlamadhyamakakārikā*.[14] In academic European philosophy to set "present" and "contained" in parallel, as seems to be done here, would lead to confusion. Besides, it is not evident at the moment whether the speaker is ruminating on time in its subjective or its objective aspect, whether (as McTaggart has it) the A-series (past, present and future) or the B-series (before, now, and after) is at issue.[15] To say these lines have an "austere exactness" is to credit them with an ambition they do not have.[16] Eliot himself is on track when he places "philosophie" in scare

---

[12] Eliot, "Dante", *Selected Essays*, 3rd ed. (London: Faber and Faber, 1951), 257.
[13] Eliot, "Charybde et Scylla: Lourdeur et frivolité", *Annales du Centre Universitaire Meditérranéan*, 5 (1951-52), 77. Eliot and F. R. Leavis agree here. See Leavis, *Education and the University: A Sketch for an "English School"* (New York: G. W. Stewart, 1948), 94. For Eliot's knowledge of the "middle way", see Cleo McNelly Kearns, *T. S. Eliot and Indic Traditions: A Study in Poetry and Belief* (Cambridge: Cambridge University Press, 1987), 76-84. See also A. David Moody, *Tracing T. S. Eliot's Spirit: Essays on his Poetry and Thought* (Cambridge: Cambridge University Press, 1996), ch. 2.
[14] See for example, "If the present and the future / Depend on the past. / Then the present and the future / Would have existed in the past.// If the present and the future / Did not exist there, / How could the present and the future / Be dependent upon it?", Jay L. Garfield, trans., *The Fundamental Wisdom of the Middle Way: Nāgārjuna's "Mūlamadhyamakakārikā"* (Oxford: Oxford University Press, 1995), 50.
[15] See J. M. E. McTaggart, "The Unreality of Time", *Mind* 17 (new series, 68) (1908), 458.
[16] Kenner, "Into our First World", 171. At the antipodes of my reading there stands A. Kron's argument in "A Semantics for the First Quartet by T. S. Eliot", *Algebra and Logic* 38: 4 (1999), 209-222. Kron formalizes the opening five lines of "Burnt Norton" and establishes their truth in a rigorous

quotes in his gloss on "la philosophie d'un poète". He is concerned with how one thinks in verse, not how one translates philosophy into poetry.

Third, we should note the speaker's modulation of temporal claims, since we slide from what is "*eternally* present" to "a *perpetual* possibility" to that which "is *always* present". The word "present" occurs four times in ten lines, and calls for vigilant reading. It would have been different in 1935, though no one now would pass easily over the word "present" in these lines. Husserl has made us conscious of different shadings of "presence" and "absence": we think of an original presentation to consciousness (*Gegenwärtigung*) that is intuitively present and of re-presentation of currently absent sides of an object (*Vergegenwärtigung*). And we think too of empty, full, and fulfilling intentions. An empty intention gives us an object, without any intuition of it, purely in language: all we have are signs, not perceptions. A full intention carries the object in its sensuous presence, while an intention is fulfilling when it refers to an earlier empty intention. All these distinctions will help us to read the opening of "Burnt Norton"; more, phenomenology will help us to understand their difficulty and appreciate their richness. Whatever further innocence we may have had with respect to presence Heidegger and Derrida, among others, have taken from us.[17] Today we are likely to question the *presence* of the present moment, what Heidegger calls its *Anwesenheit*. Also, we are likely to be more vigilant with respect to "possibility" than Eliot's first readers, for we read the poem after Husserl and not just after Aristotle, and are aware of eidetic possibilities and not just metaphysical ones, that is, of possibilities that contrast with actualities rather than realities. A poem with philosophical motifs may well resonate with the philosophical concerns of another age and *vice versa*.

On a first reading, one conducted with western eyes and ears, we might say that the opening lines pass from a philosophical to a biblical vocabulary and then back again. Certainly when we hear the conditional, "If all time is eternally present / All time is unredeemable" (ll. 4-5) we seem to be in the realm of biblical thinking, indeed a biblical thinking that is already modified by philosophical reflection. Unlike the first two statements, this third one is categorical. We think of St Paul: ἐξαγοραζόμενοι τὸν καιρόν, ὅτι αἱ ἡμέραι πονηραί εἰσιν ("Redeeming the time, because the days are evil") (Eph. 5: 16), and readers of Eliot will also recall, "Redeem / The time. Redeem / The

---

fashion. However, he translates "perhaps" by ∃ the existential quantifier, which may be questioned. See 219. Another favorable reading is offered by C. O. Gardner, "Some Reflections on the Opening of 'Burnt Norton'", *Critical Quarterly* 12: 4 (1970), 326-335.

[17] See, for example, Martin Heidegger, *What Is Called Thinking?*, trans. J. Glenn Gray (New York: Harper and Row, 1968), 102-103, and *Logic: The Question of Truth*, trans. Thomas Sheehan (Bloomington: Indiana University Press, 2010), 173. See also, for example, Jacques Derrida, *Of Grammatology*, corrected ed., trans. Gaytri Chakravorty Spivak (Baltimore: Johns Hopkins University Press, 1997), 112.

unread vision in the higher dream" from the fourth section of "Ash-Wednesday". Yet the poem gives us no right to think simply and exclusively of Christianity here: Buddhism and Hinduism are both concerned with redemption. A problem for all religions concerned with redemption, whether they are theistic or not, is how to overcome the consequences of past faults. If the presence of the past is freighted into the present and the future, all time is strictly unredeemable. Christianity resolves the problem with the doctrine of Christ's atonement; Buddhism teaches that redemption is achieved through the cessation of desire; and Hinduism proposes that many lives of selfless devotion to one's *dharma* can overcome bad *karma*, brought about by wrong doing, and finally attain *moksha* or the state of endless bliss.

"What might have been" is not only an abstraction, as Eliot says, but also almost always an empty intention: it has no intuitive content. Bypassed potential cannot be redeemed, cannot be brought into the present, because it has never entered the stream of time, the speaker tells us. So it remains "a perpetual possibility / Only in a world of speculation" (ll. 7-8), a possibility only in the sense of never being able to be realized, made real, and not in the sense of being able to be realized at any given moment. Because "what might have been" was never realized, it has not influenced the course of lived experience. And yet we know very well that such things can impinge on our lives. They inform our decisions by way of felt disappointments, regrets, remorse and lingering hopes, usually by way of the imagination. They may not have been actualities but they still have a certain reality for us. Even if they influence how we act, they nonetheless indicate the same *terminus ad quem* at any moment of our lives, the here and now where we find ourselves because of what we have done and not done. In the end, the most powerful adverb or adjective in these lines is not "eternally", which is tacitly rejected, or "perpetual", since it is sequestered to a world that can never be actual, but "always": it is the present, the passing now, that is paradoxically always with us though never with us for more than a moment. No matter what we have done or not done, even if we have brooded endlessly on choices we did not make, we are invariably led to the present moment of time.

With the next few lines the voice changes, becoming more surely embodied and personal. This is now someone who is part of a scene, however minimal it may be – a corridor with a door in it – and, what's more, one of a "we" who is also in contact with a "you" and so not speaking into a void. We are told about a memory of a choice not made, and so the poem slots itself into the terms of McTaggart's A-series:

> Footfalls echo in the memory
> Down the passage which we did not take
> Towards the door we never opened
> Into the rose-garden. My words echo
> Thus, in your mind. (ll. 11-15)

The recalled corridor echoes with remembered footsteps, though not those of the speaker and not by anyone else who is named or alluded to: profiles of the past enter the present, though only in the mode of presentation (*Vergegenwärtigung*) and, for the reader who does not have the speaker's memories, by way of an empty intention (with respect to those memories) and presentation (with respect to his or her own). Others have gone that way, it seems, actualizing possibilities that the speaker has not, even though he always knew that the door in the passage opened onto a rose-garden. The possibilities perhaps relate to two people, the "we" (which perhaps includes Emily Hale) and the speaker is either addressing this person or us, inviting the reader to contemplate missed opportunities in his or her life. Immediately, though, the speaker steps back from any consequential knowledge of the reversal of time's passage through the agency of memory: "But to what purpose / Disturbing the dust on a bowl of rose-leaves / I do not know" (ll. 15-17). The memory of the garden in the other person's mind is no more than a bowl of potpourri now covered with dust, and since "what might have been" cannot be realized now and abides "Only in a world of speculation", it will scarcely respond to the speaker's words. Yet we have passed from certainty as to an end to a disclaimer of any grasp of a possible end or purpose: the speaker may know his thoughts well but not the intentions of the person he addresses.

Suddenly the speaker passes from passivity to action, from philosophical musing to participating in a unique experience, whether internal or external. It is the consequence of an indefinite intention, one that never actually becomes definite and perhaps never turns on an actual object.[18] The sound of apparently real, not metaphorical, echoes in the present form the first prompt to action, though as we shall see there are three prompts in all, growing in intensity as we pass from the one to the next:

> Other echoes
> Inhabit the garden. Shall we follow?
> Quick, said the bird, find them, find them,
> Round the corner. Through the first gate,
> Into our first world, shall we follow
> The deception of the thrush? Into our first world. (ll. 19-24)[19]

---

[18] On indefinite intentions, see David Woodruff Smith and Ronald McIntyre, *Husserl and Intentionality* (Dordrecht: D. Reidel Publishing Co., 1982), 18.

[19] Cf. Agatha's remark to Harry, "I only looked through the little door / When the sun was shining on the rose-garden: /And then a black raven flew over" in *The Family Reunion* (New York: Harcourt Brace, 1939), 104. See also Harry to Mary in the same play: "You bring me news / Of a door that opens at the end of a corridor, / Sunlight and singing", 59. In addition, see the lines about the "Lady of silences" in part two of "Ash-Wednesday". The rose-garden as a theme in Eliot's poetry was discerned quite early. See Leonard Unger, "T. S. Eliot's Rose Garden: A Persistent Theme", *The Southern Review* 7: 4 (1942), 677-681.

These echoes, neither footfalls nor words, permanently occupy the rose-garden, at least in imagination, and presumably were the original attraction to go down the passage and perhaps the reason why the door was never opened in the first place. The second prompt comes from the speaker himself, as he responds to the recently heard echoes. "Shall we follow?", he invites (rather than asks) his companion and ourselves, meaning shall we pursue these echoes, even take them as our guides? Third, there is a bird that urgently insists, "Quick ... find them, find them". That we cannot return to "our first world", our childhood or early adulthood, and that we cannot re-live elapsed time, decide differently and remake our present selves, is known all too well by everyone concerned. We cannot even represent an object that was never present to consciousness, and must content ourselves with presentation, and so Eliot asks if we really should entrust ourselves to "The deception of the thrush".[20] The thrush's song is widely regarded as one of the most beautiful among birds, and here it entices the speaker to cross a line that he might take to be forbidden to him and to give him and us mistaken hope of changing the past and hence the present and the future.

This section of the poem has long been associated with a range of literary allusions, all of which can be discerned by the experienced reader of English literature. Eliot himself recalls *Alice's Adventures in Wonderland* (1865) and (after the fact) Rudyard Kipling's story "They" (1904), while there is also reason to think of Elizabeth Barrett Browning's "The Lost Bower" (1844).[21] To these I add J. M. Barrie's *Dear Brutus* (1917). One line from the play explains why: "A might-have-been? They are ghosts, Margaret. I dare say I 'might have been' a great swell of a painter, instead of just this uncommonly happy nobody".[22] Above all, I think, one feels the slight pressure of the thirteenth-century poem *Le Roman de la Rose* with its birds in the garden that sing like angels and also like the Sirens that deceive sailors, its garden with many roses and its sense of order.[23] Yet it is worthwhile considering that the

---

[20] In his commentary on *Four Quartets* Peter Milward suggests that the thrush is a symbol of the Holy Spirit. Yet I cannot conceive of Eliot maintaining that the Holy Spirit is capable of deceit. See his *A Commentary on T. S. Eliot's "Four Quartets"*, 23. We also remember the "hermit thrush" singing in part five of *The Waste Land*.

[21] See Helen Gardner, *The Composition of "Four Quartets"*, 39-40. Eliot himself mentions Kipling's story "They" in a letter of February 1, 1946 to a French translator of *Four Quartets*. See Eliot, *Quatre Quatuors*, 55. It is worth noting that Alice, on entering the garden down the rabbit hole, encounters a "large rose-tree near the entrance of the garden: the roses growing on it were white, but there were three gardeners at it, busily painting them red", *Alice's Adventures in Wonderland* (London: Folio Society, 1961), 68.

[22] See James M. Barrie, *Dear Brutus*, ed. and intro. William-Alan Landes (Studio City: Players Press, Inc., 2007), 35.

[23] See Guillaume de Lorris et Jean de Meun, *Le Roman de la Rose*, ed. Félix Lecoy, 3 vols, Les Classiques Français du Moyan Age (Paris: Libraire Honoré Champion, 1965), I, ll. 659-672, 1249-1256. See also *The Romance of the Rose*, trans. Charles Dahlberg, 3rd ed. (Princeton: Princeton University Press, 1995), Part 1, book 1.

three prompts lead to ἐποχή and reduction. These are weighty philosophical words now used here by Eliot but not therefore inappropriate or alien to the poetry. Phenomenology was developed and articulated in early twentieth-century philosophy, and once established lit up what many artists had always known in a pre-reflective manner. Phenomenology is not inherently philosophical in the sense of working only within an academic discipline called "Philosophy", though it is inherently thoughtful. The language of phenomenology can sometimes help us to identify and clarify cognitive moves in poetry that does not make use of any philosophy.

In the lines under consideration we have already suspended any belief or non-belief in the philosophy of time being offered to us, and now we bracket the explanatory power of naturalism and the ingrained logic of the priority of cause over effect.[24] Now this is not a thoroughgoing leading back to transcendental consciousness, as Husserl commended, or the adoption of an attitude so that one can discern being instead of beings, as Heidegger proposed; but it is surely a bracketing of the natural attitude, and involves a passage beyond it.[25] On the hither side of reduction, above or beside his natural being, the speaker experiences a shift of perspective; no longer captivated by the world, he or she can be open to everything that is in the world.[26] The reduction does not lead Eliot into another world, certainly not a spiritual world behind our own. Rather, he undergoes a change of awareness, not a change of place; he passes from experiencing the echoes in the garden to focusing on the experience in which the echoes are given.

Yet the experience Eliot is to undergo with these presences is not recollected but lived as present, something more like a hallucination than a memory. The presences are merely intentional objects, having a meaning but no independent existence, but since Eliot is writing a poem, not an essay, he figures them in terms that are appropriate to a poem. He phenomenalizes them:

> There they were, dignified, invisible,
> Moving without pressure, over the dead leaves,
> In the autumn heat, through the vibrant air,
> And the bird called, in response to
> The unheard music hidden in the shrubbery,

---

[24] On suspension of belief and non-belief, see Eliot, "Dante", 258.
[25] See Husserl, *Ideas Pertaining to a Pure Phenomenology and to a Phenomenological Philosophy: First Book*, trans. F. Kersten (Dordrecht: Kluwer Academic Publishers, 1983) §32, and Heidegger, *The Basic Problems of Phenomenology*, rev. ed. trans., intro. and lexicon, Albert Hofstadter (Bloomington: Indiana University Press, 1988), 21.
[26] See Eugen Fink, *Sixth Cartesian Meditation: The Idea of a Transcendental Theory of Method* with textual notations by Edmund Husserl, trans. and intro., Ronald Bruzina (Bloomington: Indiana University Press, 1995), 42.

And the unseen eyebeam crossed, for the roses
Had the look of flowers that are looked at. (ll. 25-31).

Note that the speaker is not neutrally conscious of these presences: they appear to him in a certain way, as respected. He recognizes them as dignified before he concedes them to be invisible. Are we to figure their invisibility in terms of intuitive presence (they are spirits) or by way of a lack of intuitive presence (they are memories or literary figures)? The lines give us no sure way of telling.[27] Yet the opening phrase ("There they were") lightly suggests a fulfilling intention, and Husserl allows fantasies to have intuitive content.[28] "What might have been" has intuitive content, then, as *meaning* but not as *object*. The presences exist not in time but in a quasi-time that cannot be redeemed. As poetry, the lines credit the "they" with phenomenality, while leaving us philosophically undecided as to what Eliot is asking us to believe. Note too that this eerie situation takes place in a time that is itself peculiar: there are dead leaves, suggesting that autumn is well along, and yet it is hot with "vibrant air." It is a day in which death and life coexist, each exhibiting its power. Thrushes would not usually sing in autumn unless, as here, it is a warm day.

The bird calls again, this time in response to "unheard music". Is this because the speaker has missed hearing some music, because human ears cannot usually hear it or because we can never hear it? We cannot say, although I tend to think that Eliot inclines us to believe that this is heavenly music that our sinful state prevents us from hearing. If we are attentive, we recall that the bird is deceptive, and so it may well be that no music is heard: the bird's song might actually respond to nothing at all. Of course, we recall Keats ("Heard melodies are sweet, but those unheard / Are sweeter"). Yet we think equally, and in a more spiritual register, of "la música callada" [silent music] that St John of the Cross evokes in his "Cantico Espiritual".[29] And in doing so we know we are dealing with signs, not intuitions. More intriguing is the line about the "unseen eyebeam", an odd expression since we do not usually think of beams of vision as being observable in the first place. "Eyebeam" is an unfamiliar word in the twentieth century. It is found in Marlowe's and Nashe's play *The Tragedie of Dido Queene of Carthage* (1594) where Dido says to Anna of Aeneas, "But tell them none shall gaze on him but I, /

---

[27] Barbara Everett is somewhat hasty, it seems to me, in figuring the presences as ghosts. See "A Visit to Burnt Norton," *Critical Quarterly*, 16: 3 (1974), 199-224, esp. 207-208, 212.

[28] See Husserl, "Psychological Studies in the Elements of Logic", *Early Writings in the Philosophy of Logic and Mathematics*, trans. Dallas Willard (Dordrecht: Kluwer Academic Publishers, 1994), 150-151, and *Logical Investigations*, II, 725.

[29] See John Keats, "Ode on a Grecian Urn", in *Poems*, ed. John Barnard (Harmondsworth: Penguin, 1988), and St John of the Cross, "Cantico Espiritual," in *The Collected Works of St John of the Cross*, eds. Kieran Kavanagh and Otilo Rodriguez (Washington DC: ICS Publications, 1979), 44.

Lest their gross eye-beames taint my lovers cheeks", as well as in Donne's lyric "The Ecstasie" (1634). Given that the lines that follow speak of an ecstasy, though one without any romantic element, it is possible that the reference to Donne is the one to keep close.[30] Of course, it could be that the eyebeam is no more than an ordinary "shaft of sunlight" that fills the pool and is styled that way towards the end of the poem.[31] At any rate, this unseen counter-gaze crosses the scene, and the speaker is partly re-shaped in response to it.

To feel the gaze of someone who cannot be seen is common in experiences of shame. Here, though, the speaker does not feel the gaze directly: it is inferred from the roses that have "the look of flowers that are looked at". In one sense, the image is straightforward: Eliot is in a garden and flowers in a garden are planted so that they may be viewed. (We might think of Proust: "les grandes roses vivantes 'posant' encore dans les vases plein d'eau".[32]) Yet there is a sense of the garden being an enchanted world, as though the flowers are posing by way of a response to a gaze.[33] It cannot be the gaze of one of the echoes or presences, since there is more than one of them and they are not individuated in any way. It may be going too far to invoke Bishop Berkeley's *esse est percepi*, but we may at least suppose that the gaze comes from the "eye of providence" or the "all-seeing eye" of God – an eye with rays of light radiating from it that is usually set in a triangle – an image that was common in Victorian parlours and cemeteries, as well as on the American dollar bill, and one that would have been very familiar to Eliot. Not that this image therefore restricts the poem to confessing the Christian triune God, for it may also be found in Buddhism.

The strong sense of the supernatural impinging on the scene – invisible presences, unheard music and unseen eyebeam – is unsettled by an alternative explanation that is entirely naturalistic, as we have been seeing. Another of

---

[30] Christopher Marlowe and Thomas Nash, *The Tragedy of Dido Queen of Carthage*, III. i, Tudor Facsimile Texts (Oxford: Clarendon Press, 1914). See Donne, "The Ecstasie":
> Our hands were firmly cimented
> With a fast balme, which thence did spring,
> Our eye-beames twisted, and did thred
> Our eyes, upon one double string.

[31] Steven Carroll proposes an entirely naturalistic interpretation of the event in a novel based on Eliot's visit to Burnt Norton with Emily Hale. See his *The Lost Life: A Novel* (London: Fourth Estate, 2009), 7, 22.

[32] Marcel Proust, "La Coeur aux Lilas et L'Atelier des Roses: Le Salon de Mme. Madeleine Lemaire", *Essais et articles*, éd. Pierre-Clarac et Yves Sandre, presentation de Thierry Laget (Paris: Gallimard, 1994), 155.

[33] Philip Wheelwright points us to the flowers in Botticelli's "Primavera" and da Brescia's "Madonna in the Rose Garden" to get a sense of flowers that seem to be looked at. See his "Eliot's Philosophical Themes", *T. S. Eliot: A Study of His Writings by Several Hands*, ed. B. Rajan (London: Dennis Dobson, Ltd., 1947), 99. I must confess, however, that I am unable to discern any visual evidence in these two paintings for the sense that Eliot proposes in "Burnt Norton".

these details that caution us against a religious reading in general and a Christian one in particular is the image of the "vibrant air". It could be that the speaker is experiencing a minor distortion of perception due to the shimmering heat. By the same token, it could be that this unseasonable heat is the trigger to make the speaker aware of things that otherwise he would not see. A similar hedging with regard to perception or misperception occurs at the start of "East Coker", where, before the speaker encounters the spirits of the dead villagers dancing around a bonfire, he walks down a lane "in the electric heat / Hypnotised", adding that he walks in "a warm haze" and "sultry light" (ll. 19-20). Yet we are not supposed to believe in the presence of the dead villagers in the way we are invited to consider the lotos rising. Even less are we asked to believe that Eliot actually encounters a "ghost" (l. 95) in the second section of "Little Gidding": the imitation of Dante makes it clear that if there is testimony here, it is folded within literature. As with the presences in the garden, it is uncertain whether the lines about the lotos result from an empty intention, a full intention, or a fulfilling intention. The imagination may be variously in play in all three: in literary allusions, in unanticipated acts of the imagination, and in using the imagination in order to fill an intention. As important as the distance taken from the natural attitude is the reserve taken with respect to what we may call the supernatural attitude. No attempt is made to code the invisible, the unheard and the unseen with creedal statements, despite the speaker's allusion to redemption in the opening lines and the later image of the eye of providence.

Yet it needs to be underlined that there is not just one reduction in the opening passage of "Burnt Norton," that which leads us *into* the garden, but also, as already noted in passing, a reduction that takes place *in* the garden itself. This does not turn on the speaker realizing that he constitutes phenomena but instead that *he* is constituted by the "unseen eyebeam" as it crosses the garden. It is only in the divine gaze that the meaning of his life may be found, and the first inkling of this occurs in his encounter with the echoes or presences.

The next section begins by repeating the existential claim, "There they were", the speaker being entirely unflustered by invisible presences. In the lines that follow it feels far less likely that either the speaker or the reader will seek naturalistic justification for what happens:

> There they were as our guests, accepted and accepting,
> So we moved, and they, in a formal pattern,
> Along the empty alley, into the box circle,
> To look down into the drained pool.
> Dry the pool, dry concrete, brown-edged,
> And the pool was filled with water out of sunlight,
> And the lotos rose, quietly, quietly,
> The surface glittered out of heart of light,

And they were behind us, reflected in the pool.
Then a cloud passed, and the pool was empty. (ll. 32-41)

This is a curious situation: we have entered "*our* first world" [my emphasis] at the particular prompt of the thrush, who has perhaps encouraged us to trespass in a world *not* our own, and now we are told that the dignified echoes who "*Inhabit* the garden" (l. 20) [my emphasis] are "as *our* guests" [my emphasis]. The echoes can be guests if they are hosted in the speaker's memory or imagination, or if the dead require the living as hosts so that they may be present to someone. And so, once again, it is not entirely clear whether we are dealing with empty, full or fulfilling intentions, though the meaning (not the object) given in imagination inclines us to think, in one direction at least, of the last option. Also, the passage moves from an "empty alley" to an "empty" pool and in between there is a sense – perhaps deceptive – of remarkable intuitive fullness; we seem to pass from memory or imagination (that is, from image as broadly conceived) to lived event. It is as though the echoes and the speaker walk ceremoniously towards the "box circle", the circle of box shrubs, where they will have a privileged view of the pool. They see the drained pool, and doubtless passively take in some details of its historical strata. (A concrete pool would have been an improvement on the original pool, if there was one, modern concrete having been invented by John Smeaton in 1756, some fifteen years after Over Norton House was burned to the ground.[34]) More important is the expression "box circle", which has a secondary sense of a place to view something staged. The presences are "*as* our guests" [my emphasis again], which underlines their condition or their capacity, and yet it can also be taken lightly to suggest that they are playing a role.

Utterly unexpected, the pool is "filled with water out of sunlight", which means at the most basic level that a sudden stream of light crosses the empty pool and makes it seem as though it has miraculously filled with water. Yet more than this appears to be intended; it is as though the speaker sees the pool as it was when the house was lived in. Even this is insufficient when read with the following lines in mind: "And the lotos rose, quietly, quietly, / The surface glittered out of heart of light". We recall Tennyson's "The Lotos Eaters", which evokes the land that "seemed always afternoon", although we primarily think of the lotos in Buddhism and Hinduism.[35] There are various possibilities: in Buddhism the white lotos symbolizes Bodhi, the state of mental purity; the red lotos, love and compassion; the blue lotos, triumph

---

[34] Joseph Aspdin invented "Portland Cement", still used today, in 1824. I am unsure as to the history of the renovations and improvements of the garden and house that Eliot visited.
[35] See Robert W. Hill, Jr., ed., *Tennyson's Poetry: Authoritative Texts, Juvenilia and Early Responses, Criticism* (New York: W. W. Norton Inc., 1971), 48.

over the senses; the pink lotos, divinity; and the purple lotos, the mystical. In Hinduism, Krishna is known as the "Lotos-eyed One".[36] The lotos *rises*, manifests itself, and by convention indicates a change of state in the speaker. If the speaker is having a spiritual experience, it is plainly not coded as Christian unless, of course, one identifies the "shaft of sunlight" with the "unseen eyebeam", and even here there is room for doubt because of the Buddhist use of the motif of the all-seeing eye. If we stall when reading the poem, the expression "lotos rose" may seem to synthesize eastern and western symbols, though it is impossible to keep both as nouns in the syntax of Eliot's sentence. We might say that as the lotos rises, so it displaces the rose, associated with England and Christianity; or, maybe, the Christian rose attains its true spiritual significance only in a verbal form.[37] Certainly the softness of the lotos contrasts with the hardness of the water's surface that "glittered out of heart of light". Again, we think of *Le Roman de la Rose* where the water's surface, in the midst of the garden, is a "miroërs perilleus" because of is capacity to seduce one to narcissism.[38] (And we recall also that "heart of light" appears in *The Waste Land* (1922) in the romantic scene of the Hyacinth garden.) For Eliot, though, there is more loss of self at issue than self-love. What the speaker sees, it seems, is not his image but that of the echoes who are reflected in the water: individuality disappears in the face of tradition. If we think first that invisible presences cannot have reflections, we are being overly literal; the distorting play of light in the pool gives the sense of broken images.

At the same time that we are oriented by *Le Roman de la Rose*, we are pointed to the end of Dante's *Paradiso*, where St Bernard of Clairvaux identifies the blessed in the heavenly white rose. Before he prays to the Virgin Mary, Bernard indicates to Dante the children in the mystic rose, and Eliot alludes to "*le voci puerili*" in the lines of dismissal from the scene: "Go, said the bird, for the leaves were full of children, / Hidden excitedly, containing laughter".[39] The "hidden music" of several lines earlier is now heard. What at first seems a peculiar reason to leave the garden, the laughter of hidden children, is a strong reason when we associate it with the children in the mystic rose, for "human kind / Cannot bear very much reality", and we would willingly believe while reading the poem that heavenly children are

---

[36] Mashaharu Anesaki, who taught Eliot at Harvard, evidently observed (in Manju Jain's words) that the lotos "is perfect because it has many flowers and many fruits at once. The real entity is represented in the fruit, its manifestation in the flower, so that there is a mutual relation of the final reality and its manifestation," Manju Jain, *T. S. Eliot and American Philosophy: The Harvard Years* (Cambridge: Cambridge University Press, 1992), 199.

[37] I expand on the significance of the lotos in Kevin Hart, "Fields of *Dharma*: On T. S. Eliot and Robert Gray", *Literature and Theology*, 27: 3 (2013), 267-284.

[38] De Lorris, *Le Roman de la Rose*, l. 1569.

[39] See Dante, *Paradiso*, xxxii, 47.

more real than children in this life. (And yet we have a lingering reservation, for the bird was introduced to us as deceptive.) There is also another strong reason: Eliot who had no children might have become a father had he chosen differently in life, by marrying Emily Hale, say.[40] (It is not wholly irrelevant that the bird, the tutelary spirit of the passage, is a thrush, since wood thrushes mate for life.) In any case, these are not children *hiding* in the shrubbery; they are *hidden* there: concealed with the suggestion of being kept safe by another in heaven or in another possible world. The shrubbery contains their laughter in the sense that only giggles that can be heard; the children themselves cannot be seen.

The passage seeks closure by returning to the terms of the opening lines, though now greatly condensed:

> Time past and time future
> What might have been and what has been
> Point to one end, which is always present.

What might have been and what has been still bring one to the present moment in time, as we heard at the start of the section, and the past flows towards the present while the future seems to pour towards the same point. Or, as Augustine showed in the *Confessions*, the past that abides in the soul is the present of the past (memory) and the future that abides in the soul is the present of the future (anticipation).[41] The present is the mode of access to the past and the future, though only in highly limited ways; and it has no presence in and of itself: such presence is to be found only out of time, the poem proposes, and is marked by divine love rather than *Anwesenheit*.

What is given to us in the opening passage of "Burnt Norton"? The question is not easy to answer, for in much of the description of the rose-garden it is unclear whether the speaker records an ecstasy of some sort or an entirely natural experience brought about through distorting heat. To be sure, the bird's injunction to leave the garden inclines us to think that the experience has been supernatural; the speaker has encountered more reality than he can bear. Yet we have been warned from the outset not to trust the bird, and we have warrant to acknowledge a distinction between object and meaning. Certainly the passage gives us no reason to look for the Christian confession alone as able to explain the event: the sudden filling of the pool does not provide adequate *Evidenz* for a Christian "mystical experience", most references allude to eastern religions as well as Christianity, while the most

---

[40] Eliot expressed regret about not having children. See Ronald Bush, *T. S. Eliot: A Study in Character and Style* (New York: Oxford University Press, 1984), 192.

[41] See Augustine, *Confessions*, trans. and intro. Henry Chadwick (Oxford: Oxford University Press, 1991), XI. xx (26).

compelling Christian reference, to the heavenly children, is literary, a matter of signs and not intuition. Nonetheless, the event in the rose-garden may still be a "religious" experience in the sense that the speaker has been converted to see things from a new perspective. Is it that he now has the world, given not pre-given, before him as a correlate of his subjectivity, and that this world is richer and stranger than he ever imagined? Or is it that his subjectivity has been challenged by a counter-experience that has made him shift his way of seeing things? Even if we were to grant that the speaker has had a full or fulfilling intuition of the "heart of light" in the garden, it would not of course protect that intuition from doxic modification. What was once felt to be certain can thereafter be regarded as partly or wholly illusory.[42] Needless to say, there must have been a perception at first for modification to occur later in the writing of the poem by way of phrasing and allusion. By the same token, the perception may have been only of "a shaft of sunlight" that was itself subject to doxic modifications of its substance and meaning so that an ordinary event became charged with religious significance.

Let us look at the final passage of "Burnt Norton" where the "shaft of sunlight" is evoked. It reflects on the very lines we have been considering:

> The detail of the pattern is movement,
> As in the figure of the ten stairs.
> Desire itself is movement
> Not in itself desirable;
> Love is itself unmoving,
> Only the cause and end of movement,
> Timeless, and undesiring
> Except in the aspect of time
> Caught in the form of limitation
> Between un-being and being.
> Sudden in a shaft of sunlight
> Even while the dust moves
> There rises the hidden laughter
> Of children in the foliage
> Quick now, here, now, always —
> Ridiculous the waste sad time
> Stretching before and after.

To return to Eliot's distinction between philosophy in the language of philosophy and in the language of poetry, one might almost wonder if he is imitating here the awkward prose of some modern philosophy (but not his beloved F. H. Bradley). A philosopher might use the word "movement"

---

[42] See Husserl, *Phenomenological Psychology: Lectures, Summer Semester; 1925*, trans. John Scanlon (The Hague: Martinus Nijhoff, 1977), 141.

three times in a short space because of the demands of verbal precision in developing an argument. A poet, concerned with precisions of other sorts, would usually seek alternatives. (The same might be said of the repetition of "presence" in the poem's opening lines.) The final lines that see endless temporality as "ridiculous" may well be a rejection of Bergson's understanding of immortality, which Eliot had earlier dismissed as an "exciting promise" that has a "somewhat meretricious captivation".[43] Yet to my ear they are a devaluation of time with respect to eternity as experienced in the rose-garden, lines whose complete confidence in isolated moments of ecstasy Eliot will weaken over the course of the *Quartets*.

The pattern is first mentioned when the speaker moves "in a formal pattern" with the presences towards the box circle, and it is found again in the pursuit of the boar by the boarhound in the second section of the poem and in the evocation of the pattern of words in the fifth section of the poem where it is asserted that the pattern is the formal cause whereby "words or music" can "reach / The stillness". Pattern presumes movement, at least in this poem, though Eliot refers us to another poem, St John of the Cross's "Una noche oscura", and specifically to this stanza:

A oscuras, y segura	In darkness, and secure,
Por la secreta escala disfrazada	By the secret ladder, disguised,
— ¡ Oh dichosa ventura! —	— Ah, the sheer grace! —
A oscuras y en celada,	In darkness and concealment,
Estando ya mi casa sosegada.	My house being now all stilled.[44]

In his commentary of this stanza in *The Dark Night*, St John of the Cross says that the secret ladder is a figure for "dark contemplation", which has ten stairs. We begin with the first step of love, which is sickness "for the glory of God", and end with the tenth step, which marks the soul's assimilation into God.[45]

To ascend this dark staircase calls for self-purgation with the aid of divine grace; it is "movement / Not in itself desirable" that is prompted by God, conceived here in the terms of perfect being theology as the Unmoved Mover, outside of time and without desire. However, this God can be "caught" in the sensuous world, grasped in and through time, in the mode of becoming, which is between non-being and being. The privileged moment is given while the dust moves on the bowl of rose-leaves, in "a shaft of

---

[43] See Eliot, "A Prediction in Regard to Three English Authors: Writers Who, though Masters of Thought, Are Likewise Masters of Art", *Vanity Fair*, 22: 6 (1924), 29. I am summarizing Jain's view in *T. S. Eliot and American Philosophy*, 227.

[44] Kavanagh and Rodriguez, eds., *The Collected Works of St John of the Cross*, 721. Eliot imitates the stanza pattern in part four of "East Coker".

[45] See "The Dark Night", *The Collected Works of St John of the Cross*, ch. 17-20.

sunlight," and allows one to hear "the hidden laughter / Of children in the foliage". Once again, nothing in these images points ineluctably to a "mystical experience"; the children could well be imagined, could well be no more than imaginative contact with one's past that has the effect of a sudden release from the power of time, as in the "spots of time" passages in Wordsworth's *The Prelude* (1805; 1850) or the moments of temporal recovery in Proust's *À la recherche du temps perdu* (1913-27). Only the theological introduction to the concluding image leads one to read the sunlight as a figure for ecstasy and to do so in Christian terms. "Burnt Norton" begins with a quasi-philosophical framing and concludes with a robust theological framing. Indeed, by the time we get to the end of the poem, the speaker is thinking in terms of cause and effect. At the start of the poem, it was the tight linking of cause and effect that seemed to stymie the possibility of redemption. Something was required to break that linkage, and at the end of the second section it turns out to occur through time itself:

> only in time can the moment in the rose-garden,
> The moment in the arbour where the rain beat,
> The moment in the draughty church at smokefall
> Be remembered; involved with past and future.
> Only through time time is conquered. (ll. 88-92)

Conquered, not redeemed: the language has become much more forceful in the second section, and the lines remain within Christian orthodoxy only if it is God who conquers time through the gift of his grace. A moment in and out of time suffices to overcome the power of time, the supposed presence of the past in the present and the future, to render us unredeemable. Once again, these lines obey the inexorable logic of cause and effect: if there is a privileged moment, then one can escape the domination of time. But this is not the case throughout the poem; the first section shows us something quite different.

After the speaker's initial meditation on time, we pass to another way of thinking of our relations with the world. We hear of "Other echoes" that "Inhabit the garden"; we hear a response to "unheard music" without a call, and long before we gather what this music really is; and we see roses that "Had the look of flowers that are looked at": effects precede causes in the garden, and the culminating event is a series of effects without an identified or named cause. We pass from the echoes to the presences, and from the look of the flowers to the divine eye that sees everything, to a sunlit pool that is filled for no apparent reason. In the garden Eliot lives phenomenologically; only outside it does he think in terms of a metaphysical philosophy or a perfect being theology. This is not to say that in the garden he enjoys full or fulfilling intuitions; it is perfectly possible that the entire experience is given in memory or even hallucination, and that he receives meanings and not objects or being or any mode of phenomenality. Thereafter in *Four Quartets* one finds many doxic modifications of the event in the rose-garden, none of them as affirmative as at the closing lines of "Burnt Norton". It happens even before the poem has ended. In the fifth section, we are invited to entertain the possibility

> that the end precedes the beginning,
> And the end and the beginning were always there
> Before the beginning and after the end,
> And all is always now. (ll. 149-152)

Here the experience in the rose-garden is not deflated by a return to that "which is always present" but instead is recoded in Augustinian terms as touching on the eternity of God before Creation.[46] We approach eternity through time, and this eternity, this "still point" or Love, is a joy rather than a burden; the "present" is not burdened with a hardened presence so as to be irredeemable.

In "East Coker" there are elders who are deceitful, and we are warned that, "knowledge imposes a pattern, and falsifies" (l. 84), which suggests that we should not trust reflections on first-hand experience, perhaps even the very passage about the rose-garden. Also we are told that, "You must go by a way wherein there is no ecstasy" (l. 137).[47] The roses are now associated with the flames of purgatory both in "East Coker" and "Little Gidding". The "intense moment" is placed in a wider context, and we are warned that "experience" and "meaning" do not coincide. In "East Coker" we are told that "echoed ecstasy" is "Not lost" but requires as a supplement "the agony / Of death and birth" (ll. 131-33). In "The Dry Salvages" the event in the rose-garden is depreciated somewhat by being called "The distraction fit, lost in a shaft of sunlight" (l. 208), and, what's more, is regarded as one of a number of "hints and guesses," the rest being "prayer, observance, discipline, thought and action" (ll. 212-14). What principally counts is not ecstasy but "Incarnation". *Four Quartets* develops by unfolding and interpreting the episode in the rose-garden, among other motifs, and this interpretation tends to downplay the event rather than magnify its significance. "To apprehend / The point of intersection of the timeless / With time, is an occupation for the saint" (ll. 201-3) we are told in "The Dry Salvages", the implication being that the author is no saint.[48]

---

[46] See Augustine, *Confessions*, XI. xiii (15).
[47] See the Sketch of Mount Carmel, *The Collected Works of St John of the Cross*, 110-111.
[48] Cf. Eliot, *The Rock: A Pageant Play* (London: Faber, 1934), 52. F. H. Bradley writes something that may have stimulated Eliot: "There will be many times, all of which are at one in the Eternal – the possessor of temporal events and yet timeless", *Appearance and Reality: A Metaphysical Essay*, 2nd ed. (Oxford: Clarendon Press, 1930), 189.

"East Coker" tells us that what is most important is not "the intense moment / Isolated, with no before or after, / But a lifetime burning in every moment" (ll. 192-94). Our aim should be to live a pattern of burning moments in life, moments of "sudden illumination" ("The Dry Salvages", l. 92). What most matters is not even localized in the life of one person: "And not the lifetime of one man only / But of old stones that cannot be deciphered" (ll. 195-96), namely, the tombstones in the graveyard of East Coker. Even in the frame of "Burnt Norton", the event in the rose-garden is not promoted simply as a "mystical experience": we are warned of deceit and the possibility of misperception. We recall the first epigraph from Heraclitus: τοῦ λόγου δὲ ἐόντος ξυνοῦ ζώουσιν οἱ πολλοὶ ὡς ἰδίαν ἔχοντες φρόνησιν ("Though wisdom [λόγος] is common, yet the many live as if they had a wisdom of their own"). If our reading of "Burnt Norton" inclines us to think of this fragment as prizing the Christian revelation over common human wisdom, a reading of *Four Quartets* may well edge us towards another interpretation: we should follow the path of mere Christianity and not seek special revelation or private spiritual consolation. For all of the involvement of Buddhism and Hinduism in the poem, it becomes more and more solidly Christian when we hear of "the one Annunciation" and "Incarnation" ("The Dry Salvages", ll. 84, 215) and as it seeks closure in "Little Gidding". At the same time, one of the developing themes of *Four Quartets* is a discrediting of *experience* as such. Quite early on in "East Coker" we hear the weary disclosure, "There is, it seems to us, / At best, only a limited value / In the knowledge derived from experience" (ll. 81-83). Individual experience is to be subordinated to tradition.

The second epigraph, we recall, is ὁδὸς ἄνω κάτω μία καὶ ὠυτή ("The way up and the way down are one and the same"). In "Burnt Norton", this fragment indicates the deep identity between what is above and what is beneath, between the immense and the tiny; the cosmic dance is beyond us and yet we participate in it here. By the time we have finished *Four Quartets*, however, we are likely to reflect also that the way to God is the path of endless humility. When we are told in "The Dry Salvages" that "the way up is the way down, the way forward is the way back" (l. 129), we are being asked, by way of Krishna rather than Christ, to "consider the future / And the past with an equal mind" (ll. 153-54), as though "all is always now" ("Burnt Norton", l. 152). We do not ascend to God through industry – by chairing many committees, for instance – but are redeemed, as we are told in "Little Gidding" (with a bow to Julian of Norwich) through "the purification of the motive / In the ground of our beseeching" (ll.. 198-99). In the fourteenth of the "shewings" (long text) we overhear Jesus say to Julian, "I am grounde of thy beseking," namely, the foundation of her prayer.[49] These lines touch lightly on the opening passage of "Burnt Norton", on the questionable motive of following the "deception of the thrush" that led us into the rose-garden. It is not the fullness of intuition granted there (if it *is* granted) that counts in a life devoted to God but rather the purification of one's motives rising from an awareness of what is likely to come to all of us, "the shame / Of motives late revealed, and the awareness / Of things ill done and done to others' harm / Which once you took for exercise of virtue" (ll. 139-42).

The final lesson of *Four Quartets* is perhaps the religious significance of a certain mode of reduction. In the phenomenological reduction the gaze is converted, and we recognize that phenomena are lodged on our intentional horizons. This kind of reduction takes place not just the once but – if we are attentive in life – continually. Yet *Four Quartets* also asks us to consider that "the ground of our beseeching" performs a reduction on *us*, one that may occur just the once or many times. It cannot be brought into focus, cannot be rendered meaningful in the usual ways, and hence mastered by us; rather, the phenomenon of divine revelation, centered in Incarnation, saturates our intentional horizon, leads us more to frustration (and thereafter humility) than to exaltation or ecstasy.[50] We are led back to find ourselves not centered in our intellects, our wills or our consciousnesses but to what is revealed, divine Love, "the unfamiliar name" ("Little Gidding", l. 208). In the end, Eliot undergoes and describes a transformation prompted by divine love: God overcomes distinctions between the real and the ideal, the real and the imagined, the real and the possible as a counterpart of Eliot purifying his motives in ordinary earthly actions. All these distinctions are displaced and set in another pattern when we practice humility before Love.

All this is said in poetry. Yet "The poetry does not matter" ("East Coker," l. 71) on its own account, as embellishment or "heightened language," or anything of the sort, but only in so far as it points to God who is capable of leading us back to our true selves in him. (Eliot may well be thinking of the poetry of the *Commedia*.) Were it to matter deeply, it would pose a serious problem for Eliot, since the imaginative use of language opens up a quasi-time that competes for our attention with God's ability to overcome time. Besides, poetry might itself be kin to the song of the thrush. So Eliot diminishes the power of poetry in the hope of being led back to a state of "being human" in God. And yet there is no doubt that his words "echo" in our minds ("Burnt Norton," l. 14) because they are poetry of a high order. The poem lives between the claim that poetry does not matter and the

---

[49] Nicholas Watson and Jacqueline Jenkins, eds., *The Writings of Julian of Norwich* (University Park: The Pennsylvania State University Press, 2006), 249.

[50] See Jean-Luc Marion, *Being Given: Towards a Phenomenology of Givenness*, trans. Jeffrey L. Kosky (Stanford: Stanford University Press, 2002), §§ 21-22.

hope that it echoes in our minds. Certainly the poetry is not desired to obscure the thinking of the poem. The movement of what I have been calling counter-reduction is the most difficult of all reductions to perform in the entire repertoire of phenomenology, whether one is a poet or not, for as "Little Gidding" teaches – and the pedagogical aspect of the *Quartets* needs to be acknowledged – it brings us to "A condition of complete simplicity / (Costing not less than everything)" (ll. 253-54). *Everything*: our sense of self-development, our hopes for the future, our regret for the past, all these things must be set aside if we are to live attentively in the now and participate in the divine simplicity. Julian came to see that, for God, the Fall of Adam and the Atonement of Christ are the one act; and she teaches "the fulhed of joy is to beholde God in alle".[51] In his turn, much influenced by Julian, Eliot comes to see that "the end and the beginning were always there / Before the beginning and after the end. / And all is always now" ("Burnt Norton", ll. 150-152). That "which is always present" (l. 10) is not just time's cursor, the now, but is the all. In reaching this insight, we are released from the chain of time, able to be redeemed, though not absolved from "prayer, observance, discipline, thought and action" ("The Dry Salvages," l. 214). For we have not yet reached the end of time "When the tongues of flame are in-folded / Into the crowned knot of fire / And the fire and the rose are one" ("Little Gidding", ll. 257-59).

---

[51] Watson, *The Writings of Julian of Norwich*, long text, ch. 51, 229.

The Call of Canterbury: The Festival Plays of T.S. Eliot and Charles Williams (1935-1936)

Bradley M. Wells

Whether it was coincidence, collaboration or calling, the commissioning of a new play as the centrepiece of the annual Canterbury Festival resulted in the production of some of the early twentieth century's most significant modern religious dramas, the greatest of which being the two verse plays written for the successive years of 1935 and 1936. While T.S. Eliot's *Murder in the Cathedral* (1935) and Charles Williams's *Thomas Cranmer of Canterbury* (1936) have had contrasting commercial and critical success in the years since, their production and reception at the time constituted an apotheosis in the religious drama revival of the early twentieth century. Furthermore, in what has been little recognized to date, the events surrounding the writing and production of these two successive plays represented a key moment in the development of an important personal and professional relationship between these two writers. Canterbury not only brought the two men closer together personally, but its shared experience became the foundation for their future professional relationship, a "still point" around which their subsequent writing would turn.

There is a notable absence in scholarship investigating the direct personal and professional relationship between Williams and Eliot. As Grevel Lindop lamented recently:

> Has any biographer of Eliot, for example, really explored the relationship of the two men, or searched archives such as those in the Bodleian which would fill out the picture? Did any Eliot scholar, when that was still possible, interview those – such as Anne Ridler – who could have informed them properly? Apparently not.[1]

And as Roma King noted in her recent Introduction to the published letters of Williams: "the full depth of his feeling for Eliot has not been fully recognised".[2]

---

[1] Grevel Lindop, "Charles Williams and his Contemporaries", in Suzanne Bray and Richard Sturch, eds., *Charles Williams and His Contemporaries* (Newcastle: Cambridge Scholars publishing, 2009), 4.
[2] Roma A King Jr, ed., *To Michal from Serge: Letters from Charles Williams to His Wife, Florence 1939-45* (Kent OH: Kent State University Press, 2002), 8.

While this paper does not claim to completely fill this void, it will attempt to trace some of the key elements of this important relationship leading up to, and immediately after, their "call to Canterbury", in order to better appreciate the impact of their Festival experience upon the development of a shared literary and theological vision.

It is generally agreed that Williams and Eliot first met in person at one of Lady Ottoline Morrell's famous literary *soirées* in London, and that this meeting was a success. According to Hadfield:

> They had met at a gathering of Lady Ottoline Morrell's soon after the publication of *The Place of the Lion* in 1931. Mr Eliot was then holding the palm of "obscurity" among poets, which CW was to wear later. They had tea together, and on and off thereafter they met about twice a year for an evening.[3]

Williams's "immediate charm and likeability [and] benevolence and amiability"[4] immediately impressed Eliot who recalled of this first meeting:

> One retained the impression that [Williams] was pleased and grateful for the opportunity of meeting the company, and yet that it was he who had conferred a favour – more than a favour, a kind of benediction, by coming.[5]

This was not their first literary encounter with each other, however. While Eliot had read two of Williams's novels (*War in Heaven* [1930] and *Place of the Lion* [1931]) before their first meeting, Williams had already published his critical work, *Poetry at Present* (1930) which contained a chapter on Eliot. While in this chapter Williams confesses some misgivings about perceived shortcomings in Eliot's poetry, there is a genuine admiration for and fascination with Eliot: "for whose work I profess a sincere and profound respect, though I fail to understand it".[6] While this early critique of Eliot's work is somewhat critically ambivalent, there is a notable sense of genuine recognition of a "fellow traveller". As Lindop notes:

> Written with a refreshing voice of the "common reader" Williams's tone verges on intimacy. There is an unsettling recognition of a familiar "expression of the horror of a particular kind of emotional bleakness".[7]

---

[3] Alice Hadfield, *An Introduction to Charles Williams* (London: Robert Hale, 1959), 156.
[4] T. S. Eliot, "Introduction' to Charles Williams, *All Hallows' Eve*" (New York: Pellegrini & Cudahy, 1948), xi.
[5] Eliot, "Introduction", ix-x.
[6] Charles Williams, *Poetry at Present* (Oxford: Clarendon Press, 1930), viii.
[7] Lindop, 9.

In this underlying tone of familiarity there is a sense of Williams's early recognition of something of the "soul mate" in Eliot who seemed to understand something of his own self. Williams recognized it in Eliot's Prufrock in particular: "Mr Eliot's poetic experience of life would seem to be Hell varied by intense poetry. It is also, largely, our experience".[8]

From these early episodes it is clear that the personal, professional and literary ties were quickly established, if not, ordained. Indeed, Eliot would later acknowledge the providential, divine and supernatural nature of their relationship:

> He [Williams] seemed to me to approximate, more nearly than any man I have known familiarly, to the saint.[9]

Eliot also quickly recognized and appreciated a fellow Anglo-Catholic in Williams, or at the least, a degree of shared spirituality. As Hadfield recalls:

> He [Eliot] noted that CW always appeared over-worked and often tired, but that one was enlightened by merely being with him. Apart from the conversation something of the spirit was communicated. He was, Mr Eliot said, a genuine Anglican, and no Papalist. Mr Eliot, himself a solitary, felt the central solitude and the darkness in CW's vivacity.[10]

By the time of the Festival commissions, it is clear that Williams and Eliot were close professional acquaintances, verging on very close friends. There was more than an assumed understanding between two Christian writers. For Williams, at least, there was a degree of intimacy and trust. After an evening meeting in November 1935, Williams writes to Eliot with a surprising degree of frankness when referring to OUP editor and colleague, Daniel Nicholson: "I have not known so happy and easy a time since the dearest of my male friends died two years ago".[11] In the same letter, Williams makes a date with Eliot for a talk on "a few modern poems on the Grail story".

If anything, Williams appears at this time to be the senior figure in the relationship. In a letter to Phyllis Jones, most likely written in 1935,[12] Williams asks, "Did I tell you I was talking with Eliot and John Hayward, and we touched on Triolus-Niphates crisis? I referred to the moment when the thing by which we lived becomes poisoned – as Othello said – and Eliot said

---

[8] *Poetry at Present*, 166.
[9] T. S. Eliot, "The Significance of Charles Williams", *Listener*, 19 December, 1946, 895.
[10] Hadfield, *Introduction*, 157.
[11] Letter from Charles Williams to T. S. Eliot, 21 November, 1935, cited in Alice Hadfield, *Charles Williams: An Exploration of His Life and Work* (New York: Oxford University Press, 1983), 128.
[12] Williams came to know Hayward (who had edited the 1926 editor of Rochester's *poems* in 1926) while Williams was writing the biography, *Rochester* (London: Arthur Barker,1935).

he didn't quite get it. So I said – 'O – Keats and Fanny Brawne', and he said, so charmingly and seriously, 'Ah I don't know that state'. But Hayward and I agreed that we did, only too well".[13]

While their relationship grew steadily in the years since their first association, it was the specific experience of the Canterbury Festival that both consolidated their friendship and laid the foundation of their future creative output. It was as if, in answering the unique call to Canterbury, that they were blessed artistically and personally.

The "call" to write the play for the Canterbury Festival came, at least formally, in the form of a commission. For Eliot, there seems to be general agreement that it was a direct approach from George Bell that initiated the process, and that it was this offer that was immediately accepted by Eliot. As Browne recalls:

> George Bell came to see *The Rock* and from his visit arose another invitation: would Mr Eliot write a play for the Canterbury Festival of 1935?[14]

While this "invitation" may have been helped by an immediate offer of one hundred pounds and performance guaranteed "at a time when commercial theatre managements were giving little incentive to the writing of verse plays",[15] it is significant that this "call" should have come from Bishop Bell, the founder of the Festival and driving force behind the English religious drama revival. Eliot had known Bell since 1930, and it was Bell who introduced Eliot to the man who would be Eliot's chief dramatic collaborator and partner, E. Martin Browne.

Was it Bell who also invited Williams the following year? After all, Williams had known Bell since attending his "invitation only" Religion and Drama conference in October 1932.[16] Furthermore, by 1935 their association had deepened due to Williams's involvement with the printing and editing of the Bishop's *Life* of Randall Davidson, former Archbishop of Canterbury (1903-1928). Bell's admiration for Williams's contribution to this book as being "a brilliant piece of work, and extraordinarily true" extended to a general admiration and attachment to Williams: "I value your eyes and your mind intensely"[17] and even led to Williams often staying with the Bishop at

---

[13] Letter from Charles Williams to Phyllis Jones (No 364), cited in Hadfield, *Exploration*, 134.
[14] E. Martin Browne, "T. S. Eliot in the Theatre: The Director's Memories", in *T. S. Eliot: The Man and his Work*, ed. Allan Tate (London: Chatto & Windus, 1967), 120.
[15] Kenneth Pickering, *Drama in the Cathedral: A Twentieth Century Encounter of Church and Stage* (Colwall: J. Garnet Miller, 2001), 100.
[16] See Martin Browne, *Two in One* (Cambridge: Cambridge University Press, 1981), 72. Martin Browne was also in attendance and was by this time leader of the Religious Drama Society.
[17] Letter from the Bishop of Chichester to Charles Williams, 18 April, 1935 (OUP file 7470) cited in Hadfield, *Exploration*, 128.

Chichester. The admiration appeared to be reciprocated with Williams writing to Phyllis Jones about one such stay: "Chichester may be Canterbury. I should mildly like to dine at Lambeth before I die; still more, I should like to hear Romantic Theology declared and defended from the Throne of Augustine".[18] With such evidence it is not surprising that Kenneth Pickering identifies Bell as the source of Williams's commission: "Bell had no hesitation in asking Charles Williams, a notable lay theologian and already a prolific writer of verse, fiction and biography, to write the Festival play for 1936".[19]

However, there is evidence that the source of the Canterbury commission came from Martin Browne. Browne certainly claims the credit in his memoir:

> Miss Babington had asked me to suggest an author, and my first choice was Charles Williams.[20]

While this memoir, written in 1981, seems to be the first claim to Browne's direct involvement in securing Williams, Hadfield echoes the claim when she writes in her revised biography that "Martin Browne suggested Williams's name as a possible author for the Canterbury play after Eliot's".[21] This view has been the accepted orthodoxy since. Thus, the involvements of Browne, Babington and Bell in directly approaching Williams are all likely, and it is further possible that it was some combination of each. However, there is also a strong likelihood that one other person was directly involved in securing Williams for the 1936 Festival, and that person was Eliot.

As has already been shown, Eliot and Williams were well known to each other by this time and were colleagues and friends. They were also mutually associated with the other key Festival players: Bell, Browne and Babington. Furthermore, it seems that there was a tradition, if not a convention, of the previous Festival playwright recommending their successor. Williams certainly suggested that his successor be Dorothy L. Sayers, and she was, so it is possible that Eliot did the same for him.[22]

Either way, it is extremely likely that Eliot was directly involved or at least gave some form of tacit approval for Williams's commissioning. While perhaps short of collusion, it could rightly be called a fruit of Exchange or Co-inherence. Even if inconclusive, the very legitimacy of this speculation is revealing. It shows the depth of Williams's and Eliot's creative and professional relationship in 1935 and 1936 and that they were both at the

---

[18] Letter from Charles Williams to Phyllis Jones (No. 092), cited in Hadfield, *Exploration*, 129.
[19] Pickering, 101.
[20] Browne, *Two in One*, 101.
[21] Hadfield, *Exploration*, 135. This claim is an embellishment on the account from her original biography that stated simply: "In 1935 [Williams] was invited to write a play for the Canterbury Festival". See Hadfield, *Introduction*, 127.
[22] According to Hadfield, *Exploration*, 211.

centre of the religious drama revival of the period, and the Canterbury Festival phenomenon, in particular.

The official Commission was not the only matter that called Eliot and Williams to Canterbury. There was much about this annual Festival, which had a play as its centrepiece, which appealed to both of them.

For Eliot, the Festival ideally suited his creative and theological desires and aims. As Barry Spurr notes:

> We can imagine that central to the appeal of this commission, for Eliot, was that he could write a poetic drama about sanctity. So, at a twentieth-century festival at quintessentially Anglican Canterbury, to be celebrating the story of Catholic Beckett, is a way of affirming the Catholic origins of Anglicanism.[23]

The shared Anglo-Catholic beliefs of both playwrights were central to the appeal of the Festival commission.[24] According to Horton Davies, Williams's and Eliot's Anglo-Catholicism were part of a broader contemporary movement that sought to bring the orthodox and the mystical closer together, to parallel a growing merging of public and private worship.[25] And both were like their fellow Anglo-Catholic, Evelyn Underhill (1875–1941),[26] in seeing their role as educating the religious public about the significance of both personal mysticism and public worship for the modern Church.[27] The Canterbury Festival provided a unique opportunity for both men to realize this vision.

On a more pragmatic level, the assurance of a Festival audience was also liberating for Eliot because it allowed him to:

> ... indulge his affection for religious symbolism without calculating, as was needful with his later plays, the odds against success if he did not compromise with the public caprice.[28]

This liberation from commercial worries was an even greater godsend for

---

[23] Barry Spurr, *Anglo-Catholic in Religion: T. S. Eliot and Christianity* (Cambridge: The Lutterworth Press, 2010), 234.

[24] After Eliot's Christian conversion in 1927 (see Spurr, Chapter 5), he made his now famous declaration of his Anglo-Catholicism in the 1928 "Preface" to *For Lancelot Andrewes* (London: Faber and Faber, 1970), 11: "To make my present position clear.... The general point of view may be described as classicist in literature, royalist in politics and anglo-catholic in religion". Unlike Eliot's mid-life conversion, Williams seems to have always been drawn to Anglo-Catholicism and had been practising the faith and attending Anglo-Catholic churches from very early in his life.

[25] See Horton Davies, *Worship and Theology in England* (Grand Rapids: Eerdmans, 1996), Vol V: *The Ecumenical Century 1900-1965*.

[26] The English mystical writer, whose letters Williams edited in 1944. See Evelyn Underhill, *The Letters of Evelyn Underhill*, ed. Charles Williams (London: Longmans, 1943).

[27] Davies, 144.

[28] Grover Smith, *T.S. Eliot's Poetry and Plays* (Chicago: University of Chicago Press, 1956), 180.

Williams. As Cavaliero notes, "The invitation to write *Thomas Cranmer* must have seemed heaven – as well as ecclesiastically – sent – a rare combination as Williams would have been the first to point out".[29] But there were other factors, unique to the Festival, which were even more attractive to the two playwrights at this particular time. Even the apparent restrictions that accompanied the Festival commission proved to be blessings, including the apparent limitations of the venue and its performance space.

One of the reasons Eliot and Williams were both sought by, and attracted to, the Festival was the timely opportunity it afforded them both to realize their vision for the reclamation of ecclesiastical buildings and their liturgical space for the purpose of dramatic performance. There could be no more apt liturgical space to incarnate their Anglo-Catholic vision than in the spiritual heart of the Church of England – Canterbury Cathedral.

Williams's and Eliot's Festival plays were written at the height of the English drama revival movement of the early twentieth century, which aimed, among other aspirations, to successfully reconcile the secular with the divine.[30] A key element of this revival was the reclamation of church buildings as legitimate spaces for modern theatrical productions. This reappropriation of the previously secular theatre within the divine space was not without its opponents,[31] but it suited both Williams and Eliot's view of the liturgical and sacramental nature of both worship and theatrical performance. As Martin Browne noted:

> The participation in a common experience, vicariously suffered, is the essence of drama, and also of worship. It is the link between them. The Eucharist, as the late Bishop Woods pointed out, is such a vicarious act, and may from that point of view be said to be the original Christian drama.[32]

Furthermore, the use of liturgical space for modern theatre assisted in achieving Eliot's much desired "unattainable ideal"[33] of a modern verse drama that breaches the "gulf between verse and modern experience".[34]

---

[29] Glen Cavaliero, "Charles Williams and 20th Century Verse Drama", *Charles Williams Society Newsletter* 24 (1981), 6.
[30] For the most comprehensive study of this revival see Gerald Weales, *Religion in Modern English Drama* (Philadelphia: University of Pennsylvania Press, 1961).
[31] In recollecting his experiences performing *Murder in the Cathedral* in church, Robert Speaight experienced opposition from various clergy causing him to conclude that nowhere "have piety and playgoing the slightest connection with each other", and that "ritual is one thing, drama is another, and they do not mix easily". See Robert Speaight, *The Property Basket* (London: Collins, 1970), 177-8.
[32] E. Martin Browne, *The Production of Religious Plays* (London: Philip Allan & Co., 1932), 9. Frank Theodore Woods was Bishop of Winchester from 1923-1932.
[33] T. S. Eliot, *Poetry and Drama* (London: Faber & Faber, 1951), 296.
[34] Christopher Innes, *Modern British Drama: The Twentieth Century* (Cambridge: Cambridge University Press, 2002), 436.

Eliot was to come close to achieving this ideal in *Murder in the Cathedral* whose success was inseparable from its setting. As Eliot would himself concede later, after having viewed a performance of *Murder* in St Paul's Chapel at Columbia University:

> I cannot conceive of the play being done on a conventional stage.... It is not, after all, a commercial endeavour. I wrote it to be performed in Canterbury Cathedral as a religious celebration, and so I would always prefer that it be performed in a consecrated setting.[35]

Subsequent productions and the experience of the cast seem to have borne this out. Robert Speaight, who played Becket in the original production, notes:

> There is something in *Murder in the Cathedral* which quarrels with a conventional theatrical setting. Is it that a play designed for the Canterbury Chapter House demands a similar hospitality of church or hall? ... Is it not significant that when Eliot began to write for a more conventional theatre he wrote a very different kind of play?[36]

The importance of the ecclesiastical and liturgical setting was just as important for the success of *Cranmer*, with Williams determined to embrace and exploit what others might perceive as being difficulties or limitations of the specific venue as prescribed by the Festival which since 1929 had been the Chapter House.[37] The limitations imposed by such a performance space were clear from the outset[38] and the organizers were quick to point out to Williams

---

[35] William Turner Levy and Victor Scherle, *Affectionately, T. S. Eliot: The Story of Friendship: 1947-1965* (London: Dent, 1968), 24.

[36] Robert Speaight, "With Becket in *Murder in the Cathedral*", in *T. S. Eliot: The Man and His Work*, ed. Alan Tate (London: Chatto & Windus, 1967), 193. Interestingly, of all the subsequent theatre productions of *Murder* performed by Speaight it was amid the "Tudor Gothic of Bonython Hall" at Adelaide University in Australia for the 1960 Adelaide Festival with its "immense crucifix" and "medieval iconography" that he deemed the most successful (192).

[37] For a discussion of the performance spaces used by each of the Festival plays from 1928–1948 see Chapter 4 in Pickering. It is also worth noting that several critics have mistakenly placed the performance of *Cranmer* in the cloisters of the Cathedral, including Hadfield (see *Introduction*, 131) and John Heath-Stubbs (see *Collected Plays by Charles Williams*, viii). Williams's play was always intended to be performed in the Cathedral Chapter House. Such confusion is unfortunate but it is also significant because it reflects, in part, the level to which criticism of Williams's play has been focused on the text rather than the play in performance, and the associated implication that setting and location are not important, whereas, place and physicality are crucial elements of Williams's integrated artistic and theological vision.

[38] Pickering explains how, at the time, "the Chapter House presented enormous difficulties to actors, producers and technicians: the high, long roof and great expanses of stone and glass caused acoustic problems that could only be overcome by careful articulation and projection; entrances and exits were confined to a central aisle, ninety feet long; and electricity supply had to be brought from the Cathedral crypt!" (Pickering, 95-96).

"the unsuitable dimensions of the space and the limitations of the staging".[39] Such limitations were compounded by specific contingencies of the Festival including how Margaret Babington[40] was "fond of crowding as many people as possible into the Chapter House, making processional passage down the centre aisle somewhat precarious".[41] Rather than fearing the crowding or cramping of the Chapter House, Williams relished the intimacy of the space and the consequent physical connection and proximity between actor and audience. Eager to extend the pioneering theatrical work of both the early Festival playwrights in particular and the wider religious drama revival,[42] Williams's play proved to be "an inspired choice"[43] which, together with Eliot's *Murder*, made a significant contribution to the ongoing liberation of modern theatre from "the stifling restrictions of the proscenium arch and velvet-curtains of the commercial theatre in the nineteen twenties and thirties",[44] and provided an opportunity to further exploit the recently legitimized practice of using ecclesiastical buildings for public theatre.[45]

Another apparent restriction imposed on the commissioned Festival playwright was the requirement that the subject of the play have a direct association to the history of Canterbury Cathedral. Again, this limitation suited, rather than stifled, both Eliot and Williams. While the famous heroic English saint, Thomas Becket, might seem an obvious choice for the Anglo-Catholic Eliot in order to fulfil his theatrical aim of creating characters that embody "something of himself",[46] the choice of Cranmer by his fellow Anglo-Catholic, Williams, might seem less obvious. Unlike Eliot's Becket, Cranmer was not the unequivocal heroic and saintly English martyr,[47] and his shifting political allegiances, conversion and subsequent recantation belie simple categorization. For Williams, however, such a figure offered enormous potential for investigating the various paradoxes of spiritual faith and physical existence. Indeed, it was this very ambiguity that appealed to

---

[39] James G. Dixon, "Charles Williams and Thomas Cranmer at Canterbury", *Seven: An Anglo-American Literary Review* 5 (1984), 36.
[40] Steward of the Friends of Canterbury Cathedral and central organizer of the Festival.
[41] Dixon, 36.
[42] See Weales, Pickering and Williams Spanos, *The Christian Tradition in Modern British Verse Drama: The Poetics of Sacramental Time* (New Brunswick: Rutgers University Press, 1967).
[43] Browne, *Two in One*, 102.
[44] Pickering, xv.
[45] For a discussion of the gradual acceptance by the Church in England in the late nineteenth and early twentieth century of public drama performances held in their ecclesiastical buildings, see Pickering, Chapter 3.
[46] T. S. Eliot, *Poetry and Poets* (London: Faber and Faber,1957), 94, cited in E. Martin Browne, *The Making of a Play: T.S. Eliot's 'The Cocktail Party'*. The Judith Wilson Lecture (Cambridge: Cambridge University Press, 1966), 44.
[47] For a useful comparison of Eliot's figure of Beckett in *Murder* and Williams's Cranmer in *Cranmer* see Browne, *Two in One*, Chapter 5.

Williams and provided him with a figure through whom he could present his theological, historical and artistic vision of the true workings of what Speaight calls the "initiatives of grace".[48] Furthermore, according to W. H. Auden, the choices of Becket and Cranmer are connected because both "Eliot and Williams are less concerned with their secular historical significance than with their religious significance as martyrs", and their ability to embody a modern incarnational figure of "permanence and newness".[49] Like Eliot, the choice of protagonist was obvious for Williams and he leapt at the opportunity when it was presented. According to Browne:

> When I took him to Canterbury, [Miss Babington] said, "Mr Williams, I have one request to make. So far, every Festival hero has been carried out dead from the Chapter House: could you choose one who needn't be?" Charles did not hesitate for a moment: "Cranmer: he ran to his death".[50]

Such "conditions" of the Festival commission became opportunities that gave licence to both playwrights to realize their personal vision for religious verse drama. The plays that resulted became their most successful to date and together marked the high point in the Festival's history. A critic from *The Times* went so far as to proclaim the two plays together constituted a new "school" of religious drama:

> If Mr T. S. Eliot may be said to have founded it with *Murder in the Cathedral*, Mr Charles Williams helps to establish its characteristics. This school of drama, written for performance in the Chapter House ... has no tradition to follow.... The Canterbury Cathedral drama could follow what course it would; and if it continues to be rather mystical than eventful, rather lyrical than dramatic, there is no reason why it should not develop on whatever lines it pleases.[51]

Whether or not these two plays constituted a unique school, they should be considered intimately connected if for no other reason than the proximity of their creation and production facilitated a greater cooperation between the two playwrights and marked a consolidation in the professional and personal relationship between the two men. Eliot's enthusiastic critical response to seeing William's *Cranmer* in 1936 was symptomatic of his now "true"[52] personal admiration and affection for his friend, declaring an urgent need to

---

[48] Cited in Browne, *Two in One*, 101.
[49] W. H. Auden, *Secondary Worlds* (London: Faber & Faber, 1968), 21,132.
[50] Browne, *Two in One*, 101.
[51] As quoted by Margaret Babington, "Cranmer of Canterbury: a note by the Management", *Canterbury Cathedral Chronicle* XXIV (1936), 11-12.
[52] See Kathleen Spencer, *Charles Williams*, (Mercer Island: Starmont House, 1986). Spencer argues that 1936 marked the critical point in the consolidation of a "true" friendship between Eliot and Williams.

take "lunch ... tea ... dinner ... supper – or breakfast at any time" in order that he and Charles could talk.[53]

After 1936 their relationship deepened and, had not Williams died in 1945, it promised to continue to flourish. The claim attributed to Eliot, as recounted in Levy, that "I [Eliot] was not intimate with [Williams], although I knew him for a good many years, informally" appears to be either a deliberate understatement or an error, for it seems at odds with other evidence which suggests a far more "intimate" relationship. [54] Williams certainly felt "intimately" connected to Eliot as a fellow writer. In a letter written soon after Canterbury, Williams rightly predicts that his literary influences will posthumously be seen as Blake, Hopkins and Eliot.[55] In 1941 this collegiality evolved into talk of collaboration between Williams and Eliot for a joint program for the BBC and by November 1943 there was even the possibility that Eliot would join Williams's Order of Co-Inherence.[56] Williams even quipped in a letter to his wife in October 1939 that Eliot's and his shared vision justified the creation of an exclusive intellectual or theological "movement" between just the two of them:

> Eliot has sent me his new book [*The Idea of a Christian Society*].... The *Dove* does not much disagree with Eliot's book; we shall be starting a Movement between us.[57]

There is also the compelling fact that it was only after 1936 that Eliot's publishing house, Faber and Faber, started to print Williams's works, including *The Descent of the Dove* (1937), *Witchcraft* (1941), *The Figure of Beatrice* (1943), *All Hallows' Eve* (1945), and the combined *He Came Down From Heaven* and *The Forgiveness of Sins* (1950).

The depth of their friendship is further evident in his statements about the scale of Eliot's loss upon the death of Williams:

> Through his premature death one lost the books he should have gone on to write – as one of his publishers I knew of his plans for the future. I regret the unwritten books, but most I regret the man. Even were I not a Christian, Charles Williams is a man in the extinction of whose spirit I could not believe.[58]

---

[53] As recorded in Hadfield, *Exploration*, 140.
[54] Levy and Scherle, 20. Apart from the time lapse between this reported conversation and Levy's publication, the reliability of this account is further undermined by the fact that, unlike the many archival letters cited in his book, this is an unreferenced conversation with no known corroboration.
[55] Letter from Charles Williams to Anne Renwick, undated (c. 1940) Bodleian MS Eng Lett. D. 452.ff 102-103, cited in Lindop, 12.
[56] See Lindop, 12.
[57] Letter from Charles Williams to Florence Williams, 24 October, 1939, in *To Michal from Serge*, 26.
[58] T. S. Eliot, interview by Ruth Spalding, "Portrait of Charles Williams", BBC radio, 9.20-10.20pm, 13 September, 1961. Wade Centre Archives, Spalding Collection. Box 1. Series 3. Folder 8. Uncatalogued.

This spiritual intimacy sprang from a shared understanding of the way true friendships intersect between the earthly and the divine.

The impact of Eliot's professional and personal admiration for, and intimacy with, Williams which developed after Canterbury was long-lasting and continued to grow well after Williams's death. This personal impact can be glimpsed in Eliot's comments recorded in September 1961 for a BBC radio feature titled "Portrait of Charles Williams":

> [Williams] could have caught one's attention in any company, not least amongst literary lions great and small. With something of the cockney volubility and lively humour, a radiation of friendliness and an ability to talk interestingly about what interested him, he must have been a fascinating lecturer, as he was a most agreeable companion.[59]

This shared "lively humour" and genuine "friendliness" can again be traced back to their correspondences soon after Canterbury, including this mock acknowledgement of their shared spirituality:

> My Dear Charles,
> (Unless you are to be addressed as the Blessed Charles, but our Secretarial Etiquette Book contains no guidance for formal approach to the presently beatified).[60]

For his part, Williams also grew in his admiration of Eliot, both personally and professionally. His praise for *The Family Reunion* in his essay "The Image of the City" recognises the shared vision of a fellow traveller: "But I do not recollect any other modern work which throws so strange a light on the true relationship of the generations, and therefore on the principles of the City".[61]

Beyond this shared personal "intimacy" there remains some dispute over the extent of their mutual influence upon each other's writing, post-Canterbury. There is much potential to investigate this and, while it is beyond the scope of this paper to do so fully, there are at least some tantalizing hints that suggest a deeper integration than previously acknowledged.

On the one hand you have Brother George Every claiming, "In the long run Williams influenced Eliot more, because his own 'effortless originality' was less open to any influence than Eliot's negative capacity, his infinite receptiveness".[62] In this same passage, Every even goes further to claim that

---

[59] "Portrait of Charles Williams", Wade Archives, Spalding Collection: 1-3-8.
[60] Letter from T. S. Eliot to Charles Williams, 14 December, 1940. Bodleian Archives, Anne Ridler Gift. Box 5, Series 2 "Letters". (MS res c.137/1).
[61] Charles Williams, "The Image of the City", in Charles Williams, *The Image of the City and Other Essays*, ed. Anne Ridler (London: Oxford University Press, 1958), 101.
[62] F. R. Leavis, *The Common Pursuit* (London: Chatto & Windus, 1958), 252.

Williams's influence was so great that it changed Eliot's attitude toward Milton.[63] Eliot confirms as much in a lecture he delivered in 1947:

> I can give only one example of contemporary criticism of Milton, by a critic of the type to which I belong if I have any critical pretensions at all: that is the Introduction to Milton's English Poems in the 'World Classics' series, by the late Charles Williams…. What distinguishes it throughout (and the same is true of most of Williams's critical writing) is the author's warmth of feeling and his success in communicating it to the reader. In this, so far as I am aware, the essay of Williams is a solitary example.[64]

What is particularly notable about these comments is that they represent a more positive development on less flattering comments Eliot made about Williams in his earlier "Milton I" lecture in 1936, which was notably just prior to the *Cranmer* performance.[65]

For his part, Williams explicitly acknowledged a debt of gratitude to Eliot for his earlier "attack" on Milton for it helped "compel the reconsideration everywhere of [Milton's] power as a poet".[66] According to a recent re-assessment of the Milton debate of the mid-twentieth century by Beverley Sherry, this "reconsideration", which became known as "the Milton controversy" expanded exponentially from 1940 to 1970, owes its own great debt to the collaboration of Williams and Eliot.[67]

In their creative work, the influence is at once more clear and more mercurial. As Newman puts it in his recent study of the influence of Williams's and Eliot's shared interest in Julian of Norwich, "one cannot discuss Eliot and Williams in terms of influence: the two poets are writing in the same key".[68]

Nonetheless, perhaps the most famous "appropriation" flowing out of their post-Canterbury association is Eliot's explicit acknowledgement that his image of "the still point of the turning world" from "Burnt Norton" (1936) in *Four Quartets* was taken directly from an episode in Williams's novel, *The Greater Trumps* (1932), where the Tarot cards dance around a still point

---

[63] See Leavis, 252.

[64] The Henrietta Hertz Lecture, delivered to the British Academy in 1947, and subsequently at the Frick Museum in New York. Subsequently published in Eliot, *Poetry and Poets*. Sometimes called Eliot's "Milton II" Lecture.

[65] Eliot, "A Note on Milton's Verse" in *Poetry and Poets*. Sometimes called Eliot's "Milton I" lecture.

[66] Charles Williams, "Introduction", in *The English Poems of John Milton*, ed. H. C. Beeching, The World's Classics (London: Oxford University Press, 1940).

[67] See Beverley Sherry, "The Legacy of T. S. Eliot to Milton Studies", *Literature and Aesthetics* 18 (1) June 2008, 135-151.

[68] Barbara Newman, "Eliot's Affirmative Way: Julian of Norwich, Charles Williams, and *Little Gidding*", *Modern Philology* 108, no. 3 (2011), 435.

marked by the Fool who appears to be both fixed and subtly turning in order to complete the dance of the cards encircling him.[69]

This influence of Williams extended to other parts of *Four Quartets* including "Little Gidding" (1942) where Knowles is right to surmise that "Eliot's last quartet is the work Charles Williams looked for in 1938, the perfect re-imagination of Dante in English style".[70] If so, Eliot seems to have taken on board what Williams asked back in 1930 in *Poetry at Present*: "Dante and St John of the Cross – what interpreters of poetry are these? Can this hell be rather the place of purgation?"[71]

In "Little Gidding", the influence of Williams is explicit in the episode of the encounter with a ghost in the second movement which Grover Smith is right to note as being reminiscent of the *Doppleganger* scenes from Williams's *Descent Into Hell* that set the "precedent for a discouraging view of the 'other' world as nothing but the simultaneous presence of times".[72] Even Eliot's later explanation of this scene suggests the direct influence of Williams's Dante scholarship. In his "Talk on Dante" in 1952 Eliot explains his style in this passage as being "the nearest equivalent to a canto of the *Inferno* or *Purgatorio*" and that he meant to present "a parallel by means of contrast, between the *Inferno* and the *Purgatorio* … and an hallucinated scene after an air–raid".[73]

While Eliot would never write another explicitly religious play after *Murder*, the influence of Canterbury and Williams can be found. In a revealing letter Eliot wrote to Williams in 1939 we find him implicitly seeking Williams's approval for his new play, *The Family Reunion* (1939), while acknowledging a shared creative mission to reconcile the secular and the divine:

> After all, one of your most important functions in life (which I have endeavoured to emulate in *The Family Reunion*) is to instil sound doctrine into people … without their knowing it.[74]

In his later play, *The Cocktail Party* (1949), Eliot's debt to Williams is even more explicit. As Grover Smith notes when accounting for Eliot's quoting from Shelley's *Prometheus Unbound* in that play:

---

[69] See Helen Gardner, *The Art of T. S. Eliot* (London: Cresset Press, 1949), 161.
[70] Sebastian Knowles, *A Purgatorial Flame: Seven British Writers in the Second World War* (Philadelphia: University of Pennsylvania Press, 1990), 117.
[71] Williams, *Poetry at Present*, 173.
[72] Smith, 289.
[73] Eliot, "A Talk on Dante", *Kenyon Review*, XIV (Spring 1952), 181, cited in Smith, 289.
[74] Letter from Eliot to Williams, 14 December, 1940. Bodleian Archives, Ridler Gift, Box 5, Series 2.

The direct source was Charles Williams' novel *Descent into Hell*, the opening chapter of which, containing some of the same lines from Shelley, is entitled "The Magus Zoroaster".[75]

This, together with its "pattern of simultaneity" and the parallels between the character of Julia Shuttlethwaite and Sybil from Williams's novel, *The Greater Trumps* (1932),[76] show how *The Cocktail Party* further demonstrates the protracted influence of the "admired friend" upon Eliot.[77]

There is clearly more work to do in tracing the depth of the impact of this unique relationship. Even this brief study shows how their coming together in a personal and professional "exchange" at Canterbury constituted a genuine manifestation of what Williams would call an embodiment of "co-inherence" which, like the Incarnation itself, had both a human and divine dimension.

While Eliot remains the better known of the two, Williams's star appears to be once again rising, as a recent lecture by Geoffrey Hill suggested when, in comparing the legacy of both writers, he ascribed to Williams the equal claim to posterity as being both a great poet and even greater literary critic.[78] Whether or not the two writers will ever again be seen as companions of equal literary status in this world remains to be seen but it is more likely that both stars will rise if they are considered existing together in the same orbit rather than in isolation. In this sense, Hadfield's image of them both now dining together in heaven as they, together with "Yeats, Landor and Donne sit late with their wine" is right to have them sitting beside each other as friends and fellow guests at the feast.[79] Either way, an appreciation of the context surrounding the production of *Murder in the Cathedral* and *Cranmer* shows how we can better understand and appreciate the individual and shared turning worlds of Eliot and Williams, if we will only peer a little more closely into the "still point" of Canterbury.

---

[75] Smith, 226-227.
[76] Charles Williams, *The Greater Trumps* (London: Victor Gollancz, 1932).
[77] Smith, 226, 227.
[78] See Geoffrey Hill, "Alienated Majesty", 2005 Empson Lecture at Cambridge. Subsequently published in Geoffrey Hill, *Collected Writings*, ed. Kenneth Hayes (Oxford: Oxford University Press, 2008).
[79] Hadfield, *Exploration*, 157.

The Sea-Wall

Robert Gray

The headland has been raided,
eaten, broken away –
a carcass that hyenas
have found. It is the quarry

for the wall, drawn from it,
a rough intestine of stone;
this jumble of shapes like
DNA or protein.

Among them, a cement lane
goes nowhere, to carry
with bold gesture to sea
just the track of a railway

that built it (now rust flakes
and the sleepers' imprint).
Added each side, more recent,
are great blocks of cement.

The purpose the wall served
has been lost, apart from
that of swimmers and paddlers,
now that ships never come.

On the wall, looking back past
broken edge and sharp angle,
the line of the headland
holds its ravaged blue metal.

Beneath that contour of
the grass, supple as wire,
unbroken panes of stone
surge, a turned-up gas fire.

I have seen the wall at dawn
from its headland – silhouette
of a stamen, weighed with seed,
amid the sea's milky-white.

The people come here early
to sit on flat roof-tops
in a street of skewed pueblos,
which they drape with bright stripes.

And here, they pluck the garden
of the sea, in its alcoves,
or snorkel above rocks,
and laugh when ocean shoves

heavily (a whale with spume)
the outer curve. They cover
just eyes and genitals,
organs of too much pleasure.

Behind them, soap flakes sprinkled;
then higher, along the sea,
soap-powder; and then lathered
clouds, a whole bright laundry.

Children ride their bikes here,
and men gut fish they've caught;
a woman on the ocean
has a red towel drawn straight

behind her, and levers it
slowly back and forth; her breasts
solemnly eye those passing.
The finest sea-spray floats

in the hair on forearms, on
a girl's lip; feet are slapped
through puddles; in chevrons
of shade, picnics unpacked.

The sea's striped purple, blue-green,
chrome. Nearby, an idle yacht;
a black dog, framed by its sail,
on a pedestal, alert.

Slightly curved, as fishing rods
are, the wall unfailingly
will sprout its riffled bristles
in the days that are holy.

Knowing Oneself and the Aesthetic Shaping of Character: German Romantic Anthropology

Stephen Gaukroger

Civilization and science have been tied together in the West since the eighteenth century, and both have suffered from the way in which they have come to be associated: science by its failure to meet ideals that it could never have met; civilization by the removal of the humanities and culture generally from its core, these becoming mere adjuncts or even leisure activities. In the latter case, this is mirrored in analytic philosophy – in philosophy of mind and philosophy of language for example – where aesthetics is considered marginal, an added extra, to what it means to be human. The common view, if only implicit, is that human beings would not be human beings without language or consciousness for example, but they would still be human beings if they lacked any aesthetic life. This stands in direct contrast to late eighteenth and nineteenth century thought, in which an aesthetic model of the human being is central. At the apex of this tradition stands Schiller's *Über die ästhetische Erziehung des Menschen* – "On the Aesthetic Education of Man" – of 1794.

The modern view is mirrored in a particular conception of what constitutes an understanding of the world. We can distinguish between propositional and non-propositional understanding. Propositional understanding concerns knowledge that something is the case, and takes the form of factual, paradigmatically scientific knowledge. Non-propositional understanding is a matter of how we encounter and come to terms with the world by means of such things as aspirations, desires, fears, raw beliefs, anxieties, responsibilities, and goals. Systematized forms of non-propositional understanding we might term mythical, in a non-pejorative sense. Myths rework and pare down experience; far from shunning ambiguity they help to bring things into sharper relief, and they feed back into ordinary life, even if the way in which this happens can be hard to specify.

The issue about mythology is whether it is an added extra or whether it is an integral part of our coming to terms with the world. Under the category of mythology, as I have defined it, I am including religions. For *philosophes* such as Diderot and Condorcet, the transcendence of religion meant that society could finally achieve a harmonious balance through a combination of individual freedom and an education based on rational, humanitarian principles, which would replace the fear- and ignorance-driven religious conformity of the Christian era. But for German thinkers such as Lessing, Herder, and Schiller one could not possibly simply live without mythology. Note however that this is *not* an argument for the permanence of religion: these thinkers tend to work with a form of anthropological humanism which is an alternative to religious forms of mythology.

I am taking Schiller's *On the Aesthetic Education of Man* as the central text in this tradition, and I want to bring out three things:

• Aesthetic experience is crucial to what it is to be a human being.

• As well as a propositional dimension to understanding there is also a mythical one, which is just as necessary.

• Mythical understanding can take a religious form, but alternatively it can take the form of a humanist anthropology, one which has an explicitly aesthetic model.

Schiller's account was not *sui generis*, however, and it depends crucially on an association between aesthetic culture and civilization that effectively dates back to mid-century, in the work of Winckelmann. Winckelmann's predecessors, Wolff and Baumgarten, had established aesthetics as an area of study, and had been concerned with matters of taste and aesthetic judgement. For these purposes, art is something abstract and ahistorical: simply a concrete manifestation of beauty and harmony. Winckelmann by contrast treats works of art as products of particular historical cultures. Integrating accounts of the sculpture newly discovered at Herculaneum and Pompeii,[1] together with his unparalleled knowledge of the sculpture of classical antiquity, as well as the detailed descriptions of art in Pliny's *Natural History*, he builds an account of the art of antiquity as a product of its age and culture, a product that can and should serve as a model for all art since that time. Classical antiquity provides what are effectively the only standards of good art, standards that will always remain valid. This is why the study of classical culture itself is so important. The next generation of German thinkers influenced by Winckelmann – Schiller, Hölderin, and Friedrich Schlegel – saw Greek antiquity as humanity's childhood, a pagan version of paradise with parallels to Rousseau's state of nature.[2]

---

[1] Winckelmann published two accounts of the newly discovered antiquities: *Sendschreiben von den herculanischen Entdeckungen* (Dresden, 1762), and *Monumenti antichi inediti spiegati ed illustrati* (2 vols., Rome, 1767).

[2] Frederick C. Beiser, *Diotoma's Children. German Aesthetic Rationalism from Leibniz to Lessing* (Oxford: Oxford University Press, 2009), 192.

In his *History of Art in Antiquity* of 1764, Winckelmann established the compatibility of aesthetic rationalism – the belief in absolute aesthetic values – with viewing the plastic arts as made possible by, and as distinctive products of, definite historical cultures. In reaction to this, Lessing subsequently set out to topple the plastic arts from the role of aesthetic standard, reinstating literature in this role, but he followed Winckelmann in the idea that it was the aesthetic products of the culture of classical antiquity that set the standard.

Herder is a key figure here. He treated myth as something that bound together the language, literature, customs, and religion of the classical world into a coherent whole. The contrast was between the beauty and the public nature of Greek religion, and the hieratic and divided Christian churches.[3] Unlike stadial theories that saw development in largely teleological terms, where the interest in the "primitive" was confined to where it led, Herder (like Vico) viewed the early stages of human history as its most aesthetically vital and religiously creative, becoming progressively debased as civilization and luxury came to predominate. Primitive language, in particular, had a richness lacking in modern forms, and Herder's pressing task was to recapture the vitality of the language of ancient fables, which dated from the time of creation and as a consequence reflected humanity's relation to the natural and human realms in a pure and fertile fashion.

Aesthetics played a crucial role in shaping Herder's anthropology. His concern with language was above all with a means of expression, rather than simply a means of representation, and it was in large part aesthetically motivated. This aesthetic concern is immediately evident in his anthropology, for, in the practical realm, philosophical anthropology was directed towards *Bildung*, the cultivation of character.[4] Herder's conception of the cultivation of character was one based on an aesthetic model, as opposed to the traditional religious, metaphysical, or humanist models, or the newer socio-political and medical ones.

Some of the more significant features of Herder's understanding of the shaping of character can best be seen by contrast with a more traditional view, which goes back to Aristotle. Like Aristotle, Herder thinks of life in terms of the realization of purpose, but whereas the Aristotelian conception fostered an idea of this realization as establishing an order and harmony which is constantly threatened by disorder and disharmony, Herder thinks of it in terms of a force or striving against a world that opposes and would seek to shape one to its own ends. So far, this sounds very much like Spinoza, and

---

[3] George S. Williamson, *The Longing for Myth in Germany. Religion and Aesthetic Culture from Romanticism to Nietzsche* (Chicago: University of Chicago Press, 2004), 9.
[4] In the tradition of German classical philology clear classical precedents for this could be identified. See, for example, Werner Jaeger, *Paideia: The Ideals of Greek Culture* (3 vols., Oxford: Oxford University Press, 1939-1945).

Herder was indeed influenced by the revival of Spinozism. There are however two significant features of Herder's account which marked it out from Spinoza's. The first is the view that one's ends are not perspicacious in their own right. They are not accessible simply through introspection. The attempt to realize these ends is a crucial part of understanding them, for struggling to realize one's ends is a way of clarifying just what those ends are: it is through action that we come to know ourselves. As Charles Taylor puts it: "man comes to know himself by expressing and hence clarifying what he is and recognizing himself in his expression. The specific property of human life is to culminate in self-awareness through expression".[5] Second, one does not act in the abstract, but rather in a particular historical context, which shapes what one can do and how. This may resist one in various ways, a resistance that one can strive to overcome, or it may offer paths by which one can come to know oneself. Whichever it is, we are always acting within a particular cultural context – typified in some respects by one's language – and within a particular type of physical context. In short, to the extent to which we come to discover and realize our purposes, that is, come to know ourselves, this is never *ab initio*, but always using the resources of a particular culture.

Bildung is, however, not just a matter of self-expression, but above all a question of moral striving. Moral striving as a feature of self-expression is a central theme in German thought from Lessing onwards. Lessing himself sums up the idea in terms of truth:

> The true value of a man is not determined by whether, in reality or not, he possesses the truth, but rather by his sincere striving to reach the truth. It is not possession of the truth, but rather the pursuit of truth that allows him to extend his powers, and in which his constantly increasing capacity for perfection is to be found.[6]

The idea of striving became reinforced in the 1790s when many philosophers, dramatists, and others took up Kant's idea of freedom as radical self-determination by the rational will. This complemented the idea, broadly shared, of one's responsibility for one's own inner development. No external factor, not even God, could constrain our freedom. This equation of

---

[5] Charles Taylor, *Hegel* (Cambridge: Cambridge University Press, 1975), 17. Taylor sees a central connection between Herder's expressivism and Hegelian idealism, but this is questionable: see Michael Rosen, *Hegel's Dialectic and its Criticism* (Cambridge: Cambridge University Press, 1982), 122-143.

[6] *Anti-Goetze: Eine Duplik* (1778) in: Gotthold Ephraim Lessing, *Werke* ed. H. G. Gölpert et al (8 vols., Berlin, 1978), viii, 32. As Nietzsche commented: "Therefore Lessing, that most honest thinker, dared to announce that he cared more for the search after truth than for truth itself": Friedrich Nietzsche, *Die Geburt der Tragödie aus dem Geiste der Musik* (Leipzig, 1872), §15.

one's moral life with absolute freedom will play an especially significant role in the development of German idealism, but it was also crucial as a complement to the notion of cultural self-expression, for which freedom of self-determination was a core objective.

Note however that the idea of "moral striving" was a general one at the time, and not restricted to those who were to follow the Kantian path. Goethe for example had no place for the Kantian conception of absolute freedom and its associated notion of radical subjectivity. He had worked closely with Herder in the 1780s, and was particularly concerned with the idea of *Bildung*, philosophically but also in a literary context: his novel *Wilhelm Meister* was the first *Bildungsroman*, setting a model for the subsequent development of German literature.[7] Moral striving is as crucial to Goethe's idea of *Bildung* as it was to those who construed this striving in Kantian terms. Of the more explicitly philosophical accounts of how one should attempt to achieve self-understanding, however, the most influential was one that attempted to integrate the Kantian conception of morality and freedom into a picture of self-expression drawn from Herder and Goethe. This was Schiller's "on the aesthetic education of man". Schiller departs from Kant on a number of questions, and the most important for our purposes hinge on the problem of moral agency.[8] First, he argues that moral worth springs not just from the agent's intention, as Kant had argued in the 1780s, but that it is also necessary that the intention derive from the moral character of the agent. It is this that makes the formation of character the central concern of his anthropology. Second, freedom for Schiller is an autonomous development not just of reason but of reason and sensibility. In contrast to Kant, freedom could not be a matter of reason alone. Third, moral agency is something which is shaped by history and sensibility, rather than just being a product of reason, insulated from the natural world. In these respects, Schiller is far closer to Herder than to Kant.

The centrality of an *aesthetic* education to Schiller's anthropology is due to his conception of beauty as reconciling the two natures of human beings: sensibility and rationality, what in Kant are respectively our sensory receptive powers and our spontaneity, and what in Letter X of *On the Aesthetic Education* take on a moral tone:

---

[7] See William H. Bruford, *Culture and Society in Classical Weimar, 1755-1806* (Cambridge: Cambridge University Press, 1962).
[8] I take the following summary points from Frederick C. Beiser, *Schiller as a Philosopher: A Re-Examination* (Oxford: Oxford University Press, 2005), 3-4. Beiser develops them in detail in the course of the book.

> So you are at one with me about this, and are convinced … that man can be drawn aside from his destiny in two opposite ways, that our age is actually travelling along both these false roads, and has fallen prey to coarseness on the one hand, and to enervation and perversity on the other. From this twofold straying it must be brought back by means of Beauty.[9]

It is in aesthetic perception that we ultimately discover our unity and integrity.[10] The significance of this cannot be over-estimated. For Schiller, life has an aesthetic dimension that is crucial to our understanding of who we are, just as his predecessors and contemporaries had considered that life has a religious dimension that is crucial to our understanding of who we are. What Schiller is proposing is in effect a replacement of a religious by an aesthetic model of human development.

In Letter X, after proposing aesthetics as the solution to reconciling sensibility and reason, Schiller asks how it can achieve this, and the remainder of the essay is devoted to this question. Actually, there are two questions: how human nature can realize itself only as beauty, and – what he calls a brief excursion into the realm of speculation – what effect the different kinds of beauty have in developing the ideal human being. In the first, art is treated as a means to an end, whereas in the second it is treated as an end in itself.[11] Schiller's aim is to establish systematic connections between the two, building up a general account of the necessity for aesthetic education.

It is classical antiquity that provides his starting point:

> The Greeks put us to shame not only by the simplicity to which our age is a stranger; they are at the same time our rivals, indeed often our models, in those very excellences with which we are wont to console ourselves for the unnaturalness of our manners. In fullness of form no less than of content, at once philosophic and creative, sensitive and energetic, the Greeks combined the first youth of imagination with the manhood of reason in a glorious manifestation of beauty. At that first fair awakening of the powers of the mind, sense and intellect did not as yet rule over strictly separate domains.[12]

---

[9] Friedrich Schiller, *On the Aesthetic Education of Man, in a Series of Letters*, ed. and trans. Elizabeth Wilkinson and L. A. Willoughby (Oxford: Clarendon Press, 1967), 63. This edition contains facing German text and translation.

[10] Cf. the other two landmark defences of art as a means of overcoming the fragmentation of humanity: "Jean Paul" [Friedrich Richter], *Vorschule der Aesthetik* (Hamburg, 1804); and Samuel Taylor Coleridge, *Biographia Literaria, or Biographical Sketches of My Literary Life and Opinions* (2 vols., London, 1817).

[11] See Beiser, *Schiller as Philosopher*, 135-168.

[12] Schiller, *On the Aesthetic Education of Man*, 31. Goethe shared this view: see Humphry Trevelyan, *Goethe and the Greeks* (Cambridge, 1941). This was to be an assessment of the Greeks that shaped the German educational system. As Lionel Gossman notes: "To the generation of [Wilhelm] Humboldt the study of antiquity was no narrow technical or scholarly exercise: it was conceived as an essential stage in the education of German youth and in the transformation and reconstruction of the German

In the classical times, there was a harmony of reason and sensibility, because the artist was still in unity with nature. The correspondence between thought and feeling has been lost in the modern age, however, so has to be re-established, albeit in a way that surpasses its original unreflective naive form, for it is now something that exists not inside oneself but outside, in the form of an idea that one strives to realize.[13] In classical antiquity, there was no specialization of knowledge, whereas in the modern era there are "whole classes of men developing but one part of their potentialities".[14] With the division of labour, not only a fragmentation of skills, but a fragmentation of the human being arose. This is associated by Schiller with a number of dysfunctions of the modern age.[15] The first is the rigorous separation of ranks and occupations.[16] Second, there is a set of connected fragmentations:

> That zoophyte character of the Greek States, in which every individual enjoyed an independent existence but could, where need arose, grow into the whole organism, now made way for an ingenious clock-work, in which, out of the piecing together of innumerable but lifeless parts, a mechanical kind of collective life ensued. State and Church, laws and customs, were now turned asunder; enjoyment was divorced from labour, the means from the end, the effort from the reward.[17]

The separation of enjoyment from labour, and of means from ends, are the crucial forms of fragmentation here as far as *Bildung* is concerned. Third, one's activity or labour or occupation no longer expresses one's humanity: instead, one merely becomes defined by one's occupation. It is true that the "outstanding individual will never let the limits of his occupation dictate the limits of his activity", but this is unavoidable in the usual case.[18] Finally, the state becomes alien to its citizens.[19]

Reconciliation of reason and sensibility cannot occur under these conditions. One's activity *(Tätigkeit)* is what constitutes one and defines what one is, so that when, as a result of the division of labour for example, this activity becomes mere toil *(Arbeit)*, when it results in a fragmentation of

---

nation; and for this reason it was built into the new educational system that Humboldt and his collaborators devised for the new Prussia." *Orpheus Philologus: Bachofen versus Mommsen on the Study of Antiquity*. (Transactions of the American Philosophical Society, vol. 73 no. 5, 1-89, Philadelphia, 1983), 76-77.

[13] See Philip J. Kain, *Schiller, Hegel, and Marx: State, Society, and the Aesthetic Ideal of Ancient Greece* (Kingston: McGill-Queen's University Press, 1982), 15-19.

[14] Schiller, *On the Aesthetic Education of Man*, 33.

[15] See the discussion in Kain, *Schiller, Hegel, and Marx*, ch. 1.

[16] Schiller, *On the Aesthetic Education of Man*, 33.

[17] *Ibid.*, 35.

[18] *Ibid.*, 37.

[19] *Ibid.*, 37.

oneself rather than in a unification, then it must be transformed. The model for this transformation is artistic production. This is because, in the case of artistic labour, we can see most clearly how labour could, in changed circumstances, be pleasurable and, above all, genuinely fulfilling. On the conception of self-knowledge that Schiller is offering, one comes to know oneself not introspectively, for "man without perception or sensations is nothing but form and empty potential"[20]; prior to one's doing anything there can be no self-knowledge because there is simply nothing to know about oneself. Rather, one comes to understand oneself through what one has produced. The paradigm form of expression here is artistic production, which for Schiller is unique among forms of production because the product is not alienable in the way that other products are.

The aesthetic model for a philosophical anthropology was to prove exceptionally fruitful in nineteenth- and twentieth-century culture. But it was always fraught with danger. Among the many variants, two different developments bring to light an inherent tension in the model, one jettisoning the idea of the uniqueness of artistic production, the other effectively aestheticizing life as a whole.

The first route was that followed most influentially by Marx in the 1840s.[21] Marx rejected the idea that artistic production is wholly distinct from other forms of production. It is not a non-alienated area outside normal production, but as subject to alienation as any other form of production. The aesthetic aspects of his conception are manifest in his statements about labour under socialism in his comments on Mill's political economy:

> In my *production* I would have objectified my *individuality*, its specific *character*, and therefore enjoyed not only an individual *manifestation of my life* during the activity, but also when looking at the object I would have the individual pleasure of knowing my personality to be *objective*, visible to the senses and hence a power *beyond all doubt*.... My work would be a *free manifestation of life*, hence an *enjoyment of life*.[22]

---

[20] *Ibid.*, 77. Compare the way Fichte, in his *Grundlage der gesamten Wissenschaftslehre* of 1794, combines, in his inimitably uncompromising way, a distinctively Herderian view of what is distinctive about humans with a Kantian conception of radical freedom, to produce a view that goes beyond either of them when he writes that "All animals are perfect and complete: man however, is merely suggested.... Every animal is what it is; man alone is originally nothing at all": Johann Gottlieb Fichte, *The Science of Rights*, trans. A. E. Kroeger (New York, 1889), 118-119.

[21] See the discussion in Stephen Gaukroger, "Romanticism and Decommodification: Marx's Conception of Socialism" in *Economy and Society*, Volume 15, Issue 3, 1986.

[22] Karl Marx and Friedrich Engels, *Werke* (43 vols., Berlin, 1956-1968), Ergänzungsband i (= vol. 42), 462-463; Karl Marx and Friedrich Engels, *Collected Works* (50 vols., London and New York, 1975-2005), iii, 227-228.

For Marx the alienation of labour was at the basis of all other forms of alienation, and with the overcoming of alienated labour all other forms of alienation would be overcome. But the aesthetic/anthropological model (one that Marx gradually moved away from, it should be said), rather than providing a goal for politics in fact leads to a disconnection from politics. We are not being given an account of how social and political problems are to be recognised, or to be posed, or the mechanisms by which we might hope to resolve them. Rather, what we are presented with is a picture of a state of affairs in which there are effectively no social problems: if there is no alienation from nature, oneself, the human species and others, then we effectively have an end of politics.

The second route, by contrast, celebrated what it took to be the liberation from politics offered by an aesthetically-modelled anthropology. It led to the valuing of cultural achievement over everything else, as it became a substitute for religion and politics. This was primarily a German phenomenon, and it led in different directions. On the one hand, the cosmopolitan nature of culture was attractive to assimilated German Jews, who, cut off from their own religious tradition but denied full participation in civic life, embraced and immersed themselves in Germany's cultural life, and were able to forge an identity for themselves independently of national politics.[23] On the other hand, it also led to a scorn for politics among intellectuals and artists, and, in the Nazi era, a substitution of culture for politics, or even an apolitical aestheticization of Nazism.[24] But although these developments are most clearly seen in Germany, they are also evident elsewhere. In Britain from the late eighteenth century, for example, German philosophical anthropology was seen by Coleridge and his circle as something purely intellectual, unconnected with any political programme, and consequently something that freed one from deciding between French revolutionary thought, with its materialism, and British reaction. It offered a politically neutral mode of engaging with the world. As Mike Jay remarks of the British reception of German idealism, "the Kantian philosophies were revolutionary, but it was a revolution that pointed the way to inner freedoms and the primacy of the life of the mind in

---

[23] Cassirer is a good case in point. See Edward Skidelsky, *Ernst Cassirer: The Last Philosopher of Culture* (Princeton: Princeton University Press, 2008). See also Ned Curthoys, "Redescribing the Enlightenment: The German-Jewish Adoption of *Bildung* as a Counter-Normative Ideal", *Intellectual History Review* 23 (2013), 365-386.

[24] See Edith May Butler, *The Tyranny of Greece over Germany* (Cambridge: Cambridge University Press, 1935); and Wolf Lepenies, *The Seduction of Culture in German History* (Princeton: Princeton University Press, 2006). See also, specifically on how this culture bore on the pursuit of science, the area with the most dangerous consequences: Alan D. Beyerchen, *Scientists under Hitler: Politics and the Physics Community in the Third Reich* (New Haven: Yale University Press, 1977); and Philip Ball, *Serving the Reich: The Struggle for the Soul of Physics under Hitler* (Chicago: University of Chicago Press, 2013).

forms that could evolve under the political lockdown of the absolutist Prussian state".[25]

The problematic standing of philosophical anthropology with regard to political questions was one of its most problematic aspects, either because, in the one case, it failed to yield the political understanding to which it aspired through its programme of uncovering how one discovered one's humanity; or because, in the other, its celebration of liberation from politics was itself in many cases a taking of a political stance. Nevertheless, despite this it offered powerful new understandings that shaped nineteenth- and twentieth-century views of how one might come to terms with the human condition. Philosophical anthropology, in the form that it came to take in Herder and Schiller and their successors, was, of all the forms of naturalization of the human, the only one to offer a plausible secular world-view on a par with the Christian one, and the only one in a position to displace the Christian one. Its power lay in its ability to replace a Christian world-view with something that was not merely non-reductionist, by contrast with the programmes of the *philosophes* for example, but more importantly was able to bear the weight of the non-propositional forms of engaging with the world: in terms of aspirations, goals, and desires, as well as fears and anxieties. It was able to do this because it provided the basis for a programme of naturalization of a range of human aspirations, including the rich dimension of human experience that had been articulated in a mythical or religious form. It encountered deep and in some cases insurmountable problems. But these were above all an indication not only of its ambition, but also of its refusal simply to reduce or ignore features of human experience that appeared to offer resistance to the direction of its enquiry.

---

[25] Mike Jay, *The Atmosphere of Heaven: The Unnatural Experiments of Dr Beddoes and His Sons of Genius* (New Haven: Yale University Press 2009), 193-194.

Do Not Forget: Memory and Moral Obligation in *Little Dorrit*

Jennifer Gribble

Enclosed within the outer case of an old-fashioned gold watch, a silk watch-paper embroidered with the initials "D.N.F" carries to Arthur Clennam's mother from his dying father a reminder of obligations variously interpreted by the characters in *Little Dorrit*, Dickens's novel of 1857. It is a palpable image of memory's housing in time, of the spatial and temporal dimensions across which memory travels, and of the histories and psychologies it holds in connection from time past and into the future of a legally-binding intent. It raises questions about "the duty of memory" that preoccupy contemporary cultural narrative.[1]

The embroidered letters signify a plot of such labyrinthine Gothic complication that successive Penguin editors have felt obliged to provide a summary. I quote, selectively, from John Holloway's "The Denouement of *Little Dorrit*", Appendix A in Stephen Wall's and Helen Small's 1998 Penguin edition:

> Many years ago, a Mr Gilbert Clennam put forward his orphan nephew (Arthur's father) as a husband for the Mrs Clennam in the story. They were married. Later, this Mrs Clennam discovered that her husband had already gone through a form of marriage with another woman, who had borne him a son. Mrs Clennam, a woman of vindictively self-righteous religiosity, demanded that the child (Arthur) be given into her custody: if not, she would expose her husband, and bring it about that his uncle would cut off his financial support. She got her way, taking possession of the child Arthur, while his true mother went mad and died, and his father went abroad and later died too.

---

[1] For a useful overview of the "turn to memory" in recent academic studies and in the framing of public policy, nationally and internationally, see Matthew Graves and Elizabeth Rechniewski, "From Collective Memory to Transcultural Remembrance", in *Journal of Multidisciplinary International Studies*, Vol. 7, no.1, January 2010. For local debate, see Stephanie Dowrick's discussion of mercy in relation to the "eye-for-an-eye" morality reflected in Indonesia's decision to exact the death penalty for two of the "Bali Nine" drug smugglers. She quotes Archbishop Desmond Tutu: "Forgiving is not forgetting…. It is actually remembering – remembering and not using your right to hit back. It is a second chance for a new beginning". It is also, Dowrick comments, "freedom at its most convincing" (*The Sydney Morning Herald,* 24 February, 2015), 16.

Meanwhile, Gilbert Clennam has heard of the existence of Arthur's true mother; but all he has heard is that she was a girl whom his nephew had loved, but had abandoned in order to marry as his uncle had wished, and that she had subsequently gone mad and died. He felt remorse at this, and as a kind of recompense has left, in a codicil to his will, a thousand guineas *to the youngest daughter of the man who had at one time acted as patron to this girl* (i.e. Arthur's true mother); or, if that man had no daughter, *to his brother's youngest daughter*....

But: Arthur's father had dictated the codicil making this change in his will, to Mrs Clennam; and it had been witnessed by herself and Jeremiah Flintwinch. Mrs Clennam, however, had concealed the codicil, hiding it in her house in a place which she alone knew. But then she became paralysed and could not get at it. Later the prospect of Arthur's home-coming from his many years in China made her uneasy: she saw that he might find the paper she had hidden. Therefore, on the very day of his return, she at last revealed the hiding place to Flintwinch, and told him to locate the paper and destroy it. But he did not destroy it. Instead, he gave it, with other papers (old letters, in fact, written by Arthur's true mother during her madness), in an old iron box, to his twin brother Ephraim Flintwinch, who was at that time staying in the house.... Ephraim Flintwinch later resided in Antwerp ... Rigaud/Blandois became one of his drinking cronies there, and when he died ... got possession of the box and so of the suppressed codicil, and was therefore in a position to attempt to blackmail Mrs Clennam as she had blackmailed her husband and Arthur's mother so long ago.[2]

The plot has still further intricacies. Holloway, focussing on Book the Second, Chapters XXX-XXXI, does not mention that the letters D.N.F have been embroidered by Arthur's birth mother as a reminder to his father of the love that has bound them, formalized in their unspecified form of marriage. Nor does he mention that the iron box, travelling from London to Antwerp and back to London via Calais, containing the original documents (as distinct from the copies made by Rigaud), passes through the hands of Miss Wade and then of Tattycoram, who delivers it to Mr Meagles who entrusts it to Amy Dorrit to return to Arthur. Amy resolves to let Arthur know all that is of import to himself, but to keep her own part of it from him: "that was all past, all forgiven, all forgotten" (2:XXXIII, 773). The relationship between forgiveness, forgetting, and remembering, lies at the heart of the novel's exploration of debt, imprisonment and atonement.

Holloway's summary does disclose, and with obvious relish, the Gothic bones of the plot and the melodramatic conventions on which it relies: "she got her way", "went mad and died", "on the very day of his return", "but he

---

[2] John Holloway, "The Denouement of *Little Dorrit*", in Charles Dickens, *Little Dorrit*, eds. Stephen Wall and Helen Small (Harmondsworth: Penguin, 1998), 189-190. All subsequent quotations from the novel will refer to this edition.

did not destroy it", "hiding it in a secret place which she alone knew", etc. We scarcely need to be reminded that Dickens was an avid reader of the Gothic novel from his boyhood, and that his close friend and collaborator in the 1850s was Wilkie Collins. The House of Clennam in its London headquarters is one of Dickens's most memorable distillations of the Gothic: a place of whisperings and strange noises; of ghostly apparitions in the chiaroscuro of flickering and guttering candles or pitch darkness; of secret spaces; stories within stories and containment within containment. The old letters in the iron box contain the pleas of a persecuted woman driven to madness by irremediable loss and solitary confinement. There are doubles (the Flintwinch twins), mysteries, repressions. All-pervasive is the story of inherited guilt recorded in the codicil, with its power to blight or to free its beneficiaries.[3] What Holloway's summary further makes clear is the elaborate contrivance that positions Amy Dorrit, at her triple remove as youngest daughter of the brother of Arthur's mother's youthful patron, as the codicil's surviving legatee. The complicated design Dickens has set himself is recorded in the number plans for Book the First, Chapters XIX and XX, in his retrospective and prospective "mems for working the story round" in the second of the Penguin edition appendices, Appendix B: the Number Plans (828-9). The melodramatically emblazoned injunction "Do Not Forget" is a reminder of how adroitly Dickens deploys popular generic conventions in pursuit of psychological and moral enquiry.

Memory plays a crucial role in this novel not only as legal obligation, but also in its psychological dimensions. The operations of memory are dramatized by an extensive cast of "fellow-travellers" within the apparent freedoms and confinements through which they travel. Miss Wade's early assertion that the prisoner cannot forgive his prison foreshadows a history and a point of view that will provide a continuing contrast with that of Amy Dorrit, albeit not the simply tendentious contrast upheld by Mr Meagles for the rebellious Tattycoram. Yet Amy's belief that the past can and should be "all forgiven, all forgotten" raises questions about what can, or should be, remembered. Dickens, remembering, suppressing, and constantly rewriting his own back-story, is self-consciously preoccupied by the work of memory as early as *Oliver Twist* (1838).[4] His Wordsworthian belief that the reclamation of primal memory is essential to psychic health flowers again as Amy Dorrit reads to Arthur Clennam in the Marshalsea, giving him access to the lost maternal presence of his infancy. In his treatment of the nervous disorder of Augusta de la Rue, in 1845, Dickens drew on contemporary theories of spectral illusion as "ideas or recollected images of the mind", as well as on

---

[3] See Randolph Splitter, "Guilt and the Trappings of Melodrama in *Little Dorrit*," in *Dickens Studies Annual*, 1977, 119-133.

[4] As Rosemarie Bodenheimer, *The Politics of Story* (Ithaca: Cornell University Press, 2000), 113, argues.

mesmeric techniques designed to access them.[5] The various accounts of the plot of the suppressed codicil, by Affery and Jeremiah Flintwinch, Rigaud, Arthur and Mrs Clennam, show Dickens well aware of the distinction drawn by Frances Power Cobbe in the 1860s, between "what is available for recall and retelling", shaped as it is by the biases and imperfect recall of the teller, and "that which lies inaccessible and unpossessed".[6]

For Dickens, however, the admonition "Do Not Forget" has an overarching ethical, and indeed, theological resonance. The Bible provides the ground on which he stands to appeal, and, by the time of *Dombey and Son* (1847), with increased urgency, to the conscience of "a Christian people ... owing one duty to the Father of one family, and tending to one common end, to make the world a better place".[7] This "duty of memory" reiterates the continuing call, in both the Old Testament and the New, to remember God's Covenant with humankind. The Judeo-Christian grand narrative of Creation, Fall, Incarnation, Redemption and Resurrection, is invoked in Dickens's novels through dense networks of biblical allusion.[8] In *Little Dorrit* he situates the history of the House of Clennam, as it emerges in eye-witness accounts, documents, conjectures and partial recollections, within the highly-contested history represented for his contemporaries in the Bible. "Set the [Old Testament] darkness and vengeance against the New Testament" is the intention noted in the number plans (833). And although the novel vigorously upholds the "Spirit" of the Gospel against Mosaic "Law", it draws on the legal terminology of will and codicil as St Paul does, to suggest how the Testator's covenant may be "added to" in the light of the fulfilment embodied in the promised Messiah.[9] Gilbert Clennam's codicil is, by turns, a metaphor for inherited guilt, for redemption of the past, for reparation for sin, and for the role played by memory in relation to the Old and New Covenants. Contending mid-Victorian scriptural interpretations shape the novel's discussion of original sin, predestination, and anamnesis.[10]

---

[5] See Louise Henson, "Investigations and fictions: Charles Dickens and ghosts," in *The Victorian Supernatural*, eds. Nicola Bown, Carolyn Burdett and Pamela Thurschwell (Cambridge: Cambridge University Press, 2004).

[6] Frances Power Cobbe, "The fallacies of memory" (1866), quoted in Jill Matus, *Shock, Memory and the Unconscious in Victorian Fiction* (Cambridge: Cambridge University Press, 2011), 92.

[7] Charles Dickens, *Dombey and Son*, ed. Dennis Walder (Oxford: Oxford University Press, 2000), 685.

[8] Janet Larson, *Dickens and the Broken Scripture* (Athens: University of Georgia Press, 1985), 3, draws attention to an impressive range of such allusions. In keeping with her deconstructionist argument, however, she finds the Bible not a source of "stable values" for Dickens, but a "locus of hermeneutic instability reflecting the changed status of the Bible in his time".

[9] See Galatians 3:15-29. Paul argues that just as in "the manner of men" (by which he means the still-prevailing Roman Law) a man could make a will and then add codicils, so Mosaic law may be seen as a codicil to the covenant made with Abraham and his seed, and "the coming of Christ" as the subsequent fulfilment of the promises of God.

[10] The element in the Eucharist which corresponds to the "remembering" aspect of the Last Supper: "Do this in remembrance of me" (Luke 22:19). Julie Gittoes, *Anamnesis and the Eucharist:*

In *Dombey and Son* the falling house of New Testament parable provides an image of the material and moral decay and final collapse of Dombey's house under its burden of familial and commercial aspiration.[11] In *Little Dorrit*, "there is something wrong in the gloomy house" of Clennam, as the old servant Affery knows. If Dickens exploits his Gothic conventions to give material representation to what that wrong is, he locates its psychological and ethical significance in the memories of its inhabitants. It is through what they have seen, can remember, can name and interpret, that he sustains the slow release of his mystery plot. The biblically-derived binaries that structure the novel, Poverty/Riches, Sunshine/Shadow,[12] lend themselves to a play of light and darkness, of eyes shut and eyes open, acted out in the borderland between sleep and waking, dream and actuality. These manifestations of a haunting past are exemplified from the outset in the confused consciousness of Affery, imprisoned in the Punch-and-Judy show of her enforced marriage to Jeremiah Flintwinch, factotum of the House of Clennam. Her "dreams" of the transference of the iron box, and her "memories" of Arthur's mother as the unseen presence who haunts the house, take on the authenticity of record when Mrs Clennam, Jeremiah Flintwinch and Riguad give their accounts of the codicil's history. The unexplained whisperings and rustlings Affery hears are finally confirmed as portents of the literal collapse of the house "with a sudden noise like thunder" (2:XXI, 757).[13]

Arthur, too, returning from his long exile with his father in the House of Clennam's China branch, knows that there is something wrong in the gloomy London house. The memories that reside in the objects and spaces he reinhabits in Book the First, Chapter III, locate clues to that wrong in the evangelical regimen of "wholesome repression", commended by Mrs Clennam. The "Home" to which he returns is associated with "the dim streets" in which it is set, "all depositories of oppressive secrets…. At the heart of it his mother presided, inflexible of face, indomitable of will, firmly

---

Contemporary Anglican Approaches (Aldershot: Ashgate, 2008), discusses the historic difficulties of precisely translating and interpreting these words.

[11] See Matthew 7: 27: "And the rain descended and the floods came, and the winds blew, and beat upon that house; and it fell: and great was the fall of it." The parable of the house built on shifting sands, in Matthew 7:24-27, concludes the Sermon on the Mount (a seed-bed for Dickens's biblical allusions and a continuing guide to his theological reflection). The version in Luke 6: 46-49, in the Sermon on the Plain, contains less of the nautical imagery that pervades *Dombey and Son* but is even more graphic in the connection it makes between ignoring the sayings of Christ and "the ruin" of the house.

[12] The parable of the Camel and the Needle's eye (Matthew 19:23-26; Mark 24-27; Luke; 24-27) underlies Dickens's satire of the Gospel of Mammonism and is inherent in the contrasting explorations of the novel's two Books. The novel's light and darkness imagery is associated with the doing of evil and the coming to light of the truth (see John 3:20-21).

[13] As Wall and Small note, such calamities were not unknown. They cite *The Times*, 4 September, 1856, 888, describing the collapse of a house close to the area in which Mrs Clennam's house is situated.

holding all the secrets of her own and his father's life, and austerely opposing herself, front to front, to the great final secret of all life" (1:X,520). Caught between crippling memory and the secrecy represented in the House of Clennam's erasure of memory, Arthur begins to find his own "will" by re-reading the past as a way of making reparation for it. He links the business practices of the House of Clennam, "grasping at money and driving hard bargains" with the unknown wrong, and reads his mother's long self-imposed imprisonment in her gloomy chamber as some kind of atonement characteristic of her "balancing her account with the Majesty of Heaven" (1:V, 60). But it is the memory of his father's eyes "looking at his son as they had looked when life departed from them" that "seemed to urge him awfully to the task he had attempted" (1:V,65). "Remember" … "remember" … "remember" (1:V, 58), he begs his mother, as though reiterating the word might prompt her to recall or divulge the purport of his father's transmission of the letters "D.N.F." "as a token you would understand" (1:V, 59). The allusion to Hamlet's task links the "duty of memory" bequeathed by Arthur's father with some undeclared foul deed and with Arthur's own deep-seated malaise. "Haunted by a suspicion" that "someone may have been grievously deceived, injured, ruined" (1:V, 59), Arthur himself, go-between and reminder of parental sin, has always shared its burden. Conjecturing that his mother's employment of Amy Dorrit might reflect some undivulged obligation, he pursues the hidden story by seeking out the little seamstress. Visiting the Dorrit family in the Marshalsea prison, and inadvertently shut in for the night, he is forced imaginatively to experience their interminable incarceration, and to link it with his mother's. As he lies between dream and waking, indelible memory feeds his moral imagination, the recollection of three people making a picture in his mind: "his father, with the steadfast look with which he had died … his mother, with her arm up, warding off suspicion; Little Dorrit, with her hand on the degraded arm" of her father. He thinks he hears his mother voicing some version of the truth of that degradation: "He withers away in his prison; I wither away in mine; inexorable justice is done. What do I owe on this score!" (1: VIII, 96)

The meaning of the enigmatic "D.N.F." begins to unfold when Mrs Clennam presents her memories of the codicil story in Chapter XXX of Book 2. As eye-witness, signatory, and suppressor of the deed, she has believed herself as much in control of its outcomes as she is of her memories. In response to Rigaud's candid summary of that hidden history, and Jeremiah's hostile account of her obduracy in relation to the document, she is blackmailed into a defence of her motives that earns the jeers of both conspirators. Dickens is on familiar ground in contesting the evangelical theology on which her claim to moral authority depends. Like Miss Barbary in *Bleak House* (1853), Mrs Clennam represents everything Dickens abhors in the narrowly Calvinist interpretation of the doctrine of original sin. And like

Miss Barbary, Mrs Clennam will be struck down and forever silenced for her sacrilege by authorial fiat. Like Esther Summerson, Arthur has the sins of the parents visited on his innocent head by a surrogate maternal authority who sees herself vindicated by her reading of the Bible: "'I was stern with him, knowing that the transgressions of the parents are visited on their offspring, and that there was an angry mark upon him from his birth'" (2: XXXI, 754). Contemporary evangelicalism's belief in infant depravity as the inescapable inheritance of the Fall finds corroboration in her appeal to an implacable God.[14] In addition, Arthur, like Esther, is made to suffer the consequences of his birth mother's sexual "fall". Mrs Clennam contrives to make mother, father, and child, instruments of mutual punishment: "'If the presence of Arthur was a daily reproach to his father, and if the absence of Arthur was a daily agony to his mother, that was the just dispensation of Jehovah. As well might it be charged upon me that the stings of an awakened conscience drove her mad, and that it was the will of the disposer of all things that she should live so, many years. I devoted myself to reclaim the otherwise predestined and lost boy; to give him the reputation of an honest origin; to bring him up in fear and trembling, and in a life of practical contrition for the sins that were heavy on his head before his entrance into this condemned world'" (2, XXX, 742). The tacit reference to Millais' painting of 1853, "The Awakening Conscience", underlines the ignominy of the "fallen woman" as a culturally-apposite image of the Fall, while the phrase "fear and trembling" provides biblical sanction for her shunning.[15]

A dramatic and theological connection is made, then, between Mrs Clennam's reading of the Bible and her reading of the codicil, suggesting that both readings are solipsistic, self-justifying, and inimical to the intentions of the framer. Her non-compliance with the legally-binding intent signified in "D.N.F" is justified by her appeal to the authority of the Bible. "'I do NOT forget, even though I do not read it as he did. I read in it, that I was appointed to do these things'" (2, XXX, 740). She acts as self-appointed scourge of a God who requires propitiation for human sinfulness: "'Do Not Forget'. It spoke to me like a voice from an angry cloud. Do not forget the

---

[14] See Exodus 20:5: "I the Lord thy God am a jealous God, visiting the iniquity of the fathers upon the children unto the third and fourth generation of them that hate me." Mrs Clennam's reference to an "angry mark" alludes to the entry of sin into the post-lapsarian world, told in the story of Cain's killing of his brother Abel, in which God's cursing of Cain is signified by the mark set upon him. See Genesis 4: 1-15.

[15] See Philippians 2:12: "Wherefore, my beloved, as ye have always obeyed, not as in my presence only, but now how much more in my absence, work out your own salvation with fear and trembling." In view of the "sacrifice" of young Arthur to Mrs Clennam's religious beliefs there is perhaps a reference here to Kierkegaard's discussion of Abraham's sacrifice of Isaac, in *Fear and Trembling* (1843). Although not translated into English until 1916, the work may well have been known to Dickens through his friendship at this time with Hans Christian Anderson.

deadly sin, do not forget the appointed discovery, do not forget the appointed suffering. I did not forget. Was it my own wrong I remembered? Mine! I was but a servant and a minister'" (2, XXX, 740). There is a gloating satisfaction in the effects of her punitive actions: "'They did *not* forget. It is appointed against such offences that the offenders shall not be able to forget'" (2, XXX, 742).

"Forgive us our debts, as we forgive our debtors, was a prayer too poor in spirit for her. Smite thou my debtors, Lord, wither them, crush them … this was the impious tower of stone she built up to scale Heaven" (1: v, 57), we are told by a narrative persona declaring himself in terms of the Lord's Prayer, as against Old Testament vengeance against the sinner.[16] If there is a case for forgiving Mrs Clennam, Dickens makes it in the account she gives of her own narrow evangelical upbringing: "the corruption of our hearts, the evil of our ways, the curse that is upon us, the terrors that surround us – these were the themes of my childhood" (2, XXX, 739). Holloway's description of her as "a woman of vindictively self-righteous religiosity" (789) simplifies her complex motivations. Underlying the cruelty of her response it is possible to detect the trauma of her discovery of the secret "marriage", and the genuine grievance that she herself has been deceived into a marriage based on a lie. What is "due" to her and what is owing to a wrathful Jehovah are barely distinguishable, however: she has her own score to settle, as well as the Almighty's. Residual guilt, self-defensiveness, religious cant, sexual humiliation and defeated maternal longings contend within her.

As Arthur has intuited, her self-imposed imprisonment acknowledges the need to make atonement for her own sins. Arthur's imprisonment for debt, following his failed business speculation, and Amy's return to care for him, in her father's old room, in her old prison clothes, more than symbolically reverses the Poverty/Riches divisions that have made obstacles for their love. Each is enabled to be the other's reparation for the sufferings they have endured as a direct consequence of Mrs Clennam's failure to honour moral obligations. When Mrs Clennam breaks out of her "cell of years", in a wild flight to the Marshalsea, her immediate purpose is self-protective: to recover the package containing the codicil and the letters of Arthur's mother left by

---

[16] Despite a commonly-held view that Dickens repudiated the Old Testament, the novels tell a more complex story. As a nineteenth-century Anglican he would certainly have known the Good Friday Collect for the conversion of "all Jews" (together with "Turks, Infidels, and Heretics"). This supersessionism (now officially renounced by both Protestants and Catholics) clearly influenced Oliver Twist's Christian solicitations for Fagin in "The Jew's Last Night Alive" (*Oliver Twist*, LII). But as I argue in "Apocalypse Now: Dickens in the Twenty-First Century," in *Dickens in the New Millennium* eds. Nathalie Vanfasse et al., *Cahiers victoriens et édouardiens*, February 2012, 273-284, the Old Covenant is invoked, for example, as the ethical framework parodied in the mercantilism of Mr Dombey. At issue in Amy's conversation with Mrs Clennam is that her reading of both Covenants is shaped by her punitive morality.

the blackmailing Rigaud for Amy to give to Arthur. Her encounter with Amy, however, is framed by the theological implications of the "duty of memory" she has travestied. In a battle of proof-texts that recalls Miss Barbary's confrontation with Esther Summerson, Mrs Clennam defends herself to Little Dorrit by a reprise of her argument: "'I have been an instrument of severity against sin. Have not mere sinners like myself been commissioned to lay it low in all time?'" (2:XXXI, 756)

But "'all time'", Little Dorrit insists, must surely include the "'later and better days'" recorded in the New Testament:

> 'O Mrs Clennam, Mrs Clennam … angry feelings and unforgiving deeds are no comfort and no guide to you and me…. Be guided, only by the healer of the sick, the raiser of the dead, the friend of all who were afflicted and forlorn, the patient Master who shed tears of compassion for our infirmities. We cannot but be right if we put all the rest away, and do everything in remembrance of Him' (2:XXX, 756).

Characteristic of the Inimitable in every stage of his writing life, stage directions underline the point:

> In the softened light of the window, looking from the scene of her early trial to the shining sky, she was not in stronger opposition to the black figure in the shade, than to the life and doctrine on which she rested were to that figure's history (756).

Amy's direct preaching is uncharacteristic of the Little Dorrit whose history we have been following. Yet her solicitous and light-bearing homily responds to the unrelenting belligerence of Mrs Clennam's self-defence. Furthermore, it sets the figure and teaching of Christ within the full history of the Judeo-Christian narrative of salvation as Dickens reads it. Amy's liturgical echo "do everything in remembrance of Him" recalls for Mrs Clennam, and for Dickens's readership, the significance of the doctrine of anamnesis. The Words of Institution in the Christian celebration of the Eucharist – "do this in remembrance of me" – quote directly the words ascribed to Jesus at the Last Supper in Luke 22:19. They remind the worshipping community of the Old Testament story of the Passover, as well as of the proleptic remembering embodied in the New Covenant, "by which the participants both *remember* the events and become participants in it. In the process they are themselves re-membered, for by receiving the life of Christ, they are made one with him".[17] The way in which Christ is present in the sacrament was the subject of intense debate between the Catholic and the Protestant traditions in Dickens's time as

---

[17] Charles Elliott, "Memory," in the *Oxford Companion to Christian Thought*, eds. Adrian Hastings et al. (Oxford: Oxford University Press, 2000), 421.

it has been throughout Post-Reformation history.[18] In keeping with Dickens's Broad Church understanding of the Thirty-Nine articles of the Church of England, however, Amy sees the redress for humankind's primal fault not only in good works, but in the prevenient grace represented in Christ's atonement, and commemorated in the Sacrament of the Eucharist.[19] "D.N.F" recalls the collective memory of the Christian faith and of its housing in time, and Amy Dorrit is its spokeswoman and the embodiment of grace offered and received.[20]

Together with the grace of forgiveness, however, Amy speaks for the need to forget. "'Forgive me. Can you forgive me?'" entreats Mrs Clennam, prompting Amy's reply, "'all forgiven, all forgotten'" (2:XXXI, 753). This, in essence, is what Amy's dealings with the world exemplify: a capacity for forgiveness which is based on a forgetting of wrongs dealt. Generations of critics have seen this kind of forgiveness as less than admirable, citing the protective fictions by which Amy seems to shield herself from the wrongs dealt her by her family: her father's self-obsessed demandingness and his pathetic affectations of status, and the selfishness of the feckless Tip and the volatile, mercenary Fanny. The burning of the codicil, when it falls at last into her hands, seems to enlist an unwitting Arthur in her apparent moral amnesia, depriving him of the very memory he has felt only as lack: the record of maternal deprivation.

---

[18] Anthony Symondson SJ, "Theology, Worship, and the Late Victorian Church," in *The Victorian Church: Architecture and Society*, eds. Chris Brooks and Andrew Saint (Manchester: Manchester University Press, 1995), 192-222, notes that the 1840s and 50s were dominated by doctrinal controversies about the Eucharist. In 1857, for example, Alexander Penrose Fox, Bishop of Brechin, was accused of heresy by three of his fellow bishops for defending the doctrine of the Real Presence in the Eucharist, instead of the prevailing Church of England view that Christ's Body and Blood are present only figuratively and symbolically.

[19] The ninth of the Articles of Religion of the Church of England of 1592 affirms that "original sin ... is the fault and corruption of the Nature of every man, that naturally is engendered of the offspring of Adam; whereby man is very far gone from righteousness, and is of his own nature inclined to evil." Articles X to XII, however, outline, within the apparently deterministic logic of the biblical story of the Fall, a role for moral agency. Article X, "Of Free will," emphasises that "we have no power to do good works pleasant and acceptable to God, without the grace of God preventing [or going before] us". *The Book of Common Prayer* (Cambridge: Cambridge University Press, 1951), 348-358. I argue elsewhere that Dickens's understanding of the theology of original sin shapes the dramatic and figural life of *Bleak House*. See "'In a State of Bondage': the Children of Bleak House," in Peter Merchant and Catherine Waters eds., *Dickens and the Imagined Child* (Farnham: Ashgate Publishing, 2015), 57-73.

[20] Debate about the precise nature of her goodness is ongoing. Lionel Trilling's extravagant phrases: "the Child of the Parable, the Paraclete in female form", in *The Opposing Self* (Cambridge MA: Harvard University Press, 1950), 57, attracted limited approval. Janet Larson, *op. cit.*, 271, is not unrepresentative of the antagonistic views that followed: "Amy belongs to a long line of suffering Dickensian innocents whose strength of renunciation it is hard to judge morally, to distinguish from the weakness of submission to powerful circumstances of the stronger wills of others. To the limited extent that Amy is identified with *this* Jesus, she elicits the reader's pity, perhaps, but not admiration".

Amy's forgiving and forgetting is by no means passive, however, nor can it adequately be described as deceiving. It is, rather, an example of what Nietzsche calls "active forgetfulness": not a kind of inertia, but "an active and in the strictest sense positive faculty" that provides for the unconscious "a little quietness, a little *tabula rasa* ... to make room for new things, above all for the nobler functions and functionaries, for regulation, foresight, premeditation ... so that it will be immediately obvious how there could be no happiness, no cheerfulness, no hope, no pride, no *present*, without forgetfulness".[21] It demonstrates the kind of hard-earned moral integrity that distinguishes Little Dorrit in all her dealings, through which she so subtly yet determinedly asserts her right to weigh the claims of all concerned and to act in accordance with her conscience.[22] In asking Arthur, on their wedding morning, to burn a document for her, she relies on his compliance with her "odd fancy". He intuits some "superstition" in the ritual fire-lighting and burning, and asks "'does the charm want any words to be said?' ... 'You can say, (if you don't mind) "I love you!"' answered Little Dorrit. So he said it, and the paper burned away" (2: XXXIV, 784). The act renounces her legal claims on the House of Clennam, and with them any lingering sense of grievance in relation to her father's imprisonment. Destruction and suppression are transformed into a demonstration of the love, trust, and new beginnings awakened in the lovers' mutual desire, and which will soon be avowed in the sacrament of marriage.

The letters of Arthur's mother are not destroyed, however, and Amy's power to fill "the empty place in his heart that he has never known the meaning of" (2: XXXI, 755) is celebrated in a lyrical passage at the start of this final chapter. As Little Dorrit reads to him, Arthur hears the healing voice of "great Nature.... At no Mother's knee but hers, had he ever dwelt in his youth on hopeful promises, on playful fancies.... But, in the tones of the voice that read to him, there were memories of an old feeling of such things, and echoes of every merciful and loving whisper that had ever stolen to him in his life".

"D.N.F" stands as a reminder of both moral and financial obligation. Yet two twentieth-century theorists influenced by the Judeo-Christian tradition

---

[21] "On the Genealogy of Morals", Second Essay, Section 1, in Walter Kaufmann, trans. and ed., *Basic Writings of Nietzsche* (New York: The Modern Library, 1968), 493-494.

[22] In her discussion of theological doctrine in this novel, Carolyn W. de la L. Oulton, *Literature and Religion in Mid-Victorian England: from Dickens to Eliot* (Basingstoke: Palgrave Macmillan, 2003), 138, seems not to have noticed the role of anamnesis in Dickens's presentation of Amy. Moreover, I dispute her view that in the exchange with Mrs Clennam Amy takes on "a purely symbolic role" yet one which is somehow morally compromising: "it is notable that this status is only available to her once she has agreed to deceive her future husband in mercy to his mother. Having made the difficult decision to compromise her own integrity in order to spare Mrs Clennam's feelings, her saintliness no longer appears disingenuous".

uncouple the moral from the economic, drawing on the doctrine of grace as unearned gift. For Mikhail Bakhtin, this doctrine makes a model for aesthetic activity: my right to a loving reception of my external form "descends on me from others like a gift, like a blessing which cannot be inwardly grounded and understood".[23] For Paul Ricoeur, in his magisterial *Memory, History, Forgetting*, "under the sign of forgiveness, the guilty person is to be considered capable of something other than his offence and his faults. He is held to be restored to his capacity for acting, and action restored to its capacity for continuing ... you are better than your actions".[24] In an occasional essay, "The Economy of the Gift", Ricoeur makes a distinction between "the logic of equivalence" represented in the "golden rule", and the "logic of superabundance" represented in Christ's "'new commandment' of love".[25] And this is what Little Dorrit's love embodies: release from the imprisonments of mammonism, eye-for-an-eye morality, and the blames, guilts, and hauntings of the past.

---

[23] "Author and Hero in Aesthetic Activity" (1920s), quoted Ruth Coates, *Christianity in Bakhtin: God and the Exiled Author* (Cambridge: Cambridge University Press, 1998).
[24] Paul Ricoeur, *Memory, History, Forgetting* (Chicago: University of Chicago Press, 2004), 493.
[25] See W. David Hall, "The Economy of the Gift: Paul Ricoeur's Poetic Redescription of Reality," *Literature and Theology* 20(2) 2006, 189-204.

A Reading of Wilfred Owen's 'Dulce et Decorum Est'

Lyn Ashcroft

DULCE ET DECORUM EST

Bent double, like old beggars under sacks,
Knock-kneed, coughing like hags, we cursed through sludge,
Till on the haunting flares we turned our backs
And towards our distant rest began to trudge.
Men marched asleep. Many had lost their boots
But limped on, blood-shod. All went lame; all blind;
Drunk with fatigue; deaf even to the hoots
Of tired, outstripped Five-Nines that dropped behind.

Gas! GAS! Quick, boys! – An ecstasy of fumbling,
Fitting the clumsy helmets just in time;
But someone still was yelling out and stumbling,
And flound'ring like a man in fire or lime …
Dim, through the misty panes and thick green light,
As under a green sea, I saw him drowning.

In all my dreams, before my helpless sight,
He plunges at me, guttering, choking, drowning.

If in some smothering dreams you too could pace
Behind the wagon that we flung him in,
And watch the white eyes writhing in his face,
His hanging face, like a devil's sick of sin;
If you could hear, at every jolt, the blood
Come gargling from the froth-corrupted lungs,
Obscene as cancer, bitter as the cud
Of vile, incurable sores on innocent tongues, –
My friend, you would not tell with such high zest
To children ardent for some desperate glory,
The old Lie: Dulce et decorum est
Pro patria mori.

                                Wilfred Owen[1]

---

[1] Wilfred Owen, "Dulce et Decorum Est" in *The War Poems*, ed. Jon Stallworthy (London: Chatto & Windus, 1994), 29

"Dulce et Decorum Est", written and revised between October 1917 and March 1918, and first published in Siegfried Sassoon's edition of Owen's poems in December 1920, is almost certainly Wilfred Owen's best-known poem.[2] In the decades following its publication (especially after Cecil Day Lewis's 1963 edition of Owen's poetry) it has been extensively anthologised, included in school literature courses throughout the English-speaking world and become a common subject of scholarly attention. At the conclusion of his biography of Owen, Guy Cuthbertson remarks that Great Britain's Prime Minister, David Cameron, has cited "Dulce et Decorum Est" as "his favourite piece of poetry".[3] Moreover, it has recently been claimed that in the context of today's knowledge of the First World War, Owen is now "far more famous than, say, Field Marshal Douglas Haig or David Lloyd George".[4] And in the light of the current focus on the centenary of the First World War, Owen's fame and interest in his poetry are likely to increase. This, it must be said, is despite some objections that Owen's poetry has possibly been overpraised, particularly by those who favour its perceived pacifism, and that it has coloured the modern viewpoint of the First World War to the exclusion of other perspectives.[5] It must also be recognised that Owen has his detractors, for example, Barry Matthews, who in 2010 published a disparaging biography, *Wilfred Owen: the Old Lie*, presently unobtainable, in which he accuses his subject of cowardice and paedophilia.

This essay first outlines the sociocultural context of "Dulce et Decorum Est" to determine Owen's probable motives in writing the poem. His revisions of the four drafts and some typical grammatical patterns in the text are then examined in order to elucidate, as far as is possible, his poetic intentions in its creation. It needs to be remembered, of course, that Owen's tragedy as a poet is not only that he did not live to write more poetry, but that he did not live to see his work through the publication process. The published versions of the poems were, of necessity, determined by his editors, beginning with Siegfried Sassoon (who took over as editor of the first collection from Edith Sitwell) and followed by Edmund Blunden, Cecil Day Lewis, Dominic Hibberd and Jon Stallworthy. The many decisions they had to take about the texts may or, indeed, may not reflect what Owen's own final

---

[2] Wilfred Owen, *The Complete Poems and Fragments*, ed. Jon Stallworthy, 2 vols, rev. ed. (London: Chatto and Windus, 2013), Vol I, 140. All subsequent references to the final published form of "Dulce et Decorum Est" will be to this version. Further references to this edition of Owen's poetry will use the abbreviation, *CPF*.
[3] Guy Cuthbertson, *Wilfred Owen* (New Haven and London: Yale University Press, 2014), 300.
[4] Nigel Jones, "Wilfred Owen by Guy Cuthbertson, review", *Daily Telegraph* (London), 27 March, 2014. http://www.telegraph.co.uk/culture/books/bookreviews/10724073/Wilfred-Owen-by-Guy-Cuthbertson-review.html.
[5] Ian McMillan, "Has poetry distorted our view of World War One?" *BBC iWonder*, accessed 24 July, 2015, www.bbc.co.uk/guides/z38rq6f

intentions would have been. For this reason, amongst others, critical discussion of Owen's work can be a contentious area.

"Dulce et Decorum Est" shocks the reader with a graphic portrayal of a gas attack on exhausted soldiers returning to camp behind the front lines. One of the men is unable to put on his mask quickly enough, is overcome with the poison gas, most probably mustard or chlorine gas, and is shown dying in agony. In the last stanza, accompanying the dreadful details of the soldier's suffering – "the white eyes writhing", "the froth-corrupted lungs" – is the poet's determined implication of the reader in that suffering and his expression of intense anger at the ignorant propagation of pro-war sentiment, especially to the young. Counterpointing the work's horrifying content is its poetic form, which has been described by Hilda Spear as that of a "double-sonnet"[6], written in rhymed iambic pentameter.

From its first line, "Bent double, like old beggars under sacks", the poem itself contrasts ironically with its Latin title, part of a famous quotation from the Roman poet Horace (*Odes*, III, ii, 13), the whole of which is used to conclude the poem: "Dulce et decorum est pro patria mori", "It is sweet and fitting to die for one's country". This quotation was very widely understood and used throughout the British Empire and Europe at the time of the First World War; it had in fact become a commonplace well before the war began. Time and again it appears as the title or subtitle of a poem expressing patriotic and warlike sentiments. For example, a poem by "J.R.", published in a Sydney newspaper of November 1841, "A Greek Mother's Address to her Son before Going to Battle" and subtitled "Dulce et decorum est pro patria mori" is typical of such verse:

> Go son, and come not back again,
> From thy first battlefield,
> Unless in victory or slain,
> And borne upon thy shield;
> Thy back shall feel no foe-man's dart
> Thy breast must guide them to thy heart! [7]

A poem entitled "Dulce et Decorum Est" by James Rhoades, a British officer at the time of the Boer War, and published in 1899, is also typical, especially in its religious overtones:

---

[6] Hilda Spear, "Not Well Content: Wilfred Owen's Dislocation of the Sonnet Form", *Durham* 77, (December, 1984), 57-60.
[7] "J.R.", "A Greek Mother's Address to her Son before Going to Battle", *Sydney Gazette and New South Wales Advertiser*, 25 November, 1841. http://nla.gov.au/nla.news-article2555122

> At last ye stand transfigured in Death's apocalypse,
> When by one deed that washes
> Each soul as white as snow,
> From less than man grown Godlike,
> To God at last ye go.[8]

In the years between 1914 and 1918, thousands of verses celebrating patriotism and glory in war were published in newspapers, magazines and anthologies across the Empire, several of them using the Horace quotation as title or subtitle or within the poem itself. Paul Norgate, in his essay, "Wilfred Owen and the Soldier Poets"[9], points out the existence of two such poems, both entitled "Dulce et Decorum Est pro Patria Mori", written by serving soldiers, Major Sydney Oswald and Corporal Harold John Jarvis. These were first published in the *Poetry Review*, a journal known to have been regularly read by Owen, especially during his period of convalescence in 1917 to early 1918, and were soon after anthologised in Kyle's *Songs of the Fighting Men* (1916) and *More Songs of the Fighting Men* (1917) respectively. Both of these poems uncritically endorsed the sentiments of the Horace quotation by celebrating and idealising participation in war. The last four lines of Oswald's poem illustrate this:

> Glory is theirs; the People's narrative
> Of fame will tell their deeds of gallantry,
> And for all time their memories will live
> Shrined in our hearts.[10]

It is indeed a possibility, as Norgate suggests, that if Owen intended his "Dulce et Decorum Est" as a direct response to another poem, that he had one or other or both of these poems in mind. On the other hand, Guy Cuthbertson has suggested that Owen's poem could be a riposte to a poem, also entitled "Dulce et Decorum Est" by an obscure poet, M.F. Laurie, published in the *Boys' Own Annual* of 1916-1917.[11] This is a much less credible possibility. Given the plethora of poems of the period featuring the same or a similar title and the same or similar patriotic and bellicose sentiments, it seems highly unlikely that Owen even read Laurie's poem, much less was moved to respond to it in particular. Furthermore, it needs to be recognised that in newspapers of the Empire at the time of the First World War, Horace's quotation would have been encountered over and over again

---

[8] James Rhoades, "Dulce et Decorum Est", *Adelaide Observer*, 16 December, 1899. http://nla.gov.au/nla.news-article162409418
[9] Paul Norgate, "Wilfred Owen and the Soldier Poets", *Review of English Studies: New Series*, Vol 40, No. 160 (November, 1989), 516-530.
[10] Sydney Oswald, "Dulce et Decorum Est pro Patria Mori", 1916, quoted in Norgate, cited above, 521.
[11] Guy Cuthbertson, 163.

within the death notices inserted by the bereaved but patriotic families of war dead.¹² So it is perhaps most likely that Owen felt that the ubiquitous saying, "Dulce et decorum est pro patria mori", in view of his actual experience of the war, required a shocking, harshly ironic answer.

It is also very probable that in his poem Owen was deliberately repudiating his earlier, inexperienced self, the self who had thought of war in more conventionally positive terms, and who had approvingly echoed Horace's quotation in a poem first called "The Ballad of Peace & War", begun in France in 1914, revised and abandoned in 1917:

> Oh it is meet and it is sweet
> To live in peace with others,
> But sweeter still and far more meet
> To die in war for brothers.¹³

However, Owen's variation on Horace in these lines is significant: it is "brothers", not the nation, for whom it is sweet to make the sacrifice of dying in battle. (It is also interesting to see the influence of Wilde's "The Ballad of Reading Gaol" in the lines.)

And what of Jessie Pope (1868-1941), children's author and writer of patriotic verses, to whom Owen's poem was at first mockingly dedicated? Pope never actually wrote a poem called "Dulce et Decorum Est" (as incorrectly claimed by Martin Winkler)¹⁴, but produced plenty of low-quality poetry encouraging "laddies" to go to war and celebrating Allied victories. Her war poems were mainly published in London's *Daily Mail* newspaper and later in three collections, including *Simple Rhymes for Stirring Times* (1916). Obviously, she was by no means the only pro-war poet of the time, hence the "etc" of Owen's original dedication, but she was one of the most prominent. Ultimately, Owen's poem can be seen as a response to anyone who would disseminate an uncritical belief in the glory of the War, whether they were combatants, as in the case of Oswald and Jarvis, or non-combatants, such as Jessie Pope.

Owen's poem differs greatly from those of the pro-war poets, not only in its viewpoint, but in its style. Unlike the typical pro-war poem of the time, which has a static, abstract quality, Owen's poem is characterised by dynamic, specific narrative. It has a filmic aspect, marked by increasingly confronting shifts in perspective. In its opening eight-line stanza, the men are shown as

---

[12] For instance, hundreds of examples of First World War newspaper death notices, using the tag, "Dulce et decorum est pro patria mori" can be located on Trove, the National Library of Australia's online database.

[13] *CPF*, Vol II, 504.

[14] Martin M. Winkler, *Cinema and Classical Texts: Apollo's New Light* (Cambridge: Cambridge University Press, 2012), 162.

scarcely recognisable, shambling figures, before being revealed as a group of exhausted soldiers on the march, in the fifth line: "Men marched asleep". The reader is at first merely observer, until the gas attack of the second stanza, which he or she is forced to experience from the perspective of the men, with the urgent, direct speech of "Gas! GAS! Quick, boys!" The focus then switches to the hapless soldier unable to don his mask in time, whose agonising death appals and continues to haunt the poet. The poet's own perspective shifts between that of alarmed participant and compassionate observer, until in the last stanza it becomes that of indignant, unsparing judge of pro-war propagandists, who would perpetuate the "old Lie". The last twelve lines of the poem are intentionally shocking, seeming to implicate the reader – and not simply Jessie Pope and her like – in a collective complicity in the soldier's agony.

So, in "Dulce et Decorum Est", Owen answers the versifying of pro-war poets, so often bristling with abstract nouns, rhetorical questions, multiple imperatives (in the case of recruiting poems), portraits of the ideal, fearless, straight-backed soldier, and visions of sanctified valour, with the specificity and harsh realism of his grim narrative. His soldiers are without soldierly bearing or dignity, "Bent double, like old beggars under sacks, / Knock-kneed, coughing like hags". They are presented as suffering victims, whose senses have been blunted by exhaustion:

> All went lame; all blind;
> Drunk with fatigue; deaf even to the hoots
> Of tired, outstripped Five-Nines that dropped behind.

The action they are shown to take is in panicked *reaction* to the gas attack, as they scramble to fit their masks and then to fling their gas-affected comrade into a wagon. In this way, the poem reflects the reality of the largely defensive mechanised warfare of the Western front. As Paul Fussell puts it, the soldier of the First World War becomes "the man whom things are done to".[15]

Unsurprisingly, the realistic use of "blood" in Owen's poem contrasts with its somewhat ornamental use by pro-war poets such as Jessie Pope. "Blood" is mentioned twice in Owen's account of the soldiers' experience. In line 6, the men who had lost their boots are described as limping on, "blood-shod", an expression used in all four of the surviving drafts of the poem. "Blood-shod" associates the men with animals, especially horses, and clearly emphasises their physical distress. The other use of "blood", in line 21, relates to the dying gas victim:

---

[15] Paul Fussell, *The Great War and Modern Memory: The Illustrated Edition* (New York and London: Sterling Publishing Company, 2009), 393.

> If you could hear at every jolt, the blood
> Come gargling from the froth-corrupted lungs,
> Obscene as cancer, bitter as the cud
> Of vile, incurable sores on innocent tongues, –

Significantly, the reader is urged to "hear" the blood rather than "see" it (as in the first draft of the poem). In this way, Owen attempts to heighten the reader's sensory perception of the blood with stress on the ominous sound as it issues from the soldier's lungs. The lines, "Obscene as cancer, bitter as the cud / Of vile, incurable sores on innocent tongues" which were only added in the final draft of the poem, reinforce the blood's ghastliness. This literary treatment of blood in a military context contrasts strongly with its emblematic, decorative and sometimes almost insouciant use in conventional pro-war poetry like Jessie Pope's: "Who's for the game, the biggest that's played, / The red crashing game of a fight?"[16] And in her poem, "Anzac", Pope praises:

> The marvellous feat of your landing,
> Your exploits by field and by deed,
> Your charges that brooked no withstanding,
> Though you poured out the best of your blood.[17]

Pope's blood in no way confronts or seeks to unsettle the reader; Owen's undoubtedly does.

A worthwhile approach to accounting for the effectiveness of "Dulce et Decorum Est", and for determining Owen's intentions in writing it, is through an examination of his revisions to the poem, evident in the four complete drafts that have survived (which includes one with revisions and underlinings by Siegfried Sassoon).[18] The general tendency of Owen's own revisions is to concentrate the poem's dramatic effect and to darken its mood. One's sense of the physical suffering of the men is heightened by the revisions, as is the impression of the swift shock of the gas attack and of the nightmarish atmosphere. In addition, in the process of revision, earlier poetic influences are rejected by the poet. An examination of these four drafts indicates Owen's increasing confidence in his technical capacity and his growing sense of an individual poetic identity.

---

[16] Jessie Pope, "Who's for the Game?" *Poem Hunter*, accessed 15 July, 2015, www.poemhunter.com/best-poems/jessie-pope/who-s-for-the-game/

[17] Jessie Pope, "Anzac", *Poem Hunter*, accessed 15 July, 2015, www.poemhunter.com/poem/anzac/6f

[18] The manuscripts of all four drafts of "Dulce et Decorum Est" are available via *The First World War Poetry Digital Archive*, University of Oxford, http://www.oucs.ox.ac.uk/ww1lit/collections/document In Volume II of the *CPF*, Stallworthy provides transcriptions of three out of the four manuscripts, 292-297.

Owen accentuates the soldiers' physical distress by changing the first line of the first draft of 8 October 1917 from "Bent [which replaced the crossed-out "Hunched"] like old rag & bone men under sacks"[19] to "Bent double, like old beggars under sacks"[20] in the three other drafts, an altogether stronger, less desultory line, featuring a reinforcing and characteristic pararhyme. There are seven different versions of the poem's fifth line in the four drafts (if crossings-out are counted) as Owen depicts the difficult progress of the soldiers back to camp. The final version of the line – "Men marched asleep. Many had lost their boots" – effectively stresses the men's exhaustion, as they appear to sleepwalk back to camp. The other drafts describe more activity: for example, "Dragging the worst amongst us"[21] which would have disturbed the somnolent mood created in the second half of the stanza. This mood serves to underscore the suddenness and shock of the gas attack in the following stanza.

Further sharpening the shock of the attack is the omission of four lines (present with only slight variations in all of the drafts) introducing it. The following version of these lines is the one bracketed and crossed out by Owen in what appears to be the last draft modified by the poet himself and the draft closest to the final published poem:

> Then somewhere near in front: Whew…fup, fop, fup,
> Gas shells? O/or duds? We loosened masks in case, –
> And listened. Nothing. Far ru-rumouring of Krupp.
> Then sudden crawling sudden poisons hit stung us in the face.[22]

The omission of this explanatory scene-setting for the attack serves to emphasise its suddenness textually, placing the reader in the position of the shocked soldiers, and it is the reader's close involvement that is sought by Owen from the poem's opening lines. (Intriguingly, Michael Williams puts forward a quite different view of the omission, despite the fact that it is very clearly a decision made by Owen. Williams argues for the restoration of the lines, offering the theory that they contribute to the "re-creation of a tragic accident caused by the mistiming of a British gas attack".[23] This view is unconvincing, as he puts forward no evidence to support the claim, such as a reference to an incident of this kind in Owen's letters.)

The nightmarish atmosphere of the poem is intensified by Owen's revisions. The "flares" of the third line are at first "feeble", "glimmering" and

---

[19] *CPF*, Vol II, 294-295, http://www.oucs.ox.ac.uk/ww1lit/collections/document/5655
[20] *CPF*, Vol II, 292-293, 296-297, http://www.oucs.ox.ac.uk/ww1lit/collections/document/5656
[21] http://www.oucs.ox.ac.uk/ww1lit/collections/document/5656
[22] *CPF*, Vol II, 292-3 http://www.oucs.ox.ac.uk/ww1lit/collections/document/5193/4551
[23] Michael Williams, "Wilfred Owen: a Poet Re-institutionalised", *Critical Survey*, Vol. 2, No. 2, Writing and the First World War, (1990), 199.

even "clawing", before becoming "haunting" in the final version.[24] The tendency of other revisions is to increase the reader's perception of the character of the nightmare as an appalling underwater horror, with the soldier victim "drowning" in the gas. "Heavy light" becomes "thick green light"; the "thick sea" or the "dark sea" becomes a "green sea"; the victim "plunges" instead of "lunges", as the poet views him through the "misty panes" of the gas mask, perhaps reminiscent of the helmet of a deep-sea diving suit.[25]

The mood of an already dark poem becomes even darker when Owen eliminates two lines which sensuously describe the victim as he had been before the war: "And think how, once, his head was like a bud, / Fresh as a country rose, and keen, and young".[26] These lines are late romantic in tone and perhaps, as Paul Fussell would say, Uranian in flavour,[27] recalling, for example, the similarly sensuous nostalgia present in Wilde's account of the guardsman in "The Ballad of Reading Gaol". Owen's instinct to remove the lines was a sound one, not only because of their lighter tone, but because they diluted the immediacy of the account of the gas attack by diverting attention to another time and place. The lines appear in all of the drafts, with minor variations, except that in the draft closest to the poem's final version (the one in which the lead-up to the gas attack is also eliminated) they are crossed out in favour of a grisly description of the victim's blood: "Obscene as cancer, bitter as the cud / Of vile, incurable sores on innocent tongues".[28] It should also be noted that in this draft, "innocent" replaces the deleted "small kissed" as if to expunge any last hint of sensuousness.

In his revisions to the poem, Owen can clearly be seen abandoning earlier, nineteenth-century influences. It is worth remembering that in a letter to his mother dated 15 August 1917, he comments: "I think if I had the choice of making friends with Tennyson or with Sassoon I should go to Sassoon".[29] In the first draft of 8 October 1917, there is a discursive, Tennysonian moment as the poet reflects on the horror of the dying soldier's distress: "I must not speak of this thing as I might".[30] Owen seems soon to have rejected the line, as it appears in no other draft. He judged well in deleting it, as it would have had the effect of dissipating the tense atmosphere already established in the poem. Also present only in the first draft is the description of the gas victim's "hanging face" as "tortured for your own

---

[24] *CPF*, Vol II, 292-297, and in all four drafts available at www.oucs.ox.ac.uk/ww1lit/collections/document
[25] *CPF*, Vol II, 292-297, and in all four drafts available at www.oucs.ox.ac.uk/ww1lit/collections/document
[26] *CPF*, Vol II, 292-293, www.oucs.ox.ac.uk/ww1lit/collections/document/5193/4551
[27] Fussell, 355.
[28] *CPF*, Vol II, 292-293, www.oucs.ox.ac.uk/ww1lit/collections/document/5193/4551
[29] Quoted in Dominic Hibberd, *Wilfred Owen: A New Biography* (London: Phoenix, 2003), 330.
[30] *CPF*, Vol II, 294-295, www.oucs.ox.ac.uk/ww1lit/collections/5655

sin"[31], with the implication that he is to be seen as a Christ figure enduring a kind of crucifixion because of the sin of pro-war propagandists. In altering this description to "like a devil's sick of sin" (admittedly not a completely satisfactory phrase), Owen has intentionally cut out this reference to soldierly, Christlike suffering. He would have encountered such allusions time and again in the pro-war poetry of his contemporaries and, indeed, he had made such references himself in earlier poems, such as the ballad first drafted in 1915, which he called "The Women & the Slain" and alternatively, "Ballad of Kings and Christs":

> When blood must pay the reckoning,
> Lest heart go unsufficed;
> When bodies are the offering
> Lest souls be sacrificed;
>
> Let everyman live Arthur King,
> And any man die Christ![32]

Owen decided in August of 1917 that he would not publish this ballad.[33] It seems that for him, the image of the soldier as the suffering and sacrificial Christ had lost meaning, was a distortion, and could no longer have a place in his poetry. Given this sentiment, it is unsurprising that he would promptly jettison the line, "tortured for your own sin". (Williams puts forward a contrary view, arguing for the restoration of the line.[34])

Much of the impact of "Dulce et Decorum Est" can be explained by its grammatical features, particularly the selection of tenses and the sentence structure.

The tense selection accounts for, at least in part, the strong impression of immediacy given by the text, placing the reader as horrified witness of the gas attack and its aftermath, which certainly appears to have been Owen's intention. Although the march of the exhausted men and the attack itself is described in the past tense, one's sense of the incident as a continuing nightmare is achieved by the extensive use of the present participle, a feature which dominates the text. Even when used as a participial noun – "an ecstasy of fumbling" – or as participial adjectives ("haunting flares", "smothering dreams", "hanging face") rather than as part of a verb construction, these present participles all contribute to create a prevailing effect of immediacy. Present participles first appear in the second and third lines of the text, but are most frequent in the narrative of the gas attack, which describes the

---

[31] *CPF*, Vol II, 294-295, www.oucs.ox.ac.uk/ww1lit/collections/5655
[32] *CPF*, Vol II, 508.
[33] Hibberd, 329-330.
[34] Williams, 201.

soldiers' panicked response and the ordeal of the soldier who failed to don his mask in time. "Drowning" is emphasised by its repetition within two lines, when the most concentrated use of present participles occurs: "guttering, choking, drowning", making it seem as if the soldier is dying several times over, in different ways, in perpetuity. While the effect of the accumulation of present participles in the poem is clearly to bring the reader closer to the action, their use also suggests horror without end, the implication being, "All this is still going on while you tell children that 'old Lie'". Indeed, it should be noted that in early drafts of the poem, Owen employs a present participle to stress the continuation of the propagandists' lying: "You would not go on telling with such zest"[35], instead of "My friend, you would not tell with such high zest".

Despite the prominence of present participles in the poem, the most commonly used tense is the past. In the first stanza, the simple past predominates, while in the second, depicting the gas attack and its victim, the past continuous is mostly used. The imperative mood and present and conditional tenses are all employed much less in the poem, and so may be regarded as foregrounded. "Gas! GAS! Quick, boys!" stands out as the only instance of reported speech in the work and because it contains the single example of imperative mood. In this way, the grammar of the text reflects the shock and suddenness of the semantic content, the warning of the gas attack. The use of the present tense in the third stanza is strongly foregrounded. This is so because: firstly, it is the one simple present-tense construction in the whole poem; secondly, because "plunges at" is a strong active verb; and thirdly, because the stanza contains only two lines and so is already prominent in the poem. It appears that these two lines are so evidently underlined as it is precisely this harrowing experience of recurring nightmare that the poet wishes to share. Conditual constructions, employing the modal verbs "could" and "would not", are used in the last stanza of the poem, contributing to its rhetorical force and intensity as a direct appeal to the reader to bear witness to the horror of war and to reconsider their enthusiasm for what Owen sees as its illusory glory.

The sentence organisation of "Dulce et Decorum Est" contributes strongly to the impression the reader gains of an intense experience and of the development of a passionate argument. (The poem comprises twenty eight lines divided into four stanzas of eight, six, two and twelve lines. There are nine sentences in the poem: four in the first stanza, three in the second, one in the third and one in the fourth.) A prominent feature of the sentence structure is cataphora, especially in the form of subordinate clauses or phrases preceding main clauses, producing a suspenseful effect. An example can be

---

[35] *CPF*, Vol II, 294-295, www.oucs.ox.ac.uk/ww1lit/collections/5655

seen in the first two lines of the poem, containing three subordinate adjectival clauses: "Bent double, like old beggars under sacks, / Knock-kneed, coughing like hags", followed by the main clause: "we cursed through sludge". In the second stanza, the subordinate adverbial phrases: "Dim, through the misty panes and thick green light / As under a green sea" precede the main clause: "I saw him drowning". Similarly, in the third stanza, the subordinate adverbial phrases: "In all my dreams, before my helpless sight", heighten the startling effect of the main clause which follows: "He plunges at me" (itself succeeded by subordinate adverbial clauses: "guttering, choking, drowning", intensifying the sense of the soldier's agony). The fourth and last stanza of the poem comprises one long, complex, tortuous sentence in which Owen makes his forceful and graphic plea to the reader, also underscored by extensive use of cataphora. The main clause of the sentence does not appear until the ninth line of the stanza, having been preceded by subordinate conditional clauses depicting the suffering of the dying soldier and urging the reader to bear witness: "If in some smothering dreams you too could pace"; "…and watch"; "If you could hear…". These clauses create the impression of a heaping-up of damning evidence against those who would distort the actual experience of war, especially of twentieth-century warfare. Finally, it is worth noting that the cataphoric sentence constructions are present in all of the drafts of the poem, suggesting that, from the outset, Owen was intent on creating, by this means, a suspenseful and tense mood throughout the work.

It seems evident that Owen's impetus for writing "Dulce et Decorum Est" was to produce a poem that, through the vividness of its unsparing narrative of a gas attack, could call to account those who would persist in disseminating the "old Lie" of the glory of warfare, especially to the young. Jessie Pope would appear to have been uppermost in his mind as a pernicious pro-war versifier but, as previously mentioned, the "etc" in the dedication of the first draft obviously includes similar writers. Moreover, his use of the famous Horatian saying also indicates a reaction against its ubiquity in newspapers, magazines and books of the time, including its frequent use as a title of pro-war poems, even when they were written by other "soldier-poets". Owen's revisions and his grammatical choices in the poem all serve to intensify the horror of the attack – which is intended to epitomise the horror of contemporary warfare – and the sharp, accusatory rhetoric of his challenge to the propagandists. There is no doubt that he wanted "Dulce et Decorum Est" to be an extreme and uncompromising poem, sparing no one's feelings, not even those of countless bereaved families across the Empire who, by convention and in a desire to receive and give consolation, employed the saying in the newspaper death notices of their loved ones: "Dulce et decorum est pro patria mori".

The Lizard

Christine Townend

You owned the garden long before I came,
a speckled streak between piled rocks,
protruding, curious head, arched neck,
wise, yellow watching eyes,
waiting for me to understand.

I threw meat. You watched, immobile,
before tasting the smell with your tongue,
and then the flashed movement, gone before starting;
you chewed with small jaws.

And so I learnt from you. You knew my feet.
You flashed your presence,
silver light across the earth, under leaves.
You came, and took from my giant hand
(which reached into the field of your being)
the small morsel of proffered cheese,
and I felt the touch of your wild lip on my finger.
You took, like kings take gifts from commoners.

This poem is dedicated to Professor Barry Spurr who has done so much to help the animal kingdom, and who has, along with others, fought against the injustices which humans inflict upon non-human animals. Professor Spurr was my associate supervisor when I was writing my Doctorate at the University of Sydney. I attended many of his lectures. I was amazed at his knowledge of poetry, and how he could hold the attention of a huge auditorium of students, talking for an hour about poetry without ever referring to notes, just reading wonderful verses and explaining how and why they were constructed.

Liturgy and Language

David Jasper

Ἔοικε δέ.... περὶ ταὐτὰ καὶ ἐν τοῖς αὐτοῖς εἶναι ἥ τε φιλία καὶ τὸ δίκαιον
Aristotle, *Nichomachaean Ethics*

I first encountered Barry Spurr long before I actually met him in the University of Sydney, as is often the way with academics, through an essay on the 1978 *An Australian Prayer Book* which he contributed to a book entitled *No Alternative: The Prayer Book Controversy* (1981).[1] It was written at a time of immense liturgical revisionary activity of which I was profoundly aware myself, partly because I had been ordained as a priest in the Church of England in 1977, but more specifically because my father, also an Anglican priest, was a liturgist and the Chairman of the Church of England Liturgical Commission which was responsible for the *Alternative Service Book* (ASB) published in 1980, the first radically new attempt at the revision of worship in the Church of England for over three hundred years since the 1662 *Book of Common Prayer*. My father, Ronald Jasper, was thus perceived by many as one of the "well-intentioned wreckers"[2] who were robbing the Anglican Church of its liturgical strengths and above all the glories of its language.

In the passage of time the ASB itself has passed into history, and the debates that focused upon the impoverishment of language in contemporary forms of worship have been largely forgotten and would seem now rather old-fashioned. But they did address real issues and may be worth returning to and their underlying significance re-examined in a more contemporary context. It was indubitably the case that the English language of the later part of the twentieth century was more prosaic and more utilitarian than the prose and verse of the sixteenth century that was to reach its finest flowering in the English of Shakespeare and his contemporaries. But equally it would be absurd to maintain that a century that gave us James Joyce, T. S. Eliot, W. H. Auden and Seamus Heaney, among others, was bereft of a linguistic instrument that could sound with subtlety and extraordinary beauty, though it

---

[1] Barry Spurr, "An Australian Prayer Book", in *No Alternative: The Prayer Book Controversy*, eds. David Martin and Peter Mullen (Oxford: Basil Blackwood, 1981), 162-174.
[2] The phrase is taken from the cover notes of another collection of essays on liturgical reform, edited by Brian Morris, *Ritual Murder* (Manchester: Carcanet Press, 1980).

may indeed be the case that the nature of the Church itself in the same time has rendered it peculiarly difficult to speak with proper resonance in the particular language demanded by liturgical utterance and practice. As it forgets its theological and spiritual richness the Church begins to speak in the language of its own nature and gets the dull liturgy it deserves. But, still, it was never simply a matter that when we ceased to speak in the language of Archbishop Cranmer we lost touch with the "markers of transcendence", as David Martin once suggested.[3] There was far more to it than that.

It is a deep irony that those who have most vigorously defended the Anglican *Book of Common Prayer* – a seventeenth-century work which is deeply rooted in the sixteenth century – on the bases of beauty, mystery and antiquity, have often done so in terms that Thomas Cranmer himself would have profoundly rejected.[4] Writing to Queen Mary during his imprisonment and awaiting death, Cranmer insisted upon the use of language in the liturgy in all its aspects that must be contemporary and easily understandable:

> ... that whether the priests rehearse the wonderful works of God, or the great benefits of God unto mankind above all other creatures, or give thanks unto God, or make open confession of their faith, or humble confession of their sins, with earnest request of mercy and forgiveness, or make suit unto God for anything; then all the people, understanding what the priests say, might give their minds and voices with them and say Amen....[5]

This was the principle upon which William Tyndale produced his English translation of the Scriptures, as expressed in his rendition of Erasmus' *Exhortations to the Diligent Study of Scripture* (1529), recalling the spiritual needs of the ploughman and the weaver and, further, "I would desire that all women should reade the Gospell and Paule's epistles, and I wold to god they were translated in to the tonges of all men".[6] Not only is the scholarly Tyndale wholly alert to the expressive word-play in *koine* Greek, as opposed to the heavy Latinate tendencies of more recent twentieth-century translations such as in the *New English Bible*, but he combines this with what David Daniell has called his "conscious use of everyday words without inversions, a neutral word-order, and a wonderful ear".[7] Tyndale's language is rarely less than natural.

---

[3] David Martin, "Identity and a Changed Church", in *No Alternative*, 17.
[4] See, David L. Frost, *The Language of Series 3*. Grove Booklet, No. 12 (Bramcott: Grove Books, 1973), 5.
[5] C. S. Meyer, ed., *Cranmer's Selected Writings* (London: SPCK, 1961), 91.
[6] Quoted in George Steiner, *After Babel: Aspects of Language and Translation* (Oxford: Oxford University Press, 1975), 245.
[7] David Daniell, Introduction to *Tyndale's New Testament (1534)* (New Haven: Yale University Press, 1995), xxi.

Cranmer was also well aware of the way in which language continually changes, and that therefore both Scripture and the liturgy must regularly be re-translated and revised, writing of the English of the Saxon Bible that when it "waxed old and out of common usage, because folk should not lack the fruit of common reading, it was again translated into the new language".[8] His observation is far from unique: it was made long ago by Thucydides writing of the Peloponnesian War at a time in Greece when words were losing their meaning; Proust writes of such linguistic deterioration in France at the end of his life in the early twentieth century. Yet change is not always a matter of decay, but may be deeply creative. Henry David Thoreau, for example, moving to live by the pond in the woods, writes of creating a new life and new language.[9]

It is one thing to delight in a glorious performance of Shakespeare, and quite another to imagine what it would be like to employ the rich and complex language of a Hamlet or a Lear in daily life today. The language of the liturgy, on the other hand, makes different and unique demands upon us. The glory of the *Book of Common Prayer* lies to a large extent upon its capacity to address the common joys and sorrows of human living. As one modern poet has well put it:

> ... This is
> what we always thought about rain;
> about dying, and marriage, and God.
> ... Words, then, said what they meant;
> they bit.[10]

But at the same time its words speak of heaven and they do so with theological delicacy and precision, a discipline by which Shakespeare was never so constrained. The pressure for liturgical reform in the Church of England was far from new in the twentieth century though its earlier obsession, most particularly in the nineteenth century, was almost entirely with theological questions and rarely with matters of language.[11] It was the twentieth century after the reforms of the Second Vatican Council and with its broader philosophical and cultural anxieties about the crisis in language that brought the dilemma of the Anglican liturgy to a head. It was not just a crisis of language, it was an issue of *liturgical language*.

---

[8] *Ibid.*, 2.
[9] See, James Boyd White, *When Words Lose Their Meaning* (Chicago: Chicago University Press, 1984), Chapter 1, "A Way of Reading", 1-23.
[10] David Scott, "The Book of Common Prayer 1549', in *A Quiet Gathering* (Newcastle-upon-Tyne: Bloodaxe Books, 1984), 36.
[11] See, Horton Davies, *Worship and Theology in England: From Newman to Martineau, 1850-1900* (Princeton: Princeton University Press, 1962); R. C. D. Jasper, *Prayer Book Revision in England, 1800-1900* (London: SPCK, 1954).

Bishop Stephen Neill once wrote that the Church of England in the twentieth century had only two great "liturgiologists": F. E. Brightman, the author and editor of the still standard work *The English Rite* (1915), and F. C. Burkitt, who once stated that he wished for only one change in the 1662 liturgy – the substitution of "and" for "or" between the prayer of oblation and the prayer of thanksgiving.[12] The only recent competitor to Brightman's work, now over a century old, is an edition of the Prayer Books of 1549, 1559 and 1662 by a professor of English Literature, Brian Cummings who, despite a fine sense of the theological, tends to present the sixteenth-century prayer books as examples of "literary revivalism" as much as or even more than "liturgical reform".[13] The problem is, of course, that no-one has ever quite decided what a "liturgiologist" exactly is. Most serious students of liturgy (and those most responsible for its reform in various churches after Vatican II) have been historians, with a proper sense of historical continuity not simply from the Reformation, but from the earliest times of the Christian Church. By far the most popular, and perhaps the most influential work in English liturgical studies in the twentieth century is Gregory Dix's *The Shape of the Liturgy* (1945), written by a man who had not the slightest interest in the problems of liturgical revision, who harboured an almost pathological hatred of Archbishop Cranmer and the Reformation, held a particular, if not peculiar, sense of theology, and was, as Neill puts it, "highly skilled in making the worse appear the better reason".[14]

Now, at a time when liturgy is barely given any space in serious theological study or ministerial training, neither theologians nor literary critics properly participate in discussions that require a delicate balance between the two fields of theology and literature. If we are to sustain the proper practice of liturgy in the midst of life – when people require meaningful words when they are married, die, seek forgiveness or celebrate things of most importance – then a careful articulation of truths that can become sour and toxic unless carefully tended by the right words must be pursued.

The study and writing of liturgical language may be one of the few genuine examples of the enterprise of "interdisciplinarity" about which so much is spoken in our universities – and so little actually done. For interdisciplinary study is caught within a dilemma, as Stanley Fish once described it in an essay entitled "Being Interdisciplinary Is So Very Hard to Do", where he points out that it usually involves the annexation of one or more fields by another, and students of literature, in particular, have become very adept at colonizing philosophy, psychology, and even theology,

---

[12] Stephen Neill, "Liturgical Continuity and Change in the Anglican Churches", in *No Alternative*, 5.
[13] Brian Cummings, ed., *The Book of Common Prayer: The Texts of 1549, 1559, and 1662* (Oxford: Oxford University Press, 2011), xxv.
[14] Stephen Neill, *op. cit.* 7.

frequently with strange results. Fish, however, with typical irony, celebrates the imperialistic success of literary studies inasmuch as "from a certain point of view, the traditional disciplines have played themselves out and it is time to fashion a new one". But the sting is in the tail, as Fish concludes:

> ... my pleasure at these developments has nothing to do with the larger claims – claims of liberation, freedom, openness – often made for them. The American mind, like any other, will always be closed, and the only question is whether we find the form of closure it currently assumes answerable to our present urgencies.[15]

And so what of the liturgy and its theological claims for liberation, freedom, salvation? Or does it also rejoice in closure and isolation? In fact, the divorce between liturgy and theology relentlessly takes us to Fish's position – celebrating the new "field" of cultural studies while neglecting the larger claims with a dangerously closed mind. The dilemma is exposed in the forms of language we are content to use, and within that the fundamental theological debates that examine how we express and find God: whether we pursue theo*logy*, beginning from human thought and speech about God, or *theo*logy, which responds to God's revelation to us.[16] Bridget Nichols, in a sadly neglected book on *Liturgical Hermeneutics* (1996), has pointed out that "in structural terms, liturgical language and secular language share fundamental grammatical conventions, as well as the characteristic of ritual or iterability".[17] Of course the overlap and commonalities are crucial if liturgical language is to remain meaningful and effective. Words in liturgy *do* things – as the poet says, they bite. Nichols goes on to point out what lies at the heart of the concerns of all those who expressed anxiety about what was felt to be the rather dull, prosaic language of twentieth-century liturgical reformers:

> The real risk in liturgical language is not that it is different, but that it is reassuringly the same. Only, it engages its user in *qualitatively more profound commitments* than they will have experienced when making similar verbal contracts in the extra-liturgical context.[18]

Liturgical language, then, is different, actually *doing* that which theologians just talk about. It may be that the genius of a Tyndale or a Cranmer got it just

---

[15] Stanley Fish, *There's No Such Thing as Free Speech, and It's a Good Thing Too* (Oxford: Oxford University Press, 1994), 242.
[16] See Kevin Hart, Introduction to Jean-Luc Marion, *The Essential Writings* (New York: Fordham University Press, 2013), 21.
[17] Bridget Nichols, *Liturgical Hermeneutics: Interpreting Liturgical Rites in Performance* (Frankfurt: Peter Lang, 1996), 258.
[18] *Ibid.*, 259. (Emphases added)

right in their day, but today liturgy has to engage fully with the hermeneutical issue of horizons, and to express a faith that is eschatalogical and forward-looking. It has to perform the task of being a vehicle that retains its continuity with the past but also promises a future within the often mundane realities of the present. What Nichols finally urges us to seek in liturgy is its capacity to preserve "the traces of the sense of the sacred origin of humanity, and the notion of ultimate worth defined by something beyond the human sphere".[19]

Here there are no simple answers. When, in 1990, in the last year of his life, I edited with my father a volume of essays entitled *Language and the Worship of the Church*, we tried to cover the outfield but, in the end, I think, we missed the heart of the matter. Essays in the book on early Christian rhetoric, Cranmer as creative writer, sociolinguistics and music all finally shied away from the essential task of rethinking theologically the very foundations of liturgical language. Perhaps the most important essay, then, was by the philosopher Martin Warner with its careful introduction to the distinction between "implicate" and "implicature", the latter stretching "wider than mere implications, for they [implicatures] are context-dependent, often in non-conventional ways. Even if the implications of what is said are entirely innocent, it does not follow that the implicatures are".[20] We have been warned – we are in dangerous territory, or rather we stand on holy ground. With such a warning we are wise to have our wits and intelligence about us in the matter of language. When, in the early 1980s, we began in Durham University the series of conferences on theology and literature that continue to the present day, we were wisely advised to have a philosopher at hand for the sake of just such precision in language and thought. Thus D. Z. Phillips warned us of the importance of good grammar, for "if we infringe these grammatical requirements we shall soon find ourselves engaged in trivialities or nonsense. The most common infringements come about by trying to sever a concept from the conditions of its application".[21]

This return to the theme of grammar is deliberate and takes me back to John Henry Newman's key work, the *Grammar of Assent* (1870). For it was Cardinal Newman who learnt from the poet Samuel Taylor Coleridge that notion of verbal tradition and the sense of language as "a living organism whose function is to reconcile the past and present experiences of a community".[22] Such language we might describe as "fiduciary" wherein, in

---

[19] *Ibid.*, 261-262.
[20] Martin Warner, "Philosophy, Implicature and Liturgy", in David Jasper and R. C. D. Jasper, eds., *Language and the Worship of the Church* (London: Macmillan, 1990), 150.
[21] D. Z. Phillips, "Mystery and Meditation: Reflections on Flannery O'Connor and Joan Didion", in *Images of Belief in Literature,* ed. David Jasper (London: Macmillan, 1984), 25.
[22] John Coulson, *Newman and the Common Tradition: A Study in the Language of Church and Society* (Oxford: Clarendon Press, 1970), 4.

both poetry and religion, we are drawn by inference to make an act of assent, a process that necessarily begins with trust (what Coleridge in his *Biographia Literaria* [1817] describes as "the willing suspension of disbelief") in expressions that are often highly elusive, symbolic or metaphorical. Thus, as John Coulson remarks, "understanding religious language is a function of understanding poetic language".[23] However, Newman (himself a poet) takes a further step that is not to be found in Coleridge. He returns us to the theological. Coulson acknowledges that Coleridge seeks to describe *how* we respond to what we might call the language of ultimate concern, but fails to make the next move which is concerned with *what* that language is about. In short, is such language finally true or false, and is it capable of sustaining an enquiry into such a distinction?[24]

It is precisely this enquiry that Newman embarks upon in the *Grammar of Assent*, and it is why this book is such a key text for our present concerns with liturgical language. In many ways the *Grammar* has its origins in Newman's *University Sermons*, delivered in Oxford between 1826 and 1843, which focused upon the theological issue of the relations of faith and reason. At the heart of Newman's careful epistemology of assent is the sense of living language that he had first encountered in Coleridge. As he moves towards his crucial notion of the Illative Sense, that is the faculty of judging from given facts by processes beyond logic, it is just such fiduciary language that underlies it. In the matter of religious assent, Newman carefully distinguishes between "certainty" and "certitude". He writes:

> Certitude is not a passive impression made upon the mind from without, by argumentative compulsion, but in all concrete questions (nay, even in abstract, for though the reasoning is abstract, the mind which judges of it is concrete) it is an active recognition of propositions as true, such as it is the duty of each individual himself to exercise at the bidding of reason, and, when reason forbids, to withhold. And reason never bids us be certain except on an absolute proof; and such a proof can never be furnished to us by the logic of words, for as certitude is of the mind, so is the act of inference which leads to it.[25]

The context for such a careful description of religious certitude can be nothing less than a form of language that is both theologically and poetically embraced by the act of worship – in short, liturgical language.

Such language, by virtue of its very energy that runs beyond mere logic, can never be "normal" as it stretches at once both from and towards the divine, yet it lives through the cadences of living, everyday (in Newman's

---

[23] *Ibid.*, 4.
[24] See Coulson, *op.cit.*, 20.
[25] J. H. Newman, *An Essay in Aid of a Grammar of Assent* (1870), ed. I. T. Ker (Oxford: Clarendon Press, 1985), 223.

word "concrete") speech. Open to change it yet develops in range and subtlety precisely by a *resistance* to new words and ideas, whereby it comes to adapt and to accommodate new patterns of thought.[26] The characteristics of such language are creativity and poetic allusiveness: as the poet Emily Dickinson teaches, "Tell all the Truth but tell it slant". For truth, she goes on, must "dazzle gradually" lest it blind us.[27] This is also the language of transcendence – that of theo*logy* rather than *theo*logy, though utterly embraced by the careful processes of theological thinking. It recognizes the necessity of continuity while at the same time it is open to the radically new, facing the future in God. It might best be described in the words of the French phenomenologist and philosopher Jean-Luc Marion as the "prolegomena to charity" within which, in the final analysis we live, breathe and have our being.[28]

And so, as I draw these few words to a conclusion, I have sought to revisit an old argument and to add a few thoughts to the finally elusive issue of the nature of liturgical language – a language close to that of the poet but always and of necessity more, and more strange – we find now, as the Churches of the West decline, that liturgical contexts grow, paradoxically, wider. In a post-Heideggarian world, liturgy becomes a form of dwelling in the presence of God (*coram Dei*) and as the Christian asks what it is to exist liturgically in the "place" of prayer, so the ancient, transgressive, sacred language of the liturgy contains the most dynamic of all words meeting the unthinkable which has given them life. Liturgy and its practice is not simply about going to church and what we do there (though that does remain profoundly important). Here, finally, theology becomes a whole way of living, its language less an affirmation or attempt at bold statement, but words that express an existence that is known as genuinely *kenotic*. In the words of Jean-Yves Lacoste, we then begin to approach "the paradoxical joy that is born of humiliation [which] may be the *fundamental mood* of pre-eschatalogical experience".[29] It is, perhaps, only then that we can enter, in time and in eternity, into the joy of the *Sanctus* until finally all human words are lost in wonder and praise.[30] Perhaps only then can we begin again to regain that faith in language that has so often in recent years seemed thin and uncreative.

---

[26] See further, Philip H. Pfatteicher, *The School of the Church: Worship and Christian Formation* (Valley Forge PA: Trinity Press International, 1995), 115.

[27] Emily Dickinson, *The Complete Poems*, ed. Thomas H. Johnson (London: Faber & Faber, 1970), 506-507. See also, John Tinsley, "Tell it Slant", *Theology*, LXXXIII (1983), 163-170.

[28] See, Jean-Luc Marion, *Prolegomena to Charity*, trans. Stephen E. Lewis (New York: Fordham University Press, 2002).

[29] Jean-Yves Lacoste, *Experience and the Absolute*, trans. Mark Raftery-Skehan (New York: Fordham University Press, 2004), 194.

[30] See further, David Jasper, *The Sacred Community: Art, Sacrament, and the People of God* (Waco: Texas, Baylor University Press, 2012).

A poet like R. S. Thomas might express his despair in face of the contemporary Augean stable of utilitarian newsprint, pompous bureaucrats and drab business style so that "when so much of that language is either vile or without flavour, the poet has no sound basis from which to work".[31] Yet, dare we say, is this not to look in the wrong place for the words of worship? We look out and live in the real world of cities and economies, we look back to the wisdom that continues to teach and inspire us, but finally we look up for the word that will be given to us.

---

[31] R. S. Thomas, "A Frame for Poetry", *The Times Literary Supplement*, March 3rd, 1966, 169.

Calumniation and Payback Theory: Wars of Words in the Breakdown of the Warrior Ethos

Garry W. Trompf

Only those who risk going too far can possibly find out how far one can go.
T.S. Eliot, Preface to Harry Crosby, *Transit of Venus* (1931).

Historians of ideas and literary critics with an historical bent have common interests in the oscillations of thought patterns. The great German *savant* Ernst Troeltsch, former Professor in Philosophy and Civilization at Berlin (1915-1923), got things going at the beginning of last century when he described the Renaissance and the Reformation as *typischten* in the alternating movements of Western cultural and intellectual propensities. "The dual origin of our European world", he affirmed, lies in "the world of Prophetic and Christian religion" and "the spiritual culture of [Graeco-Roman] Antiquity". The peculiar tension between these two trajectories amounts to "an original opposition … which recurs in ever new forms and with every emergence of great new life-problems remains unbridged". Even if through time the opposition is not thoroughgoing – for the "threads" of Biblical stricture and pagan permission often "intermingle" – still, "Christian 'Ascesis' ever anew builds her kingdom of the supersensible" and ranks all else beneath it, while "ever and again arise in [contrary] self-assertion the needs and impulses of nature" and pagan energies "more artistic than moral".[1]

In one of the most beautifully written works of historically oriented literary criticism, Edinburgh's Sir Herbert Grierson arrived at similar conclusions about English Puritanism *vis-à-vis* the Later Renaissance. Strict if nonetheless creative Protestant minds could take no more of Catholic idolatrous taints. But, as the Cromwellian revolution lost hold, and more noticeably after the 1660 Restoration, wantonness, refinement and sensuous delight were uncorked. The moral earnestness of a Milton, typifying Scriptural seriousness, gives way to the not-quite-classical, oratorically extravagant *felicitas* of a Dryden (and also to a not-quite-classical revival of scientific learning). And Grierson saw the process going on: quoting Carlyle,

---

[1] Ernst Troeltsch, "Renaissance und Reformation", *Historische Zeitschrift* 110 (1913): 19.

the eighteenth was "a Sceptical Century", overcome by "moral Doubt, ... infidelity, insincerity, spiritual paralysis". But of course in the ongoing "moderation" between "fanaticism" and "license", as Grierson himself has it, along come the Wesleys and the Evangelicals, and then "the Catholic revival, both Roman and Anglican", in a century better valuing moral respectability.[2] Such approaches to cultural-religious swings will remind us of the great Moments between Ideational and Sensate (between collective reliance more on the spiritual and more on the senses) in Pitirim Sorokin's sociological analyses. But what Troeltsch and Grierson spotted would be for him but minor fluctuations without global and macro-historical application.[3]

One problem in looking at competing energies within these frames is the investment of too much focus on changing sensibilities (often elite-generated), and not enough on the agents who are hyped up or angry for and against one outlook rather than another. Instead of then testing whether there have only been distinctly cultural *querelles* over taste – with the best source of poetic inspiration, for instance, being Homeric or prophetical, classical or Christian, immediate responsiveness to love or nature, the Muses or the hymnist's true "Captain of the Soul" – we would be looking for who is accusing which party of definite wrong – of wrong-headedness, or perhaps some "tyranny" – and under what pressures of conscience. A fear of "provocations against God", not merely a riling over impoverished style, may spark the reaction.[4] This is where "the logic of retribution" comes in, and we are asked to consider who holds "payback energies", whether negative or concessive, and in what relative intensities they are ready to express them.

This is somewhat of a theoretically under-assessed dimension in cultural, literary and aesthetics study, but it forever lurks in the background and we should readily concede how important it is to know whether any writer or historical agent works *against* disliked parties, or already belongs to a partisan cause, or even harbours petty jealousies! Ideational positions held always have to be researched, clarified, even tested for dissimulation, but, foremost,

---

[2] Herbert J.C. Grierson, *Cross Currents in English Literature of the Seventeenth Century, or The World, the Flesh and the Spirit, their Actions and Reactions* (1929; London: Chatto & Windus, 1958.), 266ff., 299-313.
[3] Pitirim Sorokin, e.g., *Social and Cultural Dynamics* (New York: American Book Company, 1941), vol. 4, 735. Of the two authors, he knows Troeltsch, e.g., vol. 1, 181.
[4] Quotations are from the renowned "Solemn League and Covenant" (1643, Long Parliament, England), sect. VI, in *The Constitutional Documents of the Puritan Revolution, 1625-1660*, sel. and ed. Samuel R. Gardiner (London: Oxford University Press, 1906), 270-271. For permutations of the *Querelle* over ancients and moderns, Garry W. Trompf, *The Idea of Historical Recurrence in Western Thought* (Berkeley: University of California Press, 1979-[forthcoming]), vol. 1, ch. 5, sect. B; vol. 2, chs. 6, 8-9; David Lowenthal, *The Past is a Foreign Country* (Cambridge: Cambridge University Press, 1985), 87-95; and *The Past is a Foreign Country – Revisited* (Cambridge: Cambridge University Press, 2015), pt. 1, ch. 4.

as borne by particular persons, not as abstractions;[5] while realizing as well (taking textual materials, for a start) that some genres are obviously more likely to expose piques and rants or sycophancy and unctuousness than others, such as diatribe and apologetics, panegyrics and orations, and not forgetting blatant satire.

What will emerge from this reframing, admittedly, cannot possibly in many cases reduce relevant conflictual attitudes to a "cultural quarrel". It will not always be the case of a Classical/Hebraic tussle. In the specific scenarios discussed by Grierson – the transitions from Charles I's pro-Catholic policies, through the Puritan Commonwealth to the Restoration – additional factors inevitably form part of the complex equations. We would straightway have to admit to a triangulation that placed Protestants and Catholics in their own struggle (for blind vitriol never made the Catholics *actual* pagans!), to be set beside a motley cohort of latitudinarians preferring to memorize the *Iliad* than the Bible, and of anti-Puritan folkish elements wanting to hold on to May Day or cock-fighting. Witchcraft and black magic would almost always amount to a "disfiguring of sin" for both Christian parties, while the best of the pagan inheritance, collective learning in the Greco-Roman classics and their *exempla* of worthy heroes and oppressive tyrants, was no more widely preserved than by clerics.[6] Thus the probing of retributive factors, and the exposure of where anyone lets their praise and blame fly, or their accusations and accolades roll, has to reckon with a much greater diversity of energies and not only high-cultural proclivities.

In this piece, in honour of my stimulating friend and colleague Barry Spurr, who has experimentally plumbed the perturbations of the English tongue, I add a little to the "payback theory" of aesthetics and literature,[7] by connecting the opening of less stressful spaces in the socio-military history of the Western world ("ancient, mediaeval and modern") with flurries of internal religious and cultural dispute. For, it is no use discussing the conflict of outlooks, or any "battle of the books", without reckoning with great shifts and shocks of civilization over the centuries. The following assessment can only be preliminary, yet it responds to up-to-date historical research into the

---

[5] For latter, note Quentin Skinner's seminal "Meaning and Understanding in the History of Ideas," *History and Theory* 8, 1 (1969); 3-53, esp. 18.

[6] Of background use, Keith Thomas, *Religion and the Decline of Magic: Studies in Popular Beliefs in Sixteenth and Seventeenth-Century England* (Harmondsworth: Penguin, 1973); Ruth Nevo, *The Dial of Virtue: A Study of Poems on Affairs of State in the Seventeenth Century* (Princeton: Princeton University Press, 1963), ch. 2 (quotation); Jessie Lander, *Inventing Polemic: Religions, Print, and Literary Culture in Early Modern England* (Cambridge: Cambridge University Press, 2006).

[7] For background, G.W. Trompf, *Payback: The Logic of Retribution in Melanesian Religions* (Cambridge: Cambridge University Press, 2008), Prelim. and ch. 5, sect. 1, 373-374; idem, "The Art of Payback", in *Before Pangaea: New Essays in Transcultural Aesthetics*, ed. Rick Benitez [Spec. Issue of] *Journal of Aesthetics and Literature* 15, 1 (2005): 195-207.

periods most heavily discussed. I will basically be testing the thesis that internal rancour follows general peace (or conditions more generally peaceful and stable than previous years allowed). Calumniation, my chief subject, with its "official" and literary-polemical expressions especially in view, cannot and probably should not be aired exclusively in peace-time, for bad leaders in periods of stress may deserve resounding reprobation; but as a heuristic "anthropological rule of thumb" it would seem that the internal negativities increase as external threat subsides.

A well-known classical (most memorably Sallustian) conceit has it that political success breeds internal conspiracy. Prefacing his account of Catiline's conspiracy (63 BC), Sallust recalls the good old days (*Catil.*, ii, 2-9) when the fine mental stuff (*ingenium*) of which empire was made – loyalty, industry, self-restraint, justice, and a life in "glorious deed or noble career" – generally prevailed. If the "mental excellence (*animi virtus*)" with which such kings as Cyrus and the rulers of Athens and Republican Rome were endowed "were as potent in peace as in war", Sallust averred, "human affairs would run an evener and steadier course, and you would not see power passing from hand to hand and everything in turmoil (*mutari*)". This initiated for us the oft-cited principle that war or external threat brings internal solidarity, "quarrels, discord and strife" being diverted toward enemies; while peace, coming after *res publica*, bore greatness through toil, yet unfortunately allows space for mental uneasiness and dissension – for the greed and covetousness found in Catiline's subversions. For Sallust, the breakdown into confusion (*misceri*) made "the writing of history one of the most difficult of tasks", because in casting blame rather than praising heroes historians themselves could also be accused of "malice and envy" (ii, 1, 3; iii, 2; ix, 2; x, 1).

Whether these Sallustian *axiomata* always apply, or do so only when certain variables are absent, will be a matter for debate. Accentuating outside threats to maintain internal cohesion has certainly been a visible ploy in modern politics, from early Machiavellians to contemporary policy-makers in the United States. In consideration of my shared interest with Professor Spurr in matters of doctrinal difference, though, the key point of this paper is to ask if similar formulae to Sallust's might be said to pertain to times of acrimonious religious debate.

It has long concerned me that, during the very time Christianity was being "established" in the Roman world, from Constantine's edicts of tolerance (from AD 313) to the settling of two orthodox Christian emperors on both sides of the Empire (a century later), we have been bequeathed evidence of the most fearsome polemics about questions of belief in Antiquity, and actually in their way quite unprecedented. Of course some of the vitriol had everything to do with a massive shift of religious life, from paganism to Christianity, and from a worship of many deities to one God. We know of struggles for such a great change in the antique past. Pharaoh

Ikhnaton tried engineering the New Kingdom from his new capital Akhetaten (in the 1340s BC). But his efforts were very shortly thereafter undone and the old gods reappeared; whereas in the later context now interesting us, not even the subtler and more philosophically trained mind of the so-called Apostate and emperor Julian could stem the massive tide toward monotheistic Christianity (AD 350s). Israel dismantled Canaanite polytheism within an entirely unique religious history and small territorial byway of Antiquity, but after all the literary –, historical – and redaction-criticism has been applied, it appears Jewish spiritual solidarity took over half a millennium to be secured. By 300, in comparison, between 10-15 million people in a Roman Empire of around 60 million were Christians, and without any conquest on their behalf (the subsequent imperially-sponsored "establishment" of the Faith then generating more growth, if with problems of ambiguous commitment).[8] But most of the fiery verbal and written interchanges after Constantine were not between pagan and Christian; they were internal to the suddenly legitimated, no-longer-persecuted churches, the clashes far outdoing even the prior written bouts between old persecutors and the Apologists.[9]

As is well known, the most contentious doctrinal issue at the time of Constantine concerned the teachings of the presbyter Arius in Alexandria that the Logos (or the pre-existent cosmic Christ) was a creation (*ktisma*) of God and therefore a secondary, even "changeable" divine entity, distinct from the Creator of All, a view thus undermining the shared essential being of the Father and the Son in the unity of the Godhead. Arius's position was very much a focus of dispute at the fabled Council of Nicaea, the First Ecumenical Council of the Church (325). And whatever we are to make out of the unruly mix of sources on episcopal behaviour during its proceedings, the rancour of the relevant debate, expectedly inflated by Edward Gibbon and deflated by Dean Arthur Stanley, would surely have involved scenes of shouting, jostling, even physical scraps, amid what was generally a very serious one-month-long wrestling for truth.[10] Constantine, who convened and financed the Council

---

[8] On the above, consult esp. Marc van de Mieroop, *A History of the Ancient Near East, ca. 3000-323 BC* (Oxford: Blackwell, 2004), esp. 3, ch. 7.4; Charlotte Booth, *The Boy Behind the Mask: Meeting the Real Tutankhaman* (London: Oneworld Publications, 2007); Siegfriend Hermann, *Geschichte Israels in alttestamenlicher Zeit* (Munich: Christian Kaiser Verlag, 1973), pt. 2, ch. 10; pt. 3, ch. 3; William H.C. Frend, *The Rise of Christianity* (London: Fortress, 1984), chs. 12-14; cf. Ralph M. Novak, Jr, *Christianity and the Roman Empire: Background Texts* (Harrisburg PA: Trinity, 2001), 103.

[9] Cf. Isaac Miller, "Idolatry and the Polemics of World-Formation from Philo to Augustine," *Journal of Religious History* 28, 2 (2004), 126-145.

[10] Edward Gibbon, *The History of the Decline and Fall of the Roman Empire* (1776-89), ed. (London: Dent, 1910), vol. 2, 276-283 (Gibbon not ruling out the poisoning of Arius, 286, n. 1); Arthur P. Stanley, *Lectures on the History of the Eastern Church* (1861), ed. (London: Dent, 1907), lect. 3, sects. 5-6; cf. Archibald Robertson, "Prolegomena," in his edited *Selected Writings and Letters of Athanasius, Bishop of Alexandria* (The Nicene and Post-Nicene Fathers Ser. 2, vol. 4) (Oxford: Parker, 1892), xvii-xx.

and who in full regalia apparently listened through it all, was deeply disturbed by dissension over what seemed to him a trifling distinction, and wrote pleading for moderation.[11] But we can hardly neglect to acknowledge that Nicaea's decisions unleashed at least a century and a half of further doctrinal skirmishing – the Arian controversy – in which eighteen distinct theological camps reared their heads, almost an ecclesiastical parallel to the twenty contending imperial usurpers of the 260s, plus a flush of disunity pagan revivalist Julian ever so readily used to his (albeit short-lived) advantage.[12] It has been strangely unacknowledged, though, that despite the destruction of many relevant documents, the Arian issue leaves us evidence of the most considerable and widespread "war of words" in all Antiquity. With other post-Constantinian bones of Christian contention added – the many pages of argument and animosity between Jerome and Rufinus over Origen on the pre-existence of souls, for one glaring example (from *ca.* 400)[13] – we have an extraordinary splash of vocal and intellectual agitation, gaining increasing public importance the more Christian bishops gained representative power and legal responsibility in their respective metropoles, regions or dioceses.[14]

This intriguing phenomenon, the very freedom to engage in such dissension, and the rapid growth of non-clerical persons – lawyers and rhetors especially – participant in its perturbations,[15] surely bespeaks a world of altering preoccupations, when matters of military matters and the use of sacrificial procedures to support imperial security gave way considerably to a quest for divine truth as a matter of necessity in its own right. The prevailing paradigm throughout Roman socio-martial history, at least for male citizens, was that of *cursus honorum*. A man of aspiration and physical ability was under pressure to serve in the army. It is well known by now that ancient writers hankering after the old system lamented that the Empire was made vulnerable through failure to maintain warrior *virtus* after Constantine; and not a little interest lies in the thesis that turning to the Christian holy life, even desert asceticism, was an attractive means by which women avoided commitment to

---

[11] Constantine, *Exhort. ad episc.* apud Eusebius of Caesarea, *Vit. Const.* iii, 21; cf. iii, 6-14.

[12] There are enumerations of positions from Louis-Sébastian Le N. Tillemont, *Mémoires pour servir à l'histoire ecclésiastiques des six premiers siècles* (Paris: Eugene Henry Fricx, 1734), vol. 6, 477 (starting from Athanasius's accounting in *De Synod.* [*Arim, et. Seleuc.*], ii-iii) to Richard P.C. Hanson, *The Search for the Christian Doctrine of God: The Arian Controversy 318-381 AD* (Edinburgh: T. & T. Clark, 1988). Cf. 'Pollio,' *Tyr. Triq.* i,1-xxxiii, 8 in *Script. Hist. Aug.* (30 in this title being an exaggeration for 20? see idem, *Gallien. Duo*, xvi, 2, in ibid.); and for Julian's use of ecclesiastical disunity, esp. Rufinus, *Hist. eccles.* x, 30.

[13] See Jerome, esp. *Apol. adv. lib. Rufin.*; Rufinus, esp. *Apol. adv. Ieron.*

[14] Consult for a start Henry Chadwick, *The Church in Ancient Society from Galilee to Gregory the Great* (Oxford History of the Christian Church, 1) (Oxford: Clarendon Press, 2001), 207-210.

[15] Note that two of the most famous successors to innovator church historian Eusebius of Caesarea were lawyers: Socrates Scholasticus and Salminius Sozomenos.

an ethos of *machismo*.[16] By a Sallustian account, divisiveness rose at a new time of peace, with the development of a New Rome (Constantinopolis) in the East, and so – not unnaturally – blame on the weakening of the Empire, in ancient, let alone modern times, has been laid on religious change.[17] We can hardly say the quest for truth to create a new vision of society was foreign to the Graeco-Roman *oikumenê*, which also possessed utopian visionaries; but whatever speculative and philosophic energies there had been to alter the whole outlook on life, their effects amounted to smaller pools in the ocean (even if they could be picked up and adapted in a new Christian *paideia*). And Christianity's biggest competitor, Mithraism, reinforced rather than subverted inherited warrior mentalities, even if seeking to endow it with mystical flavours.[18] Of course, mention of Mithraism will remind us that the Christian emperors, whether orthodox (Constantine, Theodosius 1 and II, etc) or Arianizing (the very late Constantine, Constantius II, Valens, etc.), still had wars on their hands (with northern barbarians and Persia) and thus troops to deploy, albeit with mixed success.[19] The point here is that scope reached by Christian controversialism, and its involvement of territorial or diocesan allegiances, was unprecedented.

Calumniations were very much at large between 320 and 420, then, and to the embarrassment of those wanting above all to teach the love of God and between humans, Christian bad-mouthing would seem like "reciprocally tearing one another to pieces", or so the Western Father Hilary of Poitiers despaired.[20] The torrid career of Athanasius, Patriarch of Alexandria and orthodox champion of the *Homoousian* cause (for the consubstantiality of Father and Son) provides a litmus test. For in the rich mix of his commonly polemical writings, we find him defending himself against the calumnies of Arian accusers and, in reply, calumniating against those whom he held to distort divine truth. The most oft-used relevant substantive, intriguingly, is the Greek *sukophantia* (Lat. *calumnia*), and it was unfortunate that such Greek terms as *diabolê* (severe censure), and *diabolos* (slanderer) were cognate with the developing Christian *diabolikos* (inspired by the Devil), the last word often

---

[16] Consider esp. "Count of Constantinople" P.F. Vegetius Renatus, *De re milit.*; and on women Peter Brown, *The Body and Society: Men, Women and Sexual Renunciation in Early Christianity* (London: Faber & Faber, 1990), esp. pt. 2.

[17] Start from Zosimus, *Nov. hist.*, esp. I, 1; ii, 6-7; and on Gibbon, John G.A. Pocock, *Barbarism and Religion*, vol. 6: *The Triumph in the West* (Cambridge: Cambridge University Press, 2015), chs. 1-11.

[18] For the above, e.g., Werner Jaeger, *Early Christianity and Greek Paideia* (Cambridge MA: Belknap, 1961); John Ferguson, *Utopias of the Ancient World* (London: Thames & Hudson, 1975; Adrian D.H. Bivar, *The Personalities of Mithra in Archaeology and Literature* (New York: Bibiotheca Persica Press, 1998), 12, 48-55, 64-68, etc.

[19] G.W. Trompf, *Early Christian Historiography: Narratives of Retributive Justice* (London: Continuum, 2001), 159-161, 197, 218-225, etc.

[20] Hilary, *Ad Constant. imperat.* I,1, cf. 4-5.

used beforehand of false belief in pagan gods.[21] Athanasius was generally so vehement in his self-defence and in turning bad light back on his accusers that charges, from non-Trinitarian thinker Sir Isaac Newton to the notoriously blustering yet great ancient historian Timothy Barnes, have accused him of badly dissembling, in Barnes' view, of plainly being a "theological thug"! I have retorted that Athanasius, through torrid decades of his episcopacy over Alexandria (324-373), was too consistent in his defence of truth as well as of himself to be a liar; but a shrill tone and degree of volatility can hardly be overlooked.[22] Witness, in contrast, the measured defence of the classical Attic orator Andocides against claims he profaned the Eleusinian mysteries, when he asks the tribunal to "bear in mind" the many "instances of accusations" showing up as "manifest lies that it would be much more welcome to you to punish the accusers than the accused" (*De myster.* 6). Even under the pre-Constantinian emperor Diocletian, just before his Great Persecution (and thus *ca.* 300), in the last surviving, indeed longest known debate from Antiquity – between an orthodox protagonist against six Gnostic opponents and with a pagan adjudicator – we never get Athanasian-like heat.[23] But then again, so much was at stake in Athanasius's cause that he even dared calling the emperor himself (the Arianizing Constantius II, who had banished him) a virtual "Antichrist" (*Hist. Arian.* viii, 67, 71).[24]

Space does not permit dwelling longer on Late Antiquity. We should move on and test our tentative hypothesis that religious divisiveness follows upon the dissipation of warrior ethos in subsequent times. This is not to argue that acrimonious religious debates or memorable calumniations do not arise in times of international crisis, or to deny an overlapping of political and religious crises – considering the notorious calumny and subsequent threat of

---

[21] See Geoffrey W.H. Lampe, *A Patristic Greek Lexicon* (Oxford: Clarendon Press, 1961), 344-345, 1279 for relevant usages from the time, including those in Athanasius, e.g., *De decret. Nic. syn.*, 25; *Contr. gent.* 22; *Orat. tres adv. Arian.* ii, 38; *Maced. dial.*, I, 11 *Epist ad. episc. Aegypt.* 3; *Apol. de fug. sua*, 9 (also on outrage or *hubris* in 3, 7); and see *Apol. contr. Arian.* esp. 56, 59.

[22] For the references and my debate with Timothy D. Barnes, see G. Trompf, "Church History as Non-Conformism: Retributive and Eschatological Elements in Athanasius and Philostorgius", in *Conformity and Non-Conformity in Byzantium* (Byzantinische Forschungen 24) (Amsterdam: 1997), 11-12, n. 4. Incidentally, in my approach to Athanasius, I am not wishing away the fact that there were cases of murder in the Arian controversy, and within the "hive" of his agitations.

[23] Something parallel to Andocides, though, we still do find in Athanasius, e.g., *Apol. contr. Arian.* 55, where he maintains that Arians involved in "sedition" and "maliciously disposed" should be subject "to the vengeance of the law" (*têi tôn nomôn ... ekdikia*) or "punishment that awaits the disorderly". For the debate with Gnostics see Robert A. Pretty, trans. and comm., *Adamantius: Dialogue on the True Faith in God: De Recta in Deum Fide*, ed. Garry W. Trompf, (Gnostica 1) (Louvain: Peeters, 1997), 35-185.

[24] See Trompf, "Church History as Non-Conformism", 15, and see Barnes, *Athanasius and Constantius: Theology and Politics in the Constantinian Empire* (Cambridge MA: Harvard University Press, 2001), 55. Note that Eunomian Arian Philostorgius is a good example of a vitriolic historical writer on the other side of the doctrinal fence (in his *Hist. eccles.*).

execution, for example, that faced Thomas Paine in the French revolutionary Hall of Deputies when, as an exposed ex-Quaker, he opposed the guillotining of Louis XVI.[25] And in the modifications of the Sallustian theory, we have all had to become more aware that in times of crisis, even when a nation is faced with a common enemy, authorities cannot expect internal cohesion, and so proceed to *enforce* it and to expunge dangerous non-conformity – most dramatically under Nazism, Stalinism, McCarthyism in contemporary history.[26] But we are here concerned with truly massive shifts in social history, and we should continue, concentrating upon the European world for management, by reckoning with centuries of barbarian incursions on what remained of Christian-Roman civilization, and by first gauging leftover effects of prevailing warriorhood mentalities in earlier mediaeval times.

Instructive, one immediately suspects, is the contrast between the continuing of the Eastern (Byzantine) Empire and the collapse of the Western Roman Empire to the north (especially from 476) in the face of western-moving "hordes". In a position of relative security (certainly until the arrival of Islam), religious squabbles internal to Eastern Orthodoxy went on, and, not altogether embarrassing to the external threat/internal unity paradigm, it has to be said that controversialism was heightened when Justinian I and Theodora had some success in reintegrating the old empire by the 560s (trying to mollify the Chalcedonian/Monophysite divide) and when the first onslaughts of the Muslim invasion had subsided (the Iconoclasic controversy, borne partly by Islam's aniconic pressures and by Armenian reservations).[27] In the West, however, four centuries of serious social dilapidation took Europe into a sea of constantly warring "smaller unities" that were only temporarily mitigated by early Holy Roman Emperors Charlemagne and Otto I. Despite sensational efforts at cultural preservation, renaissance, and creativity, they occurred usually in pockets and were often short-lived, and one cannot underestimate how debilitating for socio-religious life was the constant see-sawing of conflict between mobile (super-)tribes and smaller congealing territories (the original European *nationes*) across most of the Continent. The Western Catholic Church was and became the only means by which a sense of common human unity, let alone of a prospectively well

---

[25] Through Jean-Paul Marat and the Montagnards; see Elihu B. Washburne, "Thomas Paine and the French Revolution," *Scribners Monthly* 20 (1880): 779. On the much more conservative (and English) side, however, note Thomas Hearn, *A Short View of the Rise and Progress of Freedom in Modern Europe ... in Answer to the Calumnies of Thomas Paine* (London: W. Richardson, 1793).

[26] See e.g., Seymour M. Lipset, *Political Man: The Social Bases of Politics* (New York: Heinemann, 1969); Jerzy W. Borejsza and Klaus Ziemer eds., *Totalitarian and Authoritarian Regimes in Europe: Legacies and Lessons from the Twentieth Century* (New York: Berghan, 2006).

[27] Carmelo Capizzi, *Giustiniano I tra politica e religione* (Messina: Rubbettino, 1994); Andrew Louth, *The Church in History*, vol.3: *Greek East and Latin West: The Church AD 681-1071* (Crestwood NY: St Vladimir's Seminary Press, 2007), esp. pt. 1, ch.2.

governed Europe, were sustained.²⁸ Following Harold Berman's brilliant *Law and Revolution* (first ed., 1983), we see how slow and yet how crucial – indeed revolutionary – was the work of clerical lawyers in merging parts of Justinian's Codex, vernacular *leges* and ecclesiastical law to make possible a workable "Western legal tradition", and the striking accomplishment was accompanied by the relative success of the Papacy as arbiter between mutually suspicious peoples.²⁹ Relevant to our concerns, however, come the exigencies of new, ostensibly religious divisions as the external tensions eased.

All sorts of interesting developments immediately come to mind when trying to comprehend the great movement out of feudal-type arrangements for the armed defence of (relatively) small territories to the settling down of a more stable Holy Roman Empire, and to the discernable beginnings of nation states, more secure commercial and urban interactions, and a less corruptible ecclesial order. These days the scholarly tendency has been to push back the serious dissolution of the barbarian "warrior ethos" to the tenth and eleventh centuries, seeing also the foundations of nationalism, the emergence of cultural strands distinctive to Western Europe, and the great contest over demarcating imperial and church authorities (especially in the Investitures controversy), as markers of the great shift.³⁰ The transition does not make the reality of war less evident, but only less patently brutal, less forever near-at-hand, and more enshrouded by rules – by shared principles of honour or a Christian-affected chivalry.³¹ Locally focussed ecclesiastical campaigns to bring longer cessations of hostilities – starting most noticeably with the Peace of God movement at the turn of the millennium, and well documented for southern Francia ³² – increasingly gained effect, to make possible the remarkable achievements of High Mediaeval society.

For a general social revolution had to occur, in the acceptance of higher sanctions, legal principles, university standards of reasoning and scientific endeavour, better political protection and sanctuary, and collective assumptions about necessary spiritual unity, if any one of the great late Romanesque and Gothic cathedrals was going to reach so high toward the heavens.

---

[28] Jenö Szücs, *Nemzet és történelem tanulmányok* (Budapest: Gondolat, 1974), 254-279.

[29] Harold J. Berman, *Law and Revolution: the Formation of the Western Legal Tradition* (Cambridge MA: Harvard University Press, 1985).

[30] E.g., Francis Oakley, *The Medieval Experience: Foundations of Western Cultural Singularity* (New York: Scribner, 1974); Adrian Hastings, *The Construction of Nationhood: Ethnicity, Religion and Nationalism* (Wiles Lectures, Queen's University at Belfast 1996) (Cambridge: Cambridge University Press, 1997), chs. 2-5; Uta-Renate Blumethal, *Investiturstreit* (Stuttgart: Kolhammer, 1982), chs. 3-4.

[31] For bearings, Philippe Contamine, *La Guerre au Moyen Âge* (Paris: PUF, 1998), pt. 1, chs. 2-3; pt. 2, chs. 9-10; pt. 3, ch. 8; noting also Udo Heyn, "Arms Limitation and the Search for Peace in Medieval Europe," *War and Society* 2, 2 (1984): 1-18.

[32] Consult esp. Thomas Head and Richard Landes, eds., *The Peace of God: Social Violence and Religious Response in France around the year 1000* (Ithaca NY: Cornell University Press, 1992).

The "improved" or freer social space created, however, draws to mind the possibilities, nay actualities, of an internal divisiveness, especially surrounding religious or religion-related issues, attendant upon its own success. This draws to mind the important book of my historian friend Robert Moore (University of Newcastle upon Tyne), author of *The First European Revolution, c. 970-1215*, who dared to write of this turning-point in Western history as "the formation of a persecuting society", which thereafter in his view never really ever left us.[33] Since the attempt of the great Scottish Enlightenment scholar William Robertson to relieve the disparaged "Dark Ages" of some of its darkness by taking the origins of current commercial civilization to the twelfth century, through to sociologist Pitirim Sorokin's recognition of the high mediaeval period (twelfth to fourteenth centuries) as the most integrated ("idealistic") of the West's cultural super-system,[34] increasing attention has been given to the inner stresses and strains in the "immediate post-warrior-oriented" atmosphere of western European societies. Moore has no intention of reclaiming old and prejudicial depreciations of *mediaevalia*, from Quattrocento humanist reactions to Scholasticism to Voltairean hatred of Catholic clerisy, but he spots the (relative) origins of social and socio-conceptual problems that have bedevilled Western Europe from the turn of the second millennium. Recast for the purposes of this article, these problems are the creation of accusations of false belief (heresy), when greater space for dissent was created by less militarily tense circumstances, leading to the creation of inquisitions and anti-Jewish assaults, and to a diversion away from the newly created space for internal divisiveness by the crusader mentality, of uniting Christendom against Islam as despoiler of the Holy Places, the Great (and externally threatening) Other.[35]

So after the pregnant year AD 1000, "for the first Time", as Norman Cohn provocatively put it, Europe had to face its "inner demons", or became "uneasily aware of heretics in its midst". It was in 1009 that the highly volatile Fatimid Shi'ite Caliph al-Hakim bi-Amir Allah ordered the destruction of Christian churches in Palestine (including that of the Holy Sepulchre) and thus sparked Christian efforts to regain the Holy Land. And after centuries of

---

[33] Robert I. Moore, *The First European Revolution, c.970-1215* (Oxford: Blackwell, 2000); *The Formation of a Persecuting Society: Power and Deviance in Western Europe, 950-1250* (Oxford: Blackwell, 2007).
[34] For coverage and beyond, Trompf, *Recurrence*, vol. 2, chs. 7, sect. 6, ch. 8; sects. 4-5; ch.9, sect. 2.
[35] Cf. Moore, *Formation*, esp. chs. 1, 3 (with leprosy included as a great social danger). After conversations with Prof. Moore, I should clarify that he distances himself from the view that these developments have anything to do with heightened millennialist anxieties (worries accentuated by Richard Landes and producing their debate I encapsulate in the collection we all contributed to in [the special number of] the *Journal of Religious History* 24, 1 (2000): *Millennium* (ed. Hilary Carey), esp. 121-122; and I trust he will forgive the special adaptation of his arguments for my own case.

accepting the necessity of Jewry and especially its merchants as "Middle Man" between the Semitic zone of Islam and the then marginalized and largely Latinate West, Jews suddenly became incidental casualties between internal jostling and outward aggression.[36] Troublesome aspects in European history usually kept separate for discussion are now brought within the one synthetic analysis. What is most important for us about Moore's study is the role of powerbrokers – leaders of the "social elite" or great noble families – *manipulating* new as well as old divisions for their own ends, as well as the susceptibility of "simple folk" to popular rabble-rousing that exacerbated prior divisions of opinions and groups that could be played upon for socio-political advantage – in spite of asseverations by patently wiser and less guileful souls.[37] *Pace* the slow passing of the Indo-European "caste factor" or noble/commoner dichotomy that falls like a shadow over Europe's and a much wider history and has made such manoeuvring all the easier, how contemporary it all is! How generative of a fault-line through Western history, with religion (despite moderates' and Christian calls for peace and the true Kingdom) being continuously sucked into the unpredictable cracks of power-play!

The confinement of an essay obviously precludes much further detailing, but Moore's intent to introduce "a pattern of persecution" which "appeared for the first time" and was also "to make Europe become, *as it has remained*, a persecuting society", allows us to round up our general argument.[38] The danger of negativity – of recriminatory payback activity – lurks ready to pounce behind the success of ideational and "religious settlement". It arose as *intra*-Christian crusading – Western crusaders ravaging even Constantinople, quite apart from various instances of "violent communities" persecuting minorities – out of the unifying high-mediaeval ethos, but never excluding the triggering of trouble by powerfully placed independent protagonists (such as Boniface [1] of Montferrat and Raymond of Toulouse).[39] Out of the steady laicization of learning that culminated in the

---

[36] Norman Cohn, *Europe's Inner Demons* (St Albans: Paladin, 1976), 20 with in ch. 2 (quotation); Michael Brett, *The Rise of the Fatimids: The World of the Mediterranean in the Tenth Century CE* (The Medieval Mediterranean: Peoples, Economies and Cultures, 400-1450, 30) (Leiden: Brill, 2001), ch. 1; Hugo Slim, *Killing Civilians: Method, Madness, and Morality in War* (New York: Columbia University Press, 2010), 43-49.

[37] See R.I Moore, *The Birth of Popular Heresy* (Toronto: University of Toronto Press, 1975); *The Origins of European Dissent* (Toronto: University of Toronto Press, 1994); *The War on Heresy* (Harvard: Harvard University Press, 2012); esp. pt. 1, and note the quoted phrase of Robert de Arbrissel, Letter (1109) to Countess Ermengarde of Brittany, sects. 17-19, in *Robert of Arbrissel, A Medieval Religious Life*, docs. trans, and annot. B.L. Vernade (Washington DC: Catholic University of America Press, 2001), 96-97.

[38] The quotation derives from the dustjacket and internet advertisement of Moore's *Formation*.

[39] Steven Runciman, *A History of the Crusades*, vol. 3: *The Kingdom of Acre and the Later Crusades*, (London: Penguin, 1978), bk. II, ch.1; David Nirenberg, *Communities of Violence: Persecution of*

ebulliences of Renaissance humanism, came the Reformation, a phenomenon in a time-frame astounding for its literature of religious controversy, and followed up by tragic Wars of Religion between Catholic and Protestant armies – again exacerbated by German princes seeking independence from the Holy Roman Emperor and by rulers of emergent new monarchies.[40] In the space that allowed "Enlightenment" reactions to these wars came Revolutions, and even if Methodist-cum-Evangelical reactions to a religious vacuum or a threat to religion apparently forestalled the worst excesses of violent dissension in Britain, a sensitive soul might despair that even Queen Victoria's reign opened with a religious "civil war" – the Protestants still against Catholic influences, Establishment versus Dissent, low and broad church against the Tractarians (the last of later attraction to Thomas Sterns Eliot and Barry Spurr), and so on.[41] Where Protestant/Catholic tensions persisted and were played on in politics as a *Kulturkampf*, to invoke the most suggestive Continental term, secular ideological movements entered the fray as surrogate religions – Communism and Nazism most astoundingly, their respective (and terrifying) persecutory excesses following upon the flush of successful political expansionism (under Hitler and Stalin, perhaps the most powerful individual power-players of all time).[42] And still further we could go on: the strictures of McCarthyism followed up by the leisure of New Ageism in the United States, from anxiety over the waved red rag in Australia to the experimentalisms of the seventies, and so on.[43]

Not that these cuts and thrusts of changing times were without positives. I have elsewhere contended that sociology, certainly the study of new movements, was born out of heresiology. And, far from it all being "polemic" as "language as violence", how much have we unappreciatively drawn from the rhetoric of disputation in mediaeval scholarship? How impoverished we would be, as the composers of the Vatican II Documents lately came to recognize, without cogent critiques of Catholic accretions? And yet how important in any case for eventual Catholic ecclesial stability was the necessity of vitriolic apologetics of Counter-Reformist energies.[44] What

---

Minorities in the Middle Ages (Princeton: Princeton University Press, 2014); Jonathan Sumption, *The Albigensian Crusade* (London: Faber & Faber, 2010). For important related developments, e.g., Desmond Seward, *The Monks of War: The Military Religious Orders* (St Albans: Paladin, 1974).

[40] Philip Benedict and Myron P. Gutmann, eds., *Early Modern Europe: From Crisis to Stability* (Newark: University of Delaware Press, 2005), esp. ch. 5.

[41] Quoting James L. Ellis in his neo-hagiographical *Charles Kingsley* (*Men with a Mission*, 4) (London: James Nisbet & Co, 1890), 37 (within ch. 4).

[42] For the complexities, Trompf, *Recurrence*, vol. 2, ch. 9, sect. 1.

[43] Cf., e.g., Lipset, *Political Man*, chs. 1-4; Ronald Conway, *The Land of the Long Weekend* (Melbourne: Sun Books, 1978), chs. 1, 5. 8-9.

[44] Trompf, "Missiology, Methodology and the Study of New Religious Movements", *Religious Traditions* 10 (1987): 96-97; Almut Suerbaum, George Southcombe and Benjamin Thompson, eds., *Polemic: Language as Violence in Medieval and Early Modern Discourse* (Farnham: Ashgate, 2015);

glories of aesthetic creativity might have been lost without the special space between revolutionary Protectorate and reactionary Restoration that permitted it – if we may here hark back to a context in which we began. And such a diversity of thought and artistic breakthroughs came out of the interwar Weimarian culture-clashing *mêlée*.[45]

My general point here, as caveat, is not to denigrate vehement argument and discordant thought. I concur with the sentiments of Evelyn Hall, neglected *littérateur* and spinster daughter of a Canon of St Paul's, London, that we should defend to our deaths the right for people to say what is disapproved of (as she imagined Voltaire contending).[46] T'were better, to my mind, for all strong opinions to be heard even in times of threat and outer conflict.[47]

But the chief purpose of this article is to warn that during the spaces in which external turmoil has abated, the internal forces of negative payback and exchanges of calumny can breed persecution or savage outbursts of righteous indignation, and fester into violence, and at times re-ignite flames of war that all hoped had been extinguished. Not that one then despairs over all that happens in the context of such developments: as if in American history, for example, between the revolutionary and civil wars, there should have been no open debate over slavery, or as if other optimistic energies for social reform and religious revival were ill-spent.[48] I simply follow the anthropological principle that where pacification suppresses fighting, intra-directed sorcery has its better chances; and thus that when nations have been blessed with the state of peace, their leaders must be wary of the excesses of blame and acrimony, as well as new "sorceries" of corruption, greed, feathered nests, trumped-up charges, even "underbelly" assassinations, that come to the fore.

Thinking of Europe and the West as we have in this paper, under outcomes of distinctly Western impetuses, the culturo-spiritual "centre does not hold" anymore. In a world of "post-modern" plural voices, everyone or every human group more or less reacts in their own light to pinpoint where

---

[45] Alex Novikoff, "Towards a Cultural History of Scholastic Disputation", *American Historical Review* 117, 2 (2012): 331-364; Olgar Weijers, *A Scholar's Paradise: Teaching and Debating in Medieval Paris* (Turnhout: Brepols, 2015); F. Schüssler Fiorenza, "Vatican II and the Aggiornamento of Roman Catholic Theology", in *Modern Christian Thought*, vol. 2: *The Twentieth Century*, eds., James C. Livington, Schüssler Fiorenza, et al) (Augsburg: Fortress, 2006), vol. 2, esp. 257; Luc Racaut, *Hatred in Print: Catholic Propaganda and Protestant Identity during the French Wars of Religion* (Farnham: Ashgate, 2002).

[45] Esp. Anton Kaes, Martin Jay, and Edward Dimendberg, eds., *The Weimar Republic Sourcebook* (Berkeley: University of California Press, 1994).

[46] Evelyn B. Hall, *The Friends of Voltaire* (London: Smith, Elder & Co, 1906), 199.

[47] Hannah Arendt, *Between Past and Future* (New York: Viking, 1968), 94.

[48] See Keith Hampson, "'God and Mammon': Religious Protestant Educational Change from the Revolution to the Gilded Age", in *Schism and Heresy and Religious Protest* (ed. Derek Baker) (Studies in Church History, 9) (Cambridge: Cambridge University Press, 1972), esp. 355.

they see persecution or act it out for themselves. Yet still the power-players are at work, cultivating standards of political correctness, or changing and interpreting the law to shore up an allegedly necessary social security; or subtly – we can say insidiously – manipulating the available media. Where the Byzantine ambience can still be experienced, collective Eastern European *mentalités* have not yet outlived blatant uses of openly prejudicial state policy – that can more readily circumvent ideals of religious freedom if it does not suit a Kaczinski or a Putin. In the end value judgements will have to be made,[49] because where power, peace and violence are under analysis they should never escape ethical scrutiny, if any or all of us are going to have the opportunity of living life "in all its fullness."

---

[49] For one renowned rationale for this, see Norma Marshall, "Lord Acton and the Writing of Religious History," *Journal of Religious History* 10 (1979): 400-415.

Two Poems

Ivan Head [1]

Pie Apocalypse

In Stanmore where the trains speed by
I can sit and eat a pie

And wonder if the end is nigh.

And at the juicy gravy bit
I drool, lick my lips

And ponder the apocalypse.

The Lark Ascending

At each day's end
I listen to *The Lark Ascending*.
A cello bow across the strings
expresses fluttering rising wings.

At some unknown point I cease to hear
as transcendental night draws near.
I lie behind the mask of sleep
and wait in hope to wake again.

Beyond the limit of ascent
I cannot tell you
where I went.

---

[1] These poem were originally published in *Quadrant*, Vol. 51, No. 11, Nov 2007: 78

An Introduction to St Philip Neri

Ivan Francis Head

St Philip Neri (1515-1595) is not widely known today but is an important figure. I have a copy of a portrait of him notable for its inclusions. My copy is a copy of a postcard that now lacks the artist's name and date. I read the title as "St Philip walking with the young of Rome". The picture shows Philip as perhaps sixty years old or perhaps "approaching the age of retirement in modernity". He is seated on stonework from a foundation or ruin in the near countryside outside Rome. In the background, we can see faintly the relatively new dome of St Peter's. I think it captures a scene from a "walk" to the seven churches. Philip had made this journey many times himself and, in later life, developed it as a recreation for young and old, even as a counterpart to the excesses of carnival. The seven churches were St Peter's, St Paul's Outside the Walls, St Sebastian on the Appian Way, St John Lateran, Santa Croce in Jerusalem, San Lorenzo, and St Mary Major. One author suggested that this was in total an eight-hour journey by foot, which is like saying that you can drive around Tasmania in a day.

The portrait includes a group of remarkable diversity – chosen by the artist to depict Philip's distinctive quality – his capacity to draw others to himself and make them happy in his company, while retaining the deeper privacy of an inner focus. This is on what St Paul would call "the inner man" or "the spirit". This dimension of privacy, or modesty, reserve and restraint, or "deflection" in promoting religious realities was expressed in one of his regular utterances "*secretum meum mihi* – my secret is my own". But then, a lamp set on a table cannot be hidden. Philip did not actively discuss, but rather suppressed discussion of the "spiritual moments" of his own life. It seems that in the last stage of life he did discuss with the young Pietro Consolini the 1544 "Pentecostal encounter" and nocturnal turning point that occurred in the Catacomb of St Sebastian. That cannot be retro-written into what others would have known as "fact" about him. Consolini himself declined to talk to those considering the case for canonisation because he felt that this was inconsistent with Philip's way – and he had to be compelled to testify – and even then he kept silent about this "Pentecostal" encounter for almost another fifty years until 1643, and just before his own death. That an essential moment of formation remains undiscussed for one hundred years is a subject in itself.

There are ten other figures in the portrait: five younger boys (in groups of three and two), two women as young adults, and then a central group of three young men, perhaps of comparable age to the women. All are well-dressed, all attractive, and all clearly happy to be in the company of this man out in the countryside. It is not a painting of cloister or "holiness as separation". One aphorism that has survived of Philip is his response to a complaint that children were making too much noise around the Oratory with their ball games – saying, in effect, "I don't mind if they chop firewood on my back so long as they are not doing anything evil".

Three of the young boys are engaged in a little music. One plays what looks like a guitar and another a flute or piccolo. The third might be conducting or keeping time from a book of music. The other two boys have clearly been playing or about to play a bit of soccer. They have a round ball and are seated near Philip. Another picture exists of Philip himself playing a ball game with hoops. The two young women are in the rear of the group to the left and while engaged in filling jars of water from a fountain, are clearly involved in the group and attentive to it. The central group of three youths is standing around Philip who is marked by a faint and naturalistic aureole. One youth holds what looks like a large mandolin. Another holds a large book open as if to get Philip's attention and comment on something. The third observes closely, looking over Philip's left shoulder.

Perhaps they are looking at a copy of Anerio's "*Teatro armonico spirituali di madrigali*" which the composer musician later dedicated to "San Girolamo and Beato Filippo Neri".

Philip holds open a small book at knee level. It might be his Office book but it could be a book of "The Best Italian Jokes" by one "Arlotto". Philip was not known for severity or for intellectual abstraction. He preferred music, games, learning, the human world in its dignity and beauty, companionship and friendship, a piety that embraced and included and did not easily forbid. Sometimes he would box the ears of any he met whom he felt were gloomy.

Philip's century was not an easy one. I am struck by its violence and endless warfare, alliances and intrigues between the city states and the papacy, the French monarch and the Spanish King and Emperor. Half a century of bitter conflict began in 1494 when Charles VIII of France in command of an army of thirty thousand came to claim the kingdom of Naples. The 1500s began with French, Swiss, Spanish and German soldiery in conflict on Italian soil. Popes, such as Julius II, were big players in the political and military ventures, and this Pope was probably the biggest of them all.

Philip's life-work is set after the sack of Rome in 1527. He stands in utter contrast to the papal styles of Julius II and Clement VII. But he did not exit the ecclesia of papal obedience. He was the sustainer of a community of priests, held together by shared beliefs, friendship, spiritual virtues and equalities in learning and means, and not by vows of obedience. He had a love of the natural, the direct and colloquial as well as of culture and learning. He exhibited an inwardness which could seem simple and childlike, but which combined with a sharp capacity to read other people's motives and intentions, to discern the difference between appearance and the prose of reality. The *Laudi* of Animuccia and the reforms of Palestrina are associated with the Oratory. Yet his favourite distraction was said to be a kind of comic book (perhaps "*Facezie, Motti, buffonerie, et burle*") by Piovano Arlotto.

It was a difficult century for a unified ecclesia. Luther's German domains were split. Henry VIII and England were also lost under Clement VII (1523-1534). At the same time we find the cataclysm of the sacking and occupation of Rome by Spanish and German Lutheran mercenaries, acting on the orders of the Spanish King, and Emperor, Charles V; both a kind of ultimate "don't mess with the French" statement and a clear statement about how he and Spain were really running the world. It was during this period of the Pope's exile or retreat from Rome that Henry VII's ambassadors arrived in Orvieto to seek the annulment of Henry's marriage to Catharine of Aragon, Charles V's aunt.

Other figures against which Philip Neri's greatness becomes clear include Martin Luther, Girolamo Savanarola and John Calvin. These three could be described as equally great or greater figures of reform, all of whom came into profound conflict with Papal and Roman Christianity as they knew it.

Philip arrived in Rome in 1533 as an eighteen-year-old. He lived as a layman until the mature age of thirty-six and became a priest only in 1551. He was a student of philosophy for three years at the Sapienza but had left by 1538. Apparently, he was distracted by a crucifix in the classroom. Philip met, and knew Ignatius well in the mid-1540s. It seems that he became friends with Ignatius in 1544, the year that he underwent his deeper conversion.

The essentials of Philip's mission were expressed in the years that he lived in community at St Girolamo, nearby the Campo di Fiore and not far from the site they moved to in St Maria Vallicella, where would be built the "new church". While the *Chiesa Nuova* is a splendid, sumptuous, baroque Church, it is recorded that Philip wished to keep the interior simply whitewashed.

I became interested in St Phillip through a prior interest in John Henry Newman. After casting around for a way within the Roman Church of his new allegiance, Newman and colleagues spent time in Rome studying, preparing and searching for a form of life and allegiance. He was attracted to St Philip Neri and adopted his Oratorian rule and principles for his life in community in Birmingham – perhaps summarised as a collegiality of spirit and intellect informed by friendship amongst equals, whose amity and willingness to make community work minimises the need for an imposed rule.

Newman maintained that he had seen a hint of this amongst the Fellows in the Oxford Colleges at their best.

St Philip did not write treatises or tracts and he burned almost all his papers (letters and sonnets) prior to his death. A collection of aphorisms exists, but whether or not coloured by F.W. Faber, I cannot tell. His eccentric humour and self-mockery manifested itself in many ways. Polish nobility visited him and he spent the time reading Arlotto aloud. He would walk through the streets smelling deeply and, with ecstatic gesture, a bunch of yellow broom bush. He left a dignified church procession to pull and stroke the beard of a member of the papal guard. He was accustomed to wearing large whitish shoes of unfinished leather. Perhaps they were simply lambskins turned inside out, a twentieth-century Australian fashion, which everyone now takes very seriously. He caused one of his followers to wear an extravagant fur and enter the church through the main door on a hot day while the choir was singing and deliver a trivial message. He was averse to rhetoric for rhetoric's sake and once commanded that the preacher repeat the sermon seven times on the spot. He instructed someone to stand and sing the *Miserere* at a wedding banquet. He rarely criticised and was patient with fashion and excess. To a lady wearing extravagant high heels he merely said, "Be careful that you do not fall" and to a young man with an extravagant collar, he said "I could hug you better if your collar did not poke me in the eye". But all these things are circumstantial expressions, indicators of the style of a man otherwise renowned for extraordinary devotion to the ordinary pattern of prayer, eucharist, community and confession.

The words personal, democratic, idiosyncratic, direct and convivial are apt. At the same time his style was immensely disciplined and perhaps only this could transcend the ethnic, regional, national and imperial debacles of the time. He held to his vision and his calling with vigour and would anathematise any who even raised the topic of introducing vows into the community of a more perfect way. There was steel in his method and his manner, a steel called upon to sustain the greater inner freedom of the Spirit.

One should not dismiss his clowning as mere buffoonery or mere eccentricity. Perhaps Phillip was a "debunker". Perhaps there is something at the core of the gospel that requires much lampooning in many forms, even as highly serious liturgics emerge. Humour can be friendly satire.

The Pen of a Ready Writer: The Psalms of Myles Coverdale

John Bunyan

This essay is based on the scholarly work of many others, but also upon the writer's practical experience of parish ministry and chaplaincy. It has an equally practical purpose, the encouragement of a *regular* reading of the "Coverdale Psalms", singing or saying or pondering them, and providing one fairly original and enlightening means of doing this, at a time when I realise there is often little substantial knowledge of the Bible at all, even among otherwise educated people and even among "evangelical" Christians.

I mean here the Psalter in the book to the riches of which Professor Barry Spurr has so often drawn our attention, the full title of which since 1662 has been:

> *The Book of Common Prayer and Administration of the Sacraments and Other Rites and Ceremonies of the Church according to the Use of the Church of England together with the Psalter or Psalms of David, pointed as they are to be sung or said in Churches and the Form and Manner of Making, Ordaining and Consecrating of Bishops, Priests and Deacons.*[1]

That Psalter was also used with the earlier editions of The Book of Common Prayer (BCP), those of 1549 and 1552 (largely the work of Archbishop Thomas Cranmer) and those of 1559 and 1604 (to which others contributed minor but significant revision). All editions were not only filled with Scriptural allusions; large portions were printed as the "Epistles" and "Gospels"; and tables were provided for the reading of most of the Bible at Matins and Evensong, daily throughout the year.[2]

There were Scriptures in English before the sixteenth century, but the greatest English translation still is that of William Tyndale (b.1495).[3] He translated the New Testament into English but only a small part of the

---

[1] The Psalms were bound separately from the Prayer Book until 1662.
[2] "Morning Prayer" and "Evening Prayer" from the 1552 BCP onwards. Reformation Bibles included the "Apocrypha" and more than one hundred passages from the Apocrypha were to be read during the year, though very few from Revelation.
[3] John James Lowndes, *Memorials of Myles Coverdale* (New Delhi: Isha Books, 2013), 23, says that Tyndale was assisted by Coverdale.

Old(er) Testament, before he was put to death for heresy, by burning, near Brussels, on about 6 October, 1536. Much of his work was embodied in later sixteenth-century translations; and, by using modern spelling, David Daniell has made Tyndale accessible again.[4]

Tyndale's work was further made accessible by Myles Coverdale. Born in 1488, Coverdale became a priest and friar, a leading English reformer, three times exiled, a Bible translator, Bishop of Exeter 1551-1553, Rector of St Magnus the Martyr, London Bridge, 1564-1566, Puritan preacher until his death in 1569. Exeter historian, John Hooker, praised Coverdale for his gentle character.[5]

Coverdale published his Bible (at Antwerp or Zurich) in 1535, the first complete English translation of the Scriptures. His work, with revision was incorporated in the 1539 (-1541) Great Bible.[6] Having Henry VIII's Licence, it was the first "authorized version". For the parts of the Old(er) Testament for which Tyndale had not provided a basis, *including* the Psalms, Coverdale made use of the translations of Luther, Zwingli, Leo Jud, the Vulgate and a new Latin version.[7]

With minor variations, the Great Bible version was used in the BCPs of 1549, 1552, 1559, and 1604.[8] However, the Authorized Version (AV), after its 1611 publication, was adopted for the Epistles and Gospels in the ill-fated Scottish BCP of 1637 and then for those in the 1662 BCP (it is still the authorised standard of worship in the Churches of England and Australia). And in these and other English-speaking Churches, until and including the 1962 Canadian BCP, all their BCP *Psalters* are Coverdale's with some minor revision.

Why did 1662 retain – for the Psalms – a translation more than a century old, not the more accurate AV? In her recent study of the rhythms of the Coverdale Psalter, Cally Hammond, in *The Sound of Liturgy: How Words Work in Worship*, thinks that the retaining of Coverdale's BCP Psalms (hereafter Coverdale):

---

[4] David Daniell, *The Bible in English: Its History and Influence* (New Haven: Yale University Press, 2003); David Daniell, ed., *Tyndale's Old Testament* (New Haven: Yale University Press, 1992); David Daniell, ed., *Tyndale's New Testament* 1534 (New Haven: Yale University Press, 1986); David Daniell, *William Tyndale: A Biography* (New Haven: Yale University Press, 1994). Daniell wrote on Coverdale for The Oxford Dictionary of National Biography.

[5] Lowndes, *op.cit.*, 151. He and Cranmer were involved, however, in the burning to death of the two (an Anabaptist and a Unitarian) executed for their faith under Edward VI.

[6] On the *Great Bible* of 1539, see ch 13 of David Daniell, *The Bible in English: Its History and Influence*. Daniell includes a biography of Coverdale.

[7] Stella Brooke, *The Language of the Book of Common Prayer* (London: André Deutsch, 1965), esp. ch.6, "The Psalter"; and Colin Dunlop, *Anglican Public Worship* (London: SCM, 1961), 105-119.

[8] The Psalter revised for the 1568 "Bishops' Bible" was so unpopular that in the 1572 edition the 1539 Coverdale version was printed along with it, and Coverdale's printed alone in all but one of the later editions.

> ... parallels the persistence of Old Latin (i.e. pre-Vulgate) versions in the texts of the Office and mass propers, and for similar reasons. Familiarity is not a trivial matter, and what is traditional, and rendered sacred by long usage, is not easily laid aside, even in favour of some criterion of scholarly or historical 'accuracy'... [9]

except – Professor Spurr and I might add – where liturgical leadership is intolerant and pastorally insensitive! However, familiarity cannot be the chief reason. The Epistles and Gospels of the Ante Communion that then followed Matins would have been equally familiar, but were changed to the AV. David Frost says that Coverdale "was thought more rhythmical and better adapted for chanting than the new".[10] And choral chanting of the psalms was predominant in the cathedral services with which the Prayer Book revisers would have been well acquainted. Robert Willis, Dean of Canterbury, says that:

> Coverdale, in 1535, was much closer to the Benedictine chanting of the Psalms of the Latin Vulgate, than were the KJV translators 75 years later ... by which time the memory of the old ways of the Medieval Church had died out. Coverdale could still, as it were, hear the old chants as he translated; and his Psalms are far more rhythmic and suggestive of chanting than are those of the KJV.[11]

Just as the AV psalms remained unknown in Anglican churches, so too the Revised Standard and New Revised Standard Versions of the psalms are absent from Anglican worship and most Anglican devotion (N.P. Wright's recent book being an exception).[12]

Shakespeare quoted more from the Psalter than any other biblical book, and the majority of his quotations and allusions are from Coverdale, only a few from the 1560 Geneva Bible.[13] More than a century later, Charles Jennens used Coverdale for Psalm verses in Handel's *Messiah*. Indeed, *The*

---

[9] Cally Hammond, *The Sound of Liturgy: How Words Work in Worship* (London: SPCK, 2015), 166. Hammond makes some comparison of the work of Coverdale and that of Cranmer and notes, for example, small changes Cranmer made to the wording of the psalms.

[10] David Frost, *Making the Liturgical Psalter: The Morpeth Lectures 1980* (Nottingham: Grove Books, 1981) - this sentence taken verbatim from George D. Carleton, *The English Psalter: With a Devotional Commentary* (London: Mowbray, 1953), 4.

[11] In conversation with Andrew Mead, Rector of St.Thomas's, New York, quoted by Michael Potemra in the *National Review*, N.Y., 3 July, 2011.

[12] The Unitarian King's Chapel, Boston, BCP did replace Coverdale with the AV psalms in its eighth (1925) edition. The Church of Scotland and English Non-conformists generally preferred metrical psalms, and these did come to be sung also in the Church of England in addition to, and sometimes instead of, Coverdale. Coverdale published his own metrical psalms probably in 1535, very poor ones, as Lowndes, *op.cit.*, 104-105, shows. Like Cranmer, Coverdale could not write good verse!

[13] Richmond Noble, *Shakespeare's Biblical Knowledge and Use of the Book of Common Prayer* (New York: Octagon, 1970), 77-81.

Oxford Dictionary of Quotations has thirty-eight pages of AV quotations but not *one* quotation from the AV Psalms. It has over sixteen pages of quotations from the BCP, over ten of those pages with quotations (269!) from Coverdale's psalms.

However, Coverdale was not a Hebrew scholar and he relied on those later translations noted above. His mistakes became increasingly apparent, and even by 1611, let alone 1662, some wording was obsolete. Calls for moderate revision were made, suggested, for example, for Convocation's consideration in England in 1689, although no changes were made in the 1689 Proposed BCP.

In 1909, James George Carleton,[14] and his son George in 1945, provided one solution to the problem, though not suitable for a Prayer Book, printing Coverdale in one column on a page, with notes on the second – important clarifications, some more accurate wording from the 1885 Revised Version, and traditional interpretation of some psalms as referring to Jesus. Some punctuation changes were made, quotation marks inserted.

In 1961, Biblical scholar Frederick C. Grant called for slight changes in many places, "still keeping the rhythm and beauty of Coverdale's style, but releasing more of the power and triumphant faith of the ancient writers".[15] Minor revisions of Coverdale had already been published and in the US Episcopal Church official revision had long since begun with hundreds of small changes in its BCP – in 1790, 1793, 1822, 1845, 1871 and 1892, and over one hundred in 1928. In England, Psalter revision produced by a Church committee (with one hundred and seventy-six changes, many quite minor) received some approval in 1916. It was not authorised for England, although incorporated in the 1926 Irish BCP. Further revisions were approved by Canterbury Convocation in 1920 but the new House of Laity prevented their inclusion in the 1928 Proposed BCP. In Canada, minor changes were made in its BCP Psalter in 1918 and in 1962.

In 1963 *The Revised Psalter* (RP), developed with literary guidance from C.S. Lewis and (reluctantly) T.S. Eliot[16], was authorised for alternative use in the Church of England, with a chant edition in 1966. David Frost, Professor of English at Newcastle University, N.S.W., wrote that this *Revised Psalter*, aimed at "an invisible mending" of Coverdale, and that it was a "succès d'estime".[17] It sought to remove misleading or mystifying words, and, not least, as Commission member Bishop C.A. Chase noted, "to help towards a

---

[14] James G. Carleton, *The Psalter of the Church* (Cambridge: Cambridge University Press, 1909).
[15] Frederick C. Grant, *Translating the Bible* (Edinburgh: Nelson, 1961), 162.
[16] Francis Warner, "Lewis' Involvement of the Revision of the Psalter", in *C.S. Lewis and the Church: Essays in Honour of Walter Hooper*, eds. Judith Wolfe and B.N. Wolfe (London: Bloomsbury, 2011), 54, 55. T.S. Eliot "always wanted the Prayer Book version retained" with "Lewis, like Coverdale, willing to try his hand at a new phrase".
[17] Frost, *Making the Liturgical Psalter, op. cit.*, 3.

more intelligent singing" of some passages to Anglican chant.[18] It was clearly more than an "invisible" mending, such as is found in the US and Canadian revisions, and I doubt if it was used sufficiently to gain much esteem. It moved too far from Coverdale to satisfy those who, like church-people in 1662, treasured the latter; and (like the 1967 Series 2 English revised services, the 1979 Scottish Book of Common Order, and the 1984 Welsh BCP in which alone the RP replaced Coverdale) it did not satisfy those who wanted an end to traditional liturgical language and no use of the second person singular in addressing God, a usage that Professor Spurr and others have defended.[19] In the twenty-third Psalm, for example, the accurate "darkest valley" replaced "valley of the shadow of death" (long familiar also from *The Pilgrim's Progress*) – restored in the new Anglican *Liturgical Psalter* (LP).

Nowadays, for the main Sunday Communion in Anglican churches, 1662 services have often been replaced by innumerable alternative forms, in ways and by processes that provoked Professor Spurr's sharp criticism in *The Word in the Desert*.[20] And LP was developed and incorporated in the new alternative books of the Churches of England and Australia, and of some other Anglican Churches.[21] The first version, in *An Australian Prayer Book, 1978*, was revised to make the language more "inclusive" in *A Prayer Book for Australia, 1995* and in *Common Worship*.

Eight scholars formed the "Hebrew Panel" for the LP but Professor David Frost alone formed the "English Panel", his *Making the Liturgical Psalter: The Morpeth Lectures 1980*, the essential guide to understanding this revision. The Introduction to the first revision and the Preface to the Inclusive Language Version are both printed in *The Psalms: The Liturgical Psalter: New Inclusive Language Version*.[22]

The words of those scholars have more echoes of Coverdale than most modern versions in liturgical traditions not derived from the BCP, and perhaps more so than the Psalter of the 1979 US Episcopal BCP (with which W.H. Auden was associated – also reluctantly). Nonetheless, they freely used phrases from other translations. They sought to keep the Hebrew flavour but also to reflect current Hebrew scholarship, and, with Frost's expertise, to

---

[18] For example, "by allowing the stress to fall on the right word, or by avoiding an unnatural prolongation of a syllable to fit the chant". G.A. Chase, *A Companion to the Revised Psalter* (London: SPCK, 1963), 3.

[19] See also Peter Toon and Louis R.Tarsitano, *Neither Archaic nor Obsolete: The Language of Common Prayer and Public Worship* (Philadelphia: Prayer Book Society of the USA; Harleston: Edgeways, 2003).

[20] Barry Spurr, *The Word in the Desert* (Cambridge: Lutterworth, 1995).

[21] Published separately as David Frost, et al., eds., *The Psalms: A New Translation for Worship* (London: William Collins, 1977), and David Frost, et al., eds., *The Cambridge Liturgical Psalter* (London: William Collins, 1976).

[22] David L. Frost, John A. Emerton and Andrew A. Macintosh, eds., *The Psalms: The Liturgical Psalter: New Inclusive Language Version*. (London: HarperCollins, 1995).

provide a style and rhythm appropriate when psalms are said or sung aloud in church. Frost wrote that "inevitably the *Liturgical Psalter* has become the supplanter of Coverdale"; but he acknowledged the debt owed to Coverdale.[23] "The new version aims to be in the tradition of Miles Coverdale and not a betrayal of it. If a translation has merits, it is because a wren rose on the backs of eagles: on those Hebraists whose scholarship is its foundation, and on those earlier translators who have contributed to its language".[24] He comments that:

> Coverdale's psalms have commanded affection for so long because, unlike many other more perfect translations, their emotional power seemed to come direct from the English writer and was not simply an echo of some half-perceived original. Euphony and a command of rhythm and felicitous phrase were factors in Coverdale's success, but its essence was his ability to make the psalms his own. That is the fundamental criterion by which fresh translations will be judged, and it is the standard by which Coverdale was preferred to the committee work of the King James Version and to more recent translations.[25]

Bishop N.P. Wright has recently called for a much greater use of psalms in daily and weekly worship[26] and he notes that the beauty of the psalms does not get lost in translation (I would add, a *good* translation[27]). They rely for their effect, he thinks, on the way they set out the "main themes" through the use of parallelism. C.S. Lewis saw "other and more complex patterns" in them, but thought it "(according to one's point of view) either a wonderful piece of luck or a wise provision of God's, that poetry which was to be turned into all languages should have as its chief formal characteristic one that does not disappear (as mere metre does) in translation".[28]

The Liturgical Psalter has now commonly replaced Coverdale for Holy Communion (with mostly only short psalms or short portions of psalms used), the Eucharist now in many Anglican and Episcopal churches the only morning service – although sometimes a Coverdale psalm is still used. However, Frost exaggerates in suggesting that the LP has "supplanted" Coverdale.

Nowadays in England especially, 1662 Communion survives – mainly at early Sunday services, with little use of psalms (other than metrical paraphrases). And Choral Evensong, although now much less common, is still found, significantly, in all English (and most Scottish, Welsh, and Irish)

---

[23] Frost et al., *The Psalms: The Liturgical Psalter, op.cit.*, 8.
[24] *Ibid.*, 9.
[25] *Ibid.*, 4.
[26] N.P. Wright, *The Case for the Psalms: Why They are Essential* (London: Harper One, 2013).
[27] e.g. Robert Alter's non-liturgical *The Book of Psalms* (London: W.W. Norton, 2007).
[28] C.S. Lewis, *Reflections on the Psalms* (London: Collins Fontana, 1958), 12.

cathedrals – in recent times, the "growing points" of the C. of E. – and in many major parish churches. Even Sunday BCP Matins is still normally sung in some of those.[29] I have urged a restoration, on practical, contemporary, pastoral grounds, of Sunday Matins (or a flexible Matins replacing the Ante Communion).[30] In Australia there is BCP Evensong on all or most Sundays in major cathedrals (except Sydney), and on some weekdays in some larger cathedrals. And wherever BCP Matins or Evensong survives in church, so too, remarkably, do the Coverdale Psalms.

That is not all. Reading of the 150 psalms in the BCP Offices by some clerics and lay-people over the thirty days of the month, in public or, in practice, more often in private, still survives.[31] And the vitality of Coverdale (in its 1928 US BCP form) is also indicated by its use for Sunday Morning Prayer and occasionally Evensong in many churches of the comparatively small, separated "Anglican" churches of the United States and the emerging "Anglican Church of North America". Coverdale is also being used in the "Ordinariate" churches of former Anglicans who have joined Rome. And there is a largely forgotten precedent. The old Roman Catholic families of England tended to favour simple services and disliked the Italianate forms brought by Irish and other emigrants in the later nineteenth century, and with a missionary concern, some held Vespers in the English of the BCP![32]

More recently these psalms have been adopted in the new US English services of the Russian Orthodox Church Outside of Russia, in *A Psalter for Prayer: An Adaptation of the Classic Miles Coverdale Translation*.[33] Coverdale was chosen because of "the sonority of its language and its aptness for reading aloud" and because it was considered "one of the most elegant translations of the psalms ever to appear in English".

The devotional value of Coverdale is strongly emphasised in a recent book by James Jones, Bishop of Liverpool, *With My Whole Heart: Reflections on the Heart of the Psalms*. He says that the poetry of Coverdale "adds fathoms to

---

[29] e.g., Chichester, Durham, Guildford, Hereford, Lincoln, Oxford, Peterborough, Salisbury, St. Paul's, Wells, Winchester, York Minster, Westminster Abbey, and St. John's, Edinburgh; on most Sundays in Chapels Royal and the Guards Chapel, even daily, during term, in St. Patrick's in Dublin. Chelmsford and Rochester have Choral Matins twice monthly, St. Alban's monthly. The last and Chester on Sundays have BCP Choral Matins or Choral Communion. Most other cathedrals have *said* BCP Matins.

[30] John Bunyan, *Morning Prayer Matters, Celebrating BCP: A Map for the Minister*, and *Prayer Book Patterns and Principles* (Campbelltown: privately printed, 2012).

[31] Some Jews also read the Psalter over a month, but some Jews and Christians over a week, some Anglicans now over six or seven or eight weeks.

[32] J.D. Crichton, *Worship in a Hidden Church* (Dublin: Columba Press, 1988), ch.6, noted by George Guiver in *Vision upon Vision* (London: Canterbury Press, 2009), 137.

[33] *A Psalter for Prayer: An Adaptation of the Classic Miles Coverdale Translation* (New York: Holy Trinity Publications, 2011). Modified wording takes into account the (Septuagint) Orthodox text numbering, St. Jerome's Latin translation of the LXX, the Church Slavonic, and occasionally other English translations.

their theological depth" and that "it is my heart's desire that this little book would take the reader to the Psalms, to the Book of Common Prayer, to the Bible and thereby into the courts of the Lord."[34]

The Psalms have always been meant primarily to be sung and in English cathedrals, except under Mary I and Cromwell, Coverdale has been sung since 1549, and for a time after that, and from the later nineteenth century also in some parish churches. Cally Hammond comments that "there is great flexibility inherent in Coverdale's text, allowing for different schemes of pointing within the convention of Anglican chant".[35] Many musical Psalters have been compiled, including older UK and US *Cathedral Psalters*, the 1903 *Australian Psalter*, and the still standard *Parish Psalter (With Chants)*.

However, it is again significant that, although the LP and the 1979 US BCP Psalter have metrical editions, most Choral Evensongs continue to use Coverdale and so too do the newest Psalters. *The Anglican (or New St Paul's Cathedral) Psalter*[36], and *The Wessex Psalter*[37] – more widely useful and highly praised – demonstrate the vitality and dominance of the Coverdale tradition. George H. Guest has since produced *The Psalms of David: Pointed and Edited for Chanting*, using the 1928 US BCP revision of Coverdale.[38] The *All Saints Plainsong Psalter: As Used at All Saints' Margaret Street, London*[39], and the new *St Dunstan's Plainsong Psalter*[40] provide alternatives to Anglican chant.[41]

The background sketched, I come now to the practical proposal and main purpose of this exercise. Ordained in 1959, I was lax for years in daily reading of Matins and Evensong "either privately or openly, not being let by sickness, or some other urgent cause".[42] However, in 2009 I printed a

---

[34] James Jones, *With My Whole Heart: Reflections on the Heart of the Psalms* (London: SPCK, 2012), Prelude, x.

[35] Hammond, *op. cit*, 168.

[36] Hyperion has the New St Paul's on CDs. Priory's 10 planned CDs of *The Complete Psalms of David, Series 2* is not to be confused with Priory's earlier *The Psalms of David, Vols 1-10* which does not have the psalms in order.

[37] Originally designed for young people including a number of dyslexics, it has new as well as old chants.

[38] George H. Guest, *The Psalms of David: Pointed and Edited for Chanting* (Brewster: Paraclete, 2012).

[39] Walter Sidney Vale, ed., *All Saints Plainsong Psalter: As Used at All Saints' Margaret Street, London* (London: All Saints' Margaret Street, 1998).

[40] *St Dunstan's Plainsong Psalter* (Glendale: Lancelot Andrewes Press, 2002).

[41] This essay does not cover the choice of psalms at Sunday Matins and Evensong. On most Sundays, privately, I have used the psalms in sequence as in my tables. In our small but lively parish church we *sang* psalms, *not* difficult if an organist can accompany them, but (other than "proper psalms" on great holy days) appropriate psalms from *Parish Psalter* chants which could be easily sung. I have chosen as easiest chants those for Pss 8, 15, 23, 27, 43, 46, 48, 67, 81, 95, 98, 100, 114, 117, 119 (chant 197 etc), 121, 122, 126, 130 and 150. Others quite easy are chants for Pss 19, 22, 24, 37, 42, 51 (especially chant 102), 63, 65, 84, 87, 90. 93, 99, 103, 115, 116, 129 and 148. Some psalms with difficult chants (e.g. 1, 4, 104) can be sung to other chants if suitable for the words.

[42] Authorised short alternative forms of the daily office are found in *An Australian Prayer Book 1978* (AAPB), *A Prayer Book for Australia 1995* (APBA) and England's *Common Worship* (CW).

selection of ninety-seven psalms or portions of psalms, for me a more manageable diet, allocated in order over thirty-one days of the month, using Coverdale unchanged but incorporating annotations within it.[43] Using that selection ever since has encouraged my reading the daily Offices (with AV Lessons) and others may also be encouraged. However, for this essay, and, I hope, for a future book, I have prepared a fuller selection (the annotations still being revised), one hundred and eleven psalms or psalm portions, with a major re-allocation of them as set out below for the first time.

Only recently have I found that *in part* I had long been anticipated by W. Bernard Smith in his arrangement of the Psalter.[44] Like me, he omitted some psalms, included some psalms as optional, omitted some verses of small religious value, divided some long psalms into two or more portions, and numbered the sections of Psalm 119.

My work, unlike his, makes no changes to the BCP words. Norman Taylor comments that "even in their obscure moments they have the mellow beauty of some ancient, familiar window with slightly jumbled glass; one would scarcely have the imperfections put right".[45] More importantly, conservative evangelical Leland Ryken has emphasised the value of retaining the "elusive and mysterious", numinous, literary qualities and subtleties of the psalms (and other Scriptures), the frequent ambiguities in the original, and the possible "multiple meanings".[46]

I also make no changes to the BCP verse numbering, have the psalms chosen in their original order, cater for a thirty-first day of the month, and include my annotations – clarifications and corrections (and some inevitably debatable interpretations) – unobtrusively within the text itself[47], while remembering that the Hebrew itself, sometimes obscure, lacking tenses and moods, is such that often translations vary.

Regarding the use of the "cursing" and similar elements in the psalms, views differ: many churches allow their omission. I agree with John Wesley who thought some passages improper on Christian lips.[48] I omit now thirty-

---

[43] The full BCP Psalter can always be used by those who prefer it. I occasionally follow the full "diet" on the BBC, on CD, or in a cathedral.

[44] W. Bernard Smith, ed., *A New Church Psalter: Being the Church of England Prayer Book Version of the Canticles and Psalms with certain Omissions and Variations, and added Explanatory Notes* (London: Oxford University Press, 1936).

[45] Norman Taylor, *For Services Rendered: An Anthology in Thanksgiving for the Book of Common Prayer* (Cambridge: Lutterworth, 1993), 48.

[46] Leland Ryken, *Understanding English Bible Translation: The Case for an Essentially Literal Approach* (Wheaton: Crossway, 2009), especially Part Four, "The Ideal English Bible Translation", and Part Five, "The Bible in the Church". He has scathing criticism of many simplified "dynamic equivalent" versions of the Bible.

[47] Bernard Smith, *op. cit.* instead provides a brief explanatory note before each psalm and has a "pointing" of the psalms, something I leave to the chant Psalters which vary in their pointing.

[48] John Wesley, Sermon at Bristol, 9 September, 1784.

nine psalms, to provide not only a more digestible diet but a better daily balance. Remaining are still notes of judgment, and, in a world where there is evil, some expressions of desire for the defeat of enemies. Thus psalms chosen include "Upon the ungodly he shall rain snares, fire and brimstone, storm and tempest" (Ps.11.7) but omit "Blessed shall he be that taketh thy children: and throweth them against the stones" (Ps.137.9). Finally and importantly, in a proposal for mainly private daily use of the Psalter, this is nonetheless more than a matter of "personal devotion": it is rather a joining in the prayer of all God's people, and in the prayer of Jesus, not least in the person of those who may know joy, but also injustice or isolation, suffering – yet also a sense of the divine.

If one uses these psalms in the way suggested, as I have attempted for ninety-seven of them for over six years, the repetition and their language can help one to know some by heart (and through the annotations to understand them better) and, whether Jew or Christian, seeker or agnostic, to find here something of our "heart's desire" (Ps. 20.4), when on the Delectable Mountains and when "in the place of dragons" (Ps. 44.20).

A few examples of annotations

Pages in the "Psalter" being prepared at present are not cluttered with annotations but are inserted where thought useful. (They do *not* include the explanations in italics below.) In twelve of the thirty-two verses of Psalm 22, they are as follows:

1. My God, my God, [look upon me] ... *words noted in 1662 as not in the Hebrew*
5. They ... were <u>holpen</u> (given help) ...
13. as it were a <u>ramping</u> (ravening) lion ...
15. my mouth is dried up <u>as a potsherd</u> (like earthenware) ...
16. <u>many dogs</u> (a pack of curs) ... the <u>council</u> (cohort) of the wicked ...
17. I may <u>tell</u> (count) all my bones ...
20. my <u>darling</u> (dear life) from the <u>power</u> (mawling) of the dogs ...
21. the horns of the <u>unicorns</u> (wild oxen) ...
22. ye that <u>fear</u> (revere) him ... *Most translations used "fear" but it can be misleading.*
26. *unchanged, but the Hebrew is obscure and translations vary greatly*
29. all such as be <u>fat</u> (prosperous) upon earth: <u>have eaten and worshipped</u> (shall eat and shall worship). *Translations again vary greatly and APBA omits this verse.*
31. [My] seed shall serve him ...
    <u>they</u> (this) shall be <u>counted unto</u> (told of) the Lord for a generation (to come): *"to come" is added to make the meaning clearer.*

By contrast, e.g. Psalms 1 and 53, have no annotations at all, and some very few. The selected psalms or psalm portions are said or sung without any change in the words.

The Proposed Table of 111 Psalms for the Thirty-one Days of the Month

Psalms in bold, underlined, are always sung or said; those not in bold may be omitted. Verses of psalms are printed in *italics*. Verses printed within brackets ( ) may be omitted.

	Morning	Evening
1	<u>1</u>, *2.1-7*, <u>4</u>, <u>5</u>, *1-8*	6, <u>8</u>, <u>10</u>.
2	<u>11</u>, 12, <u>13</u>, <u>15</u>	16, 17, *1-13, 16*
3	<u>18</u>, *1-6, 16-25, 27-29*, <u>19</u>	<u>20</u>, <u>21</u>, *1-7, 12*
4	<u>22</u>	<u>23</u>, <u>24</u>, <u>26</u>
5	<u>27</u>, 30, <u>31</u>. *1-6*	<u>32</u>, <u>33</u>, *1-8, 17-21,*
6.	34, *1-9 (10), 11-15*	<u>35</u>, *1-4 (5-8) 9-28*
7	36, <u>37</u>. *1-11, 36-41*	<u>39</u>, *1-8, 13-15*, <u>40</u> (part = Ps 70)
8	41, <u>42</u>	<u>43</u>, <u>46</u>, <u>47</u>
9	<u>48</u>, 50, *7-15*, <u>51</u>, *1-4 (5) 6-18*	<u>53</u> (= Ps14), <u>55</u>. *1-11, 17-25*
10	<u>56</u>, <u>57</u>	<u>62</u>, <u>63</u>
11	<u>65</u>, <u>66</u>, *1-11*, <u>67</u>	<u>68</u>, *1-20*
12	<u>69</u>, *1-22, 30-37* (70=40)	<u>71</u>, *1-2, 10-20*, 72
13	<u>74</u>, *1-11, 19-24*, <u>80</u>	<u>81</u>, <u>82</u>
14	<u>84</u>, 85, <u>86</u>	88, <u>90</u>, *1-10, 12-17*
15	91, *1-6, 14-16*, <u>92</u>, <u>93</u>	<u>95</u>, *1-8a (8b-11)*, <u>96</u>
16	<u>98</u>, <u>99</u>	<u>100</u>, <u>102</u>
17	<u>103</u>	<u>104</u>
18	<u>105</u>, *1-22*	<u>105</u>, *23-27 (28-35), 36-44*
19	<u>106</u>, *1-13, 42-46*	<u>107</u>, *1-22*
20	<u>107</u>, *23-43*, <u>108</u>, *1-4*	<u>109</u>, *1-4, 20-30*, <u>110</u>, *1-4*, <u>111</u>
21	<u>112</u>, <u>113</u>	<u>114</u>, <u>115</u>, *1-9 (10-12) 13-18*
22	<u>116</u>, <u>117</u>	<u>118</u>
23	<u>119</u>, parts 1, 2, 3	<u>119</u>, parts 4 and 5, <u>67</u>
24	<u>119</u>, parts 6, 7, 8	<u>119</u>, parts 9, 10, 11
25	<u>119</u>, parts 12, 13, 14	<u>119</u>, parts 15, 16, 17
26	<u>119</u>, parts 18, 19, 20	<u>119</u>, parts 21 and 22, 98
27	<u>121</u>, <u>122</u>, <u>124</u>, <u>126</u>	<u>127</u>, <u>128</u>, <u>129</u>
28	<u>130</u>, <u>131</u>, <u>133</u>, <u>134</u>	137, *1-6*, <u>139</u>, *1-13, 23-24*, <u>141</u>, *1-4, 9-11*
29	<u>142</u>, <u>143</u>	<u>144</u>, <u>145</u>
30	<u>146</u>, <u>147</u>	<u>148</u>, <u>149</u>. 1-5a, 6a, <u>150</u>
31	45, *7-10, 14-18*	Ecclus 51. *1-3a, 7-9, 11-15, 20, 23, 26 Confitebor tibi* and **Ecclus 50**. 22-23a [49] *Et nunc orate Deum* (Vulgate names used as in the BCP.)

---

[49] I suggest as a finale for this revised schedule, Ecclesiasticus 50.22-23a, the basis of Luther's hymn, translated as "Now thank we all our God".

Spurred On

John Bunyan

Dear doctor Barry Spurr, you first observed
me – gowned beneath Red Hill in better days
when Church and school – their finest words conserved –
by goodness and by grace won worthy praise.

Among endangered species, you took care
of Prayer Book and King James, defended them
against the favoured philistines, did dare
to speak for voiceless, and tin ears contemn.

Sidere mens et seq: betimes, below
some lucky stars you laboured, through our night,
to lift young eyes to see where words can go
in this south land, for sweet sounds give delight.

Rejoice, resound, with T.S., live, my friend:
in your beginning, Barry, is your end.

The Cultic Milieu in Australia: Deviant Religiosity in the Novels of Carmel Bird

Carole M. Cusack [1]

Introduction

Carmel Bird's (b. 1940) *Mandala Trilogy* comprises three studies of what the English sociologist Colin Campbell termed the "cultic milieu".[2] For Bird, this is a subculture of alternative (or "deviant") religiosity, in which the vulnerable are caught up in the snares and delusions of charismatic leaders. *The White Garden* (1995) introduces the amoral psychiatrist, Dr Ambrose Goddard, who medically and sexually abuses patients at Mandala Psychiatric Clinic, a virtual prison over which he (as his name suggests) is "God".[3] In *Red Shoes* (1998) Petra Penfold-Knight is the leader of the Hill House Brethren, a "cult" that kidnaps patients from Mandala and steals the babies of unmarried mothers, and in which members are dressed identically and wear red shoes. *Cape Grimm* (2004) is the tale of Caleb Mean who, raised from infancy to understand himself as the second coming of Christ, incinerates his community of one hundred and forty-seven religious followers (most of whom are his relatives) in remote north-west Tasmania on his thirty-third birthday. The novels tease out connections between psychiatry and what are popularly termed "cults", and psychiatrists and the charismatic leaders of deviant religious groups. This chapter examines the *Mandala Trilogy* using social scientific models from the study of new religious movements (NRMs), including American sociologists of religion Rodney Stark and William Simms Bainbridge's three classic models of "cult formation" (psychopathology, entrepreneurship, and subcultural evolution) to illuminate the portrayal of charismatic leaders, Stanley Cohen's notion of "moral panic" to interpret Bird's identification of fringe religion with criminal behaviour, drug-taking,

---

[1] This research was originally presented at the Australian Genre Crossings conference, State Library of Queensland, 11 October 2013. My thanks are due to Helen Young and Kim Wilkins for both the invitation to this event and for their helpful feedback.
[2] Colin Campbell, "The Cult, the Cultic Milieu and Secularization", *A Sociological Yearbook of Religion in Britain* 5 (1972), 119-136.
[3] Patricia Bastida Rodríguez, "Narrative Strategies and Gender Discourses: The Empowerment of Female Characters in Carmel Bird's *The White Garden*", *Estudios Humanísticos. Filología* 26 (2004), 250.

sexual deviance, and irrational beliefs, and Campbell's "cultic milieu", mentioned above, to clarify the teachings of the charismatic leaders, and the existence of a group in society that is primed to follow such leaders, and to join such movements.[4]

A second focus of the chapter is Australia, Tasmania (a major setting in the trilogy and Bird's birthplace) in particular, and the historical displacement of the Aboriginal people by White settlers, which Bird connects to the prominent literary and artistic motif of the "lost child", which Peter Pierce has argued is a peculiarly Australian concern.[5] Tasmania emerges as a Garden of Eden in which there are many serpents: a place of extraordinary beauty, yet one in which acts of perversion, power, and violence, are committed by evildoers. The "religious" quality of Bird's fiction is reinforced by her use of myth, folklore, theology, fairy-tales, and archetypal psychology as the building blocks of these dark tales. Her knowingly aware authorial voice describes a bewildering world of bizarre family histories, peculiar religious communities, insane criminals, and children and women who are raped, tortured, abducted and murdered, in a matter-of-fact fashion that is deeply disquieting. Bird has often been compared to Angela Carter and A. S. Byatt, both writers of works that tend to be metafiction, "writing which places itself on the border between fiction and criticism, and which takes that border as its subject".[6] Bird, while a critically acclaimed writer and regular nominee for literary prizes including the Miles Franklin Award and the Ned Kelly Award, is not a popular novelist; the literary games of metafiction are a rarified taste, and one that is unappealing to a majority of readers.[7]

Tony Hughes-D'Aeth has noted that Bird's writings are morally challenging, in part due to her habit of inserting texts, appending footnotes, and employing multiple or unreliable voices to destabilise the overt "story" of the novel. These authorial tactics also have the effect of blurring the meaning of the narrative. Writing of *Red Shoes* (2001) he argues that, "the condemnation the book elicits from its readers in response to the terrible acts it describes is undermined by the decentring of the narratives in which they occur ... the stories, in gaining mythic significance by their resonance with

---

[4] William Sims Bainbridge and Rodney Stark, "Cult Formation: Three Compatible Models", *Sociological Analysis* 40, no. 4 (1979), 283-295; Stanley Cohen, *Folk Devils and Moral Panics* (New York and London: Routledge, 2011 [1972]).

[5] Peter Pierce, *The Country of Lost Children: An Australian Anxiety* (Cambridge, New York and Melbourne: Cambridge University Press, 1999). Pierce's study is divided into nineteenth-century cases, which he posits are concerned with "the discovery of the lost child", and twentieth-century cases, which he argues are concerned with "the abandonment of the lost child", xiii.

[6] Mark Currie, "Introduction," in *Metafiction*, ed. Mark Currie (Harlow: Longman Group Ltd, 1995), 2.

[7] Nor has she received much attention from critics, with the notable exception of a group of Spanish scholars, including Gerardo Rodríguez Salas, Maria del Carmen Rodríguez Fernández and Patricia Bastida Rodríguez, among others.

other older tales, also lose some of their disturbing immediacy".[8] It will be argued that Bird's fictional tropes are linked to perennial moral panics and societal anxieties, represented mostly by deviant religion emerging from the cultic milieu. Campbell states that this milieu is "the cultural underground of society ... it includes all deviant belief-systems and their associated practices ... alien and heretical religion, deviant medicine ... the worlds of the occult and the magical, of spiritualism and psychic phenomena, of mysticism and new thought, of alien intelligence and lost civilizations, of faith healing and nature cure".[9] In her fiction Bird reworks a limited range of motifs in a near-obsessional fashion, seeking a way to overcome or break open the melodramatic, dangerous, and seemingly inescapably horrifying world that she has created. In *Cape Grimm*, the most recent of the novels discussed, it seems that certain glimmers of hope are permitted to exist, and that redemptive power of love may create a different kind of world, in which it is possible not merely to survive but to flourish.

1: The White Garden

Bird's third novel, *The White Garden* (1995), has a plot partly based on the "deep sleep" therapy scandal at Chelmsford Private Hospital, in Pennant Hills, Sydney. Dr Harry Bailey (1922-1985) began treating patients with controversial deep sleep therapy (DST) and electro-convulsive therapy (ECT) in 1963. By the 1990s after the deaths of more than twenty patients in the ten years between 1967 and 1977, constant coverage by *60 Minutes* and the *Sydney Morning Herald* to name but two media organs, and a raft of law cases alleging injury and mistreatment by many other former patients, Harry Bailey and Chelmsford became the subject of a Royal Commission (1988-1990).[10] However, as will be seen, while each novel in the *Mandala Trilogy* has a real-world, historical incident that sparked Bird's imagination at its core, *The White Garden* is not about Chelmsford in any factual sense. Despite the seeming congruence of Bailey's suicide in 1985, and Bird's statement in *Red Shoes* that Goddard "shot his dogs and then he shot himself" in 1987,[11] *The White Garden* is in fact a story of how female voices and solidarity between women can reveal truths hidden by a charismatic, violent, domineering, and manipulative man in a position of authority. Mandala, a Catholic convent and school built in the 1870s, was viewed by Ambrose Goddard as "a boarding school for

---

[8] Tony Hughes D'Aeth, "Do You Want To Know More? Narrative in Australian Multimedia", *Journal of Australian Studies* 23, no. 63 (1999), 78.
[9] Campbell, "The Cult, the Cultic Milieu, and Secularization", 122.
[10] Merrilyn Walton, "Deep Sleep Therapy and Chelmsford Private Hospital: Have We Learnt Anything?" *Australasian Psychiatry* 21, no. 3 (2013), 209.
[11] Carmel Bird, *Red Shoes* (Sydney: Vintage, 1998), 209.

infantile women who are seen by those around them as unable to live ordinary lives, to rise to the demands of everyday life, unable to take part in the rituals of family, work, friendship".[12] In this environment a number of women meet their deaths. The novel tells of Laura Field's determined efforts to discover the truth about the death of her sister Vickie at Mandala in 1967.

The central image in Bird's book is that of the White Garden, a copy of that planted and tended by Vita Sackville-West at Sissinghurst in the 1930s. Goddard's wife Abigail, alienated from her husband and unaware of Mandala's secrets, speaks at length about the garden to him, as she is an enthusiast about Sissinghurst and its grounds. Goddard decides that the inmates can construct a replica garden as a therapeutic task. The garden connects Vita Sackville-West's book about the Catholic saints Teresa of Avila and Therese of Lisieux, *The Eagle and the Dove: A Study in Contrasts* (1943), which she wrote during World War II as bombs were falling on England, with two of Goddard's patients, Therese Gillis and Rosamund Pryce-Jones, who retreat from unbearable realities into the identities of Therese of Lisieux and Teresa of Avila respectively.[13] The forward thrust of the narrative in Bird's novel is constantly interrupted by the narratives of the patients, facts about the saints' lives, items from Sackville-West's biography, and a myriad other pieces of (seemingly unrelated) information that slow the reader's progress toward the culmination of Laura's quest to solve the mystery of Vickie's death.

Vickie's body was found in the White Garden at Mandala, the hospital over which her former doctor and sometime lover Goddard presided. Mandala in the 1960s was an "alternative" community: meditation and yoga took place in the former chapel, the stained glass of which had been removed; Goddard administered LSD and psilocybin to patients; wrote accounts of the alter egos of his patients, noting the irony of the saintly identity of Therese Gillis, given his sexual relationship with her. He tells her, "I am God and I am fucking a saint.... What do you think of that, then?"[14] Vickie, however, was a well-balanced and independent woman, who was not subjected to LSD, ECT or any of Goddard's dubious treatments. So how (and why) did she die? Laura Field's search for answers leads her to Michael Bartlett, whose wife Marjorie also died at Mandala, and a missing library book that Vickie never returned. Jane Wilson, who lived as a child at Mandala as her mother was matron there, tells them of another victim who died, given the identity of

---

[12] Jean-François Vernay, "The Art of Penning the March Hare In: The Treatment of Insanity in Australian Total Institution Fiction", *AUMLA: Journal of the Australasian Universities Language and Literature Association* 118 (2012), 88.

[13] M. del Carmen Rodríguez Fernández, "Representations of Religious Women in Contemporary Literature", *Feminismo* 4 (2004), 144.

[14] Carmel Bird, *The White Garden* (St Lucia: University of Queensland, 1995), 109.

"Molly Bloom", before sending them to a survivor, Rosamund, who has the missing book, a red copy of *The Eagle and the Dove*. Vickie carried this book when, at Goddard's request, she dressed herself as Vita Sackville-West and went to the White Garden to meet with Rosamund and Therese, the "saints" of whom "she" had written. This encounter caused Vickie's death, as the deranged Therese released bees (to which Vickie was allergic) that killed her with their stings. Therese later hanged herself after further deep sleep therapy; thus Ambrose Goddard is directly responsible for the deaths of both Vickie and Therese.[15]

Literary critics have drawn attention to Bird's fascination with charismatic leaders and the "halo effect" that they possess, which causes people to revere them and to engage in behaviours that would otherwise be reprehensible to them.[16] Ambrose Goddard differs from Petra Penfold-Knight and Caleb Mean in that his community, despite the meditation, yoga, and Catholic saints, is not primarily religious and he is not a messianic figure. Bird has remarked that "Ambrose is a bit different ... a bright boy in a patriarchal society where he could fairly easily rise to power in his field, having images of himself as a great elephant ... and, although he is a vile criminal who dominates, rapes and murders, his take on things is sometimes quite funny".[17] Yet to date there has been no theorizing of the workings of charisma in the novels; critics simply accept that Bird's protagonists are charismatic, and that this quality – while it may be used for good – is abused by them, and turned to evil. Bird's charismatic leaders "radiat[e] a mysterious aura and power that are ... translated into blind obedience".[18] William Sims Bainbridge and Rodney Stark, two sociologists of religion, posited a model of "cult formation" in which there are three possible triggers for the development of such deviant groups. The first two triggers, psychopathology and entrepreneurship, focus on the personality of the charismatic leader, as new ideas must first be invented by the potential leader, and then preached to a receptive audience. The third trigger, subcultural evolution, places emphasis on the existence of a group of potential members, who share common ideas having the potential to unite them, because social acceptance of new or strange ideas is essential for a movement both to form, and to continue to exist.[19]

Viewed in this way, Goddard's charisma is an expression of his

---

[15] M. del Carmen Rodríguez Fernández, "Carmel Bird's *The White Garden*: Symbols and Images In a Space of Their Own", *Journal of English Studies* II (2000), 89.

[16] Gerardo Rodríguez Salas and Margareta Carretero González, "When Charisma Breeds A Monster: Dangerous Liaisons in Carmel Bird's *Mandala Trilogy*", in *The Role of the Monster: Myths and Metaphors of Enduring Evil*, ed. Niall Scott (Oxford: Inter-Disciplinary Press, 2009), 39.

[17] Gerardo Rodríguez Salas, "'Time and Tide': An Interview With Carmel Bird", *Atlantis: A Journal of the Spanish Association for Anglo-American Studies* 28, no. 2 (2006), 127.

[18] Salas, "Time and Tide", 125.

[19] Bainbridge and Stark, "Cult Formation", 283.

psychopathology and his entrepreneurial desire to be a successful medical professional, and thus move in affluent and influential social circles. This successful façade aligns him with role playing (for example, via his marriage to Abigail, and in his dealings with the unwitting families of the Mandala patients) and requires him to conceal his deviance, leading Gerardo Rodríguez Salas and Margareta Carretera González to argue that, while his charisma may act upon the characters in the novel, he fails to convince the reader, who knows "that Dr Ambrose Goddard is a fake, a character interested in self-glorification and sexual satisfaction rather than in really treating the mental maladies of those who come into contact with him".[20] The charismatic leader in *Red Shoes* (2001), Petra Penfold-Knight, is a clearer case of the Bainbridge and Stark model of cult formation. Both psychopath and entrepreneur, she is venerated as divine by a group of "subcultural" followers who vindicate her delusions.

2. Red Shoes

Red Shoes is connected to *The White Garden* in several important ways. Vickie Field, costumed as Vita Sackville-West, dies in the White Garden while wearing red boots. Goddard, the "god" of the first instalment of the trilogy, features in this novel as a lackey of Petra Penfold-Knight, and Mandala as a recruiting ground for her religious group, the Red Shoe Cult, originally named the Hill House Brethren, founded by Dr Irving Clay. Beau, her "guardian angel", provides the detached and ironic narration of this truly grim tale. The model for Petra Penfold-Knight and her household of lost children is Anne Hamilton-Byrne (b. Evelyn Edwards in Sale, Victoria), a "guru" who taught a mixture of Hinduism and Christianity, and was regarded as the reincarnation of Jesus Christ by her followers, a group called The Family (which also had a presence in America, the United Kingdom, and New Zealand). Bird has based her narrative closely on the memoir by Sarah Hamilton-Byrne, one of the stolen babies adopted by Anne Hamilton-Byrne and brought up at Kia Lama (or Uptop), one of The Family's properties, near Lake Eildon.[21] Both Hamilton-Byrne and her adopted children of both sexes at times wore red shoes.

Penfold-Knight is beautiful and sexually magnetic but emotionally cold, she enters rooms to the tune of Handel's "The Arrival of the Queen of Sheba", wears dramatic gowns (often in shades of blue), and collects baby

---

[20] Salas and González, "When Charisma Breeds A Monster", 40.
[21] Sarah Hamilton-Byrne, *Unseen Unheard Unknown: My Life Inside The Family of Anne Hamilton-Byrne* (Ringwood: Penguin Australia, 1995). This book appears in the Bibliography at the end of Bird's novel, which is divided into the 232-page "The Narrative," followed by the 95-page alphabetical list of source material and clarifications, "The Footnote".

girls that she rears in strict conditions at Hill House. The girls, who are dressed identically in black smocks and red shoes, live in a house called New Haven and are cared for by the women who live in a house called Bethany. They are regularly dosed with a variety of drugs including tranquillisers and anti-psychotics, sexually abused, starved and beaten. One, Golden Jade, has her feet bound and endures agonising pain, and another, Celeste (who was wrenched from her mentally-fragile teenage mother Sylvie, who named her Colette), writes a truthful account of life in New Haven, and is drugged and burnt to death for doing so while exiled from the community and living under supervision in remote Tasmania. Beau notes that Penfold-Knight "developed a rule that footwear was to be red, or that the bare feet of adults were to be decorated with designs in henna, the feet of children dyed with mercurochrome.... Uniform of some kind is nearly always important to distinct groups of people, whether the people are together for religious, sporting, military or other reasons, and Petra decreed that ... her people would be marked by their red feet".[22] The Hill House Brethren are often recruited via Mandala, and Goddard, Irving Clay, and others aid Penfold-Knight in her bizarre, and criminal, activities.

Beau narrates Penfold-Knight's life story from birth in 1930 in Tasmania to her suicide at the age of fifty-five (though she claimed to be sixty-six, twice the age of Jesus when he died). The most extraordinary thing about this complex, deeply unpleasant tale is that almost all of it is true: the match between Penfold-Knight and Hamilton-Byrne is very close. Hamilton-Byrne was good-looking and vain (she had frequent plastic surgery to preserve her youthful appearance, wore designer clothes, and had a large collection of glamorous blonde wigs), and particularly favoured blue gowns. She dyed the hair of the children of The Family blonde and dressed them in identical clothes. She distributed posed photographs of herself that were worshipped by her disciples. Further, she delivered her "Thursday night sermons" at Santiniketan Lodge in Ferny Creek entering the room to Handel's "Largo" from the opera *Xerxes* (1738).[23] The original of Irving Clay is the retired University of Melbourne physicist Dr Rayner Johnson, who met Hamilton-Byrne at 1964 and was accepted within the group as John the Baptist to her Jesus. The identification of Mandala with Chelmsford Hospital is weakened when it is known that Hamilton-Byrne had doctors and psychiatrists as followers, including John McKay and Howard Whitaker, who worked at Newhaven Hospital in Kew. Sarah Hamilton-Byrne states that, "When the cult controlled Newhaven Hospital ... [p]otential cult members were booked into Newhaven and, once there, were completely at Anne's mercy. Her psychiatrists would put them under LSD for days, even up to a week ... there

---

[22] Bird, *Red Shoes*, 7.
[23] Hamilton-Byrne, *Unseen Unheard Unknown*, 116-117.

would be visitations by Anne herself.... Through your drug-induced haze Anne appeared God-like – she even said she was Jesus Christ – and you realised she offered you a way to attain the true potential of your spirituality".[24] The horrors experienced by thirteen-year-old Celeste during her initiation are eloquently described by Bird. Called the "Threshold", this is a ritual in which Penfold-Knight gives Celeste LSD for three days, and which culminates with her being raped by Goddard: "This was hell and I was in hell".[25] Readers might shrink from what they think to be the author's violent imagination, but Sarah Hamilton-Byrne's description of her own initiation, known to members of The Family as "Going-through", is scarcely less horrific, ending with a creepy doctor saying he will "mix up your insides so you will never be able to have children" and cutting her genitals with a knife.[26] The differences between the fictional Hill House Brethren and the factual Family are few and trivial compared to the similarities.

The Family were investigated in 1987 after Sarah, who had been expelled by Anne Hamilton-Byrne for rebellious behaviour, went to the police. The children were taken into protective custody and a range of legal cases resulted, though few succeeded. Hamilton-Byrne, unlike Petra Penfold-Knight, did not commit suicide, but is still alive and in an aged-care institution, suffering from dementia. There is, however, a mystery about her precise birthdate that reflects the fictional Penfold-Knight's lying about her age, as some publications give her birthdate as 1930 (the same date as that of Penfold-Knight) but others give it as 1921.[27] When the police seized the children in 1987 she and her husband Bill fled Australia, and avoided all serious charges, being convicted only of making false statements. Their estate, estimated at between ten and fifty million dollars, continues to be administered by members of The Family, under a range of names including the Santiniketan Park Association and Life For All Creatures. Further, Dr John McKay has been brought to the attention of the Royal Commission Into Child Sexual Abuse by Wayne Callister, a former Family member, but to date he has not been charged.[28]

Over forty years ago, sociologist Stanley Cohen proposed the concept of "moral panics" which are certain recurring public anxieties. These public

---

[24] Hamilton-Byrne, *Unseen Unheard Unknown*, 126.
[25] Bird, *Red Shoes*, 188.
[26] Hamilton-Byrne, *Unseen Unheard Unknown*, 144-145. Even minor details in Bird's tale, such as the children being forced to eat porridge that had been urinated in, are lifted from this memoir.
[27] Chris Mikul, *Bizarrism: Strange Lives, Cults, Celebrated Lunacy* (Manchester: Critical Vision, 1999), 48. Mikul's brief chapter, "The Family Way", is an accurate summary of the story of Anne Hamilton-Byrne and The Family, despite its hostile and sarcastic tone.
[28] Chris Johnston, "The Family's 'Living God' Fades To Grey, Estate Remains". *The Age*, 17 May, 2014. http://www.theage.com.au/victoria/the-familys-living-god-fades-to-grey-estate-remains-20140516-38fhv.html

anxieties tend to be directed towards groups that are marginal in certain ways, such as fringe religions and youth social movements that are perceived to be undesirable. He terms these groups "folk devils" and noted that they are "visible reminders of what we should not be".[29] The story of Anne Hamilton-Byrne is extraordinary; the upper-middle-class and professional socioeconomic demographic that she attracted as disciples in some sense concealed The Family from the public gaze for several decades, and permitted her to illegally acquire approximately twenty stolen children, whom she brought up in isolation to "continue her cult after the earth was consumed by a holocaust".[30] Bird's fictionalisation picks up on the fairy-tale motifs that litter her novel (the red shoes, the little mermaid and Golden Jade, the snow queen and Petra, Hansel and Gretel and so on), but does not shrink from condemning the evils that Penfold-Knight and her confederates are guilty of. Critics have noted that in Bird's novels passive women and girls are victims, they are "murdered, drugged, brainwashed and/or imprisoned", mainly by men but also by active, "perverted … and inherently corrupt" women.[31] The fictional world of Bird is driven by moral panics and folk devils: the inherent vulnerability of women, for example, is a recurrent theme in traditional religion (which seeks to "protect" women by immuring or denying them independence). Bird's is a world in which unspeakable things are done to human beings by other human beings; and where justice and restitution – often absent or delayed – are perpetual concerns, as the reader struggles in the moral chaos.[32]

3: Cape Grimm

The final novel of the *Mandala Trilogy* returns the action to Tasmania (where Penfold-Knight was born and Celeste died), and has as a focus Bird's recurrent concern for the violent dispossession of the Tasmanian Aborigines at the hands of White settlers. In 1998, the same year she published *Red Shoes*, Bird edited a "small collection of the stories contained in *Bringing Them Home* and published them under the title *The Stolen Children: Their Stories*".[33] This is

---

[29] Cohen, *Folk Devils and Moral Panics*, 2.
[30] Hamilton-Byrne, *Unseen Unheard Unknown*, 1.
[31] Odette Kelada, "'Animal Handlers': Australian Women Writers on Sexuality and the Female Body", *Outskirts: Feminism Along The Edge* 26 (2012), www.outskirts.arts.uwa.edu.au/volumes/volume-26/kelada
[32] Bird had a brief foray into writing detective fiction, which is a plausible move, considering that most of her novels have a puzzle element. In the two novels featuring the young female journalist and occasional investigator Courtney Frome, *Unholy Writ* (2000) and *Open For Inspection* (2002), motifs of incest, lost children, drug subcultures, and violence against women, are prominent.
[33] Susan Barrett, "Reconstructing Australia's Shameful Past: The Stolen Generation in Life-Writing, Fiction and Film", *Lignes* 2 (2005): 5, www.lignes.org.

unsurprising given her fascination, almost obsession, with lost children in her fiction. *Cape Grimm* unites the Goddard family of the first two novels with the Means, the central family of her earlier Tasmanian novel, *The Bluebird Café* (1990), as Sophie Goddard, Ambrose and Abigail's daughter, is the director of the Black River Psychiatric Detention Facility, in which Caleb Mean is incarcerated.[34] The story of Indigenous stolen children is related by the visionary Virginia Mean, during her recovery from the shock of her cousin and lover Caleb Mean's incineration of the people of their home village of Skye, and his failed attempt to commit suicide with her and their baby daughter Golden by riding a horse over a cliff, which was thwarted by police who arrested him for murder.

Cape Grimm takes its name both from the real geographical feature, Cape Grim in northwest Tasmania, and from the fairy stories of the Brothers Grimm, which are frequently referenced in the novel. John McLaren notes that the narrative does not so much progress as offer a "series of parallels and reversals.... The Temple of the Winds at Skye parallels the tower at Black River Psychiatric Detention Facility.... The loss of the community of settlers follows the destruction of earlier Aboriginal communities at the hands of other settlers. Behind these conjunctions lies a spirituality that is both grounded in nature and ungrounded, sustaining and destructive. Caleb is Caliban, the wild one, and a mass murderer, and the community he destroys is, like such recent historical counterparts as California's 'Heaven's Gate' sect, dedicated to a purity and perfection of life that leads to death".[35] The principal narrator of the tale is Paul van Loon, a psychiatrist who returned to Tasmania from the United States to work at Black River with Mean, who is a sort of *doppelgänger* of him (they were both born in 1959, have several encounters prior to the tragedy in Skye, and at the close of the novel Paul is the husband of Virginia and stepfather of Golden). Like *Red Shoes*, *Cape Grimm* is divided into parts; a "Prologue", the 243-page story, and two appended sections, "Time" and "Tide" (a 55-page commentary including a timeline of historical and fictional events, and the familiar alphabetical listing of myths, fairy tales and other supporting information).[36]

---

[34] Carmel Bird, *Cape Grimm* (Sydney: Harper Perennial, 2004), 212.
[35] John McLaren, "A Haunted Land", *Australian Studies* 20 (2005), 161.
[36] Regarding this device of dividing her novels into fiction (story) and (purported) fact (the commentary) Bird told Gerardo Rodríguez Salas that "[t]he question is why I did not have a similar section in *The White Garden*. I honestly work fairly unconsciously, so I find it hard sometimes to answer sensible questions. With *Red Shoes* there was the joke of the 'Foot Note' and then with *Cape Grimm* there was so much history that I had to have the end bits. I puzzled for a long time over what to call them and then one morning I woke up with the words time and tide and could not see why I had not realised this before. Another trait of my fiction is that I like to include fictitious information along with the truth; for example, the timeline in *Cape Grimm* has dates of fictitious events, which are fairly obvious, but in the Tide section there are fake stories as well as true stories. I am very interested in the borderlines that run between the true and the false, and I know that fiction is the place to

Van Loon's first-person narrative meditates on his own family history as Dutch migrants to Tasmania (or Van Diemen's Land as it is frequently referred to in the novel) and tells the almost mythic tale of the Mean family history, beginning with the survival of Scottish widower Presbyterian Magnus Mean from Skye and young Peruvian Catholic Minerva Carillo Hinshelwood, pregnant and on her honeymoon, when the ship they were aboard, the *Iris*, was wrecked off little Puddingstone Island in Bass Strait on 5 February 1851.[37] A baby, Niña, another "lost child" whose parentage is never discovered, also survived. She was wet-nursed by the Aboriginal Dolly Thunderstone, and adopted by Magnus and Minerva, who married and raised a family in Skye, the village they founded. Van Loon observes that "when there is a closed community such as the one at Skye, two kinds of folklore grow up about it, one inside the community and one outside.... As children we used to think that inside the village of Skye was some kind of old-fashioned cannibal and incest hell, fascinating and repellent.... To the people of Skye the world outside was full of the dangers of the devil's invention, and they saved themselves from all this when they left the planet".[38] Skye is a small place, which has a few remarkable features, such as the Temple of the Winds, which was built by Minerva Carrillo Mean in imitation of a similar neo-classical structure erected by Lady Jane Franklin, wife of Sir John Franklin (1786-1847), lieutenant governor of Tasmania, and himself lost at sea on the *Erebus*, which became stuck in pack ice off King William's Land in 1847, within sight of the North-West Passage that he sought to locate.[39]

The prologue to *Cape Grimm* is a (fictional) letter written to Lady Franklin by Jakob Grimm, connecting the Franklins with the Brothers Grimm's fairy tales of lost children, violent parents and step-parents. The period of Sir John and Lady Franklin's residence in Hobart, from 1837 to 1844, coincided with that of the lay preacher George Augustus Robinson's appointment as Protector of Aborigines in Port Phillip District, a position that he held from 1839 to 1849. Robinson met the Aboriginal woman Truganini, daughter of a Bruny Island chief, Mangana, in 1829, and over the years he "rounded up the remaining Aborigines and place[d] them in captivity on Flinders Island in Bass Strait".[40] Truganini, who died in 1876, is often erroneously described as the last Tasmanian Indigenous person; the fact that this is false does not lessen the sufferings the displaced Aborigines at the hands of White settlers or the extent of the depopulation that resulted. In *Cape Grimm*, Virginia Mean

---

explore these slippages and boundaries". Salas, "Time and Tide," 130.
[37] Bird, *Cape Grimm*, 88-92.
[38] Bird, *Cape Grimm*, 170-171.
[39] Kathleen Fitzpatrick, "Franklin, Sir John (1786-1847)", *Australian Dictionary of Biography*, vol. 1 (Melbourne: Melbourne University Press, 1966).
[40] Lyndall Ryan, *The Aboriginal Tasmanians*, 2nd ed. (Crows Nest: Allen & Unwin, 1996), 5.

has the ability to see and experience events from the colonial era of Tasmania, and in contrast with the false prophet Caleb, "she becomes the real prophet who can see the ghost of a black dead girl, Mannaginna, and ... witnesses the 1820s massacres of Tasmanian aborigines under the hands of white European whalers, sealers, soldiers, and farmers. While there had been only one 'white official' record of this mass slaughter by George Augustus Robinson, Virginia becomes the 'unofficial' key to understanding the real exploitation of the indigenous people, even when her credibility remains doubtful for being the mute lover of a mass murderer, and a ghost visionary".[41] Virginia's visions connect the story of the Mean family and the many lost children associated with it to the loss of a people. Susan Barrett has perceptively noted that, in Bird's books, "the removal of the children ceases to be a specific Aboriginal experience which took place at a given historical time and becomes instead a universal experience of maternal loss", and that as the children remain "lost", Bird "denies their existence as adult narrators" who are able to speak for themselves.[42] Whites writing about Indigenous subject matter is a notoriously problematic phenomenon, but Virginia's role as truth-teller is to be taken seriously, which will be discussed further below.[43]

Bird has admitted to a fascination with the Mean family, noting that the name reflects her interest in making meaning, and that in every book she has written there is "at least an epigraph from some mad book by Carrillo Mean, and then he turns up in the text, more or less unexplained".[44] Carrillo and Bedrock Mean's story, in *The Bluebird Café*, is one of an incestuous relationship between twins who were identical apart from sex, and who from their earliest childhood spoke to each other in "Meaning", a secret language they had devised. In the 1960s they lived in America, after fleeing condemnation of their relationship, but returned to remote Copperfield, where their midget daughter, Lovelygod, yet another lost child, mysteriously disappeared in 1970 aged ten. After that tragedy, Bedrock remained in Copperfield, a ghost town that became the model for a theme park, "The Historic Museum Village", built by the entrepreneurial Bests, Nancy, Oliver and Bill.[45] Bedrock and Carrillo are described as cousins of Caleb, and after the loss of his daughter

---

[41] Gerardo Rodríguez Salas, "'The Tide That Riffles Back': Spiral Femininity in Carmel Bird's *Cape Grimm*", *Antipodes: Journal of the American Association for Australian Studies* 19, no. 1 (2005), 88.
[42] Barrett, "Reconstructing Australia's Shameful Past", 5.
[43] It is worth mentioning that Bird has also indicated that the massacre at Port Arthur in 1996, in which Martin Bryant killed thirty-five people, is also a real-life inspiration for *Cape Grimm*. Linda Hassall, in "What Is Australian Gothic Theatre? Three Playwrights Enter the Conversation", *NJ (The Drama Australia Journal)* 38 (2014), singles out Port Arthur as a site that "echoes with overlapping atmospheres of previous convict and contemporary criminal violence", 29.
[44] Salas, "Time and Tide", 128.
[45] Carmel Bird, *The Bluebird Café* (South Yarra: McPhee Gribble, 1990), 4. It is worth noting that this novel, too, has a 25-page alphabetical guide to the narrative that the reader has just perused.

Carrillo Mean moved to America where he "runs some centre for finding lost children".[46] Copperfield is a town very like the later Skye of *Cape Grimm*; Philosopher Mean built the Temple of the Eye of God there, and the townsfolk were taught "the beliefs, rituals and symbolism of a diversity of faiths".[47] *The Bluebird Café* is not part of *The Mandala Trilogy*, and is referred to briefly here only because it reinforces certain themes in Bird's fiction. One clear link to *Cape Grimm* is the motif of a Tasmania Indigenous female, in this case Mathinna, a child adopted by Sir John and Lady Franklin, who later abandoned her. Mathinna is known from a portrait painted in by the colonial artist Thomas Bock in 1842, depicting her as a child of about seven, wearing a red dress.[48] At the novel's conclusion, Virginia O'Day, who knew the Mean twins as children, has written a play in which all the possible explanations of the disappearance of Lovelygod (murdered by her parents, abducted, taken for scientific experiments and so on), are presented; "six scenes and six possible solutions, providing no answers, just endless speculation".[49]

Bird often has characters called "Virginia" play the role of truth-tellers in her fiction, and O'Day is a writer who is also the narrator of Bird's manual for writing fiction, *Dear Writer* (1988). Further, her surname "O'Day" suggests that she is able to shed light on dark subjects. Bird told Salas that "you will see that I frequently use that name, since it has for me at least three meanings: Woolf, Queen Elizabeth I of England, [and the] Virgin Mary.... What I think of as 'The Virginia Effect' covers a wide range of issues in my work – issues of creativity and inspiration, feminism, image and language".[50] Virginia Mean's visions of the historical Cape Grim massacre of 28 February 1828 in which white shepherds killed around thirty Indigenous people, and of other massacres of the 1820s, situates her prophetic gift as one that is empathetic, selfless and other-centred, as opposed to the egotistical self-gratification of her former lover Caleb. She agonises over the whispered pleas for mercy of Mannaginna, and grieves as she hears "the shrieks of the mothers, the cries of the children, the agony of the men".[51] In contrast, Caleb Mean, the great-great-great-grandson of the courageous and resourceful Magnus and Minerva, was raised as El Niño, the contemporary Christ child, and has used his

---

[46] Bird, *The Bluebird Café*, 135.
[47] Bird, *The Bluebird Café*, 10.
[48] Mathinna is the subject of Richard Flanagan's novel *Wanting* (2008). See Jason Steger, "Flanagan's Book of Desire", *The Age*, 1 November 2008,
http://www.theage.com.au/news/entertainment/books/flanagans-book-of-desire/2008/10/30/1224956234497.html
[49] Shirley Walker, "All the Way to Cape Grimm: Reflections on Carmel Bird's Fiction", *Australian Literary Studies* 21, no. 3 (2004), 267.
[50] Salas, "Time and Tide", 131.
[51] Joseph Cummins, "Echoes Between Van Diemen's Land and Tasmania: Sound and the Space of the Island in Richard Flanagan's *Death of a River Guide* and Carmel Bird's *Cape Grimm*", *Journal of Commonwealth Literature* 49, no. 2 (2014), 264.

charisma from youth to dominate the community at Skye. He is sexually voracious, marking his conquests on the shoulder with a blue swallow tattoo (connected to Minerva Mean, whose first husband Edward Hinshelwood gave her a pendant made from a feather), and has fathered many children with girls who are cousins and close relatives, reinforcing the impression of outsiders that Skye is a place of weird religion, incest, and perversion. Caleb's malevolence and obvious craziness is conveyed directly in Paul's narrative, and indirectly in Virginia's diaries as she realizes that her friends and family are all dead, due to his actions, and that she desires to survive with her daughter Golden, which leads to her affirmation of life and marriage to Paul. Virginia writes, "He said to me he would sacrifice all his sons, all his other daughters first, but he would take Golden with him on his final journey. She would not burn, but would fly with us in our great leap from the cliff". [52] Paul changes the fate of Virginia and especially of Golden Mean, whose seemingly portentous name is changed to Golden van Loon, when Paul adopts her.

The incineration of a religious community is a particularly dramatic form of mass death, and it is unclear whether it should be regarded as a suicide pact (in which the citizens of Skye aware and willing) or a mass murder (in which Caleb's flock are assembled to hear him preach, but are unaware that he intends their deaths). Salas calls Skye "an organic community in which death has been transfigured into a mystical body ... discussed by German sociologist Ferdinand Tönnies, in which a community of blood-family ties coming from the Means' in-breeding – develops into a community of place (Skye) and this, in turn, into a community of spirit, or religious cult".[53] The fiery death calls to mind such ritual incinerations as that of several hundred members of the Movement for the Restoration of the Ten Commandments of God on 17 March 2000, in Kanangu, Uganda, who were boarded up inside a church that was then blown up and burned to the ground.[54] Bird associates the strange *mélange* of Christianity, Eastern religions, New Age sentiments, and apocalypticism typical of the cultic milieu that is taught by both Petra Penfold-Knight and Caleb Mean with deviant social practices such as incest, child sexual abuse, institutional violence, and murder. Skye is doomed because the Welsh motto of the community, "Heb Dhu Heb Dhim" (which was Magnus Mean's motto despite his Scottishness) means, "If I have God I have everything" and this sentiment is bound to be misinterpreted and lead to

---

[52] Bird, *Cape Grimm*, 101.
[53] Gerardo Rodríguez Salas, "A Dream Temple of the Collective Imagination: Exploring Community in Carmel Bird's *Cape Grimm*", *Australian Literary Studies* 27, no. 1 (2012), 80.
[54] John Walliss, "Apocalypse in Uganda: The Movement for the Restoration of the Ten Commandments of God Ten Years On", in *Sacred Suicide*, eds. James R. Lewis and Carole M. Cusack (Farnham and Burlington: Ashgate, 2014), 109-127.

extremism. Salas observes that "[t]he mystification of God is used as an instrument to brainwash members into performing a particular mission: a suicide pact or collective sacrifice".[55]

Caleb, while imprisoned at Black River, is still able to wreak havoc, as Sophie Goddard falls in love with him and (wittingly or unwittingly, it is not clear), facilitates his escape. Declan Dequidt, known as Dee Dee, an inmate who killed his wife and several other women, regarded Caleb as his friend, and murders Sophie after he escapes.[56] Caleb escapes in a small boat, the *Tom Thumb* (named for the boat in which George Bass and Matthew Flinders sailed around Australia) and drowns in Bass Strait, near to the site of the sinking of the *Iris*, which brought his ancestors Magnus and Minerva Mean to Cape Grimm in the first place. The death of Caleb acts a spur for Paul and Virginia to formalize their relationship and make plans for the future. Paul's attention restored Virginia's ability to speak, which she temporarily lost after the trauma. His love enables her to farewell Caleb with a visit to the ruins of Skye. They marry, and Paul takes a job in Florida. The novel ends with Golden, while digging in the sunny garden, discovering a statue of El Niño, the Christ Child, and discussing the past and the future end of the world with Paul. Salas argues that there is a move forward, a resolution, in *Cape Grimm*, in that Bird allows "the community of lovers" to triumph.[57] The positive portrayal of Father Benedict Fox, Sister Margaret, and the Catholic couple Michael and Gilia Vilez, who shelter Virginia and Golden after the inferno at Skye may also suggest that Bird accepts that there are forms of religion (and charisma, which Paul van Loon says Ben Fox, "one of those down-to-earth saints working for the poor and the downtrodden and the criminal and the mad", possesses, too) that are not inherently evil but may be facilitative of love, life, goodness, and human flourishing.[58]

Conclusion

This chapter has examined Carmel Bird's *The Mandala Trilogy* (and a related novel, *The Bluebird Café*) from the perspective of religious studies, in that ideas usually applied to the emergence of NRMs such as the Campbell's cultic milieu, the Bainbridge and Stark model of cult formation, and Cohen's folk devils and moral panics are applied to the charismatic leaders of deviant "cults" (whether of psychiatry or religion) that Bird describes in *The White Garden*, *Red Shoes*, and *Cape Grimm*. It has been demonstrated that Bird's fiction reworks a number of motifs, including sexual violence against women, child abuse,

---

[55] Salas, "A Dream Temple of the Collective Imagination", 80.
[56] Bird, *Cape Grimm*, 212-214, 240.
[57] Salas, "A Dream Temple of the Collective Imagination", 87.
[58] Bird, *Cape Grimm*, 192.

incest, amoral teachers of hybridized Eastern and Christian spirituality, torture, murder, and deviant religious communities, in a seemingly obsessive or neurotic fashion. The *Mandala Trilogy* presents three charismatic leaders, Ambrose Goddard, Petra Penfold-Knight, and Caleb Mean, who all die unrepentant and without resiling from their delusions (the first two by suicide, and it is possible that Caleb's being swallowed by the tides of Bass Strait could be understood as suicide too). In the first two novels, the survivors of their cultic groups are just that, survivors. In *Cape Grimm*, Virginia and Golden, the survivors of Caleb Mean's conflagration at Skye, literally an *auto-da-fé* (act of faith), go on to flourish and to enjoy a new life free from the oppressive, deviant religious community of their past, through the love of Father Fox, Paul van Loon, and others who demonstrate that the outside world is not Sodom and Gomorrah as the cult leaders say, but a place of beauty, opportunity, and hope.

Small Child and Art Installation

Geoffrey Lehmann

For Xaviera Duffy.

Xaviera who was the subject of the poem and is now 10 says she is happy for the poem to be dedicated to her.

Lowering her head of brown curls,
shiny brown irises and white half-moons stare up
from under knitted brows –
at three years and nine months
a midget Judy Garland.

They've built some temporary scaffolding
around a bronze equestrian statue
and at the top
there's a sitting room.
It's one of her favourite places,
the little sitting room,
as she scampers up the makeshift wooden steps.
A giant helmeted rider's head and shoulders,
and a bodybuilder's arm holding up a torch,
mottled with blue-green patina,
appear to be resting on a timber veneer coffee table
with today's newspapers
and three green apples and an orange in a bowl.

She opens the door of a cupboard
and there's a huge blue-green horse's head.
"Look!"
she tells young art-lovers
chins sprouting wisps of hair
as they crowd into the room,
and slams and opens the cupboard door.
She wrestles with the rider's bronze arm.
"Look!"

she rushes between table and cupboard
as art lovers enter and exit.
Judy Garland becomes Ezra Pound,
Gertrude Stein's "village explainer".
She holds up an apple to a visitor.
"This is fake"
(voice as raucous as a nestling).
She holds up the fruit again, repeats,
"This is fake."
Some art lovers politely dissent.
A young grandmother
with neat grey hair and child:
"What a trick! Is she yours?"
I explain our relationship.

"Look at this" (slamming and opening the cupboard door)
"This is fake" (holding up the apple)
continue as fresh recruits arrive.
The Cantos are repeating themselves.

I make an impressive announcement:
"The guard is watching."
A young man in sandals,
on a plastic seat outside the door,
hearing about himself,
starts looking in.
His glance is unsettling,
and Ezra Pound decides
to end her dissertations to strangers,
and she's Judy Garland again,
exiting the door,
cascading down the steps,
distraught and screaming.
"That's mine! Get out!"
Her older sister
is sitting in *her* stroller.
She's sobbing and raging at mother and sister
who watch with love,
a patient tableau in the dusk.

The Future of the Humanities

Michael Warren Davis

Russell Kirk, the twentieth century's great man of letters, who had the distinction of being the only American ever awarded the Doctor of Letters degree by St Andrew's University, wrote a weekly column for the conservative journal *National Review* called "The Ivory Tower". The column focused on the affairs of the Academy: outstanding academics, books, and all manner of conflict and scandal that perpetually bedevil universities. Dr Kirk kept the column going for twenty-five years, discontinuing it around the turn of the 'Eighties, having become known as the foremost commentator on academic affairs from among those who stood by what Barry Spurr called "the Old Idea of a University".[1] Following Cardinal Newman, Professor Spurr defended the academy as the home of those who "embrace the heterodoxy of human knowledge unhampered by considerations of practical application or societal constraints". This, too, was where Dr Kirk felt most at home, but undoubtedly any disciple of the Old Idea who paid such careful attention to the state of the academy between 1955 and 1980 would have found it increasingly difficult to write with any optimism about academia's future. Yet Dr Kirk, an independent scholar throughout his career, was fortunate enough not to depend on the universities for his daily bread. So he withdrew to his home in Mecosta, Michigan, and championed high culture and liberal education from the battlefield of his choosing. The *National Review*'s founding editor, William F. Buckley, Jr. recalled him resigning his post, saying simply, "I think I've done this for long enough".

For a true man of letters, the 60s and 70s must have seemed like the end of the world – or at least any world worth occupying. Dr Kirk's "Ivory Tower" years spanned the infamous events of *Mai 68*, when the French academy – along with its allies in the French Communist Party and sympathetic trade unions – virtually revolted against the government of Charles de Gaulle. But for many of the *soixante-huitards*' contemporaries, the events of May 1968 didn't confirm their faith in the Old Idea of a University: they awakened it.

Most prominent among these is Roger Scruton, perhaps the greatest man of letters of our own time. As a doctoral student in Paris during the uprising,

---

[1] Barry Spurr, "The New Idea of a University", *Quadrant* (April, 1990), 42.

Scruton was deeply disturbed to witness in action the spirit of deconstruction and alienation laid out by the likes of Louis Althusser, Jean Baudrillard, Michel Foucault, Jacques Derrida, and all those now-canonical names. And he saw not only the senseless violence, the collapse of any civil or spiritual order, but also the strange new form of "community" that sprang up among the *soixante-huitards*. From that first instinctive horror, Scruton devoted no small part of his life to articulating why (in Yeats's words) "The best lack all conviction, while the worst / Are full of passionate intensity".

Scruton's strongest indictment of the new idea of a university came in his essay "Where did it go wrong?", written for his 2014 tour of Australia. He asks, "So what is it that the humanities, as they used to be taught, lacked, that they should have been so easily and rapidly replaced by nonsense? The answer, I believe, is simple. Our traditional humanities failed to offer membership".[2] The Old Idea could offer only the pursuit of truth and accumulation of knowledge for its own sake; it couldn't "promise to make sense of the world, to bring companionship or love, still less does it bring an offer of redemption".[3] The New Idea, however, by blinding the judgmental eye of objectivity, was able to reshape the academy into the "old spot by the river, quite well known to you and me" of Irish republican lore, where self-styled revolutionaries could whip themselves into an ecstasy of music and dancing and rhetoric before clashing with the nefarious powers-that-be. Only the *soixante-huitard* revolutionaries were at no serious risk of bodily harm. Their targets weren't thugs of a repressive government, but the private property of hard-working everyday citizens. And as universities became even more insular, so too their foe needed to be abstract enough that one needn't leave the walls of the ivory tower to face them. Thus our intellectual and academic elite ceased antagonizing real, live men like the "Old Fascist" de Gaulle, bane of the *soixante-huitards*, and began instead speaking only of "the patriarchy", "the corporations", and all those sufficiently vague bogies – vaguer even than the dreaded bourgeoisie, whose shopfronts could at least be vandalized.

For pointing to this naked emperor, Scruton – who, immediately after earning his Ph.D., was appointed Professor of Aesthetics at Birkbeck College – was banished from polite intellectual society and gradually forced to abandon his academic career. After a remarkable string of occupations – one as a magazine editor, another with the Hungarian anti-communist underground – Scruton carved out a niche for himself as an independent philosopher. This is, one realizes, even more surprising than it first seems: a man who makes a comfortable living from the sale of books espousing a perfectly ordinary classicism and a gentle, melancholy traditionalism.

---

[2] Roger Scruton, *Australian Essays* (Ballarat: Connor Court, 2014), 5
[3] *Ibid.*, 6.

Melancholy, yes. Even in this evident triumph of high-mindedness over academic nihilism, there lurks a glaring and, perhaps, inevitable defeat. Should intelligent laymen endure in their ancient ardor for beauty, order, and reason (as they will do), we will follow Newman, Kirk, Spurr and Scruton in our devotion to the spirit of the university. Nothing will ever compensate for its loss; any such remnants of its noble "old idea" will pale with regard to the authentic article. Institutions themselves, as the Frankfurt School realized too soon and as men of letters realized too late, are of immeasurable value. Universities are no exception. In their worst form, as we tend to know them today, they're ideal vehicles for indoctrinating the brightest minds of a generation into certain ideological orthodoxies. But at their best, they're rightly thought to be the heart of a nation's culture. Their academics minister to the humanities for the sake of the humanities, promising no substantial reward but the perseverance of classical wisdom; their libraries, funded by tuition and endowments, promise sanctuary to invaluable books deemed valueless by popular markets. And while the liberal arts have few apparent applications in themselves, they've grounded "men of action" in greater truths than power and profit for generations, and trained our greatest leaders in politics and industry to think in terms beyond the vulgar material. This is to say nothing of the chief value of the Old Idea: the opportunity for men and women, young and old, to immerse themselves in the ineffable *goodness* of knowledge pursued for its own sake.

Before we slip into total despair, we should say that the threat posed by postmodernism isn't altogether unheard of. Academic reformists throughout history have loathed the fixation on dogma. The classic example from history is the idea of learned monks arguing over how many angels can dance on the head of a pin. If that's too parochial, we have the famed wit H.L. Mencken:

> The metaphysician is one who, when you remark that twice two makes four, demands to know what you mean by twice, what by two, and what by four. For asking such questions metaphysicians are supported in oriental luxury in the universities, and respected as educated and intelligent men.[4]

We could easily be speaking today about postmodernists asking how many sexual orientations can be crammed into a single acronym or, indeed, what we mean by four.

This postmodern elite now in power in the university system has no doubt realized this: that the dogmatism they espouse is entirely contrary to the free intellectual spirit that the university fosters, and indeed survives on. One must ask why, if they feel so certain that both right (or the remnants of rightness) and history are at their backs, do they so aggressively censor men

---

[4] H.L. Mencken, *A Mencken Chrestomathy* (New York: Knopf, 1949), 13-14.

like Scruton, whose ideas they ought to regard as being doomed by reason (or the remnants of reason) and Time itself?

We may answer this just as well for ourselves. The Old Idea – that is, the proper idea – of a university poses the gravest threat to their doctrines than any other force in our society. If unleashed, their fashionable nothings would be completely swept away in a tide of free discourse. Without cloaking the classical mind in flashing hazard signs like "reactionary", "misogynistic", and so on, our inborn yearning for the Good, the True, and the Beautiful would confound their fetishization of the Bad, the Obscure, and the Hideous.

Knowing the young mind – especially those drawn to the Old Idea of the University, which still dominates our collective unconscious – will be unsatisfied with anything *but* free discourse, they've not only called liberal leaning "reactionary", but deemed their own dogmata to be "transgressive", "radical", and the like. I know as you know, dear reader, that they're anything but.

Philosophy departments have become hopelessly narrow, embracing Marx's nihilistic view that "The philosophers have hitherto only interpreted the world, in various ways; the point is to change it". The natural conclusion of the Marxist view, as Marx himself no doubt anticipated, is the death of philosophy *as such*, and its evolution into a particularly ethereal subset of political theory and social science. Materialism is assumed; relatively orthodox theories of rationalism, empiricism, and idealism are treated as historical curiosities. The non-existence of God is a fundamental presupposition, and with Him dies (for all intents and purposes) the great religious philosophers: Aquinas, Averroes, Spinoza, et al. Even the relatively modern Pragmatists like William James and John Dewey are decidedly out of vogue. Those who thoughtfully pursue the ancient and yet-unsolved questions at the heart of the discipline – "What is the meaning of life?" "What is virtue?" "What is truth?" – are dismissed as clinging to Eurocentric and misogynistic paradigms of philosophy. (Judith Butler famously claimed that reason itself is a phallocentric construct designed to exclude women from discourse.) Academia has, instead, been staffed by radical gender and sexuality theorists, "postcolonial" race-baiters, and political utopians. It's become a haven for all those so-called materialist philosophies that students of the hard sciences find entirely untenable. It's become, to the objective observer, a discipline of fashionable pseudo-sciences.

English departments have, in turn, become muddled sub-disciplines of this new philosophy. The questions they ask and the answers they provide are essentially the same, only they're pursued by means of literary texts. Novels and poems are studied, not to illuminate structure and aesthetic, but to interrogate the representation of race, gender, and class. Of course, this approach is fraught with redundancies, namely: What makes an author's perspective worthy of such consideration? If the true value of studying literature is basically identical to that of philosophy – or what passes for philosophy – why not bypass that medium, as Hegel would have liked, and go straight to philosophy? And if such things as literary structures (or form) and aesthetics exist, where ought they to be studied if not in literature departments? These problems cannot, and will not, be solved. English departments are eagerly embracing their own redundancy.

Other humane disciplines are following suit, and when the so-called philosophies of Lacan and Foucault and Derrida are finally abandoned as muddled hogwash, the humanities themselves will collapse into themselves like a dying star. This is the way the academy ends, as Eliot might have said: not with a bang, but a whimper.

As we have said, this isn't altogether bad. The pseudo-humanities ought to die, and they will. Independent scholars like Scruton, Kirk, Dawson, and others will carry the mantle. Small liberal arts colleges, like Campion in Australia and Hillsdale in the United States, will provide a beleaguered haven for the Old Idea for as long as they possibly can. Like St. Benedict of Nursia, true academics will steal away from the chaos and depravity of the City, preserving the wisdom of ages without officialdom until the world is prepared to receive them again.

The blame can't be laid squarely on the shoulders of leftist intellectuals, however. There's perhaps an even greater threat to the Old Idea, and one that will no doubt be the undoing of the New Idea as well: the Taylorist administrations that have wrested control of the major universities. These are the men and women who've designs to transform the academy into a training institution, promising a large return for skyrocketing tuition in the form of marketable skills and high-wage jobs.

The commodification of education isn't merely a leftist byword, though it's used much differently by the Left than by the so-called "Right". Knowing that their system of indoctrination is an entirely incestuous affair with no use to anyone without the Ivory Tower, administrators' desire to lower the drawbridge and reintroduce students to the outside world is an existential threat to the intellectuals' illusion of their own earth-shattering radicalism. The idea that modern academic discourse is, or can be, taken seriously in a non-academic context is a carefully constructed fiction that the faintest glance out of the window would immediately shatter.

Proponents of the Old Idea object to this commodification on far different grounds. They needn't worry about their discipline being unmarketable as such; indeed, they pride themselves on the unmarketability of the liberal arts. They fear, rather, the continuing descent into vulgar materialism. It should go without saying that the Arts are precious exactly because they exalt a dimension of the human being that is greater than the material. The true devotee of the humanities reflects with J.S. Mill:

> A being capable of higher faculties requires more to make him happy, is capable probably of more acute suffering, and certainly accessible to it at most points, than one of an inferior type; but in spite of these liabilities, he can never really wish to sink into what he feels to be a lower grade of existence.[5]

It is precisely to feed and foster these higher faculties that we undertake a study of the humanities. And we do so for no reasons necessarily other than the humanities themselves. To put it crudely, as a utilitarian like Mill would, there are no pleasures in life higher than those afforded by the intellect. None of which, we see, is of any serious value to an employer. Whatever admissions departments say about the commercial benefits of an Arts degree – that it trains one to think creatively, write coherently, and so on – those are simply formalities of the degree. That we can speak of the "marketability of an *Arts* degree" as a totality, rather than the individual merits of the various sub-disciplines (literature, philosophy, history, and so forth) shows that the humanities are increasingly deracinated. In other words, while employers may like to hire a Bachelor of the Arts, that they would be indifferent to whether that degree-holder is trained in literature, philosophy, or history indicates an obvious indifference to the truly humane aspect of the humanities.

So attempts by university administrators to make Arts degrees marketable to employers has necessarily led to a great deal of the degree's most worthy content being simply tossed away, with funding being diverted to more lucrative degrees such as commerce and business, medicine, law, and the like. How rare it is today to find English courses devoted solely to certain great works and authors of the Western canon, or philosophy units focusing exclusively on the Hellenics! What remains, of course, are the pet projects of the postmodernists: multiple courses on lesbian and gay fiction, artworks created by the mentally ill, the philosophy of despair, the economics of the far Left, and the history of oppression and victimization.

These neo-*soixante-huitards*' obscurantism and ideological pandering make it so much easier for administrators to marginalize the Arts. Not only do so many postmodern writers scoff at the clarity of thought and expression that (in theory) makes Arts degrees marketable, but their ideas have been proven to fail by history (as with Marx et al.) or have never gained serious traction in mainstream society (as with Foucault, Derrida, and the likes). As we have said, the Arts in academia has become a wholly incestuous affair, the result being that sensible people have no desire to study them, and sensible employers have no good reason to hire those who do.

So if the great universities are determined to become training institutions for white-collar workers – as they seem to be – the humanities will need to find a new home, to seek out new champions. And no doubt they shall.

---

[5] John Stuart Mill, *Utilitarianism and On Liberty*, ed. Mary Warnock (Malden: Blackwell, 2003), 188.

There will always be a market for history's greatest ideas and artworks. Milton and Shakespeare, Herodotus and Gibbon, Seneca and Hume: all will have an eager, enduring, if increasingly small audience. Even if our civilization comes to ruins, how majestic will those ruins be, and how much seemlier than the hovels we've constructed on the plains below! There will always be men and women who look to the hills and, transfixed by those fine, haunting forms, will dare to leave the despair of ordinary life and make the long ascent. They'll wander the wreckage and the rubble, wondering what race could have created such staggering monuments in their own image. They'll find others like them who live a lonely, trying existence in that splendid waste. They'll forge a new community, a new society, free of the dying Brave New World's gross cynicism. And suddenly they'll wonder if they, too, aren't capable of such feats as the ancients'. So the humane spirit will endure, if barely, if weakly, until mankind desires to make something of himself again. In that moment the old spirit of the university – the true spirit of the university – will be reborn.

The Supervisor – Student Relationship

Henry Cooper

If a practical end must be assigned to a University course, I say it is that of training good members of society. Its art is the art of social life, and its end is fitness for the world.[1]

If fitness for the world is the best practical end of a liberal education, then by far the most profitable time I spent at University came under the supervision of Professor Spurr during my Honours year. Cardinal Newman believed that the training of good members of society was best achieved through something more than mere *teaching*; it comes through meaningful interaction between students and the faculty. He told students, "you have come, not merely to be taught, but to learn…. You do not come merely to hear a lecture, or to read a book, but you come for that catechetical which consists in a sort of conversation between your lecturer and you".[2] To adopt Newman's distinction between been taught and actually learning, I learnt more under Professor Spurr's supervision than I had in the previous three years of my degree combined. Clearly, that is not to say that I acquired a greater volume of knowledge during this period; it is instead to say that the influence upon my approach to intellectual inquiry during this period did more to fulfil the true ends of a liberal University education than the course of lectures, tutorials and assessments that came before.

The type of learning contemplated by Newman can only occur where the faculty invests time in engaging students beyond the mere passive delivery of information in lectures and weekly tutorials. F. R. Leavis thought it "absurd that last year's schoolboy should be flung into a wilderness of books and abandoned to his own devices".[3] Lectures, whilst of course essential, are not enough. For Leavis, the most fruitful time in an undergraduate course is spent in discussion. In my experience, the very best lecturers, such as Professor Spurr, were acutely aware of the danger of undergraduates being abandoned in the manner contemplated by Leavis, and evidently made a concerted effort to avoid it happening in their courses. However, it remains

---

[1] John Henry Cardinal Newman, *The Idea of a University* (New York: Rinehart, 1960), 134.
[2] *Ibid.*, 368.
[3] F. R. Leavis, *Education and the University* (London: Chatto and Windus, 1961), 47.

the case today that, all too often, interested students have their interest thwarted by a simple lack of attention and guidance from the faculty.

If the aim of a University education is to shape the character of its students in preparation for the world, then it is vital that students can get close enough to academics so as to be influenced by them. Personal contact with eminent people will often have a transformative effect on a young mind. Evidence of that can be found in the account given by a young William Hazlitt of the aftermath of a walk he took with Samuel Taylor Coleridge shortly after their first meeting:

> I tried to explain my view of it to Coleridge, who listened with great willingness, but I did not succeed in making myself understood. I sat down to the task shortly afterwards for the twentieth time, got new pens and paper, determined to make clear work of it, wrote a few meagre sentences in the skeletal-style of a mathematical demonstration, stopped halfway down the second page; and, after trying in vain to pump up any words, images, notions, apprehensions, facts, or observations, from that gulf of abstraction in which I had plunged myself for four or five years preceding, gave up the attempt as labour in vain, and shed tears of blank despondency on the blank unfinished paper.[4]

This passage illustrates the effect of a leading mind upon a student eager to be influenced. Coleridge did more than teach Hazlitt by imparting knowledge to him; he changed the way in which he thought. The workings of the young Hazlitt's mind were so changed that his previous endeavours were suddenly alien to him, as though they had been those of someone else. This is the formation of a brilliant mind in action, and precisely the type of character-forming influence that a liberal education should have as its objective.

The account that Professor Spurr has given to me of his first University lecture, delivered in Wallace Theatre by Dame Leonie Kramer on William Blake, is not unlike the experience of the young Hazlitt in the presence of Coleridge. Such was the brilliance of the lecturer that the fresh undergraduate feared that he was out of his depth, and he would have to return home to Canberra forthwith. But he persisted and determined to rise to the challenge of brilliance, rather than be thwarted by it or develop the neediness to be supported in order to cope with it. Anecdotes such as these demonstrate the irreplaceable and singular importance of personal influence by leading scholars upon young minds. The young mind is challenged to either sink or swim in newfound intellectual waters, and inevitably emerges stronger from the experience. No lecturer made such a powerful impact upon me until Professor Spurr's lectures on T. S. Eliot in my second year.

---

[4] William Hazlitt, "My First Acquaintance With Poets", in *William Hazlitt: Selected Writings*, ed. Jon Cook (Oxford: Oxford University Press, 2009), 219–220.

The first thing that anyone in Professor Spurr's lectures would be struck by is his rich and sonorous voice. His insistence that poetry must be read aloud unlocked the power and brilliance of the great poets immediately for me. The fundamental importance of the *sound* of great literature, particularly poetry, is something that I did not properly grasp until hearing Professor Spurr read Eliot's poetry aloud. "I could not have been more delighted if I had heard the music of the spheres".[5] This approach shaped the way in which I have understood poetry since. Furthermore, the insistence on reading aloud has had the happy effect that I continue to be able to recite certain lines of Eliot's poetry "by heart". Listening to a skilful reader such as Professor Spurr recite a poem makes an indelible mark on one's subconscious, such that the sounds and cadences of the work remain in one's mind long after they are first encountered. This has enabled me to carry the poetry I studied under Professor Spurr with me ever since, facilitating the discovery of new meanings and deeper appreciation over time.

I left my first lecture with Professor Spurr utterly enthralled, and feeling as though I had experienced what a University education should be. I resolved immediately to undertake an Honours year in the English Department, taking my thesis subject – animals in the poetry of W. B. Yeats – from a remark made by Professor Spurr regarding the number of crabs in Eliot's poetry. Those lectures gave me, and undoubtedly many others in the room, a joy in Eliot's early poetry that I will never lose. It also gave me an ideal of what a University-level teacher should be. This was someone who demanded the full attention of every person present by his charisma, clarity of expression, and attractiveness of presentation. These lectures were a true performance, and Professor Spurr's understanding that his task was to engage the attention of those in the room gave him a clear advantage over most of his colleagues. This focus on engaging the students carried through to his convening of the course. My tutor, a more junior academic, constantly impressed upon our group that Professor Spurr took a personal interest in our progress, and was always eager to hear the tutor's reports. This was one of those wonderful courses where the convenor had made it his mission to satisfy the students' interest in and further their appreciation of the subject at hand.

I took it upon myself (somewhat presumptuously, I feared) to write to Professor Spurr in the semester before my Honours year to seek his opinion on my proposed thesis topic. To my surprise and delight, he responded almost immediately with enthusiastic words of encouragement, and his preliminary thoughts on my proposal. His invitation to discuss it in person was more than I had counted on, but that first meeting was the first of many

---

[5] *Ibid.*, 213.

enjoyable and stimulating encounters. I was thrilled when at its conclusion, he offered to supervise my thesis.

Despite the vast difference in knowledge and experience between us, Professor Spurr always had a wonderful way of placing me at ease. He is unquestionably the greatest lecturer I ever had, but his style in one-on-one meetings was in no way reminiscent of a lecture. Our meetings were always a conversation, where my ideas were listened to, and considered responses were given. I left every meeting I ever had with him feeling more capable than I was when I had entered, and excited about pursuing the new avenues of enquiry which had arisen. I cannot think of two better qualities to instil in a student than intellectual confidence and enthusiasm.

Professor Spurr's knowledge, experience and personal interest in my progress were undoubtedly what gave me the feeling of enthusiasm that attended all of my meetings with him. After a discussion with him, my thesis was inevitably less onerous than I had previously imagined, and more interesting than I had realised. He had a marvellous way of crystallising and focussing the areas that I needed to explore. I would enter with ideas in their earliest stage, and I was constantly impressed and elated that he would understand so quickly, and refine or refocus them as necessary. In all the meetings I ever had with him, I cannot recall a single time when I was unable to convey my ideas to him. More impressively, he always communicated in such a way that I got his meaning straight away. The most remarkable and valuable skill that Professor Spurr utilised in these meetings was that he was able to use his own brilliance not to intimidate or strike awe into his student; to the contrary, his positive, warm disposition and clarity of thought made me feel more capable myself, just by dint of sharing the room and a conversation with him. These meetings are the happiest memories of my undergraduate degree, and I have no doubt that I learnt my most valuable lessons in them. My academic results improved markedly under Professor Spurr's supervision, and I have maintained those higher standards into my postgraduate study of law. Furthermore, I have enjoyed a number of extra-curricular successes that would have been unthinkable for me before I was influenced by Professor Spurr.

The year that I spent under Professor Spurr's supervision made an indelible impression upon me. He taught me the essential skills that go towards creating academic work. But more importantly, I learnt the types of lessons that can only come from faculty supervision in a liberal education. The experience changed the way in which I think. The scholarly approach of Professor Spurr gave me an extraordinary example to follow myself, and the faith placed in me by him imbued in me a confidence that has fuelled each one of my subsequent successes. The fundamental principle in Newman's idea of a liberal education is that education should influence the whole person, in a manner that goes beyond the mere acquisition of skills. For

Newman, education "implies an action upon our mental nature, and the formation of a character; it is something individual and permanent".[6] The gift that Professor Spurr imparted to me is something I consider to be a personal possession. I have acquired it, and it will forever shape my character. That he had such an impact on me shows the mark of a great educator, and the value of the engagement between faculty and students which is a necessary element of an effective liberal education. The influence that Professor Spurr had upon me fulfilled what Newman thought should be the aim of a University education: it prepared me for the world. It shaped my mind, and changed the way I think.

---

[6] Newman, *The Idea of a University*, 86.

O Where Are the Sounds? Inviting Poetry Back into the Lives of Learners

Karina Hepner

> *We shall not cease from exploration*
> *And the end of all our exploring*
> *Will be to arrive where we started*
> *And know the place for the first time.*
> T. S. Eliot, "Little Gidding"[1]

Some years ago cartoonist Bill Leak created a visual representation of the shift in modern schooling and its teaching practices. Leak's cartoon depicts a modern Australian living room with a school-aged boy planted in front of the television. Homer Simpson, at work on a hamburger, features on the screen. Standing in the corner, a frustrated father looks over at his son and shouts, "Turn that off and do your homework". The son, appearing conflicted, replies, "This *is* my homework". The cartoon, entitled "Studying Homer", comments on the raging debate about what our children should be learning in schools.[2] After all, Generation Z are the *screenagers* and they fill our middle school and high school classrooms. Many predict that at least fifty per cent of this iGen will also spill over into higher education. According to McCrindle Research, these dot.com kids are "globalised" and "digitalised", living their lives through technology and constantly consuming popular culture.[3] Moreover, they are identified as "distinctly social" and "uniquely visual" because they connect with others through social media; they tap and swipe and watch screens on their slick mobile devices.[4]

---

[1] T. S. Eliot, "Little Gidding", *Four Quartets*, accessed 24 June, 2015, http://www.davidgorman.com/4Quartets/.
[2] Bill Leak, "Studying Homer", *The Australian,* 30 September, 2005, accessed 24 June, 2015, http://theaustraliancartoonmuseum.com.au/projects/education/studying-homer/
[3] "Generation Z", McCrindle Research Infographics, accessed 20 June, 2015, http://mccrindle.com.au/resources/Gen-Z-Claire-Madden_Infographic_McCrindle.pdf
[4] Amanda Dunn, "What will adulthood be like for Gen Z?", *The Age,* accessed June 13, 2015, http://www.theage.com.au/victoria/what-will-adulthood-be-like-for-generation-z-20150612-ghlm88.html.

Arguably, for the most part, Australian educational institutions and modern curricula appear to have been investigated and restructured to accommodate the complex and changing needs of the modern student. For instance, current curricula privilege inquiry-based learning approaches and multimodal literacy for our predominantly kinaesthetic, interactive and visual (modern) students. School architects have redesigned classrooms fostering collaborative learning practices to produce students' cognitive autonomy. Most significantly, those on the front lines, the teachers, attend conferences and seminars that often promote blended learning techniques and constructivism as a paradigm for teaching and learning. Thus, the learner-centric classroom of the twenty-first century engages and connects students through blogging, posting, filming, tweeting and texting to create knowledge and to encourage students' reflecting on their own learning processes.

And yet something is rotten in the state of education. Our schools' learning support rooms are packed. And they're not brimming with screen-watching disabilities or movie-starved children or digitally illiterate kids, but the teachers, who in these rooms contend with burgeoning literacy issues. Quite simply, students are not reading enough. That the research suggests that click'n'go kids list reading as their least favourite activity should raise alarm bells. Literary reading, in and out of classrooms, has so diminished that today, whilst students pile out of schools technologically savvy and multi-tasker *extraodinaires*, they know too little of the transcendent ideals found so often in our great literary works.

Gustave Flaubert assures us why we need to read: in order to live. And students, as part of this ever-shifting, whirling universe, need to be urged to read in order to experience more enriching, meaningful and stable lives. On my own classroom wall I have these words from C. S. Lewis displayed:

> … in reading great literature I become a thousand men and yet remain myself. Like the night sky in the Greek poem, I see with a myriad eyes, but it is still I who see. Here, as in worship, in love, in moral action, and in knowing, I transcend myself; and am never more myself than when I do.[5]

At the beginning of a new school year, my classes and I enthusiastically recite Lewis's words. In Harold Bloom's book, *How to Read and Why*, he professes that:

> We read deeply for varied reasons, most of them familiar: that we cannot know enough people profoundly enough; that we need to know ourselves better; that we require knowledge, not just of self and others, but of the way things are.[6]

---

[5] C. S. Lewis, *An Experiment in Criticism* (Cambridge: Cambridge University Press, 1961), 141.
[6] Harold Bloom, *How to Read and Why* (New York: Simon & Schuster, 2000), 28.

As educators, our mission is to invite students to see this truth. Reading holds the colours, flavours, scents and pictures of living. We read; therefore, we *are*.

Above all, reading must encourage our young people to engage with and intimately know poetry. Because a curriculum is so packed with much to do, to learn, and to make in a school day, students receive, at best, only a light dusting of poetry. And classes in our primary and high schools teem with learners who know little – or nothing – of its brilliance and beauty. Yet Matthew Arnold claimed in his book, *The Last Word*, "The crown of literature is poetry...."[7] Poetry is both medicine and sustenance to the soul and spirit. Through poetry, students are offered sheer delight, vast knowledge, moral conviction, intimate solace and deep compassion.

Poetry has the power to delight. Cambridge Professor of Children's Poetry, Morag Styles, feels that children respond "innately", "instinctively", and "naturally" to poetry. Her research suggests that a distinctive feature of childhood is "taking pleasure in the rhythm, rhyme, and repetition".[8] Our primary school classes should, once again, ring with the chanting and singing of children's verse: Edward Lear's "The Jumblies", with their green heads and blue hands; "The Dong with a Luminous Nose"; and "The Pobble who has No Toes". We want them to chortle in triumph over Lewis Carroll's "Jabberwocky", while miming imaginary attacks with their "vorple" swords in hand. Allow them to savour C. J. Dennis's onomatopoeic delights in his narrative poem, "Hist". For spooky treats that will incite laughter and chills, they need to meet Charles Causley's "Colonel Fazackerley Butterworth-Toast" and Walter de la Mare's "The Listeners". And older students are equally delighted by poetry when they encounter Hilaire Belloc's cautionary tales: "Jim, Who ran away from his nurse and was eaten by a Lion" or "George: Who played with a Dangerous Toy, and suffered a Catastrophe of considerable Dimensions". I believe, as one of the teachers of great literature, it is our duty to keep the flame of poetry appreciation burning brightly and warmly. My senior students have often marvelled at their own ability to memorise and recite works such as Blake's "The Tyger", Shakespearean sonnets and soliloquies, as well as sections of Coleridge's "The Rime of the Ancient Mariner".

Disappointingly, Australia has no national poetic recitation competition for students to access. In the United States and the United Kingdom, students can compete against others in memorising and reciting both classical and modern poetic texts. Currently, Cambridge lecturers, David Whitely and

---

[7] Matthew Arnold, *The Last Word*, ed. R. H. Super (Ann Arbor: University of Michigan Press, 1977), 284.
[8] Morag Styles, "The Case for Children's Poetry", Cambridge University, accessed 24 June, 2015, http://www.cam.ac.uk/research/discussion/the-case-for-children's-poetry

Debbie Pullinger, are researching the relationships between memorisation, recitation and understanding during their three-year "Poetry and Memory Project". Their findings will be relevant for "pedagogical policy and practice [and, therefore,] contribute to wider discourses about cultural identity and locations of knowledge".[9] For students to memorise and recite poetry by heart, fosters not only a deep appreciation for literary heritage and the wonderment of language, but this almost-forgotten practice also builds students' self-confidence and a mastery of oratorical skills. Michael Knox Beran's article, "In Defense of Memorization", reinforces the value of students memorising poetry: "[I]t heightens their feel for the intricacies and complexities of the English language – an indispensable attainment if they are to go on to speak, write, and read English with ease".[10] Furthermore, whilst *generation connected* jumps online and multi-tasks with ease, Professors Gina Conti-Ramsden's and Kevin Durkin's research into children's language difficulties claims that this very generation struggles to listen:[11] our learners cannot be quiet, sit still and listen. Thus, to reintroduce the practice of oral repetition of verse, devoid of the fanfare of moving or still images, can encourage healthy listening skills.

And when I receive communication from past students, it is frequently the poetry that lingers on as the lasting fragrance of their high school English journey. Our young people, existing in an often morally ambiguous universe, with sometimes already troubled and anxious lives, deserve to meet and spend time with poetry. Percy Bysshe Shelley, in his "Defence of Poetry", invites us all to see that "Poetry is a mirror, which makes beautiful that which is distorted".[12]

Poetry gives readers knowledge. As a young teacher starting out, overwhelmed and disorientated, I stood in front of thirty-two students in a Canadian high school classroom after relocating from Australia to Vancouver. I had been given the English Literature 12 class, a survey course of the Western Canon of literature. On that first blustery fall day, I recall cautiously and anxiously opening my literary "bible", *Adventures in English Literature,* to start at the beginning: Anglo-Saxon poetry. Together, daunted teacher and excited students – thirty-one girls and one boy – discovered the "noble" Beowulf with his "heroic deeds". Next we examined Chaucer's *Canterbury Tales* and found the human foibles of greed in the "fat and personable" Monk

---

[9] David Whitley and Debbie Pullinger, "Poetry and Memory Project", accessed 24 June, 2015, http://www.poetryandmemory.com/about/
[10] Michael Knox Beran, "In Defense of Memorization", *City Journal,* Summer (2004), accessed 10 Jan., 2014, http://www.city-journalorg/html/issue_14_3.html
[11] Gina Conti-Ramsden and Kevin Durkin, "Understanding Language Difficulties: From Childhood to Adolescence" (presentation, Chatterbox Speech Pathology, Brisbane, Qld., Feb. 9 – 10, 2015).
[12] Percy Bysshe Shelley, "A Defence of Poetry" in *Critical Theory Since Plato,* ed. Hazard Adams (New York: Harcourt Brace Jovanovich, 1971), 516-529.

with his "fine grey fur"; lust with the Woman of Bath who "knows the remedies for love's mischances"; and hypocrisy in the Friar who frequents both "taverns" and "barmaids". We laughed – out loud – at the folly of humanity in the Middle Ages as we learned that there was nothing new under the sun.

What was interesting for me, while instructing this course for twelve years, was that I found that the most challenging and difficult poetical texts were the ones that taught students the most. For example, thunderous John Donne with his striking, disparate images of love in "A Valediction: Forbidding Mourning" introduces the metallurgy, geometry and cartography of the Renaissance world. Most significantly, he also presents to students a love "so much refined" and "inter-assurèd of the mind", one that transcends earthly limitations.[13] And his type of love directly contrasts the predominant love discourses manipulated by popular culture. Perhaps the greatest need of our current system is to teach our popular culture leaders, the global gen, what is least relevant to their lives. Neil Postman once urged that curriculum has to be "positioned some distance away from the influences of [young people's] own time rather than be held captive in the midst of things".[14] Through good poetry, teachers can present to students an alternative view of the world. For instance, to encounter John Milton forces readers to study the political complexities of seventeenth-century England so that they begin to understand, for example, the distinctly political voice of Satan's speeches in *Paradise Lost*. Evidently, high school students will not comprehend everything that Milton has to offer, but later on as they mature, they may encounter Milton's text again, and upon each reading, his work will provide something new and fresh. Adler and Van Doren in *How to Read a Book* assure us that "a good poem can be worked at, re-read, and thought about over and over for the rest of [our lives]. [We] will never stop finding new things in it, new pleasures and delights, and also new ideas about [ourselves] and the world".[15]

Poetry has the power to convict. We cannot deny that our society faces complex issues: terrorism threats, environmental concerns, refugee dilemmas and many more. Perhaps, however, a greater, more insidious issue confronts us: we are infatuated with ourselves. In schools, and elsewhere, self-esteem and assertive behaviour are celebrated and nurtured. As Twenge and Campbell offer in their compelling book, *The Narcissism Epidemic: Living in the Age of Entitlement*, "Americans have become inured to the incivility,

---

[13] John Donne, "A Valediction: Forbidding Mourning", *Adventures in English Literature,* ed. Fannie Safier (New York: Holt, Rinehart and Winston, 1996), 266.
[14] Neil Postman, *The End of Education: redefining the value of school* (New York: Alfred A. Knopf, 1995), 185.
[15] J. Mortimer Adler and Charles Van Doren, *How to Read a Book* (New York: Simon & Schuster, 1972), 229.

exhibitionism, and celebrity obsession caused by the narcissism epidemic".[16] Modern Australia appears no different. Poetry, by contrast, can help turn mine eyes into my very soul. Reading Eliot's "The Hollow Men", for instance, dramatises both "stuffed" and "hollow" people that possess "shape without form, shade without colour".[17] These words help shape convicting questions: am I one of those "hollow, stuffed men", speaking in a "dried voice", "quiet and meaningless"?[18] Our students need to be bothered by their own weaknesses and failures. Furthermore, Yeats's "The Second Coming" foregrounds a postmodern world where "things fall apart; the centre cannot hold".[19] What is the meaning of life? What can be done, if anything, about the "rough beast" that "slouches towards Bethlehem"?[20] These images become the listeners' mirrors, forcing them to confront the uncomfortable and the unspoken. In *Satanic Verses*, Rushdie's satirical poet, Baal, admits that "A poet's work … is to name the unnameable, to point at frauds, to take sides, start arguments, shape the world, and stop it going to sleep".[21] Poetry may not provide all the answers to students' complicated questions, yet it makes them restless and becomes the impetus to evaluate their own character and faith and to search for hope and, above all, Truth.

Poetry offers solace. Our students are forced to face the heavy burden of death and loss in their own lives or in lives of others. If they remain untouched by the confronting reality of death during their school years, their paths will surely cross it as they step into adulthood. So meeting W. H. Auden, for instance, helps one articulate the impenetrable sadness of loss. In "Funeral Blues" the grieving speaker longs to "sweep up the wood" and "pour away the ocean" – will anything now *ever* come to any good?[22] Today Western culture finds death and its partner, grief, awkward and cumbersome. Those looking on at the mourners are bewildered and silent. Consequently, this "silence" leaves the bereaved, young and old, intensely alone and the misery of loss becomes almost shameful. Yet poetry welcomes these salty tears that inevitably flow. Philosopher Alain de Botton's article, "Art as Therapy", claims that visual art teaches us "successful suffering".[23] Poetry also does just that. Auden's elegy, "Funeral Blues", does not remove young

---

[16] Jean Twenge and W. Keith Campbell, *The Narcissism Epidemic: Living in the Age of Entitlement* (New York: Atria Paperback, 2009), 8.
[17] T. S. Eliot, "The Hollow Men", in Safier, *op. cit.*, 952.
[18] *Ibid.*
[19] *Ibid.*, 934.
[20] *Ibid.*
[21] Salman Rushdie, *The Satanic Verses: a novel* (New York: Random House, 2008), 101.
[22] W. H. Auden, "Funeral Blues", in Barry Spurr, *Studying Poetry*, 2nd ed. (Basingstoke: Palgrave Macmillan, 2006), 298.
[23] Alain de Botton, "Art as Therapy", *ABC Religion and Ethics*, 20 Dec., 2013, http://www.abc.net.au/religion/articles/2013/12/20/3915563.htm

people's sadness; it does not replace their grief with joy. Yet the poetical images and euphonious sounds create a "dignified home" for outpourings of despair.[24]

Moreover, some poetry dismantles the notion of death as an enemy. Emily Dickinson's "Because I could not stop for death" reframes death by converging mortality and eternity. Here, Death is gentle, kind and welcoming. Romantic poet, Shelley, in *Queen Mab, a Philosophical Poem*, positions the reader to see "[h]ow wonderful is Death / Death, and his brother Sleep!",[25] while in one of his *Holy Sonnets* Donne rages against the power of Death, commanding that "[it] shall be no more; Death, thou shalt die".[26] Most significantly, death, as depicted by the Bible – a text often belittled or ignored in classrooms – transforms into a story of redemption and hope for humanity. Mervyn Bendle's paper, "Derrida and the Destruction of the Humanities", comments sadly that, in the humanities:

> little or nothing is said of beauty, love, hate, good, evil, tragedy, intimacy, loss, grief, aspiration, betrayal, genius, foolishness, arrogance, heroism, cowardice, the angelic, the satanic, redemption, damnation, or the pursuit of higher, perhaps transcendent ideals.[27]

Poetry provides an introduction into these "higher, transcendent ideals".

These five things are given through teaching poetry: delight, knowledge, conviction, solace, and compassion. But the greatest of these is compassion: poetry nurtures compassion. American writer, Joyce Carol Oates, believes that reading "is the sole means by which we slip, involuntarily, often helplessly, into another's skin, another's voice, another's soul." And Stevie Smith, for instance, demonstrates someone else's suffering. Her poem, "Not Waving But Drowning", differentiates between listening and hearing: "Nobody heard him, the dead man, / But still he lay moaning".[28] These striking opening lines of the poem penetrate the listener. Although we *appear* to communicate or befriend others, do we really know them? Facebook comes to mind: we are connected but often alone. Have our digitalised communities and classrooms severed intimacy with people? In the final lines of this short, yet moving poem there is a shift in the point of view from third person to first person. We *hear* from the dead man, but are we listening: "I

---

[24] *Ibid*.
[25] Percy Bysshe Shelley, *Queen Mab, a Philosophical Poem*, accessed 24 June, 2015, https://www.marxists.org/archive/shelley/1813/queen-mab.htm.
[26] John Donne, "Holy Sonnet VI", in Safier, *op. cit.*, 269.
[27] Mervyn Bendle, "Derrida and the Destruction of the Humanities", *Quadrant Online*. Web. 2 April, 2013, accessed 22 June, 2015, https://quadrant.org.au/magazine/2013/04/derrida-and-the-destruction-of-the-humanities/
[28] Stevie Smith, "Not Waving but Drowning", in Safier, *op. cit.*, 961.

was much too far out all my life / And not waving but drowning".[29] Our great wish for those whom we teach is that they will see through people's "waving" and recognise that they, in fact, may be "drowning".

Similarly, we encourage students' empathy when we present the marginalised voices in literature. Mary Shelley's creature from her iconic novel, *Frankenstein*, shares a common bond with Stevie Smith's speaker: loneliness. Canada's *The Globe and Mail* recently ran an article, "Life of solitude: A loneliness crisis is looming", where Vancouver residents claimed that "social isolation" was their gravest concern.[30] Victor Frankenstein's creation, who is never ascribed a name by his creator, knows the searing pain of loneliness. If taught well, students will never forget their first impressions when they read Victor's "hideous progeny" recounting his isolation, abuse, and suffering; his plight is unimaginable. Researchers David Comer Kidd and Emanuele Castano in their case study, "Reading Literary Fiction Improves Theory of the Mind", establish that "quality" fiction has the capacity to "promote empathy" in its readers.[31] While the creature struggles to make sense of his surroundings, he discovers poetry, Milton's *Paradise Lost*, which finally gives voice to his insufferable situation:

> But it was all a dream; no Eve soothed my sorrows, nor shared my thoughts; I was alone. I remembered [from *Paradise Lost*] Adam's supplication to his Creator. But where was mine? He had abandoned me: and, in the bitterness of my heart, I cursed him.[32]

The monster's tale of frailty and sorrow offers everyone a glimpse into the state of the human condition.

But there is not enough space and time to present all the reasons why poetry matters to twenty-first century schooling. In our learning centres, these poets' words should spill all over the shelves, sit on the walls, and run into the halls and corridors; the poets' compelling and convicting voices must whisper in students' ears, pulse in their veins and travel with them throughout their lives.

For a moment let us return to Leak's depiction of the iGen student connected to his Homer (Simpson) homework: shouldn't we, as educators, assure his father that we will gently coax his son back from his virtual world into the world of real face time, where he and his classmates can reconnect

---

[29] *Ibid.*
[30] Elizabeth Renzetti, "A Life of Solitude: a loneliness crisis is looming", *The Globe and Mail*. 23 Nov., 2013. Web. 29 Dec., 2013, http://www.theglobeandmail.com/life/life-of-solitude-a-loneliness-crisis-is-looming/article15573187/?page=all
[31] David Comer Kidd and Emanuele Castano, "Reading Literary Fiction Improves Theory of the Mind", *Science* 342.6156 (2013): 379.
[32] Mary Shelley, *Frankenstein: or, the Modern Prometheus* (New York: Signet Classics, 1983), 110.

with the Greek Homer, other transforming poetical works and with each other? I share Postman's faith that "something can be done in school that will alter the lenses through which [students] see the world".[33] Indeed, we will radicalise education by creating some unplugged classrooms to promote the power of the poetic word. The modern student is poetically malnourished; he must be fed more poems. Confronting poems. Sacred poems. Difficult poems. Hopeful poems. I do not suggest returning to the forgotten tools of learning, such as memorisation and recitation of poetry and other traditional teaching methods, out of sentiment or nostalgia, but of an urgent need to equip and empower our learners so that they will confidently, yet graciously negotiate themselves and others through the constant flux of a perplexing, irrational universe.

---

[33] Neil Postman, *Teaching as a Conserving Activity*, (New York: Delcorte Press, 1979), x.

Imagery for the End of the Day

Devika Brendon

There was a window that I lifted up
to let in the morning air
and the evening breeze:
A transversal that cut between
two consonant worlds
that would otherwise
have never met with ease.
A light that was turned on:
one of those study lamps,
that throw a golden circle
around the facts and figures that are on the table
that are relevant, and which really matter,
which are focal.
There were chance meetings, random decisions.
A choice, taken on the flip of a coin.
To be, all of a sudden,
And against all past experience,
Open.

And there is a season,
and a reason for everything.
Time to savour, time to move on
while the currents still run strong.

Imagery for the End of the Day

I reach out, with complete intent:
not like a child,
but with my action fully meant.
Watch what I am doing now:
I close the portal, in the glare of its allure.
Cut the line I have previously explored.
I turn off the golden light.
It is my right.
You may not like it.
But I want to let the night
with its clean, cold silence
heal the violence.
Illuminate the quiet.

I note that the image in this poem, of the golden circle of light cast on a page by a desk-lamp, was suggested by my memory of a story written by Thea Astley, which I read and taught to students in Sydney, many years ago.

Barry Spurr on graduation from Oxford in 1976, prior to his appointment as Lecturer in English, University of Sydney

Barry Spurr presenting a copy of the first edition of his book, *Studying Poetry*, to the Chancellor of the University of Sydney, Professor Dame Leonie Kramer, who was his first university lecturer and to whom the book is dedicated (May, 1997)

Occasional Address

Barry Spurr [1]

Deputy Chancellor, distinguished guests, colleagues, ladies and gentlemen, newly-minted graduates.

Early in the 1630s, the greatest of English poets wrote two companion poems with Italian titles, *L'Allegro* and *Il Penseroso*. The first celebrates the active life, while the second contemplates the pensive life of the reflective person. In the course of that second poem, the poet becomes particularly personal and reflects warmly upon his university years, then coming to a close:

> But let my due feet never fail,
> To walk the studious cloisters pale.

The personal touch has led some readers to conclude that he is commending the reflective life over the active life, particularly as he was about to embark on six further years of study at home, with his generous father's support, after graduating. Some of you today might like to put a similar proposal to your parents while they are in celebratory mode. Poetically and biographically, it would seem that the poet was preferring retirement from the world to involvement with it. Rather, in the course of the two poems (neither of which should be read without the other, but which co-exist in a creative tension with one another), he magnificently displays the virtues of both lives, leading his readers to appreciate that the life well-lived combines both action (including engagement with society), on the one hand, and, on the other, the consideration and evaluation of what we do and why, personally, professionally and as members of the community, in retreat from action in study and contemplation (which, of course, are actions of their own kind). As Socrates taught centuries earlier, the unexamined life is not worth living – and this is true for the individual, as for the culture at large.

A common misrepresentation of a university education and, indeed, of students' time and academics' lifetimes at university, is that it is time out from

---

[1] Occasional Address delivered at the Graduation Ceremony, The Great Hall, University of Sydney, 6 May 2011.

the 'real world' in a tower of ivory or, at least, sandstone gothic. An interstate university, mindful of this idea, declares in its current marketing slogan that it is 'a University for the real world', as if this were something innovative and unique, establishing a connection with reality while other places remain in a state of lamentable, chronic dissociation from it. One should not be too hard on the Queensland University of Technology, for the Concise Oxford Dictionary itself gives as one of its definitions of the word 'academic', 'not related to a real or practical situation and therefore irrelevant'. Common to both the slogan and the dictionary definition is that troublesome word 'real' from such use of which the philosophical, not to say the ordinary commonsensical mind should indeed reel.

'What is truth?' asked jesting Pilate. 'What is real?' we may ask and how is it that the University and the education you receive therein are separate from it. This is not only a dichotomy which, as soon as you start to think about it, is meaningless, but worse, it would dismiss what a university (and, especially, I would argue, a Faculty of the Humanities), truly engaged in its work, is doing – the analysing, discussing and evaluating of all aspects of reality. I would go so far as to suggest that there is no place on earth in which the real is more comprehensively pursued and known than in the university. As the poet Gerard Manley Hopkins said of the medieval philosopher, Duns Scotus (whose life was spent in the universities of Oxford, Cambridge and Paris): he was 'of realty the rarest-veined unraveller'. This is the purpose of a university, to probe and understand reality in all its forms and expressions.

But such probing and the conclusions that arise must be made known. All graduates in the Humanities should be philologists – lovers of the word, written and spoken – seeking, in Emily Dickinson's phrase, the 'consent of language' to embody truth and to communicate it.

In an inarticulate and verbally incoherent culture such as ours, where a veritable tsunami of misuse and mispronunciation of words, often because of etymological ignorance, syntactical muddle through grammatical ignorance, vacuous cliché, the circumlocution and obfuscation of risible euphemism and officialese in all departments of life in a society that is supposed to value plain speaking, and the simplistic misrepresentation of historical complexity in glib (usually dismissive) phraseology, often in the service of currently modish ideology, the need for clear thinking and accurate and compelling speaking and writing has never been more pressing. This is not merely a matter of elocution or even of the importance of speaking or writing correctly by this or that pedantic standard. George Orwell warned, as long ago as 1946, in his essay, 'Politics and the English Language', that 'the slovenliness of our language makes it easier for us to have foolish thoughts' and where foolish thoughts prevail, the people are ready for tyranny. This week we are celebrating the 400th anniversary of that book which, more than any other, has influenced the written and oral cultures of the English-speaking peoples:

the Authorized (or King James) version of the Bible, published on 2 May 1611. Last month, a group of graduates of this Faculty and of the Law Faculty took on the world in Washington DC and won the Jessup law mooting competition against 500 law schools from 80 countries. Knowledge is power, it is said, but as both the Authorized Version and our brilliant mooters demonstrate, language is its powerful tool. Those who are unable to use language effectively and compellingly are disempowered, silenced.

What you have received, in reading for degrees in Arts and the Social Sciences, is not some decorative embroidery on the tablecloth of life, but the fostering of the ability to acquire wisdom and to communicate it. The University is, as Philip Larkin said of churches, a place to grow wise in and that growth continues as you go into the next stages of your lives, for their enrichment and that of the community at large.

I began with John Milton, so I will close with him. A few years after he wrote *L'Allegro* and *Il Penseroso*, and had had his lengthy postgraduate period of private study across a range of disciplines, he reflected, in a polemical prose work, collapsing the distinctions between poet and poem, artist and artefact, that 'He who would … hope to write well … in laudable things ought himself to be a true poem'. As you go on your way justly rejoicing today, from this Great Hall, may your lives, too, be true poems: inspired, beautiful and meaningful.

List of Publications of Barry Spurr, MLitt (*Oxon*), MA, PhD (*Syd*), FACE

Books

'The world shall come to Walsingham': the Blessed Virgin Mary in English Poetry (Sydney: St Laurence Press, 2011)

'Anglo-Catholic in Religion': T.S. Eliot and Christianity (Cambridge: Lutterworth, 2010)

See the Virgin Blest: Representations of the Virgin Mary in English Poetry (New York: Palgrave Macmillan, 2007)

Studying Poetry, revised and enlarged second edition (Basingstoke: Palgrave Macmillan, 2006)

Successful Public Speaking, Debating and Oral Presentations (Epping: New Frontier, 2006)

Successful Essay-Writing (Epping: New Frontier, 2005)

Studying Poetry (Melbourne: Macmillan, 1997)

Lytton Strachey (Lewiston NY: Edwin Mellen, 1995)

The Word in the Desert (Cambridge: Lutterworth, 1995)

Edited journal

The Legacy of T.S. Eliot (special number of *Literature and Aesthetics*, journal of the Sydney Society of Literature and Aesthetics; volume 18, number 1, June, 2008).

Chapters in books

'Religion', in *Cambridge Companion to T.S. Eliot*, ed. Jason Harding, (Cambridge: Cambridge University Press, 2016), 187-201.

'Religions East and West', in *Cambridge Companion to The Waste Land*, ed. Gabrielle McIntire (Cambridge: Cambridge University Press, 2015), 54-68.

'Why Cats Matter', *Feline Friends: Tales from the Heart* (Sydney: Existe, 2012), 169-172.

'"Anglo-Catholic in religion": T.S. Eliot and Christianity', in *T.S. Eliot in Context*, ed. Jason Harding (Cambridge: Cambridge University Press, 2011), 305-315.

'The national curriculum for English', in *The National Curriculum: A Critique*, ed. Chris Berg. (Institute of Public Affairs [Melbourne], 2010), 29-40.

'Poetics of Incarnation', in *Walsingham in Literature and Culture from the Middle Ages to Modernity*, eds. Gary Waller and Dominic Janes (Aldershot: Ashgate, 2010), 233-242.

'Introduction' and 'The Legacy of T.S. Eliot', in *The Legacy of T.S. Eliot*, ed. Barry Spurr (special number of *Literature and Aesthetics*, journal of the Sydney Society of Literature and Aesthetics, June, 2008)

'John Donne and the Poetry of Meditation', *Symposium Papers* (Sydney: St Laurence Press, 2007), 4-13.

'What is the difference between *King Lear* and *Ginger Meggs*?', *Postmodernism in Education*, Warrane College Monograph No. 11 (Kensington: Warrane College, 2006), 8-23.

'English Studies in Crisis', in *Education and the Ideal*, ed. Naomi Smith (Sydney: New Frontier, 2004), 63-84.

'The genesis of Milton's sentences', in *Running Wild: Essays, Fictions and memoirs Presented to Michael Wilding*, eds. David Brooks and Brian Kiernan (New Delhi: Manohar: Sydney Association for Studies in Society and Culture, 2004), 43-53.

'The *via negativa* in the Poetry and Thought of T.S. Eliot', in *The Dark Side*, eds. Christopher Hartney and Andrew McGarrity [proceedings of the 2002 Australian and International Religion, Literature and the Arts Conference], (Sydney: RLA Press, 2004), 43-53.

'Eliot's quest for the centre of meaning in *Four Quartets*', *Seeking the Centre* [proceedings of the 2001 Australian and International Religion, Literature and the Arts Conference], (Sydney: RLA Press, 2002), 370-378.

'Felicity Incarnate: Rediscovering Thomas Traherne', in *Discovering and (Re)Covering the Seventeenth Century Religious Lyric*, eds. Eugene Cunnar and Jeffrey Johnson (Pittsburgh: Duquesne University Press, 2001), 273-289.

'"Marking time?": Milton's Recapitulation Revisited', in *Imperfect Apprehensions: Essays in English Literature in Honour of G.A. Wilkes*, ed. Geoffrey Little, (Sydney: Challis Press, 1996), 100-114.

'Poetry of Resurrection: Peter Skrzynecki's *Easter Sunday*', in *Religion Literature & the Arts: Australian International Conference*, eds. M. Griffith and R. Keating (Sydney: RLA Project, 1994), 364-372.

'Salvation and Damnation in the *Divine Meditations* of John Donne', in *Praise Disjoined: Changing Patterns of Salvation in 17th-Century English Literature*, ed. W.P. Shaw (New York: Peter Lang, 1991), 166-174.

'An Australian Prayer Book', in *No Alternative*, eds. D. Martin and P. Mullen (Oxford: Blackwell, 1981), [162]-174.

Articles in refereed journals

'The Bliss of Solitude: The Poetry and Poetics of Being Alone' [text of Inaugural Lecture as Professor of Poetry and Poetics], *Literature and Aesthetics*, December, 2013, 1-23.

'Anglo-Catholicism and the "religious turn" in Eliot's poetry and thought', *Religion and Literature* [US], Spring, 2012, 136-143.

'The Fame and Nurture of Poetry', *Sydney Studies in English*, 37, 2011, 1-18.

'The Language of Sport', *Arts*, 23, 2001, 82-99.

'True confessions? Ted Hughes' *Birthday Letters*', *Sydney Studies in English*, 27, 2001, 74-89.

'The Theology of "La Corona"', *John Donne Journal* [US], 20, 2001, 121-139.

'"I loved old Tom": T.S. Eliot and David Jones', *Yeats Eliot Review* [US], 17, Winter, 2001, [19]-25.

'Liturgical anachronism in *Murder in the Cathedral*', *Yeats Eliot Review* [US], 15, Summer, 1998, 2-7.

'A Preface Scrutinised', *Australian Journal of Liturgy*, 6, 1, May, 1997, 22-31.

'The John Donne Papers of Wesley Milgate', *John Donne Journal* [US], 15, 1997, 189-201.

'God or the Goddess? Christian Feminism Today', *St Mark's Review*, Spring, 1995, 25-31.

'"Sable-stoled Sorcerers"', *Milton Quarterly* [US], May, 1992, 45-46.

'Questions of Language', *St Mark's Review*, Winter, 1991, 25-28.

'Eliot and the Seventeenth Century', *Hellas* [US], Autumn, 1991, 278-290.

'"I have let things slip": A revaluation of Sylvia Plath', *Hellas* [US], 1991, 93-111.

'Camp Mandarin: The Prose Style of Lytton Strachey', *English Literature in Transition* [US], February, 1990, 31-45.

'The Analogy of Faith: The Anglican Character of John Donne's Sermons', *Arts*, 1989, 13-21.

'The Miracle of Order: Lytton Strachey's Essayist's Art', *Prose Studies* [UK], December, 1989, 240-258.

'Alienation and Affirmation in the Poetry of Philip Larkin', *Sydney Studies in English*, 1988-9, 52-71.

'Lytton Strachey and the Victorians', *Canterbury Conference Papers* [NZ], 1987, 74-81.

'The Art of Robert Lowell', *Sydney Studies in English*, 1981-2, 69-84.

'The Genesis of "Little Gidding"', *Yeats Eliot Review* [US], 1979, 29-30.

'G.M. Hopkins: The Poet as Sacramentalist', *Sydney Studies in English*, 1978-9, 38-49.

Conference proceedings

'T.S. Eliot and the Western Classical Tradition', *The Christian View of History and the Revival of the Liberal Arts* conference, *Connor Court Quarterly*, number 5/6, December, 2012, 251-269

The Legacy of Eliot's Poetry, *The Legacy of T.S. Eliot Conference*, *Literature and Aesthetics*, vol. 18, number 1, June 2008, 19-30

Commissioned website essays

'To live in Paradise alone: the Bliss of Solitude', ABC Religion and Ethics: www.abc.net.au/religion, November, 2011

'Recovering the numinous: the Bible, language and liturgy', ABC Religion and Ethics: www.abc.net.au/religion, May, 2011

'A vision of the city of God: restoring a revolutionary language of worship', ABC Religion and Ethics: www.abc.net.au/religion, September, 2010

'Deliver us from idiocy! Recovering inspiration in liturgical language', ABC Religion and Ethics: www.abc.net.au/religion, September, 2010

'The impact of T.S. Eliot's Christianity on his poetry', ABC Religion and Ethics: www.abc.net.au/religion, August, 2010

'T.S. Eliot's extraordinary journey of faith', ABC Religion and Ethics: www.abc.net.au/religion, August, 2010

Encyclopedia entries

T.S. Eliot: Chronology, Literary Encyclopedia [on-line], www.LitEncyc.com, 2013

T.S. Eliot: 'Journey of the Magi' Literary Encyclopedia [on-line], www.LitEncyc.com, 2009

T.S. Eliot: *Ash-Wednesday, 1930*, Literary Encyclopedia [on-line], www.LitEncyc.com, 2008

'W.B. Yeats', Literary Encyclopedia [on-line]. www.LitEncyc.com, 2005

'The Bloomsbury Group', Literary Encyclopedia [on-line]. www.LitEncyc.com, 2005

'Lytton Strachey', Literary Encyclopedia [on-line]. www.LitEncyc.com, 2005

'T.S. Eliot', *Encyclopedia of the Essay* (Chicago and London: Fitzroy Dearborn, 1997), 249-251.

Other articles

'Remembering Valerie Eliot', *Oxford Today* (https://www.oxfordtoday.ox.ac.uk/page.aspx?pid=2535) December, 2012, reprinted in *Time Present*, 'Remembering Mrs. Eliot', Winter, 2013, 2-3.

'Lunar Symbolism', *Hermes*, 2012, 40-48.

'"And God said": the King James Version and English Literature', *mETAphor*, 4, 2011, 3-8.

'Poetry and the Life Well Lived', *Quadrant*, July-August, 2011, 30-31.

'When the magic's all in the delivery' [commissioned article on Milton's 400th birthday], Higher Education Supplement, *The Australian*, 3 December, 2008, 35.

'Valuing Education', *Melbourne's Child*, August, 2004, 22.

'Men in the Classroom, *Sydney's Child*, August, 2004, 20.

'So Much Grandstanding', *Sydney's Child*, July, 2004, 18; *Melbourne's Child*, July, 2004, 12-13; *Brisbane's Child*, August, 2004, 18; *Canberra's Child*, August, 2004, 8; *Adelaide's Child*, August, 2004, 8.

'The Problem with men', *Animals*, Summer, 2003, 20.

'National hypocrisy', *AQ*, May-June, 8.

'Political paedophilia', *AQ*, March-April, 2003, 8-9.

'Kindy for jurors', *AQ*, January-February, 2003, 7.

'The decomposing university' (II), *AQ*, November-December, 2002, 7.

'The demise of seriousness', *AQ*, September-October, 2002, 8.

'Champion of a liberal, educated life' [obituary of Peter Bennie], *The Sydney Morning Herald*, 15 November, 2002, 32.

'Nurturing the essentials: children's reading, writing and speaking skills', *Australian Quarterly*, Nov/Dec 2001, 28-33.

'Terrorism in context', *Sydney's Child*, October, 2001, 29-30; *Melbourne's Child*, October, 2001, 10.

'The decomposing university' (I), *AQ*, July/August, 2001, 19-21.

'Oh boy!', *Sydney's Child*, August, 2001, 21-2; *Melbourne's Child*, August, 2001, 17-18.

'English studies: going the way of Greek and Latin?', *News Weekly*, 14 July, 2001, 12-13.

'The appeal of Harry Potter', *Melbourne's Child*, July, 2001, 38-9; *Sydney's Child*, August, 2001, 54-55.

'Nightmare sporting parents', *Sydney's Child*, June, 2001, 20.

'Cultivate reading', *Sydney's Child*, May, 2001, 21; *Melbourne's Child*, May, 2001, 10-11.

'English going the way of Latin and Greek' [commissioned], 'Opinion', *The Sydney Morning Herald*, 30 April, 2001, 12.

'The death of "English"', *Sydney's Child*, April, 2001, 16-17, 42 [reprinted in *Newswrite*, May, 2001, 7, 18].

'The well-mannered child', *Sydney's Child*, April, 2001, 34-35; *Melbourne's Child*, April, 2001, 22-23, 45.

'Dress Codes: the great uniform debate', *Sydney's Child*, March, 2001, 52.

'Throwaway Pets', *Sydney's Child*, February, 2001, 37.

'The Censorship Debate', *Sydney's Child*, November, 2000, 40-41.

'A tongue-tied nation', *Sydney's Child*, October, 2000, 12-13; *Melbourne's Child*, October, 2000, 8-9.

'Boys in trouble', *Sydney's Child*, August, 2000, 20-21.

'Sport 1 The Arts 0', *Sydney's Child*, April, 2000, 14, 16 *Melbourne's Child*, April, 2000, 12-13.

'Sports Mad', *The Sydney Morning Herald*, 5 February, 2000, 4s [commissioned].

'The high price of winning', *The Sydney Morning Herald*, 7 August, 1997, 15. [commissioned, reprinted in *The Age*, 4 September, 1997, 10, and as a chapter in *Issues in Society*, vol. 106 (Spinney Press: Balmain, 1999), 12-13 and reproduced in the Fairfax Education Unit's CD-ROM, *Issues in the News*, 1997, 1998].

'"Splendid words": Hardy's *Trumpet-Major* and "church verse"', *The Thomas Hardy Journal*, February, 1997, 77-82.

'Sport's Stranglehold on Australian Culture', *News Weekly*, January, 1997, 18-20.

'Why Literacy Matters', *News Weekly*, November, 1996, 11-13.

'Harold Bloom, the "Canon" and the Future of English', *Literature and Aesthetics*, October, 1996, 134-138.

'The Poetry of Joanne Burns', *mETAphor*, June, 1996, 49-53.

'"That string of excellences": Thomas Hardy and the Book of Common Prayer', *The Thomas Hardy Journal* [UK], May 1996, 38-39.

'The Banished Heart', *AD 2000*, December, 1995, 14.

'The Poetry of Jennifer Maiden', *The Teaching of English*, December, 1995, 26-33.

'"That string of excellences": Thomas Hardy and the Book of Common Prayer', *Faith and Heritage* [UK], Summer 1995, 13-14.

The Spirituality of John Donne (Melbourne: The Prayer Book Society, 1994), 15

'Psalms and Hymns and Spiritual Songs', *Machray Review* [Canada], 3, May, 1993, 37-50; *Faith and Worship* [UK], Autumn, 1992 and Summer, 1994; *St Mark's Review*, Summer, 1993, 22-29.

'The Crisis in English', *Education Monitor*, Spring, 1993, 18-21.

Literature and Spirituality: From Donne to Larkin (Sydney: Wild and Woolley, 1993), 36

'Changing Places: A School-University Teaching Exchange Program', *Education Monitor*, Spring, 1992, 5-8.

'Expert Beyond Experience: a tribute to Dame Helen Gardner', *Oxford Magazine* [UK], Trinity Term, 1992, 20, 22.

'The Book of Common Prayer and English Literature', *Faith and Worship* [UK], Advent, 1990, 15-22.

'*Hamlet* or *Emerald City*? The Future of English', *Education Monitor*, Winter, 1990, 24-26.

'The New Idea of a University', *Quadrant*, April, 1990, 42-46.

'The Language of Liturgy' (Brunswick: Christ Church Press, 1986), 7

'The Prayer of the Church', *The Seabury Journal* [US], December, 1984, 12-33.

'T.S. Eliot', *English Alive*, 1980, 35-41.

'Eliot's Longer Poems', *Sydney Studies in English*, 1977-8, 103-124.

Reviews

Michael Wilding, *Wild Bleak Bohemia*, *The Spectator*, 5 March, 2016, xi.

'Eliot on Pound and James', *Time Present* [US], Fall 2014, 9-10.

Joyce Ransom, *The Web of Friendship: Nicholas Ferrar and Little Gidding*, *Literature and Aesthetics*, December, 2012, 286-289.

Peter Steele, *Braiding the Voices: Essays in Poetry*, *The Melbourne Anglican*, December, 2012, 30.

Jan Frans van Dijkhuizen and Richard Todd, ed., *The Reformation Unsettled: British Literature and the Question of Religious Identity, 1560-1660*, *Journal of Religious History*, vol.35, no.1, March, 2011, 137-139.

Brent Nelson, *Holy Ambition: Rhetoric, Courtship, and Devotion in the Sermons of John Donne*, *Journal of Religious History*, vol.30, no.2, June, 2006, 241-242.

Ann Thompson, *The Art of Suffering and the Impact of Seventeenth-Century Anti-Providential Thought*, *Journal of Religious History*, vol.30, no.2, June, 2006, 244-245

Stephen McInerney, *In your absence*, *Southerly*, vol.63, no.3, 2003, 167-170.

Tracey Rowland, *Culture and the Thomist Tradition: After Vatican II*, *Oriens*, Winter 2003, 1-4 [reprinted in *Christian Order*, December, 2003, 764-773].

Barry Unsworth, *The Songs of the Kings*, *Sydney Morning Herald*, 5-6 October, 2002, 'Spectrum', 11.

Derek Wood, *Exiled from light: divine law, morality and violence in Milton's 'Samson Agonistes'*, *The Sixteenth Century Journal* [US], Vol 23/3, 2002, 917-918.

Kendall Taylor, *Sometimes Madness is Wisdom: Zelda and Scott Fitzgerald*, *Sydney Morning Herald*, 19 January, 2002, 'Spectrum', 10-11.

Karen Edwards, *Milton and the Natural World*, *The Sixteenth Century Journal*, Fall, 2001, 810-811.

Matters of the Mind: Essays in Honour of Leonie Kramer, eds Lee Jobling and Catherine Runcie, *Sydney Morning Herald*, 17 November, 2001, 'Spectrum', 11.

Henry James: A Life in Letters, ed. Philip Home, *The Melbourne Anglican*, May, 2000, 12.

Anthony Julius, *T.S. Eliot, anti-Semitism, and Literary Form*, *Literature and Aesthetics*, October, 1998, 150-154.

'*God speed the plough*, by Andrew McRae', *Literature and Aesthetics*, October, 1997, 195-199.

'John Donne and the Ancient Catholic Nobility', *The Sixteenth Century Journal* [US], XXVIII/1, 1997, 259-261.

'Poetic transcreations', *Southerly*, Summer, 1997-8, 215-217.

Video-Films

T.S. Eliot (Sydney: Classroom Video, 1992)

Sylvia Plath (Sydney: Classroom Video, 1992)

HIGHER SCHOOL CERTIFICATE STUDY GUIDES

Essay-writing for HSC English 2006/2007 (Epping: New Frontier, 2006)

Essay-Writing for HSC English 2005 (Epping: New Frontier, 2005)

The Poetry of Bruce Dawe (Sydney: Pascal, 2003)

The Poetry of Wilfred Owen (Sydney: Pascal, 2003)

The Poetry of Peter Skrzynecki (Sydney: Pascal, 2003)

CD-Rom: *Commentary on the Advanced and Standard NSW HSC English examination papers, 2001* (WebEd: Sydney, 2002)

The Poetry of Sylvia Plath (Sydney: Pascal, 2001)

The Poetry of John Donne (Sydney: Pascal, 2000)

The Poetry of Peter Skrzynecki (Sydney: Pascal, 2000)

The Poetry of Bruce Dawe (Sydney: Pascal, 2000)

The Poetry of Wilfred Owen (Sydney: Pascal, 2000)

The Novels of Christopher Koch (Sydney: Pascal, 1999)

The Poetry of Robert Gray (Sydney: Pascal, 1999)

The Poetry of Judith Beveridge (Sydney: Pascal, 1999)

The Poetry of Bruce Dawe (Sydney: Pascal, 1999)

The Poetry of Robert Frost (Sydney: Pascal, 1999)

The Poetry of Coleridge (Sydney: Pascal, 1999)

The Poetry of Ted Hughes (Sydney: Pascal, 1999)

The Poetry of Kenneth Slessor (Sydney: Pascal, 1999)

The Poetry of Wilfred Owen (Sydney: Pascal, 1999)

The Poetry of Judith Wright (Sydney: Pascal, 1995)

The Poetry of Bruce Dawe (Sydney: Pascal, 1995)

The Poetry of Robert Gray (Sydney: Pascal, 1995)

The Poetry of Kenneth Slessor (Sydney: Pascal, 1995)

The Poetry of Emily Dickinson [2 vols] (Sydney: Pascal, 1994)

Sylvia Plath's 'The Bell Jar' (Sydney: Pascal, 1994)

The Poetry of Philip Larkin (Sydney: Pascal, 1994)

The Poetry of Wilfred Owen (Sydney: Pascal, 1993)

The Poetry of Coleridge (Sydney: Pascal, 1993)

The Poetry of Judith Beveridge (Sydney: Pascal, 1993)

The Poetry of Rosemary Dobson (Sydney: Pascal, 1993)

The Poetry of John Foulcher (Sydney: Pascal, 1993)

The Poetry of Peter Skrzynecki (Sydney: Pascal, 1993)

The Poetry of Douglas Stewart (Sydney: Pascal, 1993)

The Poetry of John Tranter (Sydney: Pascal, 1993)

HSC English Extension Course, 2009-2012 (Sydney: Pascal, 2010):

The Orchard
Out of Africa
The Invention of Solitude
Robert Lowell
The Skull Beneath the Skin
Anil's Ghost
The Real Inspector Hound
Rear Window
Dune
Neuromancer
Brave New World
2001: A Space Odyssey
Catch-22
The Spy Who Came in From the Cold
Waiting for Godot
Sylvia Plath
Orlando

Hiroshima
Northanger Abbey
John Keats
S.T. Coleridge
The Shipping News
The Mosquito Coast
Island
Seamus Heaney
Lost in Translation
The French Lieutenant's Woman
If on a winter's night a traveller
Night Letters
Orlando
Twelfth Night
John Tranter
Elizabeth

HSC Standard English, 2009-2012 (Sydney: Pascal, 2009):

The Joy Luck Club
Heat and Dust
Peter Skrzynecki
Emily Dickinson
The Life and Crimes of Harry Lavender
Joanne Burns
A.B. Paterson
Douglas Stewart
Gwen Harwood
William Blake
Wilfred Owen
At the Round Earth's Imagined Corners.

The Namesake
Swallow the Air
Fly Away Peter
Steven Herrick

Speeches
Maestro
Into the Wild
The Year of Living Dangerously
Briar Rose
Judith Wright

HSC Advanced English, 2009-2012 (Sydney: Pascal, 2009):

Rosemary Dobson
W;t
Blade Runner
Elizabeth Barrett Browning
Jane Eyre
W.B. Yeats
Kenneth Slessor
Snow Falling on Cedars
The Justice Game
Denise Levertov

John Donne
Frankenstein
The Great Gatsby
Cloudstreet
A Doll House
Gwen Harwood
Speeches
Ted Hughes
True History of the Kelly Gang

HSC Advanced English 2004/2005 Course (Sydney: Pascal, 2003):

Reading Poetry
Huckleberry Finn
Peter Skrzynecki
Lionheart
Ender's Game
Coleridge
On Giants' Shoulders
Empire of the Sun
Imagined Corners
The Pardoner's Tale / A Simple Plan
The Justice Game

Wordsworth / *An Imaginary Life*
Brave New World / Bladerunner
Wuthering Heights
Cloudstreet
Gwen Harwood
W.B. Yeats
Speeches
Samplers
Wild Swans
Ted Hughes
True History of the Kelly Gang

HSC Standard English 2004/2005 Course (Sydney: Pascal, 2003):

Reading Poetry
Huckleberry Finn
Peter Skrzynecki
Lionheart
Ender's Game
Coleridge
On Giants' Shoulders
Empire of the Sun
Imagined Corners
Into the Wild
Raw
Komninos

Maybe Tomorrow
The Bush Tucker Man
Bruce Dawe
Itinerant Blues
We All Fall Down
Ports of Call
Briar Rose
Deb Westbury
Wilfred Owen
Australian War Memorial website
One Man's War
The Simple Gift

HSC Advanced English 2001/2002 Course (Sydney: Pascal, 2001):

Reading Poetry
Ender's Game
Imagined Corners
On Giants' Shoulders
Peter Skrzynecki
Gwen Harwood
Brave New World
Blade Runner
The Pardoner's Tale
A Simple Plan
Wordsworth

Jane Eyre
Cloudstreet
Sylvia Plath
John Donne
Speeches
Samplers
Wild Swans
Ted Hughes
The Justice Game
Two Weeks In Lilliput
An Imaginary Life

HSC Standard English 2001/2002 Course (Sydney: Pascal, 2000):

Reading Tasks
Reading Poetry
Imagined Corners
On Giants' Shoulders
Immigrant Chronicle
Gwen Harwood
Tales from the Blackboard
Maybe Tomorrow
Komninos by the Kupful
Inside Black Australia

We All Fall Down
Briar Rose
An Australian Son
Australian War Memorial website
Mouth to Mouth
Wilfred Owen
RAW
The Bush Tucker Man
Sometimes Gladness
Ender's Game

2/3 Unit Related English: Complete 1999 Course (Sydney: Pascal, 1999):

Resources and Uses of English
Reading Poetry
Judith Beveridge
Coleridge
Robert Frost
Robert Gray
Snow Falling on Cedars
Highways to a War
Robert Browning
Emily Dickinson

John Donne
Gwen Harwood
Seamus Heaney
Antigone Kefala
Tess of the d'Urbervilles
Lirra Lirra by the River
Brave New World
Cloudstreet
The Rover
A Doll House

2 Unit General English: Complete 1999 Course (Sydney: Pascal, 1999):

Uses of English	Kenneth Slessor
Reading Poetry	Debbie Westbury
Judith Beveridge	Judith Wright
Coleridge	*Empire of the Sun*
Robert Frost	*The Year of Living Dangerously*
Robert Gray	*The Spy Who Came in from the Cold*
Snow Falling on Cedars	*The Joy Luck Club*
Highways to a War	*Briar Rose*
Bruce Dawe	

2/3 Unit Related English: Complete 1998 Course (Sydney: Pascal, 1998):

Resources and Uses of English	Harwood
Reading Poetry	Robert Gray
Chaucer	Jennifer Maiden
Donne	*Adam Bede*
Keats	*Washington Square*
Browning	*Tess of the D'Urbervilles*
Hopkins	*The Tree of Man*
Heaney	*Tirra Lirra by the River*
Murray	*A Doll House*

2 Unit General English: Complete 1998 Course (Sydney: Pascal, 1997):

Resources and Uses of English	Judith Wright
Reading Poetry	Mark O'Connor
Slessor	Joanne Burns
Dawe	*The Life and Crimes of Harry Lavender*

2 Unit General English: Full 1996-1997 Course (Sydney: Pascal, 1995):

Resources and Uses of English	Judith Wright
Reading Poetry	Mark O'Connor
Slessor	Joanne Burns
Dawe	*The Life and Crimes of Harry Lavender*

2/3 Unit Related English: Full 1996-1997 Course (Sydney: Pascal, 1995):

Resources and Uses of English   Les Murray
Reading Poetry   Gwen Harwood
'The Pardoner's Tale'   Robert Gray
Donne   Jennifer Maiden
Keats   *Adam Bede*
Browning   *Washington Square*
Hopkins   *Tess of the D'Urbervilles*
Heaney
The Tree of Man

2/3 Unit Related English: Full 1995 Course (Sydney: Pascal, 1994):

Resources and Uses of English   Larkin
Reading Poetry   Heaney
'The Miller's Tale'   Dobson
Marvell   Gray
Coleridge   Cataldi
Dickinson   *Gulliver's Travels*
Tennyson   *Washington Square*

List of Contributors

Lyn Ashcroft

Lyn Ashcroft studied literature and linguistics and has taught at tertiary institutions in Australia, England, and France. Her interests include literature of the nineteenth and twentieth centuries, and humour studies, especially the literary expression of humour. She has previously published research in the field of applied linguistics.

Devika Brendon

Devika Brendon is an academic, teacher, editor, reviewer and creative writer. Her poetry and short stories have been published in academic and literary journals and anthologies in Sri Lanka, Australia, India and Italy. She published her first book of poetry at the age of 16, and was awarded the Sydney Union Poetry Prize and the Henry Lawson Memorial Prize for Poetry at the University of Sydney. Devika founded the 'English Only' teaching academy in 2001, and teaches Language and Literature to students studying the O-Level and A-Level syllabus in Sri Lanka and Australia.

David Brooks

David Brooks is a graduate of the Universities of London and Oxford. At Oxford he specialised in English literature of the Augustan period. He has taught at the University of Dundee and the University of Sydney. He is editor of *Lyrics & Satires of John Wilmot, Earl of Rochester* and co-editor of *Running Wild: Essays, Fictions and Memoirs Presented to Michael Wilding*. His interests are in Renaissance and Augustan English literature, and in literary and critical theory. He has published on Shakespeare, Dryden, Rochester, Defoe, and I. A. Richards, on Marxian critical theory and aesthetics, and on issues in literary hermeneutics.

John Bunyan

John Bunyan is a graduate of the Universities of Sydney, London, Durham and San Francisco. He is a retired priest of the Diocese of Sydney, a parishioner of St John the Baptist's, Canberra, and a member of St Stephen's Uniting Church, Sydney, and King's Chapel, Boston. After many years of parish and educational experience, he remains Honorary Church of England Chaplain at Bankstown Hospital and Honorary Chaplain of the Australian Intelligence Corps Association. He is a member of the Australian Academy of Liturgy and the Prayer Book Society, and of various historical, conservationist, and community organisations.

Henry Cooper

Henry Cooper graduated from the University of Sydney in 2013 with a Bachelor of Arts (Hons I), writing his honours thesis under the supervision of Professor Spurr on the poetry of W.B. Yeats. He is currently completing a Juris Doctor degree at the University of Sydney, and is employed as a law clerk.

Carole M. Cusack

Carole M. Cusack is Professor of Religious Studies at the University of Sydney. She trained as a medievalist and her doctorate was published as *Conversion Among the Germanic Peoples* (1998). She now researches contemporary religious trends. Her books include *Invented Religions: Imagination, Fiction and Faith* (2010), *The Sacred Tree: Ancient and Medieval Manifestations* (2011), and (with Katharine Buljan) *Anime, Religion, and Spirituality: Profane and Sacred Worlds in Contemporary Japan* (2014). With Christopher Hartney (University of Sydney) she edited the *Journal of Religious History* from 2007-2015. She also teaches adult education and makes radio and television programmes.

David Daintree

David Daintree has an academic background in Classics, but he is primarily a medieval Latinist. He taught at Geelong Grammar School, Timbertop, and St Peter's College, Adelaide. He was Principal of Jane Franklin Hall, University of Tasmania, Rector of St John's College, University of Sydney and President of Campion College, Australia's only Liberal Arts college. He has been a visiting professor at both the Universities of Siena and Venice, and a visiting fellow at St. John's College, University of Manitoba. He is the founding Director of the Christopher Dawson Centre for Cultural Studies in Hobart.

Michael Warren Davis

Michael Warren Davis is a native of Boston, Massachusetts, and was an undergraduate student of Professor Spurr at the University of Sydney. He now works as a journalist and writes a column for the *Spectator Australia*.

Bruce Dawe

Bruce Dawe was an Associate Professor at the University of Southern Queensland (1971-1993), and his first volume of poetry was published in 1962, while he was serving in the Royal Australian Air Force. He has been awarded numerous prizes for poetry since 1965, including the Patrick White Award. He has published 12 books of poetry and, in 1992, was appointed an Officer of the Order of Australia for his contribution to Australian literature. In 2001 Dawe was awarded a Centenary Medal 'for distinguished service to the arts through poetry'. His collected poems, *Sometimes Gladness*, is now in its 6th edition.

Stephen Gaukroger

Stephen Gaukroger was educated at the Universities of London, where he studied philosophy, and Cambridge, where he completed a PhD in the history and philosophy of science. He has been at the University of Sydney since 1981, where he is Emeritus Professor of History of Philosophy and History of Science. His publications include *Descartes, An Intellectual Biography* (1995), *Francis Bacon and the Transformation of Early-Modern Philosophy* (2001), *Descartes' System of Natural Philosophy* (2002), *The Emergence of a Scientific Culture* (2006), *The Collapse of Mechanism and the Rise of Sensibility* (2010), *Objectivity* (2012), and *The Natural and the Human* (2016).

Robert Gray

Robert Gray has been described as 'an Imagist without a rival in the English speaking world' and 'one of the contemporary masters of poetry in English'.

He has been writer-in-residence at Meiji University and at several universities in Australia. He has won numerous awards including the Adelaide Arts Festival award, the New South Wales and Victorian Premiers' awards for poetry and the Patrick White Award. With Geoffrey Lehmann, he co-edited two anthologies, *The Younger Australian Poets* and *Australian Poetry in the Twentieth Century*. His recent publications include his memoir, *The Land I Came Through Last* (2008) and his collected poems, *Cumulus* (2012).

Jennifer Gribble

Jennifer Gribble is an Honorary Associate Professor of English at the University of Sydney. A graduate of the Universities of Melbourne and Oxford, she has taught in the English Departments of Melbourne, La Trobe and Sydney. Her publications include *The Lady of Shallot in the Victorian Novel* (1983), *Christina Stead* (1994), and an edition of *George Eliot's Scenes of Clerical Life* (1998). She is working on a study of Dickens and the Bible, and is a member of the Editorial Board of *Dickens Quarterly*.

Simon Haines

Simon Haines is Professor and Head of English and Director of the Research Centre for Human Values at The Chinese University of Hong Kong. He is the Secretary of the Hong Kong Academy of the Humanities. His monographs include *Poetry and Philosophy from Homer to Rousseau: Romantic Souls, Realist Lives* (2005) and *Redemption in Poetry and Philosophy: Wordsworth, Kant and the Making of the Post-Christian Imagination* (2013). He co-edited the *Reader in European Romanticism* (2nd edition 2014), which won the Barricelli Prize in 2010. He is currently working on two books on Shakespeare.

Kevin Hart

Kevin Hart is the Edwin B. Kyle Professor of Christian Studies at the University of Virginia where he also holds Professorships in the Departments of English and French. His most recent scholarly books are *Kingdoms of God* (2014) and *Poetry and Revelation* (2016), and also recently published *Wild Track: New and Selected Poems* (2015).

Ivan Head

Ivan Head is in his twenty-second year as Warden of St Paul's College within Sydney University. He has been Head of an Anglican University College for more than a quarter century. He is a graduate in Philosophy from the University of Western Australia, in Divinity from the Melbourne College of Divinity and holds a PhD in New Testament Language and Literature from Glasgow. His poems have found a niche in *Quadrant* and elsewhere.

Karina Hepner

Karina Hepner has been teaching English for over 20 years. After graduating from Queensland University of Technology, she spent a year in Dijon, France, as *"une assistante en anglais"* in French middle schools. Upon her return to Australia, she taught in English and Humanities. In 1999, she took a position as a French Immersion and French language teacher in Canadian public schools. However, her role as an English 12 and English Literature 12 teacher in Vancouver cemented her belief in the intrinsic value of literature in young people's lives. She currently teaches in Queensland, and recently completed an MA in English Literature.

David Jasper

David Jasper is Professor of Literature and Theology at the University of Glasgow and Distinguished Overseas Professor at Renmin University of China, Beijing. He holds degrees in both English literature and theology from Cambridge, Oxford and Durham, and an honorary doctorate in theology from the University of Uppsala. He was the founding Editor of the journal *Literature and Theology*, and his most recent monograph is *Literature and Theology as a Grammar of Assent* (2016), a history of the study of literature and theology in the later twentieth century.

Geoffrey Lehmann

Geoffrey Lehmann's *Poems 1957-2013* won the 2015 Prime Minister's Prize for poetry. He has co-edited with Robert Gray three anthologies of Australian poetry, including the 1090 page *Australian Poetry Since 1788*, which was one of *The Economist's* best books of 2011. He was co-author of five editions of *Taxation Law in Australia* and has been chairman of the Australian Tax Research Foundation. He is currently writing his memoirs.

Stephen McInerney

Stephen McInerney is a graduate of the Australian National University, Sydney University and Cambridge University, and currently lectures in English at Campion College, Sydney. His first collection of poems, *In Your Absence*, was a *Times Literary Supplement* 'Book of the Year' in 2002, and his new collection, *The Wind Outside*, has just been published. His poems have appeared in a variety of publications and anthologies in Australia and abroad, including the *Warwick Review*, *Australia Poetry Since 1788* and *100 Australian Poems You Need to Know*.

Jonathan Mills

Jonathan Mills is a composer and festival director. He has worked in the Architecture Faculty of RMIT University in Melbourne, Australia, leading courses in acoustic design. He is the composer of several award-winning operas and works for chamber ensemble and orchestra. He has been director of various festivals in the Blue Mountains, Brisbane and Melbourne, and was the director of the Edinburgh International Festival between 2007 and 2014. He is currently Director of the Edinburgh International Culture Summit, Vice-Chancellor's (Professorial) Fellow at the University of Melbourne, Cultural Fellow at King's College, London and a Visiting Professor at the University of Edinburgh.

Stephen Prickett

Stephen Prickett is Regius Professor Emeritus of English, at Glasgow University and honorary Professor at the University of Kent, Canterbury. Previous posts include Sussex University, the Australian National University, Duke University, and Baylor University, where he was Director of the Armstrong Browning Library. He is a Fellow of the Australian Academy of the Humanities, former Chairman of the U.K. Higher Education Foundation, and former President of the European Society for the Study of Literature and Theology. He has published two novels, nine monographs, seven edited volumes, and over ninety articles on Romanticism, Victorian Studies, literature and theology.

Catherine A. Runcie

Catherine A. Runcie was a Senior Lecturer in English at the University of Sydney from 1969 to 2004, and previously taught at the University of

Toronto. Her teaching and research have been in the fields of 19th century literature and thought, literary theory, film adaptation and aesthetics. She was Foundation President of The Sydney Society of Literature and Aesthetics (1989-1998), Honorary President (1998-2015) and Co-Foundation Editor of the journal, *Literature & Aesthetics* (1990-1998). She was a visiting scholar at the Shanghai Institute of Foreign Languages in 1981, where she lectured on literary theory and the relation of literature and art in cross cultural movements, and the Xi'an Institute of Foreign Languages in 1993, where she lectured on modernism. She was co-editor of the Festschrift, *Matters of the Mind. Poems, Essays and Interviews in Honour of Leonie Kramer* (2001).

Beverley Sherry

Beverley Sherry is an Honorary Associate at the University of Sydney, formerly a Senior Lecturer at the University of Queensland. Her work crosses the disciplines of literature, history, and the visual arts, and her book *Australia's Historic Stained Glass* (1991) is her most pioneering work. Milton, however, remains her principal interest. She serves on the standing committee of the International Milton Symposium and the editorial board of *Milton Quarterly*, and has published widely on Milton since 1975. Her most recent work is a chapter for *Milton in Translation*, a forthcoming volume of essays.

Christine Townend

Christine Townend founded Animal Liberation in Australia in 1976 and in 1980, with Peter Singer, Animals Australia. She has had eight books published, and a collection of poetry, *Walking with Elephants* (2014). She holds a doctorate in poetry from the University of Sydney.

Garry Trompf

Garry Trompf is Emeritus Professor of the History of Ideas in the Department of Studies in Religion, School of Letters, Art and Media, and Adjunct Professor in Peace and Conflict Studies, School of Social and Political Sciences, at the University of Sydney. His better known works include *The Idea of Historical Recurrence in Western Thought* and *Payback: The Logic of Retribution in Melanesian Religions*. He is the Senior Editor of *The Gnostic World* project.

Bradley M. Wells

Bradley M. Wells was recently awarded his PhD from The University of Sydney where he was Hunter Baillie Fellow in English Literature at St Andrew's College then Vice-Master of Wesley College. He had the privilege of being taught by Professor Spurr as an undergraduate, before returning to be supervised by him and teaching senior undergraduate poetry with him.

Michael Wilding

Michael Wilding is Emeritus Professor in the Department of English at the University of Sydney. His books include *Milton's Paradise Lost*, *Dragons Teeth: Literature in the English Revolution*, *Political Fictions*, and the documentaries *The Paraguayan Experiment*, *Raising Spirits*, *Making Gold and Swapping Wives: the True Adventures of Dr John Dee and Sir Edward Kelly* and *Wild Bleak Bohemia: Marcus Clarke, Adam Lindsay Gordon and Henry Kendall*. His fiction includes the campus novel *Academia Nuts* and its sequel *Superfluous Men*, and the private eye novels *The Prisoner of Mount Warning*, *The Magic of It* and *Asian Dawn*. His most recent book is the memoir *Growing Wild*.

G.A. Wilkes

G. A. Wilkes was Challis Professor of English Literature from 1966 to 1996 at the University of Sydney, where he had been Foundation Professor of Australian Literature, and where he is now Emeritus Professor. He has specialized in two fields: Australian literature and English literature of the Elizabethan and Jacobean periods. He has a special interest in Shakespeare and Ben Jonson, and more particularly in Fulke Greville, Lord Brooke, whose *Complete Poems and Plays* he edited in 2008. He was editor from 1963 to 1987 of *Southerly: A Review of Australian Literature*. He describes as his hobby *A Dictionary of Australian Colloquialisms* (1978, 5th edition 2008).

www.ingramcontent.com/pod-product-compliance
Lightning Source LLC
Chambersburg PA
CBHW050125170426
43197CB00011B/1720